William of Malmesbury
THE DEEDS OF THE
BISHOPS OF ENGLAND

William of Malmesbury

THE DEEDS OF THE BISHOPS OF ENGLAND
(Gesta Pontificum Anglorum)

Translated by
DAVID PREEST

THE BOYDELL PRESS

First published 2002
The Boydell Press, Woodbridge
Reprinted 2002

ISBN 978 0 85115 884 6

Transferred to digital printing

The Boydell Press is an imprint of Boydell & Brewer Ltd
PO Box 9, Woodbridge, Suffolk IP12 3DF, UK
and of Boydell & Brewer Inc.
668 Mt. Hope Avenue, Rochester NY 14620, USA
website: www.boydellandbrewer.com

A CIP catalogue record for this title is available
from the British Library

This book is printed on acid-free paper

Contents

Preface

The *Gesta Pontificum Anglorum* (*The Deeds of the Bishops of England*) by the medieval historian William of Malmesbury has remained untranslated until the present time. It was the discovery of this lack of a translation, together with the fortunate presence of an edition of the Latin original in Hertfordshire County Library, that led me to make a start on translating William's history of the English Bishops. Three years later I regretfully approach the last few days of work on this fascinating task before, like William before me, 'bringing my boat to the shore of silence' (chapter 212). I am grateful to Shirley Hawthorn, the chief librarian of Hertfordshire County Library, for resisting the attempts of her colleagues to persuade her to dispose of the Library's Rolls series, and to Dr Christine Ferdinand, librarian of Magdalen College, Oxford, for letting me examine its manuscript of William's work. My thanks are also due to Caroline Palmer at Boydell and Brewer for her clear guidance and friendly encouragement, to Richard Sherwood and John Siswick for advice on word-processing problems, to Andrew Rossabi for much careful help on translation difficulties, to Anita Matthews for tracking down biblical references, to Lorely Burkill for her proofreading and to Sally Dormer for suggesting illuminating parallels between William and the art of his era. Above all I wish to thank my wife, Verity, who read the whole translation closely, greatly improved the English and punctuation and patiently listened to progress reports on William, often at Pizza Express, Highgate, on Friday evenings.

Introduction

William's life

The few known facts about William's life can soon be summarised. He was born c.1095 not far from Malmesbury in Wiltshire. He was of mixed Norman and English parentage, with his father being probably the Norman parent. He entered the monastery of Malmesbury as a boy and stayed there as a monk for the rest of his life. He did become precentor, and attended the Council of Winchester in 1139, but, when offered the post of abbot of Malmesbury in the following year, he refused it. He died c.1143. And that is all we know. But during these apparently uneventful days William was writing works which were to win him lasting fame as a historian of England. Some nineteen of these works are recorded, and they have as their crowning glory his two major achievements, *The Deeds of the Kings of England* and *The Deeds of the Bishops of England*, both of which were completed by 1125.

As an author William says little about himself. He writes the first 271 chapters of *The Deeds of the Bishops of England* without revealing a single fact about his own life, other than that he had previously written the *Deeds of the Kings*, or met various eyewitnesses like the 'white-haired priest' of chapter 82, so that it comes as a pleasant surprise when the last chapters do contain a few nuggets of biographical information. We might have guessed the first item, his claim in chapter 271 that following the lead of abbot Godefrey he had done more than anybody else to build up the library at Malmesbury, but chapter 275 is remarkable for revealing a few details of William's boyhood.

There is of course more evidence for William's views and character. He emerges as a kind, good-natured man. His original manuscript included attacks on such prominent people as William II, Ranulf Flambard, bishop of Durham, and Samson, bishop of Worcester. But on returning to his work later, William deleted large sections from those attacks. It is impossible to be certain why he did this, but a disinclination to be censorious may have been one factor involved. In chapter 72 he knows something to the discredit of a young monk, but says, 'I have been happy to forget it, since it is no part of a free-spirited man to jeer at the troubles of others.' Sometimes his good nature may have led him to make excuses for people at the expense of the truth. It is hard to believe that quite so many men were 'led astray by evil whisperers' as William suggests (for example, Aldfrith, king of Northumbria, in chapter 107), or committed some wrong 'through a mistake rather than because of wrong-headed stubbornness', for example, Thomas of York (second chapter 116). Occasionally we spot a twinkle in his eye. In chapter 76 he tells how bishop Ælfheah one night saw a drunken monk being battered in punishment by two demons sent by God, and adds, 'After Ælfheah told the others about this in the morning, it is not surprising that his drinking companions turned teetotal.'

His estimation of himself is as mixed as his Norman English parentage. He can play down his intellectual gifts, for example in the prologue to Book 4 referring to his 'barren intellect and scanty eloquence', whereas in the prologue to Book 5 he proudly states, 'I too have acquired something of a name and reputation.' Certainly in the last four sentences of his work he reveals himself as an unmistakable son of England, for he says, 'It has also been a terrible year for weather. Every month has had thunder and lightning. It has rained almost every day without stopping. Even the summer months were wet and muddy.'

The scope and content of *The Deeds of the Bishops of England*

The Deeds of the Bishops of England is a survey of the bishops in all the dioceses of England from Augustine's arrival in Canterbury in 597 down to the 1120s when the work was being written. For the period after Bede's death in 730 it is the most important single source for English church history. (The title is a slight misnomer, as he includes saints who were not bishops and religious houses, as well as bishops and cathedrals.) Book 1 covers the archbishops of Canterbury and the bishops of Rochester. Book 2 deals with the bishops of London, East Anglia and Wessex. Book 3 moves north to record the deeds of the archbishops of York and the bishops of Lindisfarne and Durham. Book 4 brings the roughly anticlockwise circle back to the bishops of Mercia, and finally in Book 5, 'returning home after a long journey' (Prologue Book 5), William writes of the life of St Aldhelm and the history of his own abbey of Malmesbury.

As for the aims of his work, he tells us in the Prologue that it is his 'enthusiasm for worthwhile knowledge' which has led him to compile his history of the bishops. There is an obvious sense in which a work of church history was 'worthwhile' for monks like William, but the word has a deeper meaning. Like Jane Austen, he believed that life was primarily a moral matter, and it soon becomes clear that a main aim of his writing is, as he puts it himself in the prologue of the second book of his *Deeds of the Kings*, 'to inspire readers to the pursuit of goodness or the avoidance of evil'. He paints attractive pictures of goodness, for example the blessings brought to the whole land by Dunstan, a good man as archbishop of Canterbury (chapter 14). Conversely, his description of the evil actions of bishop Ealhstan of Sherborne (chapter 79) contains the solemn warning 'The originator of the wickedness may die, but his example lives on.' He saw life as a battle between good and evil, but had no doubt that goodness always triumphed in the end, as when the Danish invaders are repelled from the abbey at Malmesbury by the spirit of Aldhelm (chapter 256).

William and his sources

William was a writer who liked to use visual evidence and who travelled widely in England. He may not have visited Tyneside (see p. 221 n. 4), but his record of a Roman inscription at Carlisle (chapter 99) and the description of Wilfrid's church at Hexham (first chapter 116) suggest that he did visit other parts of the north, and the whole of the south of England may well have been within his orbit. He would also have taken the opportunity to copy materials from monastic libraries while on his travels. Antonia Gransden interestingly suggests that the pocket-sized manuscript of *The Deeds of the Bishops of England*, now at Magdalen College, Oxford, may have been the very note book which he took with him on his journeys.[1] But probably the greater part of his information came from books in the monastic library at Malmesbury, which had recently been enlarged by abbot Godefrey (chapter 271). R. M. Thomson's *William of Malmesbury* gives details of this library. Sometimes we can observe William using more than one source, as when in his account of Wilfrid he uses Eddius Stephanus and Bede, but on other occasions he has to rely almost entirely on a single source. For example, the forty or so pages which describe the career of Anselm, apart from four small factual details, are derived wholly from Eadmer. Nor is William in the habit of giving variant versions and his reasons for preferring the one rather than the other (chapter 182 contains a rare example of this.) His basic method is to paraphrase and abbreviate his main source. Decrees and charters may be quoted verbatim, but, apart from Osbern's account of the vision of Ælfgar in chapter 74, it is rare to find him reproducing a story in the exact words of his sources.

The context of *The Deeds of the Bishops of England*

By the time that William was a young man, England had recovered from the chaos that had followed the Norman Conquest, and England and Normandy, once two separate states, had become a single political community. The church had also received an infusion of Benedictine monasticism from Normandy. The strength of the papacy had increased. The pope was claiming that the obligations of prelates to him should override their duty to their king and in England in 1107 Henry I had been forced to renounce lay investiture of bishops, thus acknowledging the secular nature of his kingship. It was a world still completely permeated by Christian thought and practice, and the mixture of devils and angels, visions, divine inspirations, desperate struggles to stay chaste, vows and miracles to be found in William's pages is unfamiliar to most contemporary readers. The miracles especially are omnipresent. Healing

[1] *Historical Writing in England c.550 to 1307* (London, 1974), p. 175.

happens at shrines, not at hospitals, for the poor but frequently for the rich and famous as well. There were plenty of sceptics around in William's own day: in chapter 149 he laments that 'our modern lack of belief is not willing to believe in miracles, even if seen with eye or touched with the finger'. And today such sceptics will have increased a thousandfold. But even for the sceptic the many accounts of miracles are at least well-told, dramatic tales, which constantly elicit sympathy for the unfortunate people of the twelfth century, who, when crippled by physical or mental illness, found their best hope lay in dragging themselves from shrine to shrine until a saint such as Aldhelm took pity on them.

The style of *The Deeds of the Bishops of England*

William did not imitate the style of his master, Aldhelm. Even in translation, Aldhelm's letters in Book 5 still reveal something of the long sentences, complicated structures and exotic vocabulary of their original Latin. William's sentences are much shorter, and, while he may not have the complete lucidity of his contemporary Eadmer, any difficulties in comprehension tend to be caused by the quick, incisive movement of his thought rather than by the organisation of his words into sentences. His writing does not alienate by being too florid or too prosaic, and seldom loses a certain deftness. He can reach heights of pathos and emotion, for example the moving chapters 227–31 about the death and burial of Aldhelm or the address to St Cuthbert in chapter 135, but he is never strident.

William had a mass of material to deal with, but he imposes upon it the clearest of topographical and chronological schemes. The reader encounters a host of characters, places and incidents on his journey through the book, but never loses his way with so sure-footed a guide.

Perhaps his most noticeable gift as a writer is his narrative skill. William, like Herodotus, is primarily a story-telling historian. F. M. Stenton[1] in his bibliographical section in *Anglo-Saxon England* berates William for the high proportion of stories to facts or documents in his work, but, even if stories are not so valuable as historical facts, they still immortalise their subjects, and we can admire the skill with which William tells them. A particularly well crafted example is the account of Aldhelm buying a bible (chapter 224). Opening with a matter of fact description of Dover harbour, it then gives us a vivid picture of Aldhelm strolling on the waterfront, and spotting a bible for sale. After an inconclusive argument between Aldhelm and the sailors over the price and the departure of the sailors, the storm at sea is described in short, staccato sentences with historic present verbs in the Latin, before longer, smoother sentences describe the stilling of the storm and the sailors' return to the shore. Finally Aldhelm's 'judgement of Solomon' and William's own knowledge of this bible bring the story to a strong close.

---

[1] *Anglo-Saxon England*, 3rd edn (Oxford, 1971), p. 699.

William also brings his characters to life; not just his leading actors, Anselm, Wilfrid and Aldhelm, but a host of minor players as well, such as Osmund, bishop of Salisbury, who did his own bookbinding (chapter 83), or Eadburg, the nun, who secretly cleaned the other sisters' shoes in the middle of the night.

Conclusion

No work so long can be without flaws. Sometimes William's habit of condensing his source makes him difficult to understand. For example, the account of Anselm's burial (chapter 66) is much clearer in the longer account in Eadmer. He also makes the occasional mistake, for example mixing up two Johns in chapter 240. And he perhaps has more good nature than insight. Being human he may show some bias towards his own saint and his own monastery: certainly he shows none of the doubt about Aldhelm's relics that he had shown about Oswald's arms at Bamburgh (chapter 155). He may be a better story teller than historical analyst. But these shortcomings are far outweighed by the liveliness of the writing and the fascination of almost all the subject matter. The fault which William himself was most anxious to avoid was that of boring his readers, and he repeatedly asks for the reader's forbearance (for example, chapters 4, 187), but, to my mind at least, this is the one fault of which he is never guilty.

Note to the Translation

This translation is of William's second version of his work, in which he excised some extensive passages of bitter invective written in his younger days. The British Library possesses a finely written but workaday manuscript of the first version (Claud. A.V.), copied soon after William's death, and a bigger, more handsome thirteenth-century copy of the second version with much more rubrication (Reg. D.V.). In 1870 the Victorian scholar, N. E. S. A. Hamilton, produced an edition of William's second version. He based his edition on the manuscript, written in William's own hand, which is now at Magdalen College, Oxford, and, while his text is the text of William's revised version, he retains the excised passages in footnotes. Thanks to his labours, which often included deciphering some fifty lines of William's handwriting crammed on to a page no bigger than 170 × 120 mm, I was able to work on the translation at home, while benefiting greatly from his marginal summaries and his generously detailed 172-page index. I should add that the chapter headings in this translation are not in William or Hamilton, but were devised by me as signposts for readers encountering the work for the first time.

William often uses many different spellings of the same name; to aid the modern-day reader, the names have been made consistent and semi-standardised, generally in line with forms found in *The Blackwell Encyclopaedia of Anglo-Saxon England*. This means that Anglo-Saxon names appear in a form consonant with (the varied) Old English orthography, except for the commonest names, such as Alfred, Edward, which appear in their modern spelling.

The brief notes accompanying the translation are mostly based on the writings of others. I am especially indebted to the books of Rodney Thomson, David Knowles, Frank Stenton, Richard Southern and Henry Mayr-Harting. To read the relevant passages of such historians is to discover the same sense of style and *humanitas* found in William himself.

.

The Deeds of the Bishops of England

Here begins the prologue of William's book about the deeds of the bishops of England

The first episcopal see after the conversion of the English was established in Canterbury,[1] where it still is. This is neither a particularly large English city nor an insignificantly small one. It is situated next to very fertile farmland. Its encircling wall is still complete. So, although it has often experienced the fortunes of war, it continues to nourish its citizens, possessing as it does a gloriously rich heritage of the remains of many saints.[2] It is lucky enough not to lack woods or the waters of a river, and as it is only ten miles from the sea it has a good supply of fish. The people are a mixture of simplicity and sophistication. More than the rest of the English they are still imbued with the spirit of an antique nobility, quicker to honour all with their hospitality, but fiercer in their repulse of injustices. The first see, established in this city, belongs to the archbishop who is the primate and patriarch of all England. We no longer know the site of the archbishopric in the time of the Britons: the passage of time has by now obliterated our memory of it. But I have decided to tell what is still remembered about the archbishops and suffragans of Canterbury. And as I formerly summarised the deeds of the kings of England,[3] it seems to me sensible now to run through the names of the bishops of England, so that with God's help I may now finally complete my long-promised work. When I achieve this, I shall consider myself to have finished a task attempted by no one else, in which I did not rely on my own powers but was led on by my enthusiasm for worthwhile knowledge. For what is more pleasant than to rehearse the gratitude owed to our ancestors by finding out about the deeds of those from whom we have received the rudiments of the faith and encouragement to live well. It would certainly be a clear sign of shameful sloth if we did not know at least the names of the leaders of our own province, seeing that our knowledge on other matters extends to the plains of India and any lands lying beyond which look upon the boundless ocean.[4] These are the reasons why both here and elsewhere I have taken my pen through the most obscure histories,

[1] For most names in the Anglo-Saxon period see Michael Lapidge *et al.*, *The Blackwell Encyclopaedia of Anglo-Saxon England* (Oxford, 2001).
[2] Twelfth-century Christians believed that only the saints went straight to heaven after death, while everybody else awaited the Second Coming. Thus they were the only advocates in heaven for the living, and their remains a material sign of their championship. See ch. 231 for a dilemma caused by this view.
[3] For this work see *De Gestis Regum Anglorum*, 2 vols., ed. and trans. R. A. B. Mynors, R. M. Thomson and M. Winterbottom (Oxford, 1998–9).
[4] William seems to have in mind the classical picture of the earth, in which it was imagined as being encircled by the ocean.

although for this work I do not have the same abundant supply of facts as I had for *The Deeds of the Kings*. There indeed I borrowed material from the chronicles which I had in front of me, and these borrowings, like a light shining from a high watchtower, kept my steps from straying by their guidance. In my present work, however, I have been almost completely without help, groping in the thick darkness of ignorance and without any lamp of history to hold before me and direct my path. But I hope that the light of my intelligence will help me to record the truth in its fullness without faltering and to preserve the brevity which is my aim. An author who does not neglect these two things will be neither absurd nor a nuisance. And so I shall keep to the same narrative framework as in my other works, and, just as in my former *Deeds of the Kings* I dealt with the kingdoms separately, so here I shall go through the various bishoprics province by province in separate books. Wherever I fall short of my aim, the reader will realise that it happened for a reason and forgive me. So this first book will deal with the archbishops of Canterbury and the bishops of Rochester, in whose reigns the kingdom first grew. The others will follow each in their turn.

The end of the Prologue. Now begins the First Book.

Book 1 Kent

Chapter 1 Augustine to Theodore (597–690)[1]

Augustine, the disciple of Gregory the Great, was the first to establish a see at Canterbury, as everybody knows. Gregory actually gave him the pallium[2] and the office of archbishop in London[3] (the evidence for this is a letter of Cœnwulf,[4] as I showed in the first book of *The Deeds of the Kings*),[5] since up to that time the Romans had not discovered that other, obscure city. But seeing that the first teacher of our church was so won over by the attentive hospitality of the king and the affection of the citizens of Canterbury that he protected the inhabitants from his throne for sixteen years while he was alive and after his death from his tomb, all honour was subsequently transferred to Canterbury. Remarkable miracles proclaim how highly God regards his virtues, and even after so many ages Augustine does not grow weary of impressing his people with signs of his activity: he is not going to allow his Canterbury, or for that matter the whole of England, to grow slack in his worship.

He was succeeded by Laurentius, who was archbishop for five years. As Bede's narrative is a brief, summary relation of all the virtues of Laurentius and his successors, probably because he was afraid of being found boring, a certain Goscelin,[6] whom I have mentioned elsewhere, wrote a full account of their virtues, based on what he could learn from the old writers but including new, quite striking and startling items, of which he had been an eyewitness. Here are their names. Mellitus also reigned for five years, Justus for three, Honorius for twenty-six, Deusdedit for ten, and Theodore for twenty-two years. Bede states[7] that Theodore, who was sent by the apostolic see, was the first of all the

---

[1] On the period covered in this chapter see books 1–4 of Bede, *The Ecclesiastical History of the English People*, ed. Judith McClure and Roger Collins and trans. Bertram Colgrave (Oxford, 1999), F. M. Stenton, *Anglo-Saxon England*, ch. 4, and Henry Mayr-Harting, *The Coming of Christianity to Anglo-Saxon England*, 3rd edn (Pennsylvania, 1991), chs. 3 and 4.
[2] A band of white wool, symbolising Augustine's obedience to the pope. See R. H. C. Davis, *A History of Medieval Europe* (London, 1989), Plate V.
[3] Gregory planned metropolitan sees at London and York, the two leading cities of Roman Britain, but the East Saxons who controlled London had reverted to paganism, and Æthelberht, king of Kent 560–616, was at that time the most powerful ruler in southern England.
[4] King of Mercia 796–821.
[5] 1:88.
[6] A monk at St Augustine's, Canterbury. His praises as a writer and a musician are sung by William in *The Deeds of the Kings* 4:342. He was the foremost hagiographer of eleventh-century England. The miracles of which he was an eyewitness probably took place when relics were translated during the rebuilding works at Canterbury.
[7] *Ecclesiastical History* 4:2.

archbishops of Canterbury to exercise pontifical powers in the whole of Britain, in the end removing and appointing bishops on both sides of the Humber just as he pleased: he even consecrated bishops for other cities in York itself, and, as we read in *The Life of the Blessed Wilfrid*,[1] by scheming or force drove Wilfrid and Chad, the archbishops of York, out of the city. We can understand and feel sympathy with those who felt sad that a person of the greatest sanctity and power could not completely shed his stubborn habits, and that the two 'eyes' of Britain were engaged in conflict.[2] My own guess is that Theodore expelled Wilfrid unjustly. After passing through many perils Wilfrid brought his complaint to pope Agatho in Rome. He showed restraint, not wanting to overwhelm with accusations someone appointed by the apostolic see or to allow his own innocence to be in question. These are the words of the appeal which he made to the pope:

> The fact that the most holy archbishop Theodore consecrated three bishops on his own authority without the agreement of my humble self or the consent of any other bishop, while I was still alive and in the see which I was governing, however unworthily, is a fact which it would be more fitting for me to forget than to complain about, granted the reverence I owe to Theodore. Nor do I dare to accuse one who was appointed by this most high apostolic see.

And so Wilfrid was judged innocent by the verdict of the Roman council and sent back to his see, but he did not hold on to it due to the violence of king Ecgfrith[3] and particularly to the actions of Theodore, who either deliberately obstructed him or turned a blind eye to what Ecgfrith was doing. I have not refrained from mentioning this, so that I might show the high regard in which Theodore was held in Rome. The apostolic see was completely unwilling to rescind his decrees, even if they had been wrongly passed.[4] My view is reinforced and supported by the evidence of the letter which Agatho sent to the sixth General Council, meeting in Constantinople. Amongst other things it says:

> I am expecting Theodore, my fellow priest and co-bishop, archbishop and teacher of the great island of Britain, to join my humble self here on a visit from Britain together with other people from the same place, and for this reason I am postponing the council for the present.

You see how highly Theodore was thought of, if Agatho was willing to put off an Ecumenical Council in expectation of his visit.

[1] By Eddius Stephanus, an edition by B. Colgrave (Cambridge, 1927).
[2] Mayr-Harting, *The Coming of Christianity*, pp. 130–9, argues that the conflict was between the Gregorian concept of more, smaller dioceses, espoused by Theodore, and the Gaulish concept of episcopal might, adopted by Wilfrid.
[3] King of Northumbria 670–85.
[4] Stenton views the council as attempting a compromise, 'restoring Wilfrid to his seat in York, but approving Theodore's policy of dividing the Northumbrian see' (*Anglo-Saxon England*, p. 136). For a longer account of this matter by William see ch. 101.

Chapter 2 A miracle of St Letard

Theodore was succeeded by Berhtwald, who reigned for thirty-seven years, and Berhtwald by Tatwine. The miracles and signs of the two archbishops I have just mentioned, together with those of St Letard, who, so antiquity asserts, had come over with queen Bertha,[1] were proclaimed in glowing terms by Goscelin (referred to earlier). Letard, says Goscelin, could do many things but he was especially good at speedily responding to appeals for rain, and a few years ago he provided an amusing spectacle. It was the middle of summer. The sun was burning the Crab, the ploughlands were dusty and dry, and the blazing Dog Star was scoring the thirsty fields.[2] When the body of the saint was brought out to a procession of expectant suppliants, he inflamed their eager wishes by his slowness in doing a miracle. Then, after he was taken in, the precentor, in his anger, shouted out with a loud cry, 'Do you see how dry and desperate the whole world is and do nothing about it?'[3] This witty insult needled the saint and he more than satisfied their eager longings by a mighty downpour of rain. Goscelin next tells of a procession of kings who with all their attendants were staying the night in Augustine's church. His apt names for them are 'lights of England' and 'senators of the English curia'. To this group of saints, the precious crown of the eternal king, Goscelin added two further jewels of inestimable glory, to shine in destruction on the wicked and in help for the needy, namely abbot Hadrian[4] and Mildrith the virgin,[5] who were equally famous for the praises given to their sweetness.

Chapter 3 Tatwine and Nothhelm (731–739)

Tatwine, who held the archbishopric for three years, died in the same year as Bede and was succeeded by Nothhelm.[6] It is said that this is the same Nothhelm who in the preface to Bede's *History of the English* is mentioned as having greatly helped Bede to compile his history when priest in the church of London by bringing to him from the archives at Rome some documents which were needed for his work.

Chapter 4 Cuthbert (740–760)

On Nothhelm's death five years later, Cuthbert, bishop of the Mercians at Hereford, took up the apostolic office.[7] He was a contemporary of

---

[1] The daughter of king Charibert, she had married king Æthelberht of Kent at Paris.
[2] This description of a heat wave owes much to Virgil, *Georgics* 4:425–8. The zodiacal sign of Cancer, the Crab, begins on 21 July. The Dog Star begins to appear in the sky on 27 July.
[3] A sentence from a prayer book used by the Canterbury monks.
[4] Abbot of St Augustine's, Canterbury, 669–708.
[5] Abbess of Minster-in-Thanet from 694. Goscelin's lives of Letard, Hadrian and Mildrith are still extant.
[6] Tatwine had been a priest in the monastery of Breedon-on-the-Hill in Leicestershire. Bede died on 25 May 735.
[7] For Cuthbert as bishop of Hereford see ch. 163.

Boniface,[1] and was responsible for summoning a great council of the English to check abuses. As I explained in *The Deeds of the Kings*,[2] he did this on the advice of Boniface and with the help of king Æthelbald.[3] I shall deal with the purpose and proceedings of this council by listing its decrees, sometimes in my own words but always using the views of previous writers. Please forgive me if I bore you, but we have few details of the activities of the archbishops and it may be worthwhile reading about the zeal of our forefathers in God's cause.

Chapter 5 The Council of Cloveeho (747)

The council, whose decrees I set out below, took place at the beginning of September near a place called Cloveseho[4] during the eternal reign of our Lord Jesus Christ, who together with the power of the Father and the life-giving grace of the Holy Spirit rules over all things. The following bishops of Christ's church, beloved of God, were present at the council: the honourable archbishop Cuthbert, Dunn the venerable bishop of Rochester, and those most reverent bishops of the Mercians Torhthelm and Hwita and Podda; also Hunfrith and Herewald worthy bishops of the West Saxons; also the venerable priests Herdulf of the East Angles and Eardwulf of the East Saxons and Milred of the Wictii;[5] also the honourable bishops Alwig of the province of Lindsey and Sigga of the South Saxons. The council took place in 747, in the fifteenth indiction[6] and in the thirty-third year of the reign of Æthelbald, king of the Mercians, who was present in person with his princes and lords. When these leading churchmen and the lesser dignitaries had assembled from the different provinces of Britain, two documents from the venerable pope Zachary were read out in which he warned the English to live more soberly and threatened to excommunicate those who ignored this. The first decree of the council stated that from now on bishops should show more care in their way of life and in their admonitions of their people. The second that they should live peaceably together, however far apart their residences. The third that individual bishops should tour their parishes every year. The fourth that each bishop should advise the abbots and monks in his diocese to live according to their rule and to love rather than oppress the priests under their control. The fifth that they should teach a life according to the rule even in monasteries which had been unlawfully seized by the non-religious but which now could not be taken away from them. The sixth that no one should be ordained, unless his life had been

[1] An Englishman from Devon who had devoted his life to the conversion of the Germans and had become archbishop of Mainz. For a stimulating account of Boniface see Mayr-Harting, *The Coming of Christianity*, pp. 262–73.
[2] 1:83.
[3] King of Mercia 716–55.
[4] In Berkshire. Its exact location is unknown, but it may have been a monastery. For the provisions of the council see J. Blair and R. Sharpe, ed., *Pastoral Care before the Parish* (Leicester, 1992), pp. 193–211. The fourth decree shows important episcopal supervision of monasteries.
[5] The inhabitants of Worcestershire (the Hwicce).
[6] A fiscal period of fifteen years, instituted by the emperor Constantine in 313.

examined first. The seventh that there should be frequent reading of holy Scripture in monasteries. The eighth that priests should not dispose of secular property. The ninth that these priests should not accept money for baptising young children. The tenth that they should learn and teach an English version of the Lord's Prayer and Creed. The eleventh that they should all carry out their ministries on the same pattern. The twelfth that hymns and psalms in church should be sung, not shouted. The thirteenth that Sunday services and saints' days should be celebrated everywhere at the same time. The fourteenth that Sunday should be properly observed. The fifteenth that the seven canonical hours of prayer should be observed daily. The sixteenth that the lesser and greater rogation days should not be omitted. The seventeenth that the feast of St Gregory and our father Augustine should be kept. The eighteenth that the four Ttmes of fasting should be kept. The nineteenth that monks and nuns should dress according to the rule. The twentieth that bishops should see to it that these decrees were not neglected. The twenty-first that ecclesiastics should not get drunk. The twenty-second that they should not neglect communion. The twenty-third that lay people also should take communion from time to time. The twenty-fourth that lay people should be examined before being made monks. The twenty-fifth that almsgiving should not be neglected. The twenty-sixth that all bishops should inform their people of these decrees. The twenty-seventh reported a discussion about the usefulness of alms-giving and the twenty-eighth a discussion about the usefulness of psalmody. The twenty-ninth stated that monastic communities should be set up according to established practice. The thirtieth that monks should not live among laity. The thirty-first that public prayers should be said for kings and princes.

Chapter 6 The martyrdom of Frederic (838)

The proceedings of this Council (I myself have only touched on the decrees) were immediately reported by archbishop Cuthbert to Boniface, archbishop of Mainz, through his deacon, Cyneberht. Boniface sent him back an elegant letter of congratulation, which the reader will find in its place.[1] As Boniface, formerly called Wynfrith,[2] has so often been mentioned, I shall commit to writing a memorable story about his disciple Frederic which has come to my ears. I do not suppose everybody has heard it, and it enables us to guess the sanctity of the teacher from the virtue of the pupil, for Boniface had Frederic lodging with him, so that he could learn not to fear the powerful and to despise death.

Willebrord,[3] the first bishop of Utrecht, who is mentioned by Bede, breathed his last amid the honours paid to sanctity and old age, and was succeeded as

[1] *The Deeds of the Kings* 1:82.
[2] His new name was given to him by the pope, indicating that his new German church was part of the papacy.
[3] A Northumbrian. He was consecrated as archbishop of the Frisians with Utrecht as his see by pope Sergius in 695. Bede mentions him in *Ecclesiastical History* 5:11.

bishop and teacher in Frisia by Boniface, with Cobanus also ordained a bishop at Utrecht. A long time went by. Both Boniface and Cobanus were now tired of life in this world and were being claimed by heaven, when all of a sudden the Frisians killed and made martyrs of the two of them, being driven on, so it was supposed, by the powers of hell. Lullus filled Boniface's see at Mainz, as I said in *The Deeds of the Kings*,[1] and Frederic, after a delay caused by the violence of the people, succeeded Cobanus at Utrecht. He owed his promotion to Louis the Pious, son of Charlemagne, who chose him as being the nephew[2] and pupil of Boniface and as one who breathed forth the perfume of his sanctity, although many others were canvassing for themselves or their family. He honoured the new bishop on the first day of his ordination by a seat on his right hand at dinner. When the meal was nearly over, the king turned to speak to Frederic, inviting him to be mindful of his recent profession and, showing the firmness of his predecessors, to speak out the truth without any respect of persons and pronounce excommunication upon those who took no notice. But Frederic replied with lowered head and down cast eyes, 'My lord king, you do right to feed the young plant of my profession with your holy exhortations. But I beg your majesty not to refuse to answer a question which I have long been pondering in the recesses of my mind. And, to avoid searching for a distant example, consider this fish on the table here. Is it better to attack it at the top or at the tail?' The king replied 'at the top' in too much of a hurry and without realising the trap into which he had fallen. For Frederic at once picked up his answer and said, 'In the same way, my lord emperor, your Christian faith and piety should surely be accusing you of your sins, or your subjects will be daring to neglect that which they have seen you tolerate with equanimity. So renounce the incestuous marriage you have contracted. That Judith, whom you have bound to your side, is too near to you in blood, and it is not right that the bed of the king should be defamed by lust.' Although Louis found it hard to take this, he kept control of himself and quietly dismissed the archbishop, allowing him to return to his see without a moment's delay.

But these words spoken in the presence of so many courtiers could not be hushed up. Disturbing reports of the conversation reached the ears of all the bishops of the region. Their hearts were troubled and their sorrow was great as they considered that the new bishop had freely and openly spoken about something which they themselves, bishops of long standing, had not even condemned under their breath. And so they were emboldened to be brave, and after many meetings enacted that the marriage should be dissolved and the emperor live in celibacy. Louis was imprisoned and his wife shut in a nunnery. As I have said in *The Deeds of the Kings*,[3] the person who took the lead in this was Lothario, Louis's eldest son. He said repeatedly that he had been guided by his Christian instincts, but his true motive was jealousy. But later the

---

[1] 1:85.

[2] Possibly his son. Davis comments that a son succeeding his father as bishop was more politely referred to as his 'nephew' (*A History of Medieval Europe*, p. 233).

[3] 2:110.

apostolic see made a pious intervention, and a more lenient council decreed that after the prescribed penitence they could enjoy a legitimate marriage in the future. The emperor willingly accepted this verdict and in the goodness of his heart gave up all grudges.

But Judith breathed out a woman's poison and complained in the circle of her cronies about the wrongs done to her by Frederic, bishop of Utrecht, pointing to him as the chief source of her troubles. She found two men who promised to undertake his murder. The bishop knew all about this, being the dwelling place of God himself, and fearlessly waited for the murderers to come. Indeed his desire for martyrdom was so keen that he blamed the villains for dallying. On the very morning he knew they would arrive, he arrayed himself for mass. He had just put on his alb when the boy whose duty it was to admit those who wanted to see his master came in and said that messengers from the empress were standing at the door. Frederic made the excuse that he was busy and told the messengers to wait in the dining room for the time being. When he had sung mass, he entered the bishop's vestry still wearing his vestments and gave instructions for the officers to be brought in there without any witnesses being present. They came in, but were so struck by the brightness of his face and his sacred robes that their hearts sank and they let fall the knives from their hands. But Frederic had already given up this earthly life for the hope of a future one, and when he noticed their dismay, of his own accord he encouraged the assassins to carry out their mission, urging them to take heart and recover their strength. Wicked men take little persuading. They attacked him where he sat, one slicing him from breast to groin, the other across his flanks. While with both hands Frederic tightly held on to his life forces as they ebbed away, he said to the murderers, 'Run, run, you poor fools, before my faithful servants find out. It'll be all up with you, once they catch you.' Fear made the murderers' feet still faster, and they hurried off to the Rhine, where their strong arms soon drove a boat across the river. When in the meantime the chamberlain came into the vestry and asked the bishop why he was sitting there so bloodless, he angrily drove him away and told him to hurry to the city wall to see if the empress's messengers had crossed the Rhine. When the chamberlain reported that their long start had made their arrest difficult, Frederic gave orders for his clergy quickly to gather round him and with steady voice and mind told the whole tragic story. He appointed the singing of the antiphon which begins 'Open for me the gates of justice' and while still alive placed himself in his tomb, winning heaven by this fair death which calls for our veneration. Besides offering my readers some material from abroad, I thought it not useless that the English[1] should be given credit and glory for bringing light to foreign lands. Sanctity is an export too.

---

[1] Frederic, as nephew or son of Boniface, was at least half English.

Chapter 7 Offa attacks the primacy of Canterbury (*c.765*)

After being archbishop for seventeen years, Cuthbert fell ill. He was on the way to death, so he ordered his people to bury him in the archbishops' palace. Because Augustinian monks stubbornly follow ancient custom and carry off the bodies of dead archbishops with a certain vehemence of lamentation, he gave orders that there should be no cries of mourning in house or city and forbade a public funeral. And so, while outsiders were kept from coming to the house in which loud laments had ceased, the body of the archbishop was carried in its grave-wrappings to the church of St John the Baptist, which he had himself built next to the main church. No demand for his body was made by the others, who saw themselves outwitted by his artifice.

Breguwine followed him as archbishop for three years, and he then left the see to Jænberht, formerly abbot of St Augustine. I have spoken about him in the first book of *The Deeds of the Kings*,[1] and I mention him now because Offa, king of the Mercians, fell out with the men of Canterbury and tried to rob Jænberht of the primacy. At the same time he made an attempt to win the glory of it for the kingdom of Mercia by prevailing upon pope Hadrian by means of letters and perhaps by gifts to elevate the bishop of Lichfield[2] to the pallium contrary to ancient custom, and to put all the bishops of Mercia under his control. The names of these bishops were Deneberht of Worcester, Werenberht of Leicester, Eadwulf of Crediton, Wulfheard of Hereford, and two bishops of the East Angles, Ealhheard of Elmham and Tidfrith of Dunwich. And the bishop of Lichfield was called Ealdwulf. On his own initiative Offa had founded many bishoprics in Mercia. He had also attacked the East Angles, having murdered their king Æthelberht. Some bishoprics he transferred elsewhere, for example the bishopric of Elmham to Norwich; some were amalgamated, for example that of Dunwich with Norwich; some have completely disappeared, for example those of Leicester and Crediton. Four bishops remained under the control of the archbishop of Canterbury, those of London, Winchester, Rochester and Selsey. This confusion persisted during the whole of Jænberht's primacy, although he spared no labour or expense to maintain the dignity of his see and crush the greed of its despoilers.[3]

Chapter 8 Æthelheard (790–803) recovers the primacy

Jænberht died after twenty-seven years and was buried in the chapter house of St Augustine. His successor was Æthelheard, bishop of Winchester, who reigned for thirteen years. He was an exceptionally industrious man who had a powerful influence among the nobles. On his advice Ecgfrith, son of Offa, made efforts to restore the honour of the primacy to Canterbury and

---

[1] 1:87.
[2] Conveniently near to Offa's 'capital' of Tamworth.
[3] For Offa's actions in this chapter see Stenton, *Anglo-Saxon England*, pp. 217–18. For a good short account of Offa see *s.v.* in *The Blackwell Encyclopaedia*.

would have done so, had not fate removed him from our midst. But Cœnwulf, king of the Mercians, after an admonitory lesson from Æthelheard and Eanbald, archbishop of York, about the great wrongs committed by his predecessor Offa, completely restored Canterbury to its former state. Cœnwulf and all the bishops of England had sent letters to pope Leo, Hadrian's successor, with Æthelheard himself energetically organising the embassy.[1] To give clearer proofs of this from the ancient evidence, I will add some relevant portions of letters from Alcuin[2] to Æthelheard.

Chapter 9 From Alcuin's letters to Æthelheard: extract I

To archbishop Æthelheard, most holy father and worthy of great reverence among the limbs of Christ, greetings in the love of Christ from Alcuin, the deacon. I have heard that you are well and flourishing and that you have had a meeting with my son Eanbald, archbishop of York. It gives me considerable pleasure to hope that, as a result of your saintly discussions, the honour of our holy church is being increased and the life of the servants of God brought under correction. And so my advice in the main points of my other letters was for your holiness to stay in the country, for I did not want the light of Britain to be put out. But God's will be done, so that the churches of Christ may profit. May God give you a successful journey, and, with his angel accompanying you, take you safely there and back, most dear and loving father. But my chief prayer is that you may remember me before the holy apostles, as I consider it my delight to remember you before St Martin.

Chapter 10 From Alcuin's letters to Æthelheard: extract II

To archbishop Æthelheard, most holy lord and most worthy of all honour. When I read the letter about your success, your safe journey and return to your country, and the kindness of your welcome from the pope, with a joyful mind and a full heart I thanked the eternal Lord God who with a great gift of mercy had directed your travels and journey so prosperously, giving you the grace of accomplishing your mission to the apostolic see before the face of the pope, and allowing you to return with your prayers answered. It was through you that he again thought it right to exalt the most holy see of our first teacher, Augustine, to its original height of honour. For an hour it seemed to have been torn apart by dissension and quarrelling and the jealous wranglings of certain people. Happy is the man who makes it his task to preserve the unity of peace in brotherly love, but much happier is he who strives with pious toil to reshape within the fastening of one body the entrails of love which have been ripped out by others. So now, under the operation of the divine grace, our limbs are

---

[1] See Stenton, *Anglo-Saxon England*, pp. 225–7 for the background to the events summarised by William in this chapter.

[2] Educated at the cathedral school in York, Alcuin played a central part in Charlemagne's revival of learning. For Alcuin see Mayr-Harting, *The Coming of Christianity*, p. 276.

fixed as a unity to their proper head, priestly worth enjoys its ancient honour, brotherly peace sheds its gleam on the highest bishops of Britain, and under the control of its two metropolitan states there flourishes a single will for piety and harmony. This I have understood from reading your grace's letter.

Chapter 11 From Alcuin's letters to Æthelheard: extract III

In another letter Alcuin begged that the bishop of the Mercians should not be stripped of his pallium while he was still alive. The passage goes like this:

> I approve of the reading of holy Scripture being renewed through your most holy care and the dignity of the church everywhere being raised up high. It is right that the holy see of Canterbury, which was broken into parts not by rational planning but by greed for power, should again be the first in sanctity and honour, as it was the first in faith. If unity can be peaceably brought about and the tear mended, it seems good that this should happen with the consent of all the priests of Christ and your co-archbishop of the church of York. The one proviso, however, is that the holy bishop of the Mercians should not be stripped of the pallium during his lifetime, although the ordination of bishops should be transferred back to that first, holy see.

Chapter 12 Æthelheard's restoration of the church

So Æthelheard was the one man who restored our church, not by delay but by enterprise, if I am allowed to adapt a saying of Ennius[1] about Fabius. It was not only Canterbury, restored by his efforts to its former honour, that was indebted to him for great benefits, but also the whole of England, which he had not allowed to be under the heel of a subordinate see. He is on a level with the highest pontiffs after the first teachers: in fact if I said that he almost ranks above them, I do not think I would be making a mistake, for it does definitely seem a greater achievement to have restored a lost authority than to preserve a recovered one, though that too deserves its praise. If anybody doubts his great holiness and the reverence in which he was held, he should read pope Leo's letter to king Cœnwulf, to be found in the first book of *The Deeds of the Kings*,[2] in which the pope calls him most holy, most worthy, most loved and most experienced. I am sure the high and holy pope would not have repeated such words if there was not evidence for them being true.

Chapter 13 Wulfred to Wulfhelm (805–942)

Æthelheard was followed by Wulfred for twenty-eight years, Feolgild for three months, Ceolnoth for forty-one years, and Æthelred for eighteen years. These

[1] An early Roman poet. He described Fabius' delaying tactics against Hannibal in the line, 'One man by delaying saved the day.'
[2] 1:89.

archbishops in unbroken succession did many things, so we believe, worthy of God and their age, but the passage of time has swallowed them all up in oblivion and nothing of them has come down to our day except a faint outline. Æthelred was followed for thirty-four years by Plegmund, tutor of king Alfred, who, as I said in the second book of *The Deeds of the Kings*,[1] ordained seven bishops at Canterbury in one day. Their names and sees can be read there by any one who wishes. Plegmund's successor was Æthelhelm, the one of the seven bishops whom he had ordained for Wells. Wulfhelm followed Æthelhelm, for thirteen years at Wells, and on Æthelhelm's death, at Canterbury.

Chapter 14 King Æthelstan makes Oda archbishop (942)

Then Oda, second bishop of Ramsbury, starred as archbishop for twenty years. I have often mentioned the five bishops of the West Saxons, consecrated by Plegmund in the time of Edward the Elder:[2] Oda was soon afterwards added as a sixth, with his see at Ramsbury and his diocese the county of Wiltshire. There continued to be a bishop at Sherborne with his diocese of the counties of Dorset and Berkshire remaining intact. It is right to pay honour to Oda's outstanding reputation for sanctity and miracles, based on the tradition which has come down to us. I am keen to do this not only for Oda, but also for other English saints, whenever I get the chance, and especially for those whose deeds are not famous everywhere. It would be madness to describe in detail the deeds of saints whose talents have been glowingly reported by other writers. So here is evidence to make Oda's saintly character clearer.

Just as a rose, as it grows, triumphs over the prickly brambles, so Oda suppressed the wildness of his Danish birth and emerged as a great specimen of goodness. His parents had invaded England at the time of king Alfred. On the death or departure of the other Danes, Oda briefly fought as a soldier for Edward, but soon took the tonsure and became a priest. As his services increased in number he became bishop of Ramsbury and attracted the friendship of king Æthelstan. And so it happened that when the king marched against Analavus,[3] the bishop was at his side to fire his spirit in times of success and to put things right when misfortunes occurred. On that tragic night when the king was almost cut off by the enemy, his very security having made him relax his caution too far, he lost his sword. (I have told this story in the second book of *The Deeds of the Kings*.)[4] Oda came at the king's call. Everything was full of a blind confusion, but Oda offered up prayers to the heavens and – a true heavenly gift – his gaze first fell upon the sword, which by divine chance had slipped from the king's scabbard. Oda gave a loud cry. The incident was

---

[1] 2:129.

[2] These West Saxon bishops were five of the seven mentioned in the previous chapter: they are listed in ch. 80. The other two were the bishops of the South Saxons and of Dorchester. Edward the Elder ruled 900–24.

[3] Analavus, king of Dublin, also called Óláfr, invaded England in 937 and was defeated at the battle of Brunanburg (probably Bromborough on the Wirral).

[4] 2:131.

immediately reported to Æthelstan and had such an affect on him that even then he did not hesitate to call Oda his life's protector and on the death of Wulfhelm elevated him to the primacy of Canterbury.

Oda struggled stubbornly against this, since he had not yet assumed a monk's clothing and he did not want it to seem that any ambition of his was infringing the customs of his ancestors, for up to that time no one had become archbishop unless wearing a monk's habit. But when the consent of all the bishops was added to the wishes of the king, our saintly hero at last tamed his unbending determination and yielded to the common will, recognising the proverb, 'The voice of the people is the voice of God.' And so he crossed the channel and became a monk at Fleury.[1] He was a good and sensible man, neither laughing at the support of the citizens nor tarnishing ancient custom. As long as Æthelstan lived, the friendship of king and archbishop flourished unimpaired. Each helped the other, Oda speaking out on matters of God and Æthelstan, if needed, brandishing the sword.

Chapter 15 Oda honours Wilfrid

But when jealous fate removed the young king in his prime, Oda enjoyed the favour of a similar friendship with Edmund and Eadred,[2] though now far advanced in years and his white hairs ennobled with sanctity. There was nothing in their behaviour against which his episcopal rigor needed to be directed. He even journeyed with them to Northumberland, not to fight battles but to bring back the holy bodies of the saints, of whom that soil had once produced such a fertile crop. During the journey it pained him to see at Ripon the church of our most famous father Wilfrid in ruins because of the Danes. He got the rubble cleared away from above Wilfrid's tomb and reverently transferred his remains to Canterbury. And so that he might set on a pedestal this brightest light of his country, he ordered Wilfrid's life to be written as an epic poem. The task was undertaken by a certain Fridegod[3] in quite reasonable verse, except that his love of Greek and detestation of Latin caused him to use many Greek words, so that an apt description of his work would be the line of Plautus,[4] 'Nobody will understand this except the Sibyl.' Oda also showed clearly that he was a literary man in the letter addressed to his bishops after a synod in the time of king Edmund. It was as follows:

Chapter 16 A letter of Oda to his bishops (943)

I, Oda, archbishop of the church of our Saviour Lord Jesus Christ, metropolitan in the city of Dorobernia,[5] with the help of the wonderful

---

[1] Oda's visit was the first English contact with this important monastery on the Loire, reputed to have the body of St Benedict himself.

[2] Brothers of Æthelstan. They ruled from 940–55.

[3] A monk of Canterbury.

[4] Pseudolus 1:1:23.

[5] Dorobernia was the ancient name for Canterbury. See ch. 29.

mercy of the omnipotent king of the heavens, wish my fellow bishops in the catholic faith and brothers in love's spiritual rigour, prosperity in this present life and beatitude in the heavenly glory. If in some way the wealth of the whole world could be put before our eyes so that through the gift of the emperor it might all be used in our service, I would gladly distribute it all to you, and for the salvation of your souls I would add myself to the pile as well, since it is from my desire for your sanctity that I long and hope to be strengthened for that task over which God has set us as workers.

After a long passage explaining the burdens of his office, he added:

I humbly pray and appeal to your sanctity, as one unworthy but concerned, that you do not show yourselves lukewarm and negligent in the care of souls. On the day of dreadful judgement let not God complain about you, saying, 'My shepherds fed not my flock but themselves',[1] and again, 'They were princes, and I knew them not.'[2] Instead let it be our concern to give food to the family of God which he has put in our charge, I mean that measure of grain in due season, which is sound doctrine. Although it is not through the quality of any merits of mine that I take it on myself to comfort and encourage you, being indeed the only unworthy one and guilty of innumerable sins, I do need and am glad to be strengthened by your brotherly admonitions faithfully given. No, it is in the ancient authority of my predecessors, Augustine of blessed memory and the other saints by whose efforts the Christian rule first became known from this archiepiscopal see to all the quarters of England, that I have decided to write this letter containing God's word for the benefit of you all. My purpose is that our most high king Edmund (to use his special title) and all his people may rejoice to imitate themselves what they hear about us and what they hear from us, and that all peoples everywhere subject to his kingly authority may follow the lead of our unblemished life in love, delight and exultation.

Chapter 17 Oda looks after his church

Edmund's son Eadwig, who succeeded to the kingdom after his uncle Eadred, was notorious for his headstrong rashness and lechery. He so angered Oda that the archbishop excommunicated him and stopped his association with a harlot by first expelling and then hamstringing her.[3] Eadwig got his own back by a furious attack on the monks of the whole of Britain. In the end only Oda and Dunstan, who was then abbot,[4] dared resist him even verbally, for, as Seneca says, 'A cock is lord of his own dung heap.'[5] In the meantime the archbishop

[1] Ezekiel 34:8
[2] Hosea 8:4.
[3] See Stenton, *Anglo-Saxon England*, pp. 364–5 for some defence of Eadwig against such monastic attacks as this.
[4] Dunstan was abbot of Glastonbury from 942 to 960.
[5] *Apocolocyntosis* 8.

fixed his mind on God and performed a flood of miracles. He regained lawful control of many estates belonging to his see which had been lost during the Danish invasion. In the end it was agreed that no archbishop before him had been Oda's equal in such matters. Osbern[1] adds some small testimony to Oda's abilities when he says that he would have been mourned for ever by the whole English world for his sanctity and energy, if Dunstan had not succeeded him. When his archiepiscopal church was without a roof, he must have covered it with non-stop prayers, for, incredible though this may seem, during the whole time the new roof was being got ready, not a single drop of rain wetted the site. What makes this more remarkable is that the heaviest rainstorms and continuous, mighty tempests shook the whole world during those days. He so convinced many doubters of the reality of our Lord's body that he openly displayed the bread on the altar turned into flesh and the wine in the chalice into blood, before turning it back again to its usual appearance and fit for human consumption. While he was blessing at Canterbury the most holy Dunstan, bishop elect of Worcester, he conducted the whole proceedings of the consecration in such a way that he seemed to be blessing not the bishop of Worcester but the archbishop of Canterbury. When the clergy muttered a mild protest, he prophesied that he knew what he was doing and that on his death Dunstan would be the head of the church at Canterbury. So, if they judged rightly, he ought not to be blamed for what divine inspiration had set on foot through his ministry. And in the end his prophecy did not fail to come true, although Ælfsige, bishop of Winchester, had tried to get in its way. For when Oda was delighting the long expectant angels with his presence, Ælfsige stole an edict from king Edgar and pushed his way into Kent with a band of supporters whom he had bribed. On the first day of his reception there he could not refrain from spewing forth the rage which had been fomenting in his mind. He stamped on the grave of the blessed Oda and insulted his soul with the words, 'At last, you miserable old man, you have breathed out your life and departed, making room, though late in the day, for a better man. Despite you I have achieved my long-standing ambition. For this my grudging thanks to you.'

But when at the day's end that breather of madness had gone to bed, he saw standing by him the ghost of the blessed Oda, reproaching him for his abuse and threatening him with speedy death. But Ælfsige thought he was being mocked by a phantom of his dreams, took no notice and hurried across the Alps to Rome to receive the pallium. But in the mountains he was frozen by the coldness of the snow and could hit upon no other remedy but to plunge the feet, with which he had violated the saint's tomb, into the still-breathing entrails of disembowelled horses. Not even so did the cold relax its grip. He grew stiff and his soul fled away into death.

---

[1] A twelfth-century precentor of Christ Church, Canterbury. Peter Hunter Blair, *An Introduction to Anglo-Saxon England*, 2nd edn (Cambridge, 1977), p. 173, suggests that Oda's reputation may have suffered through the lack of a near contemporary biographer.

Chapter 18 The partnership of Edgar and Dunstan (960–988)

So with Ælfsige dead, Dunstan, who had been long marked out by divine sign as archbishop, was courted by king Edgar,[1] who urged him to think himself worthy of the primacy because of his holiness. More than once Dunstan put aside his request with deaf ears, but at last he gave in, overcome by the united assent of all the bishops. Dunstan, the nephew of archbishop Æthelhelm, had been first abbot of Glastonbury, then bishop of London and Winchester and finally archbishop of Canterbury.[2] He had adorned the various stages in his career with unceasing virtues. The divine spirit had assuredly breathed on the heart of the king, for he looked to Dunstan's advice in all matters and unhesitatingly did whatever the archbishop was minded to command. For his part Dunstan never left out what he knew was consonant with the king's reputation and safety. When the king hesitated, he would put sharper pressure on him. Whenever he transgressed, Dunstan pointed to his own previous way of life as a model for his subjects, and he would mete out savage punishments without any respect of persons. I gave an example of one of these in *The Deeds of the Kings*.[3] Dunstan sentenced the king to seven years penance for his unlawful affair with a woman who had become a nun as a cover.[4] In this way the nobles were brought into line with the example and standard of the king, and dared to do little or nothing contrary to law and justice when they saw their master so obedient to Dunstan.

As for the common herd, you should by now have no doubt to what extent Dunstan kept them from crime, either when they wanted to buy the favour of their masters or when they wanted to avoid the harsh sentence of the law. In addition military discipline was properly tightened and the greed of thieves and the double-dealing of the money changers were suppressed by capital punishment. Absolutely nothing was omitted which might offend the internal judge.

The monastic orders in every place maintained a life which copied Dunstan's standards, especially because they were ruled by men with a vital religion and a reputation for knowledge, whom neither sloth could make sluggish nor lawlessness make headstrong. The king and the archbishop between them had everywhere promoted men like this, after long and careful weighing in the balances and using the deep insight of their rival minds. The secular clergy[5] of many churches, when given the choice of changing their clothes[6] or leaving, left their churches, thus making places vacant for better men. Over the whole

---

[1] The younger brother of king Eadwig.
[2] For Dunstan's career and importance as a monastic reformer see David Knowles, *The Monastic Order in England 943–1216*, 2nd edn (Cambridge, 1963), pp. 31–56, and H. R. Loyn, *The English Church 940–1154* (Harlow, 2000), pp. 8–18.
[3] 2:158.
[4] For this woman disguised as a nun, who was called Wulfthryth and the mother of his daughter Eadgyth, see ch. 87. Mayr-Harting, *The Coming of Christianity*, pp. 257–61 discusses penance in the Anglo-Saxon church.
[5] Men in holy orders who were not monks or friars but served as priests 'out in the world'.
[6] By becoming monks.

island religious houses rose up, the altars of the saints were piled with stores of precious metals, nor were the morals of the builders inferior to the splendour of the buildings.[1]

And so with men of every class aglow to serve God, the earth itself seemed also to rejoice in the peace. The fields responded to the farmers with rich crops. There poured forth from full horn an abundance of every good thing, nor ever in the time of Dunstan did a sick harvest find it easy to disappoint the hopes of the countryfolk. The weather smiled with happy face. Fogs were unknown. No clouds brought in diseases under a heavy sky. Fear of an enemy from over the seas was a thing of the past. All was calm and tranquil. And in the cities there was no prejudice against the poor, no discord amongst the living and no lawsuits because of the dead. The root of all these blessings of God's grace was seen in Dunstan. From Dunstan the plant pushed above ground and became Edgar and from Edgar it spread over the people. Those were happy times, with an archbishop whose deeds never fell short of his words, and a king who listened carefully to his prelate's pronouncements.

Chapter 19 Dunstan's miraculous powers

It was such achievements that won and preserved fame for our hero much more than any miracles, though with God's help he was not short of these either. I am persuaded to give just a brief list of them here by the thought that anyone ignorant of his deeds who chances to pick up this book can find out how far this saint, while still a traveller on this earthly pilgrimage, had a foretaste in his mind of the joys of heaven. His future sainthood was foretold by God, its author, in a happy omen which preceded his birth. When pregnant with him and just about to give birth, his mother was sitting in the church of the Purification of the Blessed Mary amid a large congregation of citizens. Suddenly, through accident or the will of God, all the lights went out. In the general consternation his mother's candle was lit from heaven. She passed on her light to the others and so dispelled their fear and restored their peace of mind. As a boy Dunstan was given to reading. And then, when he had mastered with his powerful intellect the books of all his schools, he more willingly and warmly embraced those things which when the character is formed lead the mind heavenwards. As a very little boy he repelled with a stick a night invasion of the devil, who had a pack of raving hounds close about him. Once, when the church was locked, he entered by being gently put down on the ground by the help of ministering angels. When he was older, his harp, which had been hung on a peg, played without human hand the tune of 'Heaven is the joy of the souls of the saints.' On hearing it he realised even then that he was being forewarned of the endurance of trials, and he trembled when they soon came along. Once as a young man at the office for the dead he

---

[1] For a short account of the tenth-century Benedictine reform movement, in which Dunstan played a leading part, see Loyn, *The English Church*, pp. 9–12, and for a longer account see Knowles, *The Monastic Order*, pp. 31–82.

received an oracle foretelling the success he would achieve in the eyes of God and the world. And so that he should not think he was being tricked by a nebulous, empty phantom, he received a sign which showed him the place where in three days time a priest was to be buried who was not yet even sick or ill. The king's horse bolted and carried him towards a precipice. At death's door the king cried out the name of the absent Dunstan, who rescued him by checking the horse's gallop at the very edge of the steep gorge.[1] Thanks to careless workmen a huge beam was slipping down. From far off Dunstan stretched out a sign of the cross, and put it back in its place. When he was now archbishop and primate of Britain, he needed water for a service. He made it spring forth from a natural bowl of rock, which has produced a perpetual stream of water to this day.

He clearly foresaw all the tricks of the devil and ably eluded them. Once, when the devil was whispering feminine filth, he singed him with some glowing tongs. And when the devil was attacking him verbally in the form of a wolf or a bear, he would drive him away with his stick. One day the devil was jeering at him loudly and repeatedly out of joy at his exile. Dunstan checked him with threats and put his threats into effect, for, when he returned from exile, he won souls for God, which caused the devil great losses. Informed by gleeful evil spirits that king Edmund was about to die and that Eadwig's death had taken place, he buried the body of Edmund at Glastonbury and rescued the soul of Eadwig from the attacks of his enemies. And there is something more remarkable. I should relate with the awe of great reverence how with his physical eyes he caught sight of the Holy Spirit in the appearance of a dove and saw him come to the help of a woman in agony of mind who was saying masses for herself, and then with welcome flight settle on the tomb of the most blessed Oda. At every possible future opportunity he called Oda 'the good', using 'Oda the good' as his proper usual name. And then, good God, there was the familiar way in which the heavenly spirits appeared to him and the close conversations they had with him, enlivening with their holy encouragement the weariness of one who even then was sighing for his 'country'. He knew of the birth and future felicity of king Edgar from a choir of angels and of the death of king Eadred from an unusually fierce onset of storm clouds. The significance of their awful clashings was proved by the immediate death of the animal on which he was sitting. He saw and proclaimed the happy departure for heaven of an absent pupil. He was a clear-eyed prophet, and never suffered the setback of a false prediction. He foretold the future trouble of king Æthelred, the successive deaths of Eadgyth[2] the maiden and bishop Æthel-wald.[3] He appointed the holy Ælfheah as Æthelwald's successor, on the advice

---

[1] This miracle took place in the summer of 940. The king was Edmund and the precipice Cheddar Gorge. Edmund had been intending to send Dunstan into exile, but this incident persuaded him to make him abbot of Glastonbury instead.
[2] King Edgar's daughter. See ch. 87.
[3] Æthelwald was bishop of Winchester (d. 984), and another leader of the monastic reform movement of his century.

of the apostle Andrew. For he especially enjoyed Andrew's help, whether in avoiding defeats or taking successes calmly.

But what topped all previous miracles and put everything else in the shade was that when awake he saw as a miracle present before him our Lady, Jesus' mother, inviting to Christ's praises her companions of modesty, amongst whom was his own mother, and repeatedly singing in tuneful voice the famous chant of Sedulius,[1]

> Friends, let us sing, let us sing praises unto the Lord:
> Let the sweet love of Christ resound from pious lips.

This story is truly wonderful and completely amazing, but it is not divorced from the stability of truth: wrapped in a yellow mantle he actually saw with his eyes and drank in with his ears things which through God's great gift are granted to the saints in the life to come, but for which in this life he gently encourages them with the happy caress of blessed hope. I even believe, and I am sure it is true, that he also heard the song of the angels chanting the Kyrie eleison, a chant which is now gladly taught and learnt in English churches.

So Dunstan, rich in triumphs, victorious and famous, to his own great glory but the immense grief of his country, was lifted up to heaven in the twenty-seventh year of his archbishopric. At once the weather's happy face disappeared and the peace, won by his wisdom, vanished with the arrival of the Danes, despite those great miracles with which he alleviated the catastrophes falling upon his sons. One of these miracles I heard told the other day by a certain monk of Christ's church, although I have not seen a written account of it. A thief was condemned to being thrown over a precipice and cried aloud for help to St Dunstan. Pushed backwards by his executioners, he jumped over the edge blindfold, but was not hurt. Then the blessed Dunstan actually spoke to him and undid his blindfold. The poor wretch was heartened by this help and escaped by rough paths to higher ground. He was stopped from slipping back by the efforts of a hand which he did not see but which upheld his uncertain body. But because I am writing about the turbulence of the times in my work and you can read about the miracles of the saint in the books of others,[2] I shall go back to the line of archbishops.

Chapter 20 Æthelgar, Ælfric, Sigeric and Ælfheah (988–1012)

Dunstan was succeeded for one year by Æthelgar. The blessed Æthelwald had made him the first abbot of the new monastery at Winchester. After this he had also been bishop of the South Saxons with his see at Selsey (since removed to Chichester). On his death, he was succeeded for eleven years by Ælfric, formerly bishop of Ramsbury and before that abbot of Abingdon. Some[3] say that as archbishop of Canterbury he drove out the priests and established

---

[1] A Latin Christian poet of the fifth century.
[2] For example in the lives of Dunstan written by Osbern and Eadmer.
[3] The Anglo-Saxon Chronicle for 995.

monks there, but I do not think this is true. For it is well known that there were monks in the church of St Saviour in the time of archbishop Laurentius who succeeded the blessed Augustine. Evidence for this is in a letter of pope Boniface to king Æthelberht, which will be given later.[1] Sigeric succeeded Ælfric.[2] He had been bishop of Ramsbury for five years, and, as I said in *The Deeds of the Kings*,[3] it was on his advice that king Æthelred sold the liberty of his conscience for a price to the Danes, trying to buy peace from his enemies with silver whom he could have expelled with the sword, if he had not lacked the guts. The result was the payment of an impossible tribute placed on England, which completely impoverished the people.

His successor, Ælfheah, formerly bishop of Winchester, refused to do this for the six years and seven months of his archbishopric, not wishing to buy soft peace for himself at the expense of his unhappy subjects. He was captured, thrown into prison, and finally, when stoned to death by the Danes themselves, he committed his soul to heaven.[4] His life describing his many virtues and miracles was written by Osbern.[5] He reports a remarkable miracle which took place when Ælfheah was staying at Rome: he announced to his companions with complete accuracy the death of Cœnwulf, his successor at Winchester. Moreover, when the day of his glory dawned and he was now about to slake the fury of his enemies with his death, he had a vision of Dunstan declaring his punishment would soon be over and promising him future glory. I have said elsewhere[6] that his body, showing traces of blood which is still fresh, has to this day not known the stain of putrefaction, but there is no need to follow the crowd and tramp again down this well worn path.

Chapter 21 Some last English archbishops (1013–1050)

Lyfing, also called Æthelstan, succeeded Ælfheah for seven years. He was promoted from bishop of Wells to archbishop with the help of king Æthelred. Æthelred was still alive.[7] His many misfortunes had shown him all too clearly the truth of the prophecy of the blessed Dunstan I referred to earlier.[8] He was a man who saw his country overwhelmed before his eyes and himself in the end driven into exile without hitting upon any remedy. Some put this down to his feeble body, others to his sluggish mind. But, however posterity may take my words, I am absolutely sure that a great sign of his future troubles had been his failure to bring help to the archbishop when he had been imprisoned

---

[1] In ch. 30.
[2] William is mistaken here. In fact Sigeric (990–4) preceded Ælfric (995–1005).
[3] 2:165.
[4] The Danes killed him on Saturday 19 April 1012. According to the famous account of the Anglo-Saxon Chronicle, 'They pelted him with bones and with ox-heads, and one of them struck him on the head with the back of an axe, so that he sank down with the blow'.
[5] Around 1080, at the request of archbishop Lanfranc.
[6] *The Deeds of the Kings* 2:165.
[7] In 1013, having become king in 978.
[8] In ch. 19.

for seven months. Neither the majesty of the archbishop nor the indignity of the catastrophe had stirred him to act as his avenger. So I could use of Æthelred the old proverb, 'The lightning flash of goodness produces dull darkness.' For when did England have anyone comparable to his father Edgar in goodness, or to his son in sloth? So, as I have said, Lyfing took the place of the dead Ælfheah. After him, for eighteen years Æthelnoth was archbishop: I said a few things about him in my history of Cnut.[1]

Æthelnoth was followed for eleven years by Eadsige, who made Edward king after the death of Harthacnut. He gave his authority and blessing to the efforts of earl Godwine and did not listen to the prayers of the Danes who were opposing the appointment. He was soon attacked by an incurable illness, and of his own free will resigned his office while still alive, having first in secret council with the king and the earl proposed that Siweard, abbot of Abingdon, should succeed him. But Siweard was so ungrateful to the proposer of the honour that he even deprived the sick man of necessary food, and so was eliminated as successor designate. He was given the bishopric of Rochester, to make his shame less and to comfort him for his loss.

Chapter 22 Robert, the first Norman archbishop (1051–1052)

The king had already made Robert, a monk from Jumièges, bishop of London. He now made him archbishop, in which office he lasted two years. The king gave him this very great reward as a recompense for the goods which Robert had once given to the king when he was in exile in Normandy.[2] So Robert used their old friendship and his new honour to claim first place in the king's counsels, deposing some and elevating others, just as he wished and pleased. I am telling a story known in England and repeating things I have said elsewhere.[3] But the envy of the English against a Norman made the king's goodwill less effective. Robert, however, stubbornly fought his corner, until he had banished from England the leading nobles, I mean Godwine and his sons, accused before the king on a charge of treachery. There were other causes and other authors of the banishment, as I have explained elsewhere,[4] but it was Robert who blew the loudest trumpet and took the lead in the accusation. And now he had the pleasure of seeing his decisions put into effect. But next year the exiles' cause won the support of the people, and they were brought back. The archbishop knew very well that this reconciliation would be harmful to himself, and he went off to Rome to escape judicial proceedings. He was on his way back from there with a letter proclaiming that he was innocent and should be reinstated when he died at Jumièges.[5]

---

[1] *The Deeds of the Kings* 2:184.
[2] Edward the Confessor was in Normandy during the reign of Cnut (1016–36).
[3] *The Deeds of the Kings* 2:197.
[4] *The Deeds of the Kings* 2:199.
[5] For the events of this chapter see Loyn, *The English Church*, pp. 58–9.

Chapter 23 Stigand as archbishop (1052–1070)

There was a certain Stigand who was waiting for such an opportunity and he seized it. Some time ago when he had been deprived of the bishopric of the East Angles, Stigand had set his mind on higher office and grabbed the bishopric of Winchester. Now he got around the innocent and simple-minded king, and added the archbishopric to his other great honours for seventeen years. In other matters indeed he was not lacking in judgement or inefficient. But where his ambitions were concerned, he gave no thought to proper behaviour. He snatched all that he could from others, stored it away for himself and never put any check on his greed. The sacred offices of the church were bought for himself or sold to others after persuasion, with bishoprics and abbacies actually up for sale in the open market. His avarice only acknowledged any limits when what he wanted was not available. You will surely say that animal greed[1] is the right description for the man who was in sole personal possession of the bishopric of Winchester, the archbishopric of Canterbury and many abbacies besides, when a good man would have been more than satisfied with one of these. My opinion is that Stigand's sin was just a mistake rather than deliberate. Like most or just about all the English bishops of those times he was illiterate[2] and did not realise how wrong his actions were, assuming that the business of ecclesiastical affairs could be transacted just like political ones. He would never have earned a pallium from Rome, despite his bribery being busily at work there as well, if a certain Benedict had not illegally seized the apostolic see. Benedict sent him a message of congratulation for calling him pope, when the other archbishops treated him as a joke. But Benedict was soon deposed, his acts made null and void and a decree passed in a proper council that the pallium could not have been legally bestowed by someone who was not legally pope. This did not bring Stigand to his senses. He continued to think as little of the salvation of souls as if he had been enjoying political office.[3]

Meanwhile duke William of Normandy came to England and conquered the country. The will of God was on his side and he had collected various pretexts which he personally regarded as valid. When his victory at the battle of Hastings and his capture of Dover castle had spread the terror of his name, he came to London. Stigand and the English nobles went out to cheer him on arrival and show their support. After talks together William received Stigand as father and archbishop and Stigand received William as king and son. But the king refused to take the crown of the realm from Stigand's hand,[4] with his usual cunning summoning men from the apostolic see to prevent this. And on soon sailing to Normandy, he took a reluctant Stigand with him on the pretext of doing him honour, to prevent treachery mushrooming in England in his

---

[1] For Stigand's avarice see also *The Deeds of the Kings* 2:199.
[2] For illiteracy in England see *The Deeds of the Kings* 2:123 and 3:245.
[3] Loyn, *The English Church*, pp. 60–1, finds more good to say about Stigand.
[4] The king in fact received it from Ealdred, archbishop of York. See ch. 115.

absence by Stigand's hand. In this situation it is difficult to assess the value of the courtesies performed to him by the king, when he ceremoniously rose to his feet for Stigand on every occasion, and when he made him walk side by side in a long series of processions through all the bishoprics and abbacies of Normandy.

But whatever was concealed in these wrappings burst forth into the light of day when Ermenfred, legate of pope Alexander and bishop of Sion,[1] came to England. By the king's wish he summoned a council and deposed Stigand, who protested his loyalty to William and cried out against such violence. William blandly excused himself by alleging orders from the pope, but did nothing about changing the decision to depose Stigand, and in fact kept him in prison at Winchester for the rest of his life. There Stigand kept himself alive on short commons: very little food was supplied by the state and with typical stubbornness he refused to allow anything to be brought from his own resources. When his friends, especially king Edward's widow, queen Eadgyth, urged him to wear nicer clothes and eat nicer food, he swore by all the oaths there are that he had neither money nor wealth. But the vast quantities of riches found after his death in underground cellars showed this oath was very far from the truth. The key which locked the desk for his papers and which was hanging round the dead man's neck enabled information about these riches to be found. For when the key was put in the lock, it revealed through the papers found inside both the quality and quantity by weight of his precious metals.

Chapter 24 King William makes Lanfranc archbishop (1070)

Stigand had not yet breathed his last, when Lanfranc, abbot of Caen, was chosen by king William to be archbishop.[2] He was a Lombard by race, and his origins not all that obscure and lowly. He was very famous for his scholarship. He brought the liberal arts from Italy to France, where they had long languished, and gave them fresh polish with his intellect. He spent his younger years on worldly matters, but as he grew older he turned his mind to holy Scriptures. He was so influenced by their teachings that he set no value on the smoke of the world and the bombastic eloquence of the gentiles and developed a deep longing to become a monk. He spent a long time looking round many places, but of all the many abbeys in Normandy his choice fell upon Bec: he was attracted by the poverty of the place and the spirituality of the monks. Indeed the day he happened to arrive there he caught sight of the abbot, a man called Herluin, with his habit tucked up and his hands smeared with clay about to bake bread. So he became a monk there. He was a man who knew nothing about winning a living from the soil, so he taught dialectic in lectures open to

---

[1] In Switzerland.

[2] See D. J. A. Matthew, *The Norman Conquest* (London, 1966), pp. 170–3, for possible reasons for William's deposition of Stigand and appointment of Lanfranc. See also R. Allen Brown, *The Normans and the Norman Conquest*, 2nd edn (Woodbridge, 1987), pp. 216–17.

all,[1] taking the edge off the poverty of the monastery by means of the generosity of his scholars. His reputation aroused interest in the furthest quarters of the Latin speaking world, and Bec became a famous and important centre of letters. The glory of his praises aroused envy in the ungenerous, and William's chaplains, who saw they were his inferior in knowledge, stirred up the mind of the duke against him, because he had laughed openly at the ignorance of letters of one of them.[2] Lanfranc received an edict telling him to free Normandy of his high-handed behaviour. But he came to court and soon won the duke's pardon. With his keen insight William immediately perceived Lanfranc's wisdom, inferring his inner resources from the dignity of his countenance and the wit of his replies. He soon made him abbot of Caen, where he had built a completely new monastery to St Stephen, and, when raised to the throne of England, William appointed him archbishop, as I have said. But Lanfranc will explain this better in the words of his own letter which he wrote about his ordination and the origin and settlement of the dispute between himself and Thomas of York.

Chapter 25 Lanfranc's dispute with Thomas of York

In 1070 Lanfranc, abbot of the monastery at Caen, came to England, at the advice and orders of William, glorious king of the English, and Alexander of happy memory, high pontiff of the whole church of God. A few days after his arrival he took up the care of the church at Canterbury. On 29 August he was consecrated in the mother see by the bishops of that see, William bishop of London, Walkelin of Winchester, Remigius of Dorchester or Lincoln, Siweard of Rochester, Herfast of Elmham or Thetford, Stigand of Selsey, Hereman of Sherborne, and Giso of Wells. The other bishops were absent, but gave reasons for their absence in letters brought by envoys.

In the same year Thomas was elected archbishop of York and came to Canterbury to be consecrated by Lanfranc according to ancient custom.[3] But when Lanfranc, in accordance with the practice of his predecessors, asked him for a written profession of obedience together with an oath, Thomas replied that he would never do this, unless he first read the written authority for it, saw witnesses who vouched for this piece of antiquity, and heard sensible reasons for this which required him to do it justly and sensibly without prejudice to his own church. He was doing this more out of ignorance than because of a proud, stubborn spirit. For as a stranger completely ignorant of English customs he was relying on the words of flatterers more than was right and proper. But Lanfranc in the presence of the few bishops who had assembled for this

---

[1] Stenton comments on Lanfranc's luck in coming across an individualist abbot like Herluin, who allowed him to open a school for all comers, contrary to monastic custom (*Anglo-Saxon England*, p. 662). For a moving tribute to Herluin see Knowles, *The Monastic Order*, p. 91.

[2] The chaplain mocked by Lanfranc was called Herfast. William tells the story at greater length in ch. 74.

[3] This was a good opportunity for Lanfranc to recover the primacy of Canterbury over York, which had been lost when king William had been crowned by the archbishop of York.

consecration made his demands clear. Thomas refused them all and departed unconsecrated.

When the king heard of it, he took a serious view of the matter. He thought Lanfranc was making unjust demands, and putting more trust in his knowledge of books than in truth and reason, although Thomas himself was not without a knowledge of letters, gained by hard work and a good brain. A few days went by and Lanfranc came to court, sought audience with the king and gave reasons which soothed the king's feelings. He also won over the foreigners present when he urged the justice of his case. For the Englishmen who knew about the matter consistently said that there was evidence for all Lanfranc's claims. And so it was decreed by royal edict and the common decision of all that Thomas should return to the mother church of the whole kingdom, write a profession of obedience, read out what he had written and during his examination hand what he had read to Lanfranc in the presence of the bishops: in this profession he was to promise unconditionally complete obedience to Lanfranc's commands in all matters concerning the Christian religion. But his successors were not bound in the same way, unless in interview with the archbishop of Canterbury or in the council of bishops they were first given an adequate statement of the case which proved with complete clearness that their predecessors had made this profession, as they were duty bound to do, to the primates of the church at Canterbury. So Thomas returned to Canterbury, did as he had been ordered, and went back home a consecrated archbishop. A few days later Lanfranc asked for and received professions of obedience from all the bishops of England who had been consecrated at different times and places by other archbishops or by the pope during the time of Stigand.

In the following year he and Thomas went to Rome, where Lanfranc was honourably received by the apostolic see. He received one pallium from the altar according to Roman custom, and a second from pope Alexander, who, as a mark of his affection, gave to Lanfranc with his own hand the pallium in which it was his custom to celebrate mass. Thomas in the presence of the pope made an accusation concerning the primacy of the church of Canterbury and the subjection to it of the three bishops of Dorchester or Lincoln, Worcester and Lichfield which is now Chester: he claimed that the churches of Canterbury and York enjoyed equal honour in turn and that according to the constitution of the blessed Gregory neither owed any obedience whatsoever to the other except that the archbishop of either church should rank higher than the one who was known to have been consecrated later: but the three bishops mentioned above had been subject to his own see and his predecessors from time immemorial. Lanfranc was not pleased when he heard this claim but it was with wise self-control that he replied that Thomas's words had not a grain of truth in them and that Gregory had not promulgated his constitution for the churches of Canterbury and York but for those of London and York. Much was said on both sides about the matter and the three bishops, but pope Alexander decreed that this case should be heard in

England and decided by the testimony and verdict of the bishops and abbots of that whole kingdom.

Although Lanfranc considered that Thomas was bound to him during his archbishopric by the profession he had made, all the same he preferred to make efforts on behalf of his successors rather than to pass on for their handling in the future this important accusation undiscussed. Both archbishops went to the king during the festival of Easter and when both sides had openly stated their case there, the royal court gave its judgement on the matter.[1] Then it was decreed that a document should be drawn up, containing the conclusion of the whole case. Lanfranc sent pope Alexander a letter, in which he wrote for him a brief, truthful account of the history of the whole affair. Both the document and Lanfranc's letter are appended below, although first is quoted the profession of obedience which Thomas personally handed over to Lanfranc in the presence of the king and his council.

Chapter 26 Thomas's profession of obedience

Every Christian should obey Christian laws and not for any reasons go against the regulations laid down for the good of all by the holy fathers. For this only leads to angry quarrels, jealous disputes and the other sins which plunge those who love them into eternal punishment. And the higher a man's rank, the more earnestly should he obey the divine precepts. And so I, Thomas, now ordained metropolitan archbishop of the church of York, having heard and understood the reasons, make an unconditional profession of canonical obedience to you, Lanfranc, archbishop of Canterbury, and to your successors, and promise to carry out all the just and canonical commands laid upon me by you and them. When I was waiting to be ordained by you, I had my doubts on this matter, and that is why I have promised an absolute obedience to you but a conditional one to your successors.

Chapter 27 The document containing the decision of the council

In 1072, the eleventh year of the pontificate of our lord pope Alexander and the sixth year of the reign of William, glorious king of England and duke of Normandy, in the presence of the king himself and his bishops and abbots there was discussion of the matter of the primacy which Lanfranc archbishop of Canterbury proclaimed as a right for his see over the see of York. Also discussed were the ordinations of certain bishops, it being by no means certain who particularly had the right to do this. After different authorities had been quoted for the different sides, it was at long last approved and shown that the church of York should be subject to the church of Canterbury, and should obey the commands of its archbishop as primate of all Britain in all matters pertaining to the Christian religion. But the metropolitan of Canterbury

---

[1] This was the Council of Winchester held at Easter 1070.

granted to the archbishop of York and his successors that he should receive obedience in perpetuity from the bishop of Durham, that is of Lindisfarne, and of all the regions from the boundary of the diocese of Lichfield and the great river Humber up to the southern boundary of Scotland and whatever on this side of the Humber is properly in the province of the church of York. And so if the archbishop of Canterbury wants to call a council in whatever place he thinks fit, the archbishop of York with all the bishops subject to him shall attend this council at the nod of the archbishop of Canterbury and give obedience to his canonical regulations. Moreover Lanfranc, archbishop of Canterbury, showed that, in accordance with the ancient custom of his predecessors, the archbishop of York is obliged to make a profession of obedience to the archbishop of Canterbury together with an oath; but because of love of the king he had waived the oath for Thomas, archbishop of York, and only received the written profession of obedience, though this without prejudice for his successors who might want to demand an oath from Thomas's successors together with their profession. If the archbishop of Canterbury dies, the archbishop of York is to come to Canterbury and legally consecrate, aided by the other bishops of the said church, as official primate of England whoever has been elected to the office. But if the archbishop of York dies, his appointed successor, when he has accepted the gift of the arch- bishopric from the king, is to go to Canterbury or any other place chosen by the archbishop of Canterbury and to be ordained by him according to canonical custom.

Chapter 28 William introduces Lanfranc's letter to pope Alexander

If at this point I give Lanfranc's letter to pope Alexander in its entirety, it will definitely be very tedious. So I will quote only the relevant section, though also adding the privileges from the apostolic see which Lanfranc himself asserts had been very useful in proving his case. Nor will anybody have the right to sustain an accusation against me of stealing another's fame by filling up my work with such documents. A right-thinking person will rather forgive the necessities placed upon a historian. The studious reader should even thank the writer for finding gathered in this history all the facts which it would be laborious to examine in their many documents, even supposing he could ever happen to find them, which is doubtful. Also, the disagreement between the two metropolitans has not died down but is still the subject of lengthy lawsuits, so that when I reach the times of the present dissidents I shall not have to show which side is supported by the truth, since I shall already have dealt with the matter in the time of Lanfranc.

Chapter 29 The letter

To pope Alexander, lord and great overseer of the whole Christian religion, all due obedience and service from Lanfranc, archbishop of the holy church of Canterbury. At the council in England called on your authority in which archbishop Thomas aired and put forward his complaints, reference was made to the ecclesiastical history of the English people written by Bede, priest of the church of York and teacher of the English. The passage was read out which showed to the satisfaction of all that, for the space of almost 140 years from the times of the blessed Augustine, first archbishop of Canterbury, up to finally the age of Bede, it was my predecessors who had the primacy over the church of York and the whole island called Britain including Ireland. They had pastoral oversight over all men. They often held ordinations and councils in York itself and in appropriate places near by. The archbishops of York were summoned to these councils, and, when necessary, made to give account for their actions. Also the bishops, whose subjection Thomas brought into question, for that same space of 140 years were consecrated and summoned to councils by archbishops of Canterbury, with some of them, if their faults required it, being deposed by them with the authority of the Roman see. There are many things of this kind which I cannot set out in detail in the moderate length of a letter. Various councils, summoned by my predecessors for different reasons at different times, were given over to reading them. Even if they did not contain the same material about their institution, they did contain the same material about the primacy and the obedience of bishops. The details of the elections of the very bishops over whom there is a question mark were read out as having been made before my predecessors, and also the details of the consecrations by those predecessors of those who had left to the church at Canterbury written declarations of their obedience. For the city now called Canterbury was in ancient times called Dorobernia by the people of the place themselves. We also possess chronicles which reveal that, at the time of the division of England into several kingdoms, the king of Northumbria, in whose kingdom York was situated, sold the bishopric to a simonist for a bribe, and for this crime it was the archbishop of Canterbury who summoned him to a council and, when he refused to come, passed the sentence of excommunication on him for his disobedience. The whole church of those parts was freed from communion and fellowship with Canterbury, as long as it attended councils and repaired mistakes.

Finally, as the strong foundation of this whole case, various privileges and documents were produced,[1] which were given or sent at various times for various reasons to the bishops of the church of Canterbury and the kings of England by your predecessors Gregory, Boniface, Honorius, Vitalian, Sergius, another Gregory, Leo and John. For the other copies of other papal decrees, just as authentic as the former, were completely destroyed in

[1] These documents, given by William in chs. 30–9, are generally regarded as forgeries made by the monks at Canterbury. Even if they are forgeries, the monks may have thought of them as a justifiable means of maintaining their rights and privileges. See R. W. Southern, *Western Society and the Church in the Middle Ages* (Harmondsworth, 1970), pp. 92–3, and R. W. Southern, 'The Canterbury Forgeries', *English Historical Review* lxxiii (1938), pp. 193–226.

that devastating fire which our church suffered four years ago. When these and other points, which cannot be explained in detail in a few words, had been put forward on the side of our church, Thomas made very few points against the great weight of evidence of so many authorities, the chief one being the production of the letter in which the blessed Gregory decreed that the churches of London and York were equal and neither should be subject to the other. Since everybody at once decided unanimously that this document was irrelevant, seeing that I was not the bishop of London, and the question at issue did not concern the church of London, Thomas turned to other weak, skimpy arguments which were soon in the light of Christ overthrown by a few counter-arguments, etc.

Chapter 30 Pope Boniface IV to king Æthelberht (610)

Pope Boniface, servant of the servants of God, to Æthelberht,[1] most excellent lord and pre-eminent son. The genuineness of your Christianity in its attention to its founder has so increased that it shines out far and wide, and news is brought to all lands of your advances in work worthy of God. And so we have given hearty thanks to God, the giver of all good gifts, who has looked down upon you from on high and lifted you to this peak of virtues. And so, glorious son, we grant with willing mind the request that you made of the apostolic see through our fellow bishop Mellitus. With our complete permission, you of your kindness can establish a dwelling place for monks living in all things according to the rule in the monastery set up in the town of Canterbury which your holy teacher Augustine, pupil of Gregory of blessed memory, consecrated to the name of the holy Saviour and which we know our dearly beloved brother Laurentius is in charge of at this moment. With apostolic authority we decree that your preachers as monks should join the company of the monks and adorn their life with the sanctity of their behaviour. Should any of your successors, whether kings or bishops, clerical or lay, try to rescind our decree, he will be subject to the punishment of anathema from Peter, the first of the apostles, and all his successors until he has repented with a fullness pleasing to God for his rash deed of daring and made genuine amends for the disturbance caused.

Chapter 31 Pope Boniface V to archbishop Justus (625)

Pope Boniface, servant of the servants of God, to my dearly beloved brother Justus. We have received a letter from your dear self in which we find among other things that very many of the heathen out of the people living there have been converted to Christianity thanks to the help of Almighty God and our Lord Jesus Christ, especially in the districts of Kent, and we congratulate you warmly on bringing these people to faith in our true God

---

[1] King of Kent and the first king in England to be converted to Christianity.

through your efforts. And that the feet of king Eadbald himself[1] were put on to the path of the recognition of truth, for this we praise Almighty God who does not ignore vows in his name and the rewards of your labour. For as he himself truly promised to the preachers of the gospel, 'Lo, I am with you always even unto the end of the world.'[2] Great is the mercy of God and greatly has it been shown among you, when the hearts of foreign peoples are opened to receive the unique mystery declared in your preaching. For that they should prosper, their salvation has been procured by your merits. As our Lord says, 'He who perseveres to the end, shall be saved.'[3]

You have told me in your letter that our predecessor Gregory of blessed memory granted the city of Canterbury, capital of the whole nation of the English from the days of the pagans, to Augustine and all his future successors as the original metropolitan see. And now indeed through the revelation of Jesus Christ, the source and head of Christianity, that city is exalted and the most excellent root of the true faith has been planted there, so that from that crop all the islanders may be able to reap the rich fruit of the good work for the food of the kingdom of heaven. Happy is the city which has been worthy to have Christ live in it. Happy is the city, happy the people, when the heavenly mercy has not disdained to visit those whom he predestined before the creation of the world to unite with himself. And so let all Christians refrain from removing or changing now or in the future any of the statutes of our predecessor lord pope Gregory concerning that city of Canterbury, however the affairs of men be shaken. Rather do we on the authority of the blessed Peter, first of the apostles, decree and confirm that the metropolitan see of the whole of Britain shall always in the future be placed in the city of Canterbury, and that all provinces of the kingdom of England shall be subject to the metropolitan church there. Our decree is to last unchanged for ever. And as this church exists under the special power and protection of the holy Roman church, if anyone tries to harm it and takes away from it any of the powers lawfully granted to it, let almighty God remove his name from the book of life and let him know that he is bound in the chains of anathema. God keep you safe, reverend brother.

Chapter 32 Pope Honorius I to archbishop Honorius (*c.*634)

Pope Honorius, servant of the servants of God, to my dearest brother Honorius. In the letter I received from you, beloved son, I found that your careful shepherding of the flock entrusted to you was suffering through great fatigue, and that, as troubles and secular responsibilities increased, bringing with them much toil and anxiety, your mental problems were often a great burden. We urge you, beloved, to persevere in the work of the gospel which you have undertaken, as it calls for effort and persistence on your

[1] King of Kent 616–40.
[2] Matthew 28:20.
[3] Matthew 10:22.

part rather than shirking. Bear in mind the Gospel precept which says, 'I have prayed for you, Peter, that your faith should not fail; and when you have come to yourself, strengthen your brothers.'[1] And again, as the apostle Paul says, 'Be firm and steadfast, knowing that your work is not in vain in the sight of the Lord.'[2] We humbly give you this advice, beloved brother, so that from your faith and work in the fear and love of God the gains made by you and your predecessors, tender shoots from the seeds once planted by pope Gregory, should recover and grow more widely, so that the promise spoken by our Lord himself may summon you to eternal joy, 'Come to me all you who labour and are heavy laden, and I will give you rest.'[3] And again, 'Good and faithful servant, enter into the joy of your Lord; because you have been faithful over a few things, I will set you over many things.'[4]

Meanwhile you have asked for the powers of your see to be confirmed by a privilege issued on my authority. This we grant freely and immediately, it being right that we in our turn should confirm those very things which we know to have been decreed and established by our predecessors. And so, following in their footsteps, according to the usage of the ancient custom which your church has kept from the times of your predecessor Augustine of blessed memory up till now, we grant you and your successors, Honorius, by the authority of the blessed Peter, first of the apostles, the holding of the primacy over all the churches of Britain. We decree that all churches and districts of England are subject to the sway of your jurisdiction, and that for ever more the metropolitan see, the archiepiscopal office and the head-quarters of all the churches of the English are to be kept in the city of Canterbury. Let nobody with evil words of persuasion change these to another place. But if some prelate with inborn arrogance disobeys our command and, acting otherwise, tries to oppose the privileged concessions made to the church of Canterbury, he must know that he has been cut off from sharing in the body and blood of our Lord and Saviour Jesus Christ. God keep you safe, reverend brother.

Chapter 33 Pope Vitalian to archbishop Theodore (608)

Pope Vitalian, servant of the servants of God, to my most beloved brother Theodore. Among the many things which you ordered to be made known to us through your letter I read as well of your wish to be confirmed in the diocese which is placed in obedience to you, seeing that you desire in all things to shine as a result of a privilege granted by our apostolic see. We grant your petition. It is consistent with our pastoral care for the churches of God that we should wish with unshakable conviction that the privileges which we understand were granted by this apostolic see in former times

[1] Luke 22:32.
[2] 1 Corinthians 15:58.
[3] Matthew 11:28.
[4] Matthew 25:21.

should be protected and upheld for ever both by us and by our successors. Our reasons are irrefutable and we want our successors, just as much as ourselves, to protect and uphold them for ever. And so it seemed good to us to encourage you, and for the present to entrust to your most wise and holy person all the churches belonging to the island of Britain. We grant you for ever all those things which were decreed and confirmed for Augustine, his chaplain, by our predecessor the holy Gregory, or even permitted to him by the sacred use of the pallium. You are to hold the city of Canterbury, where through the revelation of our Lord Jesus Christ the Catholic faith was first established according to the ordinances of our sacred canons. And in accordance with the authority of the blessed Peter, first of the apostles, to whom was given by our Lord God the power of binding and loosing in heaven and earth, we, though unworthy, holding the office of that same blessed Peter key-bearer of the kingdom of heaven, grant to you, Theodore, and your successors, to hold unchangeable in your own metropolitan see in the city of Canterbury the rights granted in perpetuity in ancient times. If anyone, whether bishop or priest or deacon, tries to go against our wishes and the authority of our apostolic decree of privilege, we decree with our apostolic authority that a bishop shall be removed from office and priests or deacons be told that they have lost their posts. And lay people, kings or princes, great or small, must know that they are banned from sharing in the body of our Lord Jesus Christ. This document containing our privilege, based on authority from the blessed Peter, first of the apostles, whose ministry we perform, we send to you and your successors, Theodore, to be kept for ever. God keep you safe, most beloved brother.

Chapter 34 Pope Sergius I to the kings of England (*c*.693)

Pope Sergius, servant of the servants of God, to Æthelred, Aldfrith, and Aldwulf, kings of England.[1] The gift of spiritual grace kindles the hearts of the faithful by the enlightening from the Holy Spirit, restores and renews them, strengthens them with a wonderful, lasting goodness and brings it about that they eternally deserve the help of the benefits of heaven, while nonetheless being on their guard against the final destruction of things unstable. The holy fathers through their use of this gift of God's mercy shine round the whole, round world like blazing lights of the stars of heaven and have deserved after the happy joys of this present life to be gloriously enrolled among the number of the elect. And do you, a holy people, a chosen race, a purchased nation, sons of light, a royal stock, the shoots of faith and the growths of goodness, rejoice and exult in the Lord, that Peter, first and foremost of the apostles and firmest rock of faith, is not unmindful of your zeal and rejoices in the wealth of your minds and consciences and knows and remembers your names. Indeed we are confident that he also

---

[1] Kings of Mercia, Northumbria and the East Angles.

opens the door of the kingdom of heaven for those on whom he has so
signally bestowed the favour of power and who, under the auspices of God,
are pre-eminent among the nations. And so do you, most Christian and
beloved sons, receive with eager hearts and obedient minds Berhtwald,
whom we give to you on Peter's authority as head of the see of Kent and
chief pontiff of the whole of Britain. You can be sure that all who receive
him as a prophet will receive the reward a prophet gives. Should some
arrogant person spring forth and reject him (may this never happen!), he
will reject not Berhtwald but the one who sent him, and, as our Lord says,
will be condemned without any to help him. May you be clear and free of
such awful, hot-headed actions! May the old enemy never find the ugly face
of disobedience among you, whom the holy church of God has thought
worthy to be gathered into the bosom of the sons of adoption. And we pray
that our Lord Jesus Christ with his accustomed mercy will make you
ineffably exalted with the honour of serving his royal eternal majesty and
keep you safe in the test of the judgement which is to come.

Chapter 35   Pope Sergius I to the bishops of England (*c.*693)

Sergius to his most beloved brothers, all the appointed bishops of Britain.
The divine pity has thought us worthy of receiving the care and rule of the
pastoral office begun by the blessed Peter, first of the apostles. Not only does
there stand before us a brother to respect who was unknown before, but
also the news of the good state of your most holy college of bishops has
brought us a double portion of jubilation. We give boundless thanks to our
Lord God, author of all good things, for the discovery of faithful brothers in
the bosom of holy mother church whose unanimity is firm and unshaken
and who enjoy a mutual fellowship of fervent love and affection. For men
are known to please God with their wise and prudent behaviour when they
offer him pure libations and when, kindling the fire of the true light on the
altar of their hearts, they do not make mock of the mind with enticements
or provoke and goad the hearts of the brothers or make decisions with
minds that harm their neighbours, but instead as servants of God by the
uprightness of their life and behaviour show themselves an example to their
people. If they do this, they will find God supporting them in adversity and
the wiles of the enemy will not be able to harm them or rob them of
anything. For when God is at hand to help, all the hostility of the spirits of
evil is put to flight.

And so, showing with fatherly words our joy in the holy unanimity of
your brotherly love, we inform you that our most beloved brother
Berhtwald, archbishop of the province of Canterbury, who was chosen to
succeed to the see of Theodore of blessed memory, the former archbishop,
according to the rite of the ancient custom which has been kept by his
church from the times of Gregory, bishop of Rome and our lord and
predecessor of blessed and venerable memory right up till now, has

obtained from us, or rather from blessed Peter, first of apostles, the primacy of all the churches of Britain and has been entrusted here with that office according to the holy usage of pallium and venerable dalmatic.[1] And, my dearest brothers, his appointment was not unsuitable nor inappropriate, for he obtained this great honour worthily, not through any boastful arrogance or self-importance but with a lowly mind and humble heart. Brothers, you are a community consecrated by God, and we urge and advise you with salutary counsel that, on account of your love of God and your hope of future change, you learn how to pay proper service to this same brother as archbishop of your province, as if it were owed to us, and how to obey him, as being a prelate efficiently carrying out his primacy. Do not be ignorant of what is indicated by him being a chosen vessel, 'Obey those put in authority over you.'[2] And again, 'Who resists authority, resists God's ordinance.'[3] And so, brothers, basing our precepts on this apostolic authority, we give warning to you and all the ranks of your orders that nobody should presume to oppose now or in the future these decrees once made by this apostolic see, but that always the powers granted to the above mentioned church should be preserved unimpaired for ever. And because our minds have an unshaken confidence that you, with the aid of the divine mercy, will carry out the religious commands which we have decided to impose upon your fraternity, we make prayers to the ineffable power of our Saviour that he may grant you always to show the power of true religion, to rejoice in everlasting joy, and in the happiness of brotherly affection to join the saints in their reward of eternal bliss. God keep you safe, dearest brothers.

Chapter 36 Pope Gregory III to the bishops of England (*c*.732)

Pope Gregory, servant of the servants of God, sends greetings to the bishops of England. We praise the greatness of the boundless goodness of almighty God, who has thought it right for the glory of his majesty to be so spread abroad that already the sound of his preachers has gone forth into every land and their words to the bounds of every land. Thanks to the ineffable grace of his goodness, just as we know ourselves as physically born, so also we are adopted, carrying the mystery of our holy rebirth into the hope of the glory of the sons of God through Jesus Christ our Lord. And so rejoicing in the consecrated community of you, reverend bishops, we urge you to be found stable in faith and efficient in your work, in honour preferring one another, bearing each other's burdens because thus will you fulfil the law of Christ, and in love of God and your neighbour having that unending charity without which it is impossible to please God. And so I have been given great joy that our brother Tatwine has arrived in England, appointed to the church of your teacher Augustine of blessed memory. For in the time in

---

[1] An ecclesiastical vestment, with wide sleeves and marked with two stripes.
[2] Hebrews 13:17.
[3] Romans 13:2.

which he was with us we found him to be a holy man of great integrity. Accordingly, when we heard his petitions, we ordered a search to be made in the sacred archives for the rights of his position, and when we found that what he had asked for was just, with our apostolic authority we handed him the sacred pallium together with the venerable use of the dalmatic, also granting him all the rights of his office which his predecessors are known to have held since the time of Augustine of blessed memory.

So just as the decree of our holy father Gregory, Roman pontiff, put Augustine, his chaplain and your teacher, in charge of all the bishops of England, so we, with the authority of God and of blessed Peter first of the apostles, although unworthy to hold office in his name, put you, Tatwine, archbishop of the city of Canterbury, and your legitimate successors in charge of all the churches of Britain and their rectors. And with our apostolic authority we order every man in the whole of England to obey your canonical commands and to know that you, to whom we have entrusted the discharge of all our functions in that country, are the overseer and primate of the whole island. Moreover we keep under the special protection of our hand your church established at Canterbury as Christ's primary and personal offshoot in your province. We want it to flourish in the tranquillity of peace, and for the rights and privileges of its position to be preserved unharmed for ever. As the first church established in your province, it is the mother and head of all the others, to the honour of the holy Saviour, our Lord Jesus Christ. For as it is written, 'No one is holy as God is holy.'[1] And where the head is vigorous, the other members are vigorous and stronger. So do you, my brothers, with the alacrity of reverent obedience give heed to and carry out these commands of our apostolic authority, and work with our brother as your archbishop in the harvest of God. But if anyone wishes to overthrow these commands and strives to destroy and violate the statutes decreed by us, he should know that he is working against the Saviour of the world himself and against the authority of the blessed Peter, and that, unless he comes to his senses, he is incurring the sentence of everlasting damnation. God keep you safe, most beloved brothers.

Chapter 37 Pope Leo III to archbishop Æthelheard (802)

Pope Leo, servant of the servants of God, to Æthelheard archbishop of the church of Canterbury for ever. It is especially proper for the pope at his discretion to give audience to the heads of his churches according to their irreproachable faith, and to give effect to those things which they have desired to have from the blessed Peter, first of the apostles, and from us and which will not infringe canon law, in order that when they obtain what they desire they may burn more brightly in the love of their religion. And so we

---

[1] 1 Kings 2:2.

urge and command you to cherish the dioceses of England entrusted to your care, their bishops and their monasteries, and both monks and clerics and nuns. And the rights which your church has possessed since ancient times and which we have found after search in our sacred archives, these we confirm can be held by you and your successors. Gregory, holy and excellent teacher, decreed and universally confirmed that all the churches of the English should be subject for ever to the blessed archbishop Augustine, his chaplain, according to the sacred custom of the pallium. And so both because of the authority of the blessed Peter, first of the apostles, to whom the power of binding and loosing was granted by the Lord God when he said, 'Because you are Peter, upon this rock I will build my church and the gates of hell shall not prevail against it; and I will give you the keys of the kingdom of heaven, and whatever you bind on earth shall be bound in heaven, and whatever you loose on earth shall be loosed in heaven'[1] and also because of the established power of canon law, we, though unworthy to hold the office of the same Peter, key-bearer of the kingdom of heaven, grant with irrevocable right to you, Æthelheard, and to your successors that all the churches of the English, just as they were in former times, should by confession of obedience be for ever under your control in your metropolitan see. If anyone, which heaven forbid, tries to go against our authority in this statute or apostolic privilege, we decree with our apostolic authority that, if he is an archbishop or bishop, he is to be removed from his position of power. And the same goes for a priest or deacon or any other holder of a sacred ministry. But if he is a lay person, then, whether king or prince, whether of great or small importance, he must know that he is banned from sharing in our holy communion. This document containing our privilege we give to you, Æthelheard, and to your successors to keep for ever. It comes with the authority of the blessed Peter, first of the apostles, whose office we perform. To show its genuineness, we have written a subscript in our own hand, and ordered the document to be signed with our own name. We instructed it to be written by our secretary Sergius in the month of January. Dated 18 January, by the hand of Eustachius, notary of the holy apostolic see, in the reign of our lord Charlemagne, most pious consul, crowned Augustus by God, great emperor of peace, and in the second year after the consulship of the same lord and the tenth indiction.

Chapter 38 Pope Formosus to the bishops of England (c.894)

Formosus to all the bishops of England, his brothers and sons in Christ. After hearing that wicked pagan rites had sprung up again in your country and that you, like dogs unable to bark, had kept quiet, we had determined to strike you from the body of the church of Christ with the sword of separation. But now that our beloved brother Plegmund has told us that you

---

[1] Matthew 16: 18,19.

have woken up at last and decided to resow the seeds of God's word, once reverently planted in the soil of the English, we have pulled out the sword-point of our renouncement and send you the blessing of Almighty God and of the blessed Peter, first of the apostles. And we pray that you may continue in your good designs. For you are the brothers of whom the Lord spoke when he said amongst other things, 'You are the salt of the earth, and if the salt loses its savour, with what will it be salted?'[1] And again, 'You are the light of the world.'[2] Our Lord wished to show by these wise words that it is your duty to add savour to the minds of men and in the behaviour of your lives to let your zeal for goodness shine as the lamp of faith by which men may see how to walk carefully on the path to eternal life, and so that they may be able to run without stumbling and arrive at the promise of eternal bliss. So now gird yourselves and keep watch against the lion who prowls 'seeking whom he may devour'.[3] Do not allow any longer in your country the Christian faith to be damaged by the shortage of pastors or the flock of God to wander, dispersed and scattered, but when one pastor dies let another who is suitable be immediately chosen in his place according to canon law. For according to the law several have been made priests, for the very reason that death prevents them being permanent. David thought of this, and because he saw that in the spirit of Christ the church would last to the end of time, he said, 'Sons are born to you in place of your forefathers, and you will make them princes over all the earth.'[4] So when a priest departs this life, let there be no delay in choosing another. As soon as a brother's death has been announced to him who is known among you to be in charge of the other bishops because he holds the primacy of the head see, another should be elected according to canon law and be consecrated to take his place. Since ancient times there has been no doubt who among you should hold the primacy or which episcopal see should have the power and primacy over the others. For according to the writings of the blessed Gregory and his successors it is laid down that the metropolitan city of the kingdom of the English and the chief episcopal see, which it is known our worshipful brother Plegmund now rules, are in Canterbury. We forbid the honour of his position to be diminished in any way and we entrust to him the complete performance of apostolic functions. Just as the blessed Gregory decreed that all the bishops of the English were subject to Augustine, first bishop of your people, so we confirm that the same honour is given to our aforementioned brother of Dorobernia or archbishop of Canterbury and to his legitimate successors. With the authority of God and of the blessed Peter, first of the apostles, we order and command that all should obey his canonical decisions and that no one should violate the privileges granted to him and his successors by apostolic authority. But if anybody does attempt at any

---

[1] Matthew 5:13.
[2] Matthew 5:14.
[3] 1 Peter 5:8.
[4] Psalm 45:16.

time to attack these decrees and diminish them, he must know that he will certainly be punished with a serious anathema, and that, unless he comes to his senses, he must be separated from the body of the holy church which he has striven to disturb.

Chapter 39 Pope John XII to archbishop Dunstan (960)

Pope John, servant of the servants of God, sends to his brother Dunstan, archbishop of Canterbury, wishes for the lasting salvation of eternal life in Christ. If shepherds of sheep are willing to endure sun and frost day and night for the sake of their flock, seeing with watchful eye that none of the sheep go astray and get killed or are savaged and seized by the mouths of wild beasts, with what care and effort should we, who are called the shepherds of souls, keep watch over their safety! So let us be careful to do our duty in looking after our Lord's sheep, and not run away frightened when the wolf comes, lest, on the day of the divine judgement before the great shepherd, torment is in store for us because of our sloth and for you because of your negligence. For we are judged on a higher plane than everybody else if only because of the reverence for our office.

We fully confirm you in the primacy which the blessed Augustine and his successors as archbishops of Canterbury are known to have had, and in which it is fit for you to perform the functions of the apostolic see according to the custom of your predecessors. And so according to custom we entrust you with the pallium for the celebration of the rites of the mass for your fraternity and we permit you to use it not otherwise than with the use appointed by our predecessors, with the privileges of your church staying the same as they always were. And you or anybody else is wise enough to know that the distinction of the pallium inspires awe depending on the moderation of its wearer's actions. These adornments go hand in hand with the goodness of your life, so that, with God's help, you can be so conspicuous that your life is a benchmark for your sons, which they can use to straighten any crookedness in their own lives, recognising in it a model to follow.

And the letter ended:

May the Holy Trinity surround your brotherhood with the protection of its grace, and so put you on to the path of fear of it, that after the bitterness of this life, we may deserve to arrive together at everlasting bliss. This was written by the hand of Leo, secretary of the apostolic see, on 1 October in the twelfth year of the reign of pope John.

Chapter 40 Thomas states his case

The reading of these holy charters from the apostolic saints in the council of all England then greatly strengthened the primacy of the church of Canterbury. I myself have inserted them here, not inappropriately, provided the reader has not been bored stiff. Thomas, archbishop of York, had little ammunition to bring to bear against them. Even if he brought whole classes of supporters, he had very little room left for evasive manoeuvre. But he argued that it was to Augustine alone that the blessed Gregory had granted the privileges of having subject to him through the authority of our Lord Jesus Christ not only the bishops whom he ordained himself, nor even only those ordained by the archbishop of York, but also all the priests in Britain. But after Augustine's death, so Thomas argued, the bishops of London and York would take it in turns to exercise the grace, and the recovery of ordination would indicate the superior greatness of the office. Gregory, indeed, said Thomas, had wanted Augustine to establish his see in London, but Augustine, influenced by his affection for king Æthelberht, had personally placed his see at Canterbury. If he had seen that it was suitable, it would not have been difficult for Gregory to put a stop to ambiguity and controversy by saying in a few words, 'I grant these privileges to you, Augustine, and to all your successors.' But because he saw that reason rejected this, he was unwilling to scatter his words to the winds.

Chapter 41 Lanfranc replies

Thomas was going on to say more of the same kind of thing as this, finding weapons for his speech from his lack of knowledge of antiquity and the necessity of putting forward a case, when Lanfranc joined the battle of words and attacked Thomas with the following very sharp reply:

> There is no truth in the argument upon which you rely, namely the claim that it was to Augustine alone that authority was granted over all the bishops of Britain and even over those who had been ordained by the archbishop of York. That would be a very limited and poor honour for a pope to bestow upon his old friend and new Englishman, especially since in Augustine's lifetime the archbishop of York performed no ordinations of men who could then be subject to Augustine, seeing that no archbishop of York existed at that time. Indeed it was only in the time, not of Augustine, but of Justus the fourth archbishop of Canterbury that the blessed Paulinus was sent to York as the first archbishop of that city. Anyone who does not know this can learn it from *The Deeds of the English*.[1] The most holy occupants of the apostolic see were aware of these facts when they confirmed the successors of Augustine in this authority over all the bishops of England, as the decrees read out have testified. As they said, it was Gregory's decision that they were adorning in their expansive language and his example that they were following in their generous munificence. They were arbiters for the same see, and, as its patrons, they gave the same

---

[1] See Bede, *Ecclesiastical History* 2:17, 20.

opinion. They thought it right that all the churches of the English should obtain the discipline of their lives from the place from whose tinder they had struck the flame of belief. For everybody knows that belief in Christ flowed from Canterbury to York and to the other churches in England.

As for your point that the blessed Gregory could, if he had wanted, have confirmed with a word the successors of Augustine in the grant which he had given to Augustine, this is absolutely true and undeniable. But, I ask you, what advantage would this prior judgement have brought to the see of Canterbury? I will give you an analogy. When our Lord and Saviour Jesus Christ said to the blessed Peter, 'You are Peter, and upon this rock I will build my church, and I will give you the keys of the kingdom of heaven,'[1] he could, if he had wanted, have added 'and I grant the same power to your successors.' But the omission of these words has in no way diminished the reverence paid to the successors of Peter. Will you challenge and bring arguments against these words of our Lord? For the consciences of all Christians have been instructed to stand in awe of the threats of Peter's successors no less than those of the blessed Peter, and to rejoice and be glad when those successors grant them the favour of their cloudless kindness. Indeed the arrangements of all ecclesiastical affairs are only ratified when they have been approved by the judgement of the successors of the blessed Peter. What does this show except that the power of the divine generosity has through our Lord Jesus been poured out by the blessed Peter upon his vicars? And so, Thomas, if you understand logic, you will come to a similar conclusion about similar matters.

Further, what is true of the whole is true of the part, and what is true of the greater is true of the lesser. The church of Rome is, as it were, the totality of all churches and other churches its parts. For just as, in one way of looking at it, a man is the collection of his atoms, and yet in each atom is present the complete uniqueness of the complete man, so in one respect the see of Rome is the collection and totality of all churches, yet in each church there reigns the complete fullness of the complete Christian faith. The see of Rome is itself greater than all churches and what is valid for her should be valid for the lesser churches, so that the authority possessed by the earliest head of each church should pass down to his successors, unless a personal exception by name is made. Therefore, just as Christ said to all popes of Rome what he said to Peter, so Gregory said in the case of Augustine what he said to all his successors. From this it follows that just as Canterbury is subject to Rome, since it received its faith from it, so York is subject to the Canterbury which sent its preachers there.

And then as for your allegation that Gregory wanted Augustine to reside in London, this is clearly a dubious point. For how could Augustine have been sure of this when he goes against the wishes of his master and ignores his decision? I refuse to remove my belief in a story which has been

[1] Matthew 16:18.

confirmed by the assent of so many. Anyway, suppose he did move from one place to the other; what has that got to do with me, who am not a bishop of London? For it makes no difference to me, except that ancient usage does not permit you to share the honour of the primacy with the bishop of London. If on that question you wish to air the matter in a lawsuit before a third person with peace between us, I shall not fail in my jurisdictive capacity to put forward a sound case.

Chapter 42 Lanfranc's visit to pope Alexander and his Council of 1075

Thomas yielded to this reasoning. Moderating his case, he willingly agreed to the conditions that the northern bank of the river Humber should be the beginning of his diocese, and the southern bank the limit of the diocese of Canterbury. Lanfranc was jubilant in his triumph. As he was the winner, he had the whole matter written down, for, if these recent happenings faded away into forgetfulness, posterity would be deprived of the knowledge of some crucial information. The written account was a sober document, not omitting the essentials but not fulsome either. A display of eloquence in praise of himself would have been distasteful. My own opinion is that no one else could have settled such a vexed question so clearly,[1] no matter what effort and industry he put into it, and even though he was helped, as Lanfranc was, by having justice on his side. For at that time Lanfranc was very famous both for his learning and for his worldly wisdom. Even pope Alexander respected and looked up to him. On Lanfranc's arrival in Rome, he paid him a great mark of honour: putting aside that famous Roman pride and hauteur, he condescended to rise to his feet, declaring that he was showing this respect not to his archbishopric but to his erudition, and that as he had shown Lanfranc a sign of honour, Lanfranc ought to show him a sign of obedience and, like all archbishops, prostrate himself before the feet of the vicar of St Peter. Lanfranc did his duty. He had experienced such clear signs of affection that he immediately performed whatever demands the pope had thought he should make. Lastly, on this journey, Lanfranc by his prayers got restored to office his two companions, Thomas archbishop of York and Remigius bishop of Lincoln. The pope had stripped them of crosiers and rings, Thomas because he was the son of a priest, and Remigius because he had been made bishop for help given to William on his arrival in England, obtaining spiritual office for deeds of war. In fact pope Alexander put off the responsibility for his action and transferred to Lanfranc the judgement of whether restoration was right or not: if Lanfranc wished it, he would renew their investitures, but if not, he would do what he knew was proper. And so it was from the hand of Lanfranc that they got back

---

[1] R. W. Southern, *St Anselm and his Biographer* (Cambridge, 1963), p. 136, is less impressed by Lanfranc's settlement of the case. He had failed to get an oath of obedience from the archbishop of York except during his lifetime; and he had failed to get papal confirmation of the position established in 1072.

their crosiers and rings[1] before making a happy return to their homeland in his company. Gregory,[2] Alexander's successor, took the trouble to treat Lanfranc with no less care and affection. He transacted many matters after advice from Lanfranc, and often put before him for judgement issues which were kept secret from his own staff. Evidence for the truth of what I say is a letter sent to England at the beginning of Gregory's papacy and found among the letters of Lanfranc. King William also showed respect to Lanfranc on all occasions, for he was pleased with all men like Lanfranc whom he heard were fervent for good. He permitted him to hold councils. This is an account of one of them.

In 1075, the ninth year of the reign of William, a council was held in London, presided over by Lanfranc archbishop of Canterbury, and with Thomas archbishop of York and the other bishops also being present with him. The church of Rochester was without a shepherd at that time. The bishop of Lindisfarne, who is also the bishop of Durham, had a legitimate excuse and could not be present at the council.[3] And because for many years previously the holding of councils in England had died out, some practices laid down by canons in ancient times were revived. And so, according to the fourth council of Toledo, the council of Milevia and the council of Braga,[4] it was decreed that individual bishops should sit in order of the date of their ordination, except for those who had the more important sees, either because of ancient custom or because of the privileges of their churches. The senior bishops who were advanced in years were asked what they had perhaps seen with their own eyes on this issue, or what truths they had in all probability heard from still older and more ancient bishops. They asked for a stay in proceedings to consider their answer, and were given until the next day. On that day they all said with one accord that the archbishop of York should sit on the right hand of Canterbury, the bishop of London on his left and the bishop of Winchester next to the archbishop of York. If the archbishop of York was absent, London should sit on Canterbury's right and Winchester on his left.

According to the Rule of the blessed Benedict and the ancient custom of monastic houses monks should not exceed the bounds of their position by owning property. If a monk with property died unconfessed, he should not be buried in the cemetery. According to the decrees of the high pontiffs, Damasus and Leo, and according to the councils of Sardica and Laodicea,[5] which had banned bishops residing in villages, it was granted with kingly munificence and synodical authority that the following bishops should move from villages to cities, Hereman from Sherborne to Salisbury, Stigand from Selsey to Chichester and Peter from Lichfield to Chester.[6] According to many decrees of the

---

[1] Conveniently for Lanfranc, this symbolised their dependence on him.

[2] Gregory VII, 1072–85.

[3] This absentee was Walcher, bishop of Durham 1071–80. For him see ch. 132.

[4] In Spain, Africa and Portugal respectively.

[5] Damasus II was pope in 1048 and Leo I was pope 440–61. The councils were held in 347 and 366 respectively.

[6] Loyn sees the need for defence and security and the need for improved administration as being the main reasons for this urbanisation of episcopal sees (*The English Church*, p. 75).

bishops of Rome and the authority of various sacred canons it was decided that nobody should admit to office or keep a clerk or monk from somewhere else without letters of commendation. To check the effrontery of certain tactless persons, it was sanctioned by a general decree that nobody, apart from bishops and abbots, could speak in the council without permission given by the metropolitan. According to the decrees of Gregory I and Gregory II it was decided that nobody could take as a wife from his own family either someone on his dead wife's side or someone who was the widow of a blood relation, until kinship on both sides was seven stages away.[1] Also that no one should buy or sell sacred orders or ecclesiastical office. And that no one should perform sortition or divination. According to the council of Elvira and the eleventh council of Toledo it was decreed that no bishop, abbot or clerk should sentence a man to be killed or have his limbs lopped off or approve of such a sentence.

Chapter 43 Lanfranc and his cathedral

At the time when father Lanfranc was using all his virtues to strengthen his spirit and prepare his mind, it is said that his particular prognostic was about alms, namely, 'Give alms, and all things are open to you.'[2] The prognostic was greeted with acclaim, and Lanfranc with a happy face said to God, 'So let us have a competition between ourselves, you as giver, I as distributor.' The heavenly piety answered the prayer of the praiseworthy archbishop and the amount of alms that flowed in could have filled or more than filled any space, however big. Nor was Lanfranc himself slow in giving alms; he completely eradicated from his own character the familiar Lombard vice of avarice. He did not give thoughtlessly. As his generosity was seasoned by the good sense of a sharp mind, it did not go to waste. The light from his countenance did not fall to the ground, but was as welcome to the receiver as the sunrise at day's beginning which scatters the clouds, calms the winds and makes bright the sky. So he bought bread and shoes for the poor and all that was needed to keep them alive and clothed. He was too wise and sensible to deal with them by giving them money. He knew that such people, when their purses are stuffed, endure hunger with a dry mouth. He avoided giving money for food as though it were something sacred and he did not wish to lessen its amount. For the clergy and monasteries which were in need he did pile up a vast store of wealth and often encouraged the shamefaced to ask for it. Nor did he think it beneath him to tuck up his archiepiscopal robes and hand out bread to the needy, or to bring scholars of the poorer sort to a battle of words. After such a discussion, both parties went away happy, the winner receiving a reward for his knowledge and the loser comfort from his modesty.

---

[1] For the difficulties which this decree posed for laymen see Matthew, *The Norman Conquest*, p. 192. For the council of 1075 in general see Stenton, *Anglo-Saxon England*, p. 666.

[2] Luke 11:41. Immediately after a bishop's consecration the Bible, which was being held open by the assistant bishops, was inspected to find a verse which would serve as a 'prognostic' and foretell the nature of his bishopric.

A short while beforehand a devouring fire had consumed the buildings of his cathedral.[1] The heaps of the walls and the pieces of the roof were a pile of ruins. Lanfranc dug up the old foundations and rebuilt everything on a larger scale. It would be impossible to say whether the beauty or the speed were the greater. For the hard work involved in the speed increased the glory of his good intentions. The monks, after first living in confined, temporary quarters, were afterwards housed in magnificent, elaborate buildings. I could indeed write at length about all the ornaments which were gathered there, or of the robes and vestments on which the skill of the embroiderers in gold outdid the money spent, as the materials took second place. Or I could tell of the many-hued pictures where the remarkable skill and the gleam of the colours captivated and enthralled the mind of the onlooker, as their grace and beauty took his eyes up to the ceilings.

He brought back under the jurisdiction of his house the control of all those estates which owing to the neglect of his predecessors or the rapacity of robbers were groaning under alien masters. The king helped and supported him in this, to such an extent that he even won by a lawsuit[2] lands which were being illegally held by the king's brother, Odo bishop of Bayeux and earl of Kent. For his crafty, deceitful mind had gazed greedily on properties belonging to the church of Canterbury, and he definitely would have destroyed them, if Lanfranc had not prevented him. Lanfranc's outstanding characteristic was liveliness of spirit, but he also had shed on him the favour of the blessed Dunstan. For whenever he was hesitating over some matter and putting off and delaying his decision so that it did not turn out badly, Dunstan would appear to him in a dream, revealing the tricks of his enemies and showing him the paths of escape. Once, even, when he was ill and tired of his lingering life, by means of a dream in which he seemed to have fought a wrestling match with Dunstan, he was rescued from his crisis by Dunstan and restored to good health.

Chapter 44 Lanfranc's monastic reforms

Like all English monks of that time,[3] the ones at Canterbury were no different from ordinary human beings, except that they did not give up their chastity easily. Hounds were a favourite pastime. They hunted birds by launching falcons through the air to seize them. They rode hard on foaming horses, they shook dice, they indulged in drinking. Living elaborately civilised lives of some luxury, they knew nothing of frugality and spurned economy. There were other things of the same sort, so that judging by the number of their servants

---

[1] In 1011. See *The Deeds of the Kings* 2:165.

[2] See Loyn, *The English Church*, p. 99 for this famous lawsuit at Penenden Heath near Maidstone. Marjorie Chibnall believes that the monks had actually lost their lands to earl Harold before the Conquest and that the lands had passed from Harold's estate to Odo. See her *Anglo-Norman England 1066–1166* (Oxford, 1986), p. 24.

[3] Knowles expresses doubts about this sweeping condemnation of English monks by William (*The Monastic Order*, pp. 79–80).

you might describe them as magnates rather than monks. Lanfranc saw this, but for some time endured it with patience, not wanting to scare and frighten them with loud cries of austerity. For being very skilled in that art of arts which is the control of men's souls, he knew that custom holds second place to nature, and that weaker brethren are greatly upset by a sudden change in the rules of behaviour. And so, by friendly admonitions at intervals and by withdrawing now these privileges and now those, he sharpened their rough minds on the whetstone of virtue to a point of goodness, and rubbed off from them the rust of vice. Wherever he uprooted the growths of evil, he immediately planted there the seeds of goodness. And he did not stop until the monks had renounced the adulterous growths of sin and of their own accord adopted the progeny which is born of virtue. There are today, as is only fitting, more monks at Canterbury than anywhere else in England, their piety quite on a par with that of the Cluniacs. Lanfranc is still very much with them. They often talk of the man, of his great devotion to God and the warm welcome he gave to those who came. Still remembered and never to be forgotten is his love, shared out among all but unique for each. He would never allow anyone to remain sad. If he saw somebody under the weather, he would at once ask the reason and investigate. When he had found it, his remedy was swift. Of his own accord he gave the young monks money to deal with their lack of personal necessities. If by chance what he gave failed to double, he also secretly commanded others to take care of this.

Actually he provided for monks throughout the whole of England. He did not want them crying out for essentials or lapsing from the rule. For by now the spite of the bishops was on the increase, and they wished to exclude monks from their episcopal sees and to bring in secular clergy.[1] Walkelin, bishop of Winchester, was the leader of this party. In other respects he was a good man, but on this matter he had been persuaded to do evil by the counsel of whisperers, and had equipped more than forty canons with cap and surplice. He had brought the king over to his opinion, and there had been so much delay in carrying out his plan that he was trying to win the consent of the archbishop, never doubting that he would gain it. But the archbishop was appalled when he heard of the scheme, and with one look he dissolved the plans and contrivances of all these potentates as though they were so many spiders' webs. In fact, to stop the deed being dared in the future, he got pope Alexander to prohibit it by decree. It is also greatly to his praise that he did not allow the things begun by the busy goodness of the saints in the time of king Edgar to lose momentum. However unfair the comparison, his achievement should be set alongside theirs. They, on the one hand, achieved their wishes easily, as they were masters of all England, and even the king smiled upon them: he, on the other, dealt with the matter and won the day in a lone battle against numerous opponents.

---

[1] Matthew discusses the reasons for this change and its disappointing results (*The Norman Conquest*, p. 185).

It was he who brought the abbey of St Albans to its present state through the appointment there of abbot Paul. In the diocese of Rochester the number of clergy at work could scarcely make up a quartet, and, left to themselves, they were daily short of bread. Lanfranc supported them at his own expense through their bishop Gundulf. He also brought in fifty monks, gave them a spacious house, and saw to it that, far from being subject to poverty, they could even rejoice in the abundance of their supplies. Outside Canterbury to the south he built houses of stone for all those in need, and to the west houses of wood for those wasting away with the king's disease, even appointing regular canons at St Gregory's to say divine office for them.[1] There were separate houses for men and women, their expenses were provided for and servants appointed.

He began these operations in the reign of William I, who only turned down a few of the requests he thought he ought to make. For although the king was less civil to the rest, he was charming and affectionate towards Lanfranc. As he saw him working for justice, he gave him his hand so that he should not slip over the edge, although often complaining to his friends about the tedium of his own life. Being a shrewd man of mature years he looked into the present and foresaw and prophesied future ruin. Nor was he mistaken in his opinion. For when William II succeeded to the throne on the death of his father, he found Lanfranc distinctly uncompliant, but mollified him by great promises of holding fast to justice and the right and so won him over to his side. But once in possession of the kingdom and torn by many anxieties over the rebellion of almost all the nobles, he ignored his promises. Reminded by the archbishop of his pledges, he angrily replied, 'Who can carry out all his promises?' Nauseated by all this, Lanfranc did not drag out his life much longer. After nineteen years as archbishop he caught a fever. The doctors who were consulted recommended the appropriate draught. Lanfranc first fortified himself with confession and sacrament, and then, taking the cup but turning it upside down, he breathed his last. He had gained the death he had always longed for. For he used to confess to his household that he prayed to God for a death from an attack of fever or dysentery, as these diseases brought neither loss of memory nor impairment of speech. What a man! Canterbury will tell of his industry; Western christendom will marvel at his learning among his pupils; all the years to come will preserve his greatness. For he himself left few memorials of his powers, just some letters containing decrees, and particularly the one against Berengarius.[2]

---

[1] Knowles discusses the spread of canons living under a rule in England after the Conquest (*The Monastic Order*, pp. 141–2).

[2] For Berengarius of Tours, who denied that the bread and wine laid upon the altar were after their consecration by the priest in truth and substance the Lord's body, see *The Deeds of the Kings* 3:284–6. Lanfranc's controversy with him, his only serious excursion into the field of theology, was over long before he came to England. See Knowles, *The Monastic Order*, p. 509. The same writer gives an excellent summing up of Lanfranc's strengths and weaknesses on pp. 108–11 and 142–3.

Chapter 45 The early years of Anselm

After Lanfranc the archiepiscopal see was vacant for more than four years. For the king put more trust than was right in the counsels of wicked whisperers and added all its revenues to his own. But I have spoken about these matters elsewhere,[1] with much regard for the king's majesty, as is proper. For the present I am engaged in the different task of setting down the series of events concerning Lanfranc's successor. I do not intend to copy out tracts word for word but just to give a summary of the facts, for I very willingly and gladly take second place to Master Eadmer,[2] who has written such a lucid account of all the events that they seem as it were to have been placed before our eyes.[3] The story concerns Anselm. He was born in Aosta, which is the town you come to first on crossing the Alps from France, and by the torch lit by his virtues he lifted his humble birthplace into the clearest light of fame. As a boy he devoted himself to letters. Having left boyhood behind, he was never unchaste, not even with a lustful look. In his adolescent years he was given the opportunity of leaving his home town by the anger of his father. Completely unable to calm his father down, and afraid that the family quarrel might end in some violation of nature, he forestalled this by going away. He crossed the Alps and was anxiously turning over in his mind where to go, when his uncertainty was cleared up by the divine grace. He was to go to Lanfranc in Normandy. If he stayed with him, his life there would be made smooth both by the tie of birthplace and their enthusiasm for books. On his arrival at Bec he was warmly received by Lanfranc and became a great help to him in looking after his schools. In the meantime his goodness and his years increased together, as did his industry and ability.

And now his springtime was just on the verge of moving into the strength of his young manhood (he was twenty-seven) when he was set aglow with a longing for the monastic life. He had also had the same desire long ago when a small boy – a remarkable ambition in one so very young. His prayer to God for the handicap of a serious illness had been answered: both his parents were terrified at this, and devoted their son to God. Now later on he spent a long time thinking whether it was better to become a hermit[4] or a monk. If he became a monk, would a rich place or a poor place be better for his soul? A rich place with its wealth of resources would of course provide him with leisure, but he would continually be having to ask forgiveness for enjoying a ready supply of life's essentials. A poor place,[5] on the other hand, would shake

[1] *The Deeds of the Kings* 2:312–14.
[2] A monk at Christ Church, Canterbury. For his life of Anselm see *The Life of St Anselm by Eadmer*, ed. and trans. R. W. Southern (London, 1962) and R. W. Southern, *St Anselm and his Biographer*.
[3] Southern, *St Anselm and his Biographer*, p. 303, sees a 'touch of envy' in William's description of Eadmer's gifts. We do not have to agree.
[4] See Southern, *St Anselm and his Biographer*, p. 28, for the Italian eremitical movement of the eleventh century.
[5] Eadmer, *The Life of St Anselm* 1:5 names this poor place as Cluny.

the lust out of him because of the work required,[1] but it would be a tax on his strength and would increase the whispering against him. Also, would it be better to be a monk at Bec or elsewhere. If at Bec, he had devoted his abilities to books in vain, since there was no one there whom he could teach: Lanfranc's reputation overshadowed anybody else's knowledge, however great. If in some other place which had only a few learned men, he could become proud, through being the only one who knew so much. After he had thought long and hard about these things, at a suitable moment he poured them out into the bosom of his friend, Lanfranc,[2] who decided to send him to Maurilius, archbishop of Rouen. Maurilius was a monk, and had been in the religious life so long that he was an expert judge of all its pathways.

Chapter 46 Anselm as a monk at Bec

In the end, after the pros and cons had been stated and discussed, he chose the life of a monk over all other religious lives: only monks lived under the command of another, taking the vow of obedience and renouncing their own will. The place he chose was Bec. As it was neither too richly nor too poorly endowed, he would not be broken by toil or enervated by soft living. The comparison with Lanfranc would suppress his growing pride: it was no part of being a monk to acquire fame through learning or to sell literature out of a thirst for glory. So he became a monk at Bec, and when three years later Lanfranc was moved to Caen, Anselm was made prior by abbot Herluin. During his fifteen years in this office his daily life displayed all the virtues. He took an especial care of the young, for he knew that their tender years could either be formed for goodness by hard work or for evil by sloth. He grew so accustomed to eating frugally that later on in life his digestive system, through its constriction then, could not have coped with richer food, even if he himself had wanted it. He uprooted the vice of individuality from himself by his will, and from other people by his exhortations. He used to say that it was this sin alone that had driven the devil from heaven and man from paradise, for they had fled from the command of God and pandered to their own desires. And so removing from himself any indulgence in the decisions of his own mind, he added to his store nothing at all from the outside world. Indeed he shunned every kind of sin so much that he said he would rather be in hell without sin than in heaven as a sinner. This saying was greeted with applause at the time, but nowadays it needs an interpreter. However, we must look for somebody to explain it another time.

The importance he placed on prayers and meditations is shown by his book of them, composed, so we believe, under the guidance of the Holy Spirit, whose fullness he had thirstily drunk into his inmost being. There are also

[1] Knowles takes this work to be incessant liturgical observances rather than physical labour (*The Monastic Order*, p. 149).
[2] See Eadmer *The Life of St Anselm* 1:6 for Lanfranc's influence over Anselm. Lanfranc does seem to have been Anselm's only master.

books of soliloquies and addresses to God. These surpass the thoughts of all his predecessors, or, to put it more kindly, collect them between two covers. Previous writers had aimed to force belief from us by their authority. Anselm used reason to strengthen our belief, demonstrating with invincible arguments that the things which we believe are so and could not be otherwise. By his good sense and patience he won over his rivals, who had been annoyed that Anselm had been preferred to them. By his concern over the death of a young man, he kindled the feebleness of the rest into goodness and aroused them to hard work.

Nor in the meantime did his religion live quietly in his heart without producing miracles, for God showed his favour towards him by many signs. One night he was considering[1] how God could have shown past, present and future to the prophets in one moment, when the same gift was given to him: the barriers of all the walls between the dormitory and the church were taken away and he saw the monk, whose job it was and who had got out of bed, take hold of the bell rope, which he used to warn the brothers to wake up. It was his gaze alone which restored to health diseased genitalia. It was when a leper had drunk from the water in which Anselm had washed his hands that the ghastly pallor disappeared from his skin. A monk was sick and near to death. Seeing himself surrounded by huge wolves and about to be devoured by the jaws of the beasts, he uttered piercing screams. But Anselm came up, scattered the wolves, and put the monk into a peaceful sleep. He cured another monk of a fatal illness by sprinkling him with holy water. A third monk escaped from the enticements of the flesh after being blessed by Anselm. This monk was Boso, then a young man, later abbot of Bec, who converses with Anselm in his book *Cur Deus Homo* (*Why God Became Man*). Anselm had made him a monk when he was still young, and he was experiencing boredom as a result of his recent profession, and recognised with groans the marks of the old flame which for the time being had died down.[2] He confessed his hot lusts to his father and received no response but 'God have mercy on you, my son.'[3] No sooner had Anselm said this than a clear light flowed into the victim's mind and untied and loosened the knot of vice.

Chapter 47 Anselm sails for England (September 1092)

Next, after the death of abbot Herluin, Anselm received a greater office, for he was chosen as abbot of Bec by all the monks, although he tried with many excuses to get out of the job. With his particular virtues he was of still more service in this post, and it would seem right to glance at some of these qualities, considering that he spent fifteen years in this office as well.[4] But as my intention is rather to describe the events of his archbishopric, I will skip this period and

---

[1] As he lay awake on his bed in the dormitory. See Eadmer, *The Life of St Anselm* 1:7.
[2] These words recall the description of Dido's experience at Aeneid 4:23.
[3] Genesis 43:29.
[4] He had also spent fifteen years in his previous office of prior.

draw a veil over it. The limits of the work I have undertaken are opposed and inimical to the sort of detailed approach which would make me appear to be going over ground already covered by the brightest of intellects. And yet, as I have said elsewhere,[1] it may not seem ridiculous to include a list of his virtues and achievements; for the reader who cannot lay his hand on those weighty tomes may learn from such a summary.

Well then, when Lanfranc had been taken up into another life, the churches all over England suffered extortions and had their property proscribed, and the mother church at Canterbury was added to the royal treasury and was fleeced annually, and even often monthly, by collectors of taxes. For it seemed almost more tolerable to groan under the continuing command of one man they had got used to[2] than to be subject to new masters who were ever succeeding one another. All this time the bishops kept completely silent. There were no dogs who were able to bark. Suffering found no voice and justice was stifled inside men's thoughts, all because of the fear of one man. For what was the point of speaking when words aroused hate and brought no gain. There was some hope that an end could be put to these troubles if ever they saw as archbishop of Canterbury one who would be the voice of all, a standard-bearer to go before them, and the shield of his people. Rumours spread among the crowd, in my opinion not without the mind and power of God, that Anselm was to become their archbishop, a man of deep holiness and exact scholarship who would bring happiness to England with his blessings. The remarks of this kind that came to his ears kept him in Normandy for five whole years, although he was frequently invited across the sea, as the reasons for it increased. The need of so many people was an inducement for going, but he was held back by the fear that he might be thought to have been seized by an ambition for the archbishopric and to have forgotten the nobler part. Finally, when he could now no longer delay without the loss of souls, he sailed for England, sacrificing to God the purity of his conscience. At least what men there said about him would be based on the evidence of their own eyes, when, by the long years of his good life among them, he had turned aside their criticism that the archbishopric was very much in his own interest. And at the same time the rumour about his archbishopric, which had once been full of threats for him, had by now after such a long time died away.

Chapter 48 The attempt to force Anselm to become archbishop

There were several understandable reasons for his coming, but these were the chief ones. He wanted to strengthen the abbey at Chester, which Hugh, earl of Chester,[3] desired to fill particularly with monks from Bec. He wanted also to

---

[1] William made similar remarks in chs. 19 and 28.
[2] William Rufus.
[3] Hugh of Avranches, nephew of William I. By 1080 he was one of the only four earls left in the kingdom. In 1093 he ejected the secular canons from St Werburg's, Chester, and replaced them with a Benedictine abbot and monks from Bec.

visit this Hugh, who had been ill for a long time, and who, although he was in
a position of great power, was ceasing to be arrogant, so everybody said, and
was longing for Anselm: if he were actually dying, he would bequeath to
Anselm a token of their old friendship. Anselm also wanted to soften the king
by his intercessions and so lighten the taxes on his own estates. He saw to the
first two things at once.

To discharge the third, he hurried to the court. He did not, like other people,
search out a tactful time for an audience. As soon as he arrived, he was
admitted into the inner sanctum, such was the reverence for his sanctity. Given
this opportunity of a private audience, he unhesitatingly disclosed to the king
all the things of which rumour accused him.[1] He also gave a restrained account
of his own needs. The king settled all the matters concerning the church at Bec
according to the wishes of its abbot, but laughed away the harshness of
Anselm's other remarks. He said he could not squash a reputation for
licentiousness, but that a man of sanctity ought not to believe it. For the
king had no wish at that time to snuff out Anselm with some more aggressive
reply, knowing how highly his father and mother had been accustomed to rate
him when they were alive. For this also, he said, ought to be accounted
magnificent in a king: that, when he had the power to do anything at all, he
chose to diffuse some things with a joke and transferred many matters from the
sentence of his decision to the realm of wit. For example, when the bishops
suggested that he should allow prayers to be made throughout the kingdom for
God to deign to inspire him to support the mother church with a shepherd, he
concealed his anger with a laugh and replied jokingly, 'Pray as you like; I shall
do as I please, since no man's prayer will ever change my mind.'

On another occasion, when Anselm was being discussed at a meeting of the
nobles and one of those present contributed the remark that he was the only
man of his day who was not ambitious for any office, the king pulled a face and
said, 'What? Not even for the archbishopric of Canterbury?' And when this
was equally denied by the speaker, the king declared that Anselm would do
everything with the utmost vigour, if ever he was inspired to any hope of
obtaining that honour. 'But, by the holy face of St Luke,' he said, 'both Anselm
and all the rivals for the archbishopric will for the present take second place to
me, for I shall be archbishop myself.'

He frequently repeated such jests, but soon he felt a strong, heavy pain. It
grew worse, and after a few hours he took to his bed. As it happened, Anselm
had by then taken himself away from the tumult of the court, but was roused
by a speedy messenger, direct from the king, and at the king's request
presented himself at court. With the agreement of the bishops he heard the
king's confession.[2] William was sorry for his sins, and Anselm commanded
him to send by means of the bishops, who had then all gathered together, a
crosier to the altar as a surety indicating his penitence. He was also to appoint

---

[1] This presumably refers to the homosexual vices of the king's court.
[2] This gathering at what was thought to be the king's deathbed took place on 6 March 1093.

pastors to the churches without them, to bring back exiles and to free prisoners. The king did all of this, with as scrupulous an obedience as if it had been commanded by God. His increasing sickness spurred him on, and people expected Anselm to exact punishment for his sins. Then the sick man made an appropriate speech to those standing around his bed about bringing relief to the church at Canterbury and transferring consideration of the matter to the bishops. His words were greeted with applause, and the cries went up to heaven of those wishing the king prosperity and recovery. But they handed back to the king the right of deliberating on the matter, and with submissive minds they waited for the king's approval, all determined to accept whomever the king pronounced worthy. And so William, raising himself up on his elbow, said 'I chose this holy man here, Anselm.' A huge outburst of applause followed his decision.

When Anselm heard it, fear drained the composure from his breast and at the same time his face grew pale. But as he tried to contrive excuses on the matter, the bishops took him aside, and at first calmed him with such words as these: Anselm should rejoice in this opportunity, which had no doubt been the work of God himself, intending that now, through his archbishopric, all the evils throughout England could be cut out and a proper limit placed on all her disturbances. He should announce what he wished to happen in the matters of God, and they would not fail to support him. He would pray to God on their behalf, and they themselves would undertake for him such secular tasks as needed doing. So Anselm should cheerfully take up the office to which, it seemed, that headstrong king, inspired by God, was appointing him, in order to avoid the blame for all the wickednesses then appearing in the land. Such was their case.

But Anselm, foreseeing the future, sidestepped all their arguments and nimbly replied that the weaknesses of his years made him unfit for such a burden; it would be presumptuous for any young man to attempt this great task, and much more so for one whose blood ran sluggishly and whose strength had been nibbled away by envious old age.[1] Furthermore, he knew nothing of secular affairs, as ever since he had become a monk he had refused to get to know people whose occupations made him shudder. His ideal was a free mind, devoted to the pleasures of holy Scripture. Their intentions involved a discrepancy: for the plough of holy church, which in England ought to be drawn by two strong oxen, namely the king and the archbishop of Canterbury, both working for the good with equal strength, would be wrenched aside from the straight path, if an old sheep was now yoked with an untamed bull. 'I', he said, 'am the old sheep. If I were left in peace, I could perhaps give pleasure to some with the milk of the word of God and the covering of my wool. But if you yoke me with this bull, you will see the plough leave the path when drawn by such unequal partners. So you will gain nothing from this appointment. On the contrary, with your own lips sealed in fear, you will see the church lacking a

---

[1] He was in fact about sixty.

lively shepherd, and all because you want to make a decision for her which is a bad decision. Besides all this, I am abbot in another country, so you see how inappropriate and full of ambition it is for me to let down the monks to whom I owe protection, and to dishonour the archbishop to whom I owe allegiance.' At this they put still greater pressure on him, promising to deal speedily with all his objections. Even the king, when he heard of Anselm's stubborn refusal, begged him by his friendship with his mother and father not to go on persisting in his opinion to the loss of his soul. When finally all threw themselves at his feet, Anselm too fell on his face, but, hero-like, was unmoved by any tears[1] and unpersuaded by any promises. He felt such distress at that moment, that, as he later said, calling upon the deity as his witness, he would have preferred to have stopped breathing, if that had been God's will, rather than be tossed on such a surge of anxiety. He even tearfully called for help from those of his own monks who were present, until the bishops, encouraging each other, joined in an attack on Anselm as though he were an enemy. Some in the rear, some in front propelled him towards the bed of the sick king. They took hold of the fingers of his hand, which Anselm was keeping tightly curved up in his palm, and tried to lift them up. For some time their labour was in vain, as anger and pain lent him strength, but then they just about managed to lift his index finger and put the pastoral staff in it, while Anselm uttered cries of pain at this rough treatment. All the time keeping a tight hold on his hand so that he did not throw the staff away, they dragged him rather than led him into the church, following the customary solemn rites. And although the joyful sound of everybody singing *Te deum laudamus* filled the air, Anselm shouted as loudly as he could, 'Your actions are null and void. I refuse. I do not agree.'

Returning to the king, he said that he would soon have a better view of the matter: as he, Anselm, had been forced into it against his wishes, everything which had happened to him concerning it could and should be annulled. When he had said this, he left the court escorted by the nobles and went to his lodging, in floods of tears and in deep pain and sorrow. Such behaviour, an indication of his inner thoughts, inflamed the determination of the invalid all the more, so that he at once gave orders for Anselm to be proclaimed archbishop to the people and to be invested with all rights pertaining to the revenues of the church of Canterbury. Moreover the city of Canterbury, which archbishop Lanfranc had had as his benefice, was given to Anselm with undisturbed tenure. This happened on Sunday, 6 March 1093.

Chapter 49 By June 1095 Anselm has received the pallium as archbishop

And so Anselm left for the estates given him by ecclesiastical law, while the king shook off his illness and grew better. For he energetically proceeded with his plan of establishing Anselm in the archbishopric. He sent messengers into

---

[1] Just as Aeneas was unmoved by Dido's tears in *Aeneid* 4:438–9.

Normandy with letters from the king for the archbishop of Rouen and the monks at Bec, asking them to agree to release Anselm. The monks also carefully weighed the pros and cons of this request in the scales, but after thrashing the matter out in some prolonged discussion, they finally consented. But Anselm's ordination was held up by a quarrel which came upon himself and the king for this reason: the king had asked Anselm with winning words to give his willing agreement to the ownership of some possessions of the church of Christ, which the king himself had appropriated, being permanently granted to the king's own clients, who after the death of Lanfranc had marched in upon them as the royal gift. Anselm refused to inflict a loss upon the church to which as yet he had contributed nothing.[1] This aroused the king's anger. He postponed and almost cancelled the arrangements for Anselm's consecration, which previously he had been promoting with the greatest enthusiasm and urgency. Joy sprang up in Anselm's noble heart: he hoped that, as he had performed all the functions of his abbacy, he could now start leading a private life. For he had already handed in his crosier and resigned his abbacy, from which he had been set free by archbishop William of Rouen. On that occasion and at other times he was often heard to declare that he did not have the strength for any office except that of prior of a monastery; he took delight in the freedom from business, and, although he was not up to other tasks, he did have a tongue which was prompt to bless. But, as much time went by, the king was made anxious by the complaints of everybody that the churches were going to rack and ruin through their lack of a leader, and with great difficulty he persuaded Anselm to undertake the archbishopric, with a keener desire for it as he would have the king's support in everything. The king indeed was lavish with splendid promises which weighed down the winds themselves, and these influenced and won over Anselm as he hesitated. So on 25 September 1093 he acquired his temporal powers from his sovereign according to the custom of that time and was enthroned at Canterbury, while on 4 December he received his solemn episcopal powers from all the bishops of England. His prognostic was, 'He invited many, and at the hour for dinner sent his servant to bid those who had been invited to come, because all was ready. And they all together began to make excuse.'[2]

Soon afterwards the king went across the sea. There were two rivals for the papacy at Rome at this time, Wibert and Urban.[3] Both were outstanding men of great stature, and neither was of the sort to give way to the other. English opinion fluctuated uncertainly, but people rather favoured Wibert because of

---

[1] For the importance of this principle in Anselm's thought see Southern, *St Anselm and his Biographer*, pp. 127–8.

[2] Luke 14:16. In his later revision of his original manuscript William cut out material which on second thoughts he considered offensive, including at this point a long attack on William Rufus in which he quotes the king's remark, 'his abbeys were his and he would do what he liked with them'. See Knowles, *The Monastic Order*, p. 347.

[3] Henry IV, the Holy Roman Emperor, had deposed pope Gregory VII in 1084 and elected Wibert, archbishop of Ravenna, as pope in his place. Urban II had been elected as the Roman pope in 1088 and was recognised as such by the whole of France, including Anselm as abbot of Bec.

their fear of the king. Anselm had long been a supporter of Urban, and on being chosen archbishop had mentioned this support, without the king making any objection. But, on Rufus' return to his kingdom, having failed in his scheme to deprive his brother[1] of his province, the archbishop went to him and asked permission to go to Rome to receive the pallium from pope Urban. The king was always likely to get heated, and he found fresh fuel for his anger in this request. In an evil temper he shouted that Anselm could not be properly maintaining the allegiance he had promised him, if he were calling Urban or anybody else pope without his permission. Anselm replied that the question of whether he was infringing his loyalty to his earthly master if he called Urban vicar of St Peter merited serious discussion and should be postponed to a larger assembly. And so the matter was discussed with heated arguments and much emotion on both sides. This was the king's reasoning: it is the custom of my kingdom, instituted by my father, that no one shall be called pope without the permission of the king. The person who ignores the customs of the kingdom, also violates my royal power and crown. The person who removes my crown is behaving towards me as an enemy and traitor.

Anselm replied: God has a different opinion, and has already solved and unknotted this problem by two precepts. He himself tells us what loyalty we owe to the vicar of the blessed Peter, 'You are Peter, and upon this rock I will build my church; and I will give you the keys of heaven, and whatever you bind on earth shall be bound in heaven and whatever you loose on earth shall be loosed in heaven.'[2] And as a general command to everybody, 'Who hears you, hears me, and who spurns you, spurns me.'[3] And again, 'Who touches you, touches as it were the pupil of my eye.'[4] And then he elsewhere declares what we owe to the king, 'Render to Caesar the things which are Caesar's, and to God the things which are God's.'[5] So in what concerns God I shall render obedience to the vicar of the blessed Peter without giving any offence, and in those matters which affect the earthly dignity of my master I shall not deny him my loyal support and counsel to the best of my knowledge.

In these discussions[6] all the bishops of England refused to side with Anselm, acting the part of mercenary fugitives from freedom. And as if this was not enough, they denied him all obedience and loyalty. Their instigator and standard-bearer was William, bishop of Durham.[7] A ruthless orator of dangerous ambitions, he hoped to make his way into the archbishopric, if Anselm was deposed. And so he pressed on with his wicked attempt all the

---

[1] Robert, duke of Normandy.
[2] Matthew 16:18, 19.
[3] Luke 10:16.
[4] Zechariah 2:8.
[5] Matthew 22:21.
[6] For these discussions, held at Rockingham on 25–8 February 1095, see Southern, *The Life of St Anselm by Eadmer*, pp 84–5.
[7] Southern discusses this bishop's apparent inconsistency in appealing to Urban II in 1088 when accused of treachery by William Rufus (see ch. 133) and opposing Anselm for appealing to Urban II now (*St Anselm and his Biographer*, pp. 148–50).

more and promised the king that it would be through his cleverness that Anselm would voluntarily return ring and crosier and give up his office. But he devised these plans in opposition to God, for after he and his supporters had pondered all these schemes in lengthy discussions, Anselm squashed them by one retort: if there was any one who presumed to prove that he had denied allegiance to his earthly king by appealing to the vicar of the blessed Peter, he was ready to make reply in person to whom and when he ought. At this their minds were more cast down. They realised that Anselm had more discernment than they thought, because he knew that an archbishop of Canterbury ought not to be brought to judgement except in an apostolic consistory court. And so subtly scheming men, using all their intelligence, fought in vain against the man helped by God. For whatever points they thought of making, Anselm would at once find an answer and demolish them, as if he were giving a vigorous blow at some spiders' webs. He was so calm in his mind and free from anxiety, that when his enemies withdrew and turned over his words this way and that, he would lean back against a wall and take a nap. His expression remained the same, his mind stayed undisturbed. Anger did not remove his control, or fear make him anxious, but the cheerfulness of his countenance bore witness to the tranquillity which he professed. The bishops turned to shouting as their anger rose, and the bishop of Durham openly declared that the man who could not be checked by reason should be overcome by force. The nobles protested loudly against this, as they, much more than the bishops, were of the opinion that they should refrain from harming the archbishop. Finally, when commanded to deny him obedience, they completely refused, saying that they were Christians and had no wish to resist the will of their archbishop on any matter. Although the king was extremely annoyed at this, he bit back his anger through fear of a greater disturbance. And as the bishops' promise had not gone well,[1] he relied on their plan of using force, aiming to deprive Anselm of crosier and ring and drive him from the land. But when the king could not achieve this by force, as Anselm declared that, although he was leaving England, he was not giving up his insignia and title, the whole matter was peaceably postponed from the current 15 March to the octaves of Pentecost.

The nobles brought this news to Anselm just when he was beginning to think about his vacation. He heaved a sigh, and groaning loudly replied, 'Although through past experience I am not without knowledge of the future, all the same I do not want to press on with everything according to my own wishes, and so I accept the peace and will not deviate from it, however much it is in my interest to do so. He who breaks the peace will see for himself how important this is in God's eyes.' This off-the-cuff reply turned out to be completely true. Before the date agreed on, he had been subject to many attacks. His chamberlain was hurried off to punishment before his eyes. Some counsellors that he especially relied upon were banished overseas. Cunning, wicked schemes aimed at

---

[1] The promise that Anselm would voluntarily return ring and crosier.

diminishing his honour were thought up and put into practice. Two especially crafty operators were sent as messengers to Rome to explore the lie of the land and then to ask the pope to send the pallium to king William, so that he could give it to whomever he pleased. Anselm knew nothing of all this, and in fact suspected nothing less than this. The messengers carried out their orders with force and energy, and on the instruction of pope Urban brought back to England Walter, bishop of Albano. He landed at Dover. He went to court without Anselm knowing about it, and glutted William's voracious appetite with extravagant promises. If Urban were accepted as pope in England, he would confirm with the privilege of his apostolic see whatever the king thought to ask of him. But he gave no help to Anselm's cause, except that when he was asked to banish him, he replied that it was impossible for a man with such a widespread reputation for sanctity and knowledge to be deposed, especially since he had been legally appointed archbishop and was guilty of no crime. So an edict was immediately published throughout the land stating that men should consider and talk of Urban as the rightful pope. Anselm heard this, and so was extremely surprised when a crowd of bishops turned up, sent to him by the king. By gradual degrees they tested him, to see if he was still opposed to renewing friendship with the king. When they discovered that nothing had changed, they revealed their secret, telling him how the lord king by his own efforts and expense had acquired the pallium from Rome, and through his own initiative had completed a business which had cost him many marks in money. So, they claimed, it was right that Anselm should respond to the king's great kindness with a duty which was worthy of the gift. Anselm heaved deep sighs as he heard the words of the bishops, upset that a cunning trick should have been put into effect, and told them that it would not persuade him to make any concessions, as he set little store by a service whose importance they themselves valued so highly. This incident taught the king that it was completely impossible to weaken the force of Anselm's determination and persuade him to become his friend, so, still showing a king's magnanimity, he asked Anselm straight out to be reconciled and Anselm agreed. He was publicly given the authority to exercise freely throughout the whole kingdom the rights of his primacy, and a day was appointed on which the bishop of Albano should come to Canterbury with the pallium. He came, bringing the sacred garment in a silver case. The crowd shouted their applause, and Anselm met him, barefoot but dressed in his priestly robes. Then at the altar of our Lord, the Saviour, he received the pallium, arranged it around his blessed shoulders as consecrated archbishop and proceeded to celebrate mass. It was a Sunday, 10 June 1095, and some people thought it a great miracle that it happened that the Gospel for the day was his own former prognostic, 'A man made a great supper and called many. At the hour of supper he sent his servants to bid those he had invited to come, as all things were now ready. And they all began at the same time to make excuse.'

Chapter 50 Anselm departs for Rome (October 1097)

And so friendship was established between them, and when the king went overseas, for that whole year the calm tranquillity of peace removed the cares from Anselm's mind, and lightened the anxieties of good men. But later on when William returned, there was another thunderstorm and a hurricane of hatred blew up anew. For the king, being pleased with the happy outcome of events, had at once marched against the Welsh. In all his undertakings he was finding God's favour greatly helping him and he was enjoying the smiling playfulness of fortune in everything to such a degree that it seemed God was vying with him in doing good. If he attacked in battle, he brought back rich spoils. If he wanted to sail when the sea was stormy, the winds at once set aside their fury. Anselm saw all this and was glad. He hoped that because of this abundance of blessings the king would one day make the church free. And so, when the king returned from his Welsh expedition, Anselm was thinking of putting some gentle pressure on him, but the king got in first. He upset the archbishop with reproachful messages, referring to the small numbers and feebleness of the knights he had sent against the enemy.[1] Upon the receipt of this message, all hope of reforming the king died down in Anselm's heart. He sent back the messenger without an answer. He did not want to open up the plain for battle again by an exchange of messages.

Fortune, spurred on, I suppose, by the devil, was raging hard against the archbishop, and plots were being hatched against him for the next court session. Anselm evaded and nullified all of these by asking permission to go to Rome, having first made many attempts to test the king's will on the state of the church. So, intending to communicate this to the pope, he asked permission, as I have said, to go to Rome. But two or three times he asked in vain. The king's answer was, 'I think permission should be forbidden. I know he is not weighed down by some grave sin, for which he must ask absolution at Rome. Nor does he need any advice there, seeing that there is no branch of knowledge of which he is not a master. Indeed I would be more inclined to say that Urban comes behind Anselm in wisdom than that Anselm has need of Urban. But if he stubbornly persists in his purpose, I shall transfer all his archiepiscopal revenues into my treasury. For he is breaking his promises, by which he bound himself loyally to keep all the customs of my kingdom. And it is not one of my customs that any of my nobles should go to Rome, except at my express request. And so he must either swear to me that he will never again for any purpose appeal to the apostolic see, or leave the kingdom. You, my loyal servants, are to tell him this. If you see that he is willing to give up his journey, then he must experience the force of the justice of my courts, seeing that he was not afraid to give me endless trouble about a matter which he was unwilling to bring to a conclusion.'

---

[1] Southern discusses this apparently small incident and Anselm's reasons for visiting the pope (*St Anselm and his Biographer*, pp. 159–60).

Anselm thought he should not reply to this by messengers, so he went in to the king in person and sat on his right hand according to custom. He spoke as follows, 'You say I should not go to Rome, as I have not committed any grave sin and am a man of wide learning, although I should not claim either thing to be true, but commit them to the examination of God's scales. I agree with your point that I promised to keep your customs, but I require conditions. I actually said that I would keep them with exceptions, only keeping such as were consonant with the laws of God as having been rightly instituted. As for your saying that I am disloyal because I went against your customs and am appealing to the apostolic see, saving your highness' reverence, another would have said this was not true. For the loyalty which I owe to you, O king, I have from my loyalty to God, whose vicar is the holy Peter, to whose see I am appealing. You say that I should swear not to appeal to Rome for any reason in the future, but I proclaim publicly that a Christian prince is wrong to demand such an oath from his archbishop. For if by my oath I forswore the holy Peter, I would be denying Christ. And when indeed I deny Christ for any reason, I shall not be slow in satisfying you of a sin that requires me to ask for permission to go! But perhaps, if I were to go to Rome, God would bring it about that the property of the churches would only for a short time swell your coffers, and so nullify your threats.'

The king and the nobles shouted Anselm down as he said this. Their main complaint was there had never been any mention of God or the right in the obligation of keeping the customs of the king. Anselm remained courteous and his face almost broke into a smile as he said, 'Heavens above! If, as you say, there has been no mention of God or the right, whose customs are they? Never let any Christian be in the position of keeping and upholding laws or customs which are known to be contrary to God and the right.' At this utterance, it was as though their shameless foreheads had been struck by a hammer. Their lowered heads and silent voices testified to their sense of wrongdoing. For Anselm remained completely unmoved. Whenever they shouted, he stayed silent, and then calmly reverted to the main point. The king, however, could not stop himself from hurling at him the cruel threat that he would not be taking anything with him from his kingdom. Anselm fearlessly replied, 'I will go barefoot and naked, if anyone says that my horses and clothes are yours.' This remark made the king feel ashamed, and he blushed as he said, 'I didn't mean that. Simply, when in ten days time you get to the channel port, my messenger will tell you what to take and what to leave.' Anyone else would have been angry, but Anselm remained unruffled. He said that the king's anger made him upset and sorry, but that, if the king could bring himself to believe it, he was looking for a way, still incomplete, to further the good of his soul. He then offered the king his blessing, and the king did not refuse it.

On this matter as formerly the bishops had recourse to subterfuge. Anselm summoned them and asked for their support. They replied that he was a holy and wise man. As he was wise, he did not need their counsel, but would know best what to do. As he was holy, he unerringly wanted and was able to do the good. They could not rise against their master: for the sake of their positions and the parents whom they loved they were not willing to forfeit his favour. Anselm was free of all worldly taint and greed, and should follow the cause of God which he had taken up. He would have the silent good wishes of his bishops, even if none of them expressed support openly. But if he would listen to them and was open to better advice, they judged the pleasure of being snug and peaceful at home preferable to being involved in the toils and labours of being an exile from one's country and position. Then they all went away. Only two asked for his forgiveness before he crossed the sea, and he generously forgave them. Their names were Osmund of Salisbury and Robert of Hereford.[1] He stayed at Canterbury for one day. Then, as was usual, he took up the staff and scrip, the stay and sign of his journey. He came to Dover, and was kept there against his wishes for fifteen days by unsuitable winds. During this time, the messenger, whom I have said was sent by the king,[2] untiringly tracked down the inn where he was staying and kept secret the reason for his arrival. But when favourable waves were now summoning the ships to the open sea, the messenger, on the king's instructions, ordered all Anselm's bags and baggage to be brought out into the open and searched. It was a cruel and pitiful sight to see the primate of England, the head of all religion and wisdom, treated like a pirate! But nothing was found except goods needed for the journey. There was no money. The messenger was sorry for his actions, which he had carried out unwillingly, and allowed Anselm to depart unharmed.

Chapter 51 Anselm's journey to Rome

They set sail and a south wind carried their ships out to sea, but at first so slowly that when the wind changed they seemed to be sailing back to England. Father Anselm could not look upon this with dry eyes for the pain in his heart. He lifted up his hands to the sky and drew down help from heaven. For the force of the winds abated, the seas grew calm and they set sail towards Flanders. With a favouring breeze their ships cut through the waves and they soon reached Wissant. He was first given hospitality by the monks of St Bertin, and his popularity supplied him with everything else he needed, as all the bishops and abbots vied in giving him invitations and even detaining him against his will. Anselm's reputation had preceded him, blowing with the breeze of sweetness into the hearts of those who heard of it. And so when I try to describe the love with which all men welcomed him and the kindnesses with which his heart was soothed, words fail me and my pen falters. A topsy-turvy world indeed, when he was given more honour in a foreign land than as a citizen in his own country or as archbishop in his own church!

The apostolic legate in France, archbishop Hugh of Lyons, a man of great repute and power and not lacking in sanctity, was quick to meet Anselm in

[1] For these two bishops see chs. 83 and 164–5.
[2] The messenger was William of Warelwast, a chaplain of William II.

person, when he heard that he was coming to Lyons. He devotedly attended to his wants and it was on Hugh's advice that Anselm stayed in Lyons and sent messages to Rome to pope Urban which explained his whole position. A sudden illness had required him to rest, and it also seemed sensible in the meantime to keep out of the way of Wibert's robbers. For the rumour was widespread that the archbishop of Canterbury had come from England on his way to Urban at Rome with his bags stuffed with money: the archbishop, it was said, was carrying huge sums with him, as his English province was the richest of all. This rumour had caused much excitement among Wibert's men, and by now they had blocked all the roads by seizing the narrow places to stop Anselm slipping through. It would be a great advantage to their master, they thought, if they captured one who was a champion of Urban. So Anselm denied them their booty, and allowed the lapse of time to quench their ardour. In the end the robbers went back home, believing that the rumour had been false, and deprived of their loot by Anselm's plan.

But by now the messenger had returned from Rome with orders from the pope that Anselm was to set aside all excuses and obediently come to Rome. Anselm did not know how to contravene his vow of obedience and he set out upon the journey, feeling bolder because of his hope of the mercy of God. For the return of health and strength had built up his courage, and his old age, which was green and vigorous and on this side of senility, still allowed him to endure exertions successfully. He crossed the Alps and arrived safely in Rome without loss of man or animal from his party. On the whole journey he had had only one nasty moment, and even this turned out well and increased his fame. For the duke of Burgundy had been seized with the same hope as Wibert's men and was all on fire with a great eagerness to rob Anselm. But just one look from Anselm softened him. All his arrogance evaporated and he became as humble as before. Indeed Anselm's sweet look, gentle countenance and peaceful grey hairs so captivated the onlooker that he would at once win the love of anyone on whom he cast the grace of his gaze. As soon as the duke saw Anselm, his passion, fired by the words of rascals, died down in his heart. At once he was received with a kiss by the archbishop and voluntarily asked him for his blessing. He summoned one of his nobles (for he had come attended by many of them amid great commotion) and instructed him to lead Anselm safely through his lands and everywhere to serve Anselm as faithfully as himself. So, having sealed a friendship with Anselm, the duke departed, repeatedly uttering oaths against evil counsellors and invoking the redoubled anger of God upon the person who had persuaded him to attack the angel of God. So Anselm passed safely through Cluniac country, and soon, as I have said, came to Lyons and from there to Rome.

Chapter 52 Anselm in Rome (summer 1098)

The pope received him magnificently and before his council extolled him with lavish praises. In the whole of Western Christendom, he said, Anselm was the master in the liberal arts and in piety they would not find his equal. He had suffered many insults for the Roman faith and after a journey full of danger and death had at last arrived at Rome to ask for help from one who was more in need of his wisdom. During this effusive speech of Urban Anselm kept quiet, modestly looking at the ground. When the pope came to the end of his praises, Anselm was given the opportunity to speak and gave a truthful account of his whole case. Pope and council alike promised their help. A letter was written to William, king of England, in which he was commanded to reclothe Anselm in all his vestments. For as soon as Anselm had crossed the sea, the king had given orders for the transferring of his whole archbishopric to his own control and for the annulment of all Anselm's decisions. The reply to the letter was a command that the archbishop was to remain with the pope. But Anselm was not minded to stay in Rome for a long time because that city's air was unhealthy for foreigners. So he accepted the invitation of a certain John, once his monk at Bec but then appointed abbot by Urban of the monastery of the Holy Saviour near Telese, to avoid the summer's heat by staying in his village called Sclavia.[1] This village was situated on the very top of a mountain and was kept cool almost every hour by the moderate temperature which surrounded it on all sides, so that the atmosphere was completely healthy. So Anselm enjoyed his enforced stay there, for he saw that he had regained the one thing which he had missed for so long, namely leisure. His long dormant interest in theology was awoken and he finished there the famous book, whose title and theme is *Why God Became Man.* All men loved and honoured him. The king of England had sent a letter to Roger, duke of Apulia,[2] trying to make accusations against Anselm, but even Roger, so far from listening to these complaints, completely ignored them and switched his support to Anselm, offering him houses and castles and finally promising him whatever he wanted provided he would bless his land by staying there.

In his attendance on the pope Anselm was always given second place to him in processions and at the stational churches,[3] and greetings and gifts came to him after the pope. Everybody heard him gladly, and when his thunderous words were aimed at the bishops, they did what he commanded. This gave him especial pleasure, for he would say that the fruits of wisdom consisted in other people making progress in the good life as a result of your teaching when you spoke well. And so he was seized with a great longing to lay down his archbishop's powers so that he could devote himself to God. But when he begged and pleaded with the pope for permission to do this, he got a direct refusal. 'No,' said the pope, 'By your vow of obedience I command you, wherever you are, not to lay down the title and office of archbishop of Canterbury. It is the feeble soldier who runs away before the war; it is no

---

[1] This village was renamed Liberi in the enthusiasm for liberty in 1860.
[2] Roger, duke of Apulia 1085–1111, was the son and successor of the Norman, Robert Guiscard.
[3] On certain solemn days the pope processed from the Lateran Palace to celebrate mass at one of the basilicas of the city. The basilica whose turn it was for the service was the 'station' for the day.

part of the duty of the steadfast Christian to surrender to mere threats and fears before he suffers any wound.' Anselm replied, 'I do not refuse you obedience, father, nor in God's cause am I frightened of blows or even death itself, unless by chance my courage fails me. But, I ask you, what can I do in a place where justice is not only tottering but has already been wholly overthrown? Where my bishops, who should be my loyal supporters, not only do not help me because of their fear but even attack me to win favour?' 'I am minded', replied the pope, 'to hold a council at Bari about these and other such matters. I desire your presence and need your help.'

Chapter 53 The Council of Bari (October 1098)

When the council assembled, the pope, wearing chasuble and pallium, took his seat to the front of the body of St Nicholas on a platform which was covered in cloths and palliums; the others, wearing caps, also took their seats. They each laid claim to their customary seat, but Anselm who was highest in humility sat where he could. The pope had forgotten in all the hustle and bustle to assign him a place. But he was reminded of his mistake when he had to deal with a question put by the Greeks who wanted to establish that the Holy Spirit does not proceed except from the Father. He was getting into ever greater difficulties as he tried to answer this question, while the Greeks raised very valid objections. But then he thought of Anselm and cried aloud. The size of the building and the numbers of people present magnified the thunder of his powerful voice. 'Father Anselm, scholar and archbishop of England, where are you?' When he heard his name called, Anselm got to his feet, and the pope said to him, 'Now, master, we need your learning and the help of your eloquence. Step forward, come up here and defend your mother church against the attempts of the Greeks to overthrow it. So come to our help, sent here it seems by God himself.' At once the whole gathering, both those standing and those sitting, asked who it was. He was raised up to the pope's platform by the efforts of those nearest and was commanded to sit beside the archdeacon of Rome, who customarily sits in front of the pope. 'Let us include Anselm in our sphere, as a kind of pope of his other sphere', said pope Urban. Without delay he openly told them all of Anselm's parentage and birthplace, of his learning, eloquence and piety, and of all his sufferings in his loyalty to the see of Rome. Consideration of the question was put off to the next day, although Anselm was very willing to answer it at once. But when the council met earlier than usual on the following day and Anselm was brought up on to the platform, he was so successful in dissipating the fog and in getting to the heart of the matter as he considered both sides of the question, that the Latins showed their joy in shouts of applause while the Greeks felt ashamed that they had been made to look ridiculous. And no one after that left the hall at a loss and empty of knowledge. He later gave a clear exposition of the arguments of his speech in a book called *Concerning the Procession of the Holy Spirit*. When he finished speaking, all turned their eyes and faces on him. Some praised his faith, others his learning, but all praised his eloquence. When the uproar caused by these praises had died down, the pope turned towards him and said, 'Blessed be your heart and your perception, blessed be your mouth and the words of your mouth.'

Anselm did not waste time when thus strengthened by everybody's approval, but hurled the thunderbolt of excommunication against his opponents and a discussion began about the king of England. Grisly crimes were brought into the light of day. To his contempt of men were added his offences against heaven, for two or three times he had shown no amendment when admonished. And the pope was just about to excommunicate him with everybody shouting their support when Anselm threw himself at his feet and begged for a delay of sentence, which he with difficulty obtained. This act won for Anselm great favour from all who witnessed it, for they saw a demonstration of Anselm's goodness, which surpassed his fame and reputation. They marvelled at Anselm begging forgiveness for the man who had treated him so badly.

Chapter 54 Anselm stays in Rome until the Council of 24 April 1099

No sooner had the pope returned to Rome, with Anselm as a member of his entourage, than a messenger arrived,[1] sent by the king of England in order to disprove Anselm's allegations and deny the charges brought against him. And yet the king by now had thrown off all sense of shame, being immensely arrogant and with little concern for what people said about him. These were the messenger's words to the pope, spoken in the presence of the archbishop, 'My master cannot understand why you have even thought of ordering the reinstatement of Anselm, seeing that he expressly warned him what would happen if he left England without the king's permission.'

'Does he accuse him of something?' asked the pope.

'He does not,' was the reply.

'So you took upon yourself all the labour of coming here, just to tell me that the primate of your country has been stripped of all his powers because he appealed for justice to the pope? If you love your master, go back quickly and tell him that, if he does not want to be excommunicated, he is to take immediate steps to get Anselm reinvested with all his powers. And so as not to keep you in suspense about the expiry date, you are to bring back his answer to the council to be held in this city the third week after Easter. And I can tell you, the expeller would already have been excommunicated, if his expelled victim had not interceded for him.'

The messenger was taken aback by this unexpected answer, and replied that he would communicate to his master in private the duty demanded of him by the pope. For he was very keen to do something which would win him greater friendship with the king. He achieved this by using his expert skill in bribing

---

[1] This was the same William of Warelwast who had searched Anselm's baggage at Dover at the end of ch. 50.

individuals by gifts and promises, and got the terminal date fixed at Michaelmas for the king. Urban was very reluctant to make this concession. Anselm's piety and the gifts offered him warred against each other in his mind, but in the end money won. Money, you can depend on it, comes out on top in all her battles! Nor is it pretty that in the mind of a great man like Urban there should be so little care for his reputation, with his reverence for God taking second place as money outweighed justice. So Anselm decided not to waste any more time waiting on so venal a man, but to return to Lyons. But he was foiled, for the pope would not allow him to go but kept him in Rome, so that by offering Anselm some comfort he could alleviate the unpleasantness of his action. So he got him to stay with him until the council which was held in his papal palace, and gave him a house with perpetual rights of hospitality there. The pope often visited him. They talked together of matters grave and gay. You might have said they were members of one establishment, not two.

But now the time for the council had arrived. All the French bishops found their seats, but nobody had remembered that an archbishop of Canterbury was attending this Roman council. A chair was placed for him in the circle, just as I described happening previously, and assigned to him and his successors as a perpetual right. The council met in the church of St Peter. So many people came that there was a tremendous hubbub from the onlookers[1] which made it difficult to hear the decrees being read. So the pope instructed Reinger, bishop of Lucca, to use his powerful voice to make everything audible to the throng, Reinger rose to perform the task given to him, and when he opened his mouth, he was not defeated by the noise that had sprung up. His voice reached and penetrated the ears even of those standing on the edge of the crowd. He had read out the great part of the decrees, when suddenly, as if struck by a sudden thought, he began speaking of a different matter, which seemed to have nothing to do with the business in hand. 'Oh dear! What are we doing? We are loading our subjects with instructions, but bringing no help to our suppliants. There will be sorrow and lamentation throughout the whole world, because the head of the whole church does not share the sorrow of its members. Look! Over there, sitting modestly and quietly amongst us, is a man whose silence cries loudly to God. This is the second year that he has been waiting for the power of the apostolic see to come to his aid. His powers have all been unjustly taken away from him, and what help, I ask you, has he received? Anselm is the man I speak of, the archbishop of England.'

As he said this, he heavily struck the floor with the staff which he was holding, as though to emphasise the enormity of the injustice. The pope turned towards him and said, 'Stop being angry, brother Reinger. This matter will be put right.' Reinger, now thoroughly worked up, said, 'It had better, if you want a just judge to approve the case', and returned to reading out the list of decrees which had been interrupted. Anselm was amazed at these words, for he knew that no complaints from him or his followers had persuaded Reinger to

---

[1] Largely pilgrims to the tomb of St Peter, around which the council was arranged.

speak them. In this council the pope, with the approval of eve
sentence of excommunication against laymen who gave
churches, against those invested by laymen, against those wh(
people so invested and against those who did homage to
ecclesiastical honours.[1]

Chapter 55 Anselm dissuades the barons from turning to Robert of Normandy

On the next day of the council the archbishop began his return journey. He
made his way to Lyons by high paths over the mountains, an extremely
arduous and perilous route. He could not go direct, because he heard that
Wibert had sent a painter to Rome with instructions to make a portrait of him,
so that he could not escape notice, no matter what disguise he adopted for his
flight.[2] He got to Lyons and found Hugh as friendly as before. The bishop
treated Anselm not as a foreigner but as the rightful lord of the place, gave him
complete authority indoors and out without him asking for it, and forced him
to accept it. He gave him primacy in meetings, showed him affection when
they were alone and reverence in public, and served him in all things. He
comforted him in his distresses and shared with him his powers, or rather put
them completely at his disposal. He even served him as his suffragan when
Anselm was celebrating mass, and sat at his feet whenever Anselm preached.
He showed generosity and firmness in thus daring to despise wealth and
challenge fortune. So Anselm stayed with him for all the time that Urban and
William remained alive. But not long afterwards death took both of them.[3]

When he heard of the king's death, Anselm shed tears as marks of his
affection and indicators of his duty, and then, being at once invited back home
by Henry,[4] the new king, he thought it right to return to England. On his
arrival he even at the king's wish often held assemblies of rebellious nobles and
won many to allegiance to the king. The guilty were afraid, but the others with
clear brows and eyes full of life cheered and hung on Anselm's words. In the
end, when by now the king's brother Robert had landed and many were
plotting rebellion, Anselm climbed up to a high place surrounded by the whole
army and spoke to the people. The crowd was stirred, as if by a trumpet, and
with loud voices promised their goods and allegiance to the king, provided that
he removed the abuses committed by the younger William and passed just
laws. The king offered Anselm to them all as a surety that he would do this and
gave them his word. Because of this they were all encouraged to support the
king more zealously than ever, so that, if the need arose, with united hearts and

---

[1] See Southern, *St Anselm and his Biographer*, pp. 165–7, for a discussion of these decrees which
were to prove so important in the history of the relations between church and state but which
receive their first mention here without accompanying trumpets.
[2] This portrait incident is one of the few factual additions made to Eadmer's account by William.
[3] Urban in 1099 and William Rufus in 1100.
[4] Rufus had been killed on 2 August and Anselm reached Dover on 23 September.

dedicated hands they would rush on swords to save the king. When this became known Robert gave up the fight and abandoned an enterprise which had depended more on the treachery of others than his own efforts. He had presumed to hope for the kingdom, but he now embraced peace with open arms and gladly became his brother's loving friend.[1]

Chapter 56 Anselm refuses homage to king Henry (1100–1101)

Next the king, following the custom of his predecessors, asked the archbishop to pay homage, but the archbishop delayed because of the excommunication which had been passed at Rome.[2] So both sides sent envoys to Rome. In the meantime the king commanded Anselm either to pay homage or without any excuses for delay to leave the kingdom. Anselm replied, 'Rather, we should look at the pope's letter and do what it says.' For by now the envoys had got back from Rome. But the labour of their journey had been in vain for pope Paschal with unshakable firmness repeated the opinion of his predecessor. 'What does the pope's letter have to do with me?', said the king. 'I refuse to give up the rights of my kingship.' The discussion turned into a quarrel as Anselm declared that he would not leave the country, but would go to his church and give judgement against anyone who offered violence against himself or his people. On that occasion they parted in anger, but some days later a more pacific dispatch from the king summoned Anselm to put aside his anger and present himself at court: if they talked the matter over, all future disagreements could be avoided. Anselm did not refuse to go, in case God's finger had touched the mind of the king.

So envoys were sent to Rome once more, bearing a joint message from the two of them, to try to modify or rescind such a harsh sentence. The envoys of the archbishop were Baldwin and Alexander, both monks.[3] The king's envoys were Gerard, archbishop of York, Herbert, bishop of Norwich, and Robert, bishop of Chester. Gerard and Herbert were also concerned about matters of their own, Gerard about the receiving of the pallium and Herbert about the recovery of the privilege of the abbey of St Edmund, which abbot Baldwin after many efforts had obtained for his monastery from pope Alexander.[4] This privilege stated that the abbot of St Edmund's abbey was subject neither to the bishop of Norwich, in whose diocese he was recognised as being, nor to anybody else except the primate of England. Herbert's aim was to remove this privilege, but through some unlucky chance or other he got separated from his

[1] See Southern, *St Anselm and his Biographer*, pp. 161–4 and 169, for Anselm's attitude on his return to England.
[2] Anselm had not refused to pay homage to Rufus in 1094, but he had not then been aware of a papal decree banning such homage. For the struggle over the next two and a half years between Anselm and Henry see Eadmer, *Historia Novorum in Anglia*, ed. Martin Rule (Rolls Series, 1884), pp. 120–47.
[3] Baldwin and Alexander were monks from Canterbury.
[4] See Matthew, *The Norman Conquest*, pp. 187–8, for the struggle between the bishop of Norwich and the monastery of Bury St Edmunds.

companions, wandered from the pathway and fell into the hands of robbers. After a payment of forty marks he ended his captivity and was free to resume his journey. But first he was forced to swear an oath by all that was said to be sacred to Guido (that was the name of the leader of the robbers) that he would do nothing at Rome which was to the disadvantage of his lord, archbishop Anselm. So he handed over the cash and hastily followed after his companions, with a freer feeling of ease because of his lighter purse.

Chapter 57 The return of the embassy to the pope

Herbert rejoined his companions. They hurriedly finished their journey and were given audience with the pope. They did whatever they could by means of presents and promises to effect the king's wishes, but without success. Paschal remained unmoved and refused, as he said, to rescind the statutes of the holy fathers to suit the will of one man. In fact the only thing achieved by the efforts of the envoys was to create dissension in England when they disagreed among themselves. For the king had seen that the letter brought him by the bishops opposed his wishes and so thought he ought to conceal it, while in the unconcealed statement which he published abroad the episcopal envoys declared it as the truth that the pope was happy with investitures made by the king, provided that Henry carried out the other duties of a good ruler: the pope had been unwilling to put this view in writing, in case other rulers should seize it as an opportunity to protest to him. But the two monks made loud public protests, complaining that the pope's instructions were being dealt with deceitfully. Certainly, the letter which they had brought for Anselm was now being read out to the people, and in this letter it was shown that Paschal, besides not approving of the investitures, was stubbornly stressing the statutes of Urban and advising that they should be kept. So the whole court was a buzz of people saying that no attention should be paid to two monks who would willingly hide the truth in a pack of lies just to please the archbishop: it was the bishops whose office and words counted, whereas the monks had lost the right to give evidence on secular matters. 'But this is not a secular matter', protested Baldwin.[1] The nobles replied, 'We know that you are a good and wise man, and that you are not one of that huge crowd of monks that bring disgrace on your order by their sinful lives, but all the same human and divine reasoning demands that more trust should be placed in three bishops than in the testimony of two monks.'[2]

So for a long time Anselm hesitated, uncertain which way to turn: it seemed arrogant to call in question the evidence of bishops head on, but foolish not to believe the letter which bore the apostolic seal. Finally he made up his mind and replied that he would send to Rome to find out the truth on the matter.

---

[1] The logic of this sentence seems to need a 'not'. The required negative is not in Hamilton's text or in the Magdalen College manuscript, but it does appear in the British Library MS, Reg. 13 D.V.

[2] For this disagreement see Matthew, *The Norman Conquest*, pp. 198, 235–6. He describes the quarrel as 'the most stark example of the mutual repulsion between monks and bishops'.

Meanwhile he would not refuse communion to those who were invested, but neither would he give them his blessing. Those chosen as bishops had been Roger, the king's chancellor, as bishop of Salisbury,[1] and Reinhelm, the queen's chancellor, as bishop of Hereford. More recently William Giffard had also been chosen on Henry's authority as bishop of Winchester, but it had been by force. William had not agreed to his election but had attacked the electors with abusive threats. However, on Anselm's return, he had received his pastoral staff at his hands and been inducted into his church. So Anselm did willingly give his assent to blessing William. The king was rather upset and commanded Gerard of York to consecrate all of them. He would have been willing to do this, if the bishops themselves had not shown themselves higher minded and refused. Reinhelm soon gave back his ring and staff to the king and resigned from his episcopate. William did the same, except that he did not return the ring. But Roger with admirable good sense kept the matter so well balanced that he did not annoy the king or wrong the archbishop.

Chapter 58 Anselm goes once more to Rome (1103)

Anselm completely refused to give up his plan. He declared that not even to save his life would he go against the decisions of the apostolic see, unless that same see helped by providing absolution. So all the storm and trouble of the affair settled on his own head. King, bishops and nobles all agreed that Anselm himself was the right man to go to Rome and to finish in person what others had left incomplete. The apostolic see had such a high opinion of him that he would not fail to carry out his wishes. He should undertake just this one more task for his country, to bring back peace to its church and honour to its king. Anselm knew how to be persuaded. He did not want to seem to presume to be deciding everything by his own judgement, and so he agreed: he would go, so as not to disappoint the wishes of all, and seeing that the shortage of envoys had forced them to choose one old man, weighed down by years and feeble in body. But they should know that he would make no suggestion to the pope which tarnished the fair fame of his predecessor or infringed his statutes. 'Only go,' they said, 'and in the presence of the pope agree with the king's envoy, if he speaks the truth, giving evidence that he does so backed up by your authority.'

So agreement was reached, and both sides went away. At once Anselm with favouring winds passed over the perils of the sea, and also completed the land journey all the way to Rome without mishap. Welcomed with warmth by the pope and by a large crowd of officials, for a few days he enjoyed peace and quiet on the pope's orders. When he had regained his strength from the rest, he went to the Lateran Palace on a day appointed. Also present was an envoy, already known at Rome,[2] William of Warelwast, bishop elect of Exeter, who

---

[1] Roger was reputedly the fastest singer of the mass known to Henry.
[2] See p. 67 n. 1.

had arrived a few days before Anselm. Using all the powers of his eloquence he was pleading the king's case, aiming to get restored to him all the customary rights enjoyed by his father and brother. England, he said, was a special province of the Roman church and payed her taxes every year; its king was as noble as he was generous; it both seemed and actually was a disgrace for him if he lost the rights of his predecessors, whom he far surpassed and outstripped in both nobility of spirit and abundance of wealth. And so the pope should be careful to honour this king and also to look after his own interests, seeing that there was no doubt that he would deprive himself of great sums of money, unless he was thinking that he should abstain from the severity of his statutes. By these and other powerful arguments for his case William won over the Roman council to his side. Giving him firm support, it declared that the wishes of the king should be fulfilled. Meanwhile both pontiffs were silent, carefully taking in the rhetoric of the pleader and the foolish talk of his flatterers, but secretly smiling. The envoy took their silence for consent, and full of confidence burst out with, 'Much could be argued on both sides, but the crux of the matter is that my master will not allow the power of investiture to be taken away from him, as the loss of his kingdom is involved.' 'And I', said the pope, 'will not allow him to have it unopposed, as the redemption of my soul is involved.'[1] The tenor of this statement caused the envoy's supporters to view the matter otherwise and giving a different opinion they said, 'Blessed be the firmness of your heart, and blessed be the words of your mouth.' Utterly confused, the envoy fell silent. But he did bring it about that some of the rights of his father were extended to king Henry, and that in the meantime the king should be immune to excommunication for making investitures, and that those invested should obey the statutes in all their strictness. Anselm was asked to judge that these decisions were satisfactory.

Chapter 59 Anselm returns to Lyons (December 1103)

By now Anselm had received his permission to go back home, but William put off his return journey, saying that he had to fulfil a vow at the tomb of St Nicholas.[2] But his intention was contrary to his words, for he was in fact trying to get the pope to change his decision by some means or other. But when he saw he was achieving nothing, he took a short cut and got to Piacenza before the archbishop. For a few days they journeyed on together. When they came to the parting of their ways, William spoke out and revealed what he had previously kept hidden, 'My master gives you this mandate: if you behave towards him as your predecessor did to his father, he is glad and willing for

[1] Southern notes that not only has the king got his supporters in the Roman curia but that even pope Paschal is now omitting to mention the decree forbidding clerical homage to laymen, and that the seeds of compromise were beginning to take root. He describes William of Warelwast as being the first in a long line of professional civil servants in the history of the church (*St Anselm and his Biographer*, pp. 169–72).
[2] At Bari.

you to return to England; but if you do not, I am speaking to a wise man and you know the consequences.' So William hurried to England, and Anselm to Lyons. From there he wrote to the king to elicit the truth of William's words. There was an exchange of letters, sent by the pope to the king and Anselm, by Anselm to the king, and by the king to Anselm. This correspondence grew to an immense size. I have decided not to include it here. People who want to read it can go to Eadmer's book.[1] He included the letters, so that no one could accuse him of lying and so that the solid truth of his words should remain unassailed. Also, Eadmer had plenty of time, as his intention was to describe the career of Anselm only, whereas 'I have a greater work afoot'[2] and am trying to cover the deeds of many. So I will just pick out the main points, in my concern to avoid boring my readers.

Chapter 60 Anselm's exile at Lyons (December 1103 to April 1105)

So the king took possession of the archbishopric, but he did so with more careful restraint than his brother had done, and delegated the administration of ecclesiastical affairs to the archbishop's own men rather than to outsiders. Anselm stayed at Lyons for a whole year and four months. All this time he received nothing from the pope but letters urging him to stand firm, and nothing from the king except reasons for delay. For the king's messengers were going frequently to Rome and returning without obtaining anything besides various postponements, which merely prolonged the exile of a good man and impeded a solution. Anselm understood his position clearly and at last even his heart, for all its rich stores of piety, was stirred to thoughts of revenge, and he considered excommunicating the king.[3] The king found out about this from a letter sent by his sister Adela, countess of Blois, and entreated Anselm to come with the countess to Normandy, where he himself was staying at that time. Anselm came. The king showed him much favour and reinstated him in all his possessions. But Anselm's return to England was delayed because of his unwillingness to communicate those lately invested. So the king went back to England and Anselm to Bec.

William of Warelwast and Baldwin the monk were now[4] sent as envoys to Rome, and by their rare integrity brought to a close a controversy which had bubbled away for so many years. For the pope conceded that the king should accept homage from men elected as bishops, even though he was not to invest any with crosier and ring.[5] While the envoys were still in Rome, frequent complaints reached Anselm from England of the depravity which was seething

[1] The book is *Historia Novorum in Anglia*.
[2] Words used by Virgil at *Aeneid* 7:44 to introduce the second half of his epic poem.
[3] Southern attributes Anselm's sudden aggression to the king's seizure of the lands of Canterbury (*St Anselm and his Biographer*, pp. 176–7).
[4] Early in 1106.
[5] For the possible effect of this compromise solution on Anselm see Southern, *St Anselm and his Biographer*, pp. 178–9. For the first time since he became archbishop in 1093 Anselm was free of any cause of dispute with the king.

and spreading everywhere. He was asked to hasten his return, especially by the bishops who by now were disgusted at the crimes which were actually being committed. For even some priests, yes, priests, had scandalised the council of London[1] held before Anselm's departure by inviting to their lodgings some new women or reinviting old ones, and the king was thinking of imposing a fine of money upon them. Anselm thought the king's interference in this was not to be borne, and wrote a letter asking him to refrain from this punishment, saying that the faults of servants of the church should be dealt with by the actions of bishops rather than the civil authorities. By this time the king had become less hasty and more mature in all matters, thanks to his own good sense and the advice of count Robert of Meulan. He received Anselm's salutary counsels courteously and wrote him a gentle reply, saying that he would come to Normandy very soon and by his obedience put right any wrongs he had committed over these and other matters. So when the messengers returned from Rome, he did not search around for many reasons for delay, but met Anselm at Bec. And then all the controversies which up to that point had kept the pair apart were by the grace of God brought into the open and resolved. The churches upon which Henry's brother William had imposed taxes were given back into Anselm's hands free of the taxes, and the king promised to receive nothing from them during periods while they were without a pastor. He so repaired the losses of priests who had paid money that for a whole three years they were free of all taxes, while he decreed that those who had failed to pay should pay nothing further; and he gave a solemn pledge and promise that on his return to England he would give back all the things taken from the archbishopric.

Chapter 61 Anselm returns to England (September 1106)

Anselm was carried back to England by favouring breezes. His countrymen had wanted him back, and in no way did he disappoint the good hopes which they had of him. Without any delay those renting land from churches were ejected, simonists condemned, priests stopped from having concubines, sex between blood relations banned, and many other illegalities which formerly had flourished unreproved were punished. The happiness of these times was increased by the good luck of the king who just then in Normandy captured and imprisoned his brother Robert,[2] together with many others whom he now hated for their importunity or feared as potential rebels. Robert was thought to be paying his brother a just penalty for having caused him trouble when his kingdom had been at peace. At the same time the king judged that his gentle character made him unfit for governing a country. Henry could see that Normandy, the birthplace of them both, was being gobbled up by grasping scoundrels because of Robert's ignorance of ruling. So the king straightaway

---

[1] For this council, held at Westminster in 1102, see ch. 64.
[2] Robert spent the last twenty-eight years of his life as his brother's prisoner.

wrote a letter, telling Anselm of his joy in this victory. It does not seem to me odd to include it here, as one sign of the king's devotion.

Chapter 62 Henry's letter to Anselm about Tinchebray

Henry, king of the English, to Anselm, archbishop of Canterbury, greetings and friendship. To you, holy father, we announce that Robert, earl of Normandy, at the head of all his forces of knights and infantry that he could assemble by prayer and payment, has fought with me a bitter battle before Tinchebray on a day determined and agreed upon. In the end through the mercy of God the victory was ours, and with few losses. In short, the divine mercy has given into our hands the earl of Normandy, the count of Moreton, William Crispin, William de Ferrers, the aged Robert de Stuteville and up to four hundred other knights and ten thousand infantry, together with the province of Normandy. The numbers of those killed by the sword are not to hand. I do not in arrogant pride claim this victory as due to my own strength, but consider it as a gift sent by God. And so, venerable father, I fall before your holy knees in supplication and devotion and beg you to pray to the heavenly judge, through whose will and wish I was given this glorious and beneficial triumph, that it may have been given me, not for my own loss and downfall, but for the beginning of good works and the service of God, and for maintaining and strengthening the state of God's holy church in peace and tranquillity, so that from now on it may live in freedom and be shaken by the storms of war no more.

Chapter 63 Anselm at last consecrates bishops who had paid homage to Henry

This letter shows how much material for good there was in the king's heart, if someone made the sparks of this noble faith flare up with the kindling of words and made it burn stronger with good advice. So the king returned, all splendid with trophy held aloft, and in his triumphal glory rode to London. He handed over church investitures to Anselm in perpetuity, with Anselm conceding that no one should be refused his blessing just because he had paid homage to the king. So on 11 August at Canterbury Anselm consecrated these five bishops: William of Winchester, Roger of Salisbury, Reinhelm of Hereford, William of Warelwast of Exeter and Urban of Llandaff. There were also present to assist him the following suffragan bishops of the senior see: Gerard of York, Robert of Lincoln, John of Bath, Herbert of Norwich, Robert of Chester, Ralph of Chichester and Ranulf of Durham. And so thanks to Anselm, man of God, freedom returned to the churches and peace shone down from a cloudless sky. But there is no point in mentioning the decrees of the councils which he held, since we know they have all disappeared into oblivion by now. Indeed, so men thought, it was not by chance but by some divine inspiration that both at Anselm's consecration and his receiving of the pallium these words were read,

'At supper time he sent his servant to tell those who had been invited to come, as everything was now ready; and they all at the same time began to make excuses.'[1] For never was he properly obeyed. People made excuses on almost all matters which Anselm had either explained by his teaching or banned by his threats. But following the example of the servant in the Gospel who went out twice and filled the wedding reception from those who had not been invited, Anselm himself twice left England and by his preaching won and lifted up to heaven the souls of many. But I do not want to appear to disappoint serious students,[2] so I will consider it a small matter to spend some time in describing what happened at a council which he held.

Chapter 64 Anselm's council at Westminster in 1102

In the year of our Lord 1102, the fourth year of pope Paschal and the third year of the reign of Henry, glorious king of the English, with Henry's permission and the common consent of the bishops and abbots and nobles of the whole kingdom, a council was held in the church of the blessed Peter in the west part of London. It was presided over by Anselm, archbishop of Canterbury and primate of the whole of Britain. Seated alongside him were those venerable men, Gerard archbishop of York, Maurice bishop of London, William elected as bishop of Winchester and other bishops and abbots. Present also at this council were the nobles of the realm. Anselm had requested this of the king, in order that whatever decrees were made on the authority of this council should be ratified and kept by the common, careful efforts of both orders. This was necessary, since, for many years previously, with the synods stopping their cultivation, the brambles of vice had grown up thickly and throughout England the warmth of the Christian faith had frozen hard. So first of all on the authority of the holy fathers the crime of the heresy of simonism was condemned by the council. The people found guilty of this fault and deposed from office were Guy of Pershore, Wimund of Tavistock and Aldwine of Ramsey. Others who had not yet been consecrated were removed from their abbacies, namely Godric of Peterborough, Haimo of Cerne and Æthelric of Milton. Richard of Ely, Robert of St Edmunds and the abbot of Muchelney were removed from their abbacies, not for simony indeed, but for various individual reasons.

It was also decreed that bishops should not undertake duties in secular courts; that, as befitted persons of the cloth, they should wear the garments of the ordained and not look like lay people; and that always and everywhere they should have respected people as witnesses of their way of life. That archdeaconries should not be rented out and that archdeacons should be deacons. That no archdeacon, priest, deacon or canon should marry a wife or keep one he had married. That any subdeacon not a canon, if he married after

[1] Luke 14:17.
[2] It is typical of William, himself a 'serious student', to give details of legislation which had already become a dead letter by the time of writing, *c*.1125.

a profession of chastity, should be bound by the same rule. That a priest, as long as he lived illicitly with a woman, should not be legally a priest or celebrate mass, or, if he did celebrate it, the people should not hear it. That no one should be ordained subdeacon or to any higher rank unless he had made a profession of chastity. That sons of priests should not inherit their fathers' churches. That no clerics should be in charge of secular affairs or proctors or judges in capital cases. That priests should not go off to drinking bouts or drink 'to the pegs'.[1] That the clothes of clerics should be of one colour, and their shoes standard. That monks or clerics who had left their orders should either return or be excommunicated. That clerics should be tonsured. That tithes should not be paid except to churches. That neither churches nor prebends[2] should be bought. That new chapels should not be built without the consent of the bishop. That a church should not be consecrated until the necessary things had been provided for both priest and church. That abbots should not create knights, and that they should sleep and eat in the same building as their monks, unless prevented by some necessity. That monks should not enjoin penitence on anyone without the permission of their abbot and that their abbots could not give permission for this unless the people concerned came within their care of souls. That monks should not be god-fathers or nuns godmothers. That monks should not rent manors. That monks should not accept churches except from their bishops, nor, when they were given them, should they so beautify them from the revenues that the priests who served in them suffered shortages of those things necessary for themselves and their churches. That any marriage pledge entered upon privately by a man and a woman without witnesses should be regarded as null and void if either party denied it. That the long-haired should so be shorn that some part of their ears was visible and their eyes were not covered. That relations up to the seventh degree of kindred should not have intercourse, or, if they had intercourse, should not remain together, and if anyone knew of this incest and did not reveal it, he should regard himself as sharing in the same offence. That bodies of the dead should not be taken outside the parish for burial, as the priest of the parish would lose what was justly owing to him from the burial. That nobody through an ill-advised wish for novelty should pay holy reverence to the bodies of the dead or to springs or to other things, which we know has happened, without the authority of the bishop. That nobody henceforth should presume to engage in that wicked business, by which up to that time it had been the custom in England for men to be sold like brute animals. Those committing sodomy or willingly helping others to commit it were condemned in this same council under a heavy anathema, unless they deserved absolution by their confession and penitence. Indeed it was decreed that a person publicly proclaimed to be a sodomite, if he was a religious, should not be promoted to

---

[1] Pegs were placed inside a drinking vessel to divide its capacity into equal portions, one of which was taken by each individual at the feast, as the cup was passed round.

[2] The portion of the revenues of a cathedral or collegiate church granted to a canon or member of the chapter as his stipend.

higher office and should be deposed from any office which he held, and if he was a lay person, should be deprived of the legal dignity of his rank throughout the whole of England. And that henceforth no one, unless he was a bishop, should presume to grant absolution for this crime to those who had not taken the vows of some religious order. It was also decreed that every Sunday in all churches throughout England the excommunication previously mentioned should be renewed.

Chapter 65 The death of Anselm (1109)

Right up to the end of Anselm's life his bodily strength and fervent piety continued unimpaired. He died in the year of our Lord 1109, in the ninth year of the reign of king Henry, in the sixty-sixth year of his age[1] and the sixteenth year of his archbishopric. He was buried first at the head of his predecessor Lanfranc, but afterwards was given a more worthy mausoleum in the eastern porch. He surpassed all the men we have ever seen[2] in wisdom and piety. Sin was completely foreign to him. He once told a close friend of mine, whom I believe implicitly, that after he became a monk he had never been so goaded by anger as to hurl an insult at anybody – well, this had happened to him just once. He had never except once spoken a word, of which the memory made his conscience sore. At supper one day, realising that he had eaten raw herring, he struck his breast and lamented his sin, that against the rule he had eaten raw flesh. But Eadmer, who was sitting next to him, said that the salt had drawn out the rawness of the herring. Anselm replied, 'You have cured me of being tormented by the memory of my sin.' He had always carefully observed his vow of obedience. So when his archbishop's power gave him freedom, he asked pope Urban to suggest someone by whose commands he could arrange his life. The pope produced Eadmer, and Anselm regarded his orders so highly that when Eadmer had put him to bed, not only would Anselm not get up without a command from him, but he would not even turn over on to his other side.

In ordinary conversation his speech was a fast-flowing torrent of eloquence. Not even when eating would he take a break from theological talk. He took the greatest pleasure in testing the wits of his opponents by putting forward questions. On almost all issues he would either explain his own position by illustrations or parry the arguments of others. By now, indeed, on secular matters he would deliberately give an appearance of dullness, and when tossed about by a fierce storm of such issues would even find his limbs go weak. But when his domestic chaplains noticed this, they would send away the crowds, and find someone to sharpen his blunted wits on the whetstone of theological niceties. And at once Anselm, his mind aroused, would turn towards the questioner with sparkling glance and regain his strength for dealing with both

---

[1] According to Eadmer, *Life of St Anselm* 2:67, Anselm died in his seventy-sixth year.

[2] A rare mention of personal experience by William, assuming his words are to be taken literally.

worlds. For his books prove how deeply he penetrated both the secrets of men and the complexities of the divine mind. The ill-feeling towards him has long since disappeared, and the whole of Western Christendom now applauds those books.

Chapter 66 Anselm's miracles

Anselm did not take a holiday from doing his usual miracles just because of the burden of his archbishopric with its mass of important business. A fire, started by lightning on a pile of timber, was now burning the neighbouring buildings when Anselm, making the sign of the cross with his outstretched hand, reduced it to ash. Campania gazed in amazement at a new spring bubbling from a rock, when, at his blessing, a hollowed out stone poured forth water. A hare, surrounded by its enemies, sought refuge at the feet of the animal on which the saint was sitting. It escaped safe and sound. For when Anselm gave the order, he deprived the hare's open-mouthed pursuers of their bark and at the same time baffled their attempts to give chase. He rubbed some spit on to the blank eyes of a blind woman and filled them with clear light. He stopped a severe attack of fever by giving the sick man bread.[1]

When Anselm had now breathed his last, Baldwin was asked by Ralph, bishop of Rochester, who was present, if he had even a few drops of balsam with which at least Anselm's head could be anointed and so avoid the taint of future corruption. Baldwin produced a flask with a very little drop of balsam still in the bottom. When this amount of precious liquid was poured into Eadmer's hand, it scarcely wetted the middle of his palm. It was quickly used up. But then Eadmer stared in amazement when as much again poured out. In fact this eager plunderer did not stop putting pressure on the miracle by repeated bold attempts until he had properly covered the whole body in all its parts with the balsam ointment. You will applaud this miracle still more, when I tell you that, after the sacrament of anointing had been solemnly completed, the flask which had so often been emptied, now by turning its belly upside down, now by twisting sideways its curved neck, was found more than half-full. When Anselm's body was being laid out for burial next day, they had the misfortune to find that the stone which was to receive his body had been carelessly hollowed out and was a full handsbreadth too shallow. There was a muttered general discussion. To find another stone would not be easy, but neither did they want to do injury to the body, the vessel of the Holy Spirit, by curving it. Then, all of a sudden, they saw the stone was of the right size, and the body, without help of human hand, slipped fittingly into its sarcophagus.[2] A cry of joy arose from the bystanders and struck the stars. It was not so much the solemn appropriateness of the miracle, remarkable

---

[1] Eadmer, *Life of St Anselm* 2:61 says the patient sent a messenger to ask for some bread which had been blessed by Anselm.
[2] Eadmer, *Life of St Anselm* 2:68 says the miracle happened when a monk started to draw the staff of Ralph along the top of the sarcophagus.

though that was, that prompted this cry, but the speed of the help which had not even been asked for.

Anselm passed to another world on 21 April. But he did not leave his friends exposed to the world without any help from him. He still fights for them, when they call upon him. It is hard to find anybody going to his tomb in eager hope, who does not come away again with his prayers fully achieved. Then there is the miracle which happened at Lyons recently.[1] There lived there, shut off from the world, two old women, the embodiment of piety and concord. Anselm courteously visited them, when he was staying at Lyons, and frequently poured into their ears injunctions to virtue. But after his death, as happens with women, a quarrel broke out between them over a small matter. It broke their peace and split their harmony. As they were carrying on the quarrel day and night with spiteful asides and provocative, stinging slanders, it gradually escalated. Their furious anger supplied their tongues with insults to hurl. They were both involved in this stupid behaviour, but the responsibility for it lay more with the one who had begun the quarrel. One night Anselm stood by her bed, but the expression on his face was greatly changed from the gentleness which she had seen on it when he was alive.[2] Force was given to his words by his cold look and by his severity, which seemed to have been borrowed from a distant stranger. 'A nice job you have made of keeping my commandments', he said. 'The religion you have professed or your love for my zeal should have reminded you to keep them. But instead you quarrel continuously and awake each other's hate, forgetful of your reputation, the reverence you owe to me and the success of all three of us. So you have wearied me into coming to you through all those intervening lands, to restore peace if you stop, but with threats of punishment if you persist.'

This vision soothed her quarrelsome spirit and quietened her anger. Later that same night, when, tired out after continual tears she had sunk into sleep, she had an extended vision of heaven. The clouds of her earthly senses were dispersed. She clearly saw herself standing alongside our Lady, St Mary, and at her command sat at her feet. Our Lady graciously gave her the chance of asking any question she liked. Encouraged by a spirit of happy daring she asked what could be hoped for by Hugh, the archbishop of her own city, who had recently died.[3] 'My daughter,' said Mary, 'it will soon be well for him through the mercy of God and forgiveness is already at the door.' 'And what can we know of my lord Anselm, archbishop of Canterbury?' 'Of Anselm,' she replied, 'never doubt that he is in the great glory of God.' None of you, please, should laugh at these words when you hear them, as though they were the figments of an old woman's dream, or mock and make fun of them. Everybody knows that those women had always been equal to any saints in the austerity of their complete abstinence and the saving quickness of their conscience.

---

[1] Eadmer visited Lyons with archbishop Ralph at Christmas 1116.
[2] Similarly the ghost of Hector appears to Aeneas in a dream at *Aeneid* 2:270–97 'greatly changed' from his appearance when alive.
[3] Hugh had died on 7 October 1106.

Chapter 67 Ralph chosen as archbishop (26 April 1114)

So after Anselm of blessed memory had escaped from the knots of our body of clay and said farewell to this life, the archbishopric lay vacant for a full five years. During this whole period, whenever the king was advised to do something about the widowhood of his mother, the church, he would put the matter off with the gentle reply that the archbishops sent by his father and brother to the post had been of the best, and he himself did not want to fall below the standard of the happy choices made by his forbears; therefore the decision ought to be taken only after great consideration, so that he might appoint as archbishop a man who would keep up with his predecessors on the same path of virtue, or at least match the most recent. Such replies seemed completely fair and proper, and indeed they were so. After long and detailed discussion of the question, he summoned a council at Windsor where he would put the finishing touches to the business.

His own intention was to choose Faricius, abbot of Abingdon, who was very sharp and remarkably hard working in completing tasks. But he would not follow his own wishes, at least in the election of an archbishop, and referred the choice to the decision of the council. The fact that the king was known to have shown the same remarkable self-control on other occasions besides the present would influence them in their dealing with this religious question and affect the spirit in which they discussed the choice delegated to them. So when they wanted to elect someone from the order of priests, it was objected that no priest had ever been archbishop of Canterbury except only Stigand, and he had been a rogue from the beginning and rightly deposed. There was no need to ignore a custom of such great antiquity, especially when doing so could not be approved of without going against their faith. They were thrown by this argument, and, as they had their suspicions of Faricius' severity, they concluded as follows. If a Lombard[1] was archbishop, quarrels and lawsuits would break out again. He would have no mercy on any of the English, especially as the king looked up to him just as if he had been sent down from heaven. But such things could not be said openly. Nothing must be said which would wound anyone's feelings. So they argued that there had been more than enough foreigners as archbishop of Canterbury, while there existed an abundance of men of their own tongue who could recall Lanfranc by their knowledge, display the piety of Anselm and resemble both in their wearing of monkish habits. There was Ralph, bishop of Rochester, who in reputation equalled the ancients, and in humble friendliness surpassed both men of old and men of the present day. If his lineage was investigated, he came from a famous Norman family. If his life was examined, his record would be found to be unblemished. He was the only one whose religious life could not be attacked by envy because it was perfectly orthodox. If his knowledge of

[1] Like Faricius.

literature was probed into, he had imbibed a whole university's worth.[1] Ask about his eloquence. The words flowed from his mouth in a honeyed stream; they were also in the grammatical, well-groomed speech of his native town of Le Mans. These arguments deserved support. The result was that the king at once changed his mind and agreed to their wishes. This council took place five years and five days after the death of Anselm.

Chapter 68 Ralph's early career

Ralph in the first flower of his youth had taken the vows of a monk at Séez, an abbey in Normandy. As his good qualities grew and increased, he became first sub-prior, then prior, and finally abbot. It was Ralph who made this quite small and insignificant spot justly famous at home and abroad. At first he received support from Robert of Belleme, the lord of that district,[2] who allowed him the freedom to be vigilant for his faith. But as soon as Robert, as I have described elsewhere,[3] was driven out of England by king Henry and withdrew to Normandy, he began to demand the oath of homage from the abbot. Robert pressed his request persistently: the other, as he had heard the pope's veto on this matter, refused point-blank. So he left his abbey, sailed to England and got through and wasted much time in doing a circuit of our abbeys, where his personality and preaching deservedly made him a welcome guest. He did not think it a good idea for a free man to return to Normandy and to Robert, as he was a bottomless cesspit of all filth and foulness. But neither did he judge it right to enjoy hospitality for a long time anywhere in England, fearing that his importunity might appear to make the natives sick of him. For at that time the country had been swamped by a crowd of Norman abbots, who brought to England the speeches they had planned and polished in their own country and who, now here, now there, destroyed our slow-moving days of peace and caused the loss of other things, being accustomed to sell their tongues and to chase after the breeze of favour.[4]

Ralph avoided giving those causes of annoyance with as much restraint as possible and spent more time with the archbishop, as ever since his youth he had been well known to Anselm's God-fearing household. And so it came about that when Gundulf, bishop of Rochester, died, Anselm chose Ralph in his place, having first received from him homage and the promise under oath that he would be faithful to the holy church of Canterbury. As the day of his consecration came near, Anselm, so the story goes, prayed strenuously to God, that, as Ralph was his own choice as bishop, God would produce for Ralph a prognostic which would enable him to rejoice that his decision was in harmony

[1] Literally 'He had drunk the whole of Athens.' Athens had been the Oxbridge of the classical world.
[2] This Robert is king Henry's elder brother, whose defeat was described in ch. 62.
[3] See ch. 55 and *The Deeds of the Kings* 5:396.
[4] See Matthew, *The Norman Conquest*, pp. 289–94, for an examination of William of Malmesbury's theory of a cultural divide between Anglo-Saxons and Normans.

with the divine will. The holiness of the Godhead heard his simple prayer and provided the verse, 'They will be like the angels of God.'[1] So Ralph was made bishop. He did not fall short of the opinion of his goodness which men had had of him, but put it into effect as he carried it out into public life. So that when the choice of archbishop was being discussed, everybody with enthusiastic goodwill and also with complete unanimity agreed upon the election of Ralph. He was led to his see, and soon afterwards earned the pallium, thanks to the kindness of the Roman see.

The pallium was brought to him by the legate Anselm, a nephew by his sister of Anselm the archbishop. For at the start of Henry's reign Guy, archbishop of Vienne, who later became pope,[2] had come to England as papal legate; after him Anselm; and soon a certain Peter.[3] They all went back to Rome, having accomplished nothing as legates, but with great gain for themselves, especially Peter, seeing that everybody took precautions to arouse his interest, as being the son of Peter Leo, prince of the Romans. So embassies came frequently to England from Rome, making attacks on Ralph's unfitness for office, but Henry was wary and they were all sent packing. For he refused to go against ancient custom and to receive in England any legate except the archbishop of Canterbury,[4] while the legates willingly suspended their efforts because of the excessive bribes they received. But Cono, the legate in France, was not so easily dissuaded. He involved in a sentence of suspension all the bishops and abbots of Normandy, because three times they had not obeyed a summons to attend a council in Rome.

After a discussion of this matter archbishop Ralph[5] and Herbert, bishop of Norwich, were sent to Rome to bring order by their efforts into the great confusion caused by the legates. But when they got to the castle called La Ferté, an extremely nasty carbuncle erupted and swelled up on Ralph's face, a sure sign of his future paralysis. 'Carbuncle' is Pliny the Elder's word for that particular facial disfigurement which either eats away the skin down to the bone, or, if stopped by medical attention, leaves behind an ugly scar. So he took to his bed for many days. But later, when the pain had abated, or rather, when his death had been put off, he arrived at Rome. At that time pope Paschal was away from Rome, staying in Benevento. The intervening hills were occupied by the followers of the emperor,[6] who was then for the second time frightening Rome with his troops, and the archbishop could not obtain an audience with the pope except through messengers. The following letter will show how the messengers fared with the pope.

[1] Mark 12:25.
[2] In 1119 as Calixtus II.
[3] See Southern, *St Anselm and his Biographer*, pp. 129–30 for the failure of Anselm to keep papal legates out of England.
[4] This position was ultimately agreed to by the pope in 1125. See Loyn, *The English Church*, p. 110.
[5] Ralph was accompanied on his journey by the faithful Eadmer.
[6] This was Henry V, emperor of Germany 1106–25. His death is mentioned in ch. 278.

Chapter 69 Letter of pope Paschal to Henry and his bishops (1117)

Pope Paschal, servant of the servants of God, to his venerable brothers, the bishops of England, and to his dearest son, the illustrious king Henry, greetings and apostolic blessing. While our most dear and respected brother, the archbishop Ralph, was still on his way to us, we learnt of your embassy to us through our venerable brother, Herbert, bishop of Norwich. Indeed these same brothers and fellow bishops have been completely unable to come to see us, stopped from doing so by serious, troublesome weaknesses. But we have received their suit in writing through the persons of their reliable, respected messengers, and have noted their requests and the prayers of your embassy. Their wish and request was that the church of Canterbury should not be deprived of its powers during the time of our papacy, and that we should not diminish or allow to be diminished the powers which it has apparently held ever since it was established by the blessed Gregory through the blessed Augustine. In addition to this material in the letter, the messengers who were sent to us, being sensible, active men, made their own wise declarations in an energetic and efficient manner. We, I assure you, have kindly and cheerfully received the persons of your legates and their declarations and the requests of all of you, as being our dearest brothers. Therefore we wish it to be known to your love that we are not diminishing or thinking of diminishing the powers of the church of Canterbury. For we pay reverence in all things to the blessed Gregory, pontiff of this apostolic see, as being a special member of the body of Christ our Lord, and the shepherd and teacher of the people of Christ and minister of eternal salvation, and we desire the decrees which he instituted to remain binding. So, I assure you, we are in no way diminishing the powers which the church of Canterbury received from Gregory through the blessed Augustine, and which our brother Anselm of holy memory is known to have held rightly and with lawful possession, but we wish the church of Canterbury to remain in the same position, so that its authentic privileges, as laid down in the canons, may not be disturbed or harmed in any way. Given at Benevento, the 24 March.

Chapter 70 Ralph in Normandy

If in this letter the pope had explicitly said 'The church of Canterbury has such and such powers and I confirm it in these same powers', he would have settled the argument and ended the controversy. But as his words were, 'We in no way diminish any authentic privileges possessed by Canterbury', he left the matter undecided and still in mid-air. Those cunning, charming Romans knew they were using orators' tricks and they left their wishes unclear because of the futile ambiguity. They did not mind involving other people in trouble, provided they had looked after their own interests. And so Ralph stayed on in the neighbourhood of Rome for several days, being either, though with the pope's permission, with the army of the emperor, or waiting for a meeting with the pope at Sutri, where, according to the widespread rumour, he was about to arrive at any time. Ralph wasted a lot of money while held up at Rome through these expectations, for the pope never came. So Ralph returned to Normandy, and stayed near the king for more than a year. He was intending to meet Gelasius, Paschal's successor, when he came north of the Alps, so that he might dispel the attacks of his enemies by defending his own case in Gelasius' presence. For Thurstan, bishop-elect of York, was refusing to make a profession of obedience to the archbishop of Canterbury and was vigorously stirring up the minds of the Romans in his support. Indeed when Gelasius was taken from among us and Guy, archbishop of Vienne, had succeeded him (being called Calixtus as pope) and was holding a council at Rheims, Ralph sent messengers to him to state his case. The pope on the surface received them more fulsomely but in secret tricked them more cunningly than was fitting for such a great man, by ignoring all the ancient rules and consecrating the archbishop elect of York himself.[1] When I reach my review of matters at York, I shall not neglect to give an account of the ways in which Thurstan, even with the opposition of the king, promoted his own schemes.

Chapter 71 The death of Ralph (1122)

When Ralph returned to England, his paralytic attack, which I have mentioned, caused him daily ever more pain, though not so much that he gave up his duties. Although he found it more difficult to speak, he still made valuable suggestions at meetings. He was more inclined to outbursts of anger, just because that disease usually makes a man bad-tempered. When attacks were made on the rights of his church, he would be very annoyed and take a sharp revenge. But he did not stay long in this life, as the illness, every day getting worse, hastened his end. He died on 20 October 1122, in the ninth year of his patriarchy. Such was the end of Ralph, a man second to none in piety, of outstandingly accomplished scholarship, and without a doubt easily first of all in friendliness. He was very rich. He had, in fact, never made any addition to his wealth unless to be more able to help those he wanted to, but ordinary people thought every accession of riches correspondingly diminished his fame. He was never marked by even the smallest suspicion of wrongdoing, except that he was more inclined to a laugh and a joke than seemed to be suitable for his dignified position. But, whatever the reason for this, in Ralph's case, at least, it will have been a good one. To suspect Ralph of doing anything underhand is to fight against God's goodness.

---

[1] See Southern, *St Anselm and his Biographer*, pp. 305–7, for the struggle of Henry and Ralph with the papacy and Thurstan.

Chapter 72 An account of the bishops of Rochester

Rochester comes next after the church at Canterbury, not in power and authority but in geographical proximity.[1] Long ago it drank in the faith when Canterbury supplied the milk, and still now strives to copy its mother and follow in the line of her virtues. The site of the town is extremely confined, but because it is on a steep hill and washed by a powerfully flowing river, it cannot be approached by enemies without danger. Very few, in fact hardly any, of the deeds of the bishops of the town I have come across seem to me worth recording, so I ought not to be censured for just giving a list of bare names. Nobody will raise his eyebrows when brief descriptions are caused by shortage of deeds.

The first bishop there, appointed by the blessed Augustine, was Justus. On the death of archbishop Mellitus, Justus ascended the throne of Canterbury. Romanus was chosen by Justus as his successor at Rochester, but he lost his life when he was drowned in a storm at sea while on a mission to pope Honorius. Paulinus succeeded to the empty see. Always up till now Paulinus' praises have been sung, extolled and magnified by our predecessors. He was a Roman by race, sent to England with others by the blessed Gregory in the service of the Word. Archbishop Justus appointed him apostle and ordained him bishop to the people of Northumbria. He brought a reluctant king Edwin to the faith by telling him of the divine sign,[2] which the approval of the divine mercy had once shown to the king and which the spirit of prophecy now imparted to Paulinus. Paulinus received his own pallium from pope Honorius, and then consecrated Honorius as archbishop of Canterbury after Justus. After much booty had been carried off for the devil from the people of the north, Paulinus was driven from his see by a fierce enemy attack[3] (so that a retired soldier might still face the test of persecution) and withdrew to Kent. Then, as I have said above, he took over the control of the church at Rochester, as both archbishop Honorius and king Eadbald approved of this most holy priest and surrounded him with their support. He undertook the task which the love of his brothers' minds suggested, and content for the intervening period with the throne of a lesser place, he went the way of all flesh, when his time came nineteen years, two months and twenty-one days after his ordination at York. He was buried at Rochester, in the church which had been built from its foundations by king Æthelberht in honour of St Andrew the apostle, the saint still honoured and worshipped by that see. He is a famous saint in that province, loved and revered by all for the speed of his untiring response to prayer.

Paulinus' place at Rochester was taken by Ithamar, appointed and

---

[1] John Blair says that the proximity of two such tiny dioceses suggests that Kent was a recent amalgamation of two distinct kingdoms (*The Blackwell Encyclopaedia*, s.v. 'Rochester').

[2] For the full story of the sign see Bede, *Ecclesiastical History* 2:12. At 2:16 Bede records an eyewitness description of Paulinus as 'tall, with a slight stoop, black hair, a thin face and a slender, aquiline nose'.

[3] Edwin was killed in battle against Penda of Mercia in 633.

consecrated by archbishop Honorius. He was actually an Englishman by birth, but you would by no means find him lacking in anything required for full sanctity of life or for a Roman refinement of learning. He was the first to bring to his land in the person of an Englishman the grace of the episcopal office and so added considerably to the prestige of his people. He ordained Deusdedit[1] as archbishop of Canterbury in succession to Honorius. This was properly the duty of the archbishop of York, but, as I have said, Paulinus had been driven out and nobody had taken his place. For the Scots,[2] who with the support of the Northumbrian kings had filled that province, were accustomed to lurk ingloriously in marshes rather than dwell in lofty cities, and because they had a crazy attitude towards many things but especially towards the observation of the Catholic Easter, the remnants of them were on their guard against receiving people ordained by erroneous Romans at Canterbury. On Ithamar's death Damianus took over, appointed bishop by archbishop Deusdedit. Damianus, on Theodore's order, was succeeded by Putta, who was as suited to the ecclesiastical calm as he was sluggish and slow in matters of state. In the end, when he was repeatedly thinking of retiring from his bishopric as a profound peace still reigned, he gladly used an enemy attack as an excuse. For Æthelred, king of the Mercians, had been enraged by some insolent reply or other from the Kentish king. He was attacking the whole of Kent with fire and sword and had marked out all the lands of the bishopric of Rochester for destruction as well. Putta took this trouble on his shoulders very patiently, and withdrew to Sæxwulf, bishop of the Mercians, through whose generous gift he obtained a country church with a plot of land. There he passed the rest of his life peacefully, taking his public school of ecclesiastical song wherever he was asked to go. Cwichelm was ordained in his place, but soon also resigned, distressed by his shortage of essentials. His substitute Gebmund put up with permanency. His successor was Tobias, who, according to Bede,[3] was filled to the very brim with learning. He was so familiar with Greek as well as Latin, that he could say whatever he wanted in them just as readily and eloquently as in his own language. When he died, his successor was Ealdwulf, who, of course, is the last bishop to be mentioned by Bede in his list of the bishops of Rochester.

I have followed Bede so far, but will now add the names of others, listed in the documents: Dunn, Eardwulf, Deora, Wærmund, Beornmod, Burgric, Ælfstan, Godwine, Siweard. Siweard was bishop[4] when the Normans came to England. He lived on for a few days and then died, leaving the church poor and empty, lacking everything inside and out. There were barely four canons. They eked out an existence, wearing the cheapest clothes and living poorly from hand to mouth as they acquired food from their prayers or fees charged.

---

[1] Deusdedit was ordained in 655 and was the first native Anglo-Saxon archbishop of Canterbury, just as Ithamar was the first native Anglo-Saxon bishop.

[2] For the people designated by the term 'Scots' see p. 267 n. 2. For the incursion of Scottish Christians into Northumbria see p. 140.

[3] *Ecclesiastical History* 5:23.

[4] Stenton calls him 'the inconspicuous occupant of the smallest of English sees' (*Anglo-Saxon England*, p. 660).

In his wish to remove these troubles archbishop Lanfranc in his great wisdom gave them as bishop a monk called Arnost. But when he was taken away by a speedy death, Lanfranc brought in Gundulf,[1] who was also a monk. Under him the church made a magnificent recovery. The monks grew to more than fifty. They were lovers of the rule and had an abundance of all essentials. This was set down to Gundulf's glory and especially to the hard work of Lanfranc, who even bought out of his own pocket the estate of Haddenham[2] and handed it over freehold for the use of the monks who were servants of the holy Apostle. Gundulf was also deeply religious, not unlettered, sharp and clear-minded in secular matters, and apparently picked out by God himself for the award of this office. For in the days when he was still listening to the holy Scriptures at Caen, it happened that he was sitting holding the Gospel next to the master with two other monks. The name of the one was Walter, the name of the other has been forgotten. For the time being the master was busy with something else, so, playing a game amongst themselves, they said, 'Let's turn the pages and find out which of us will be an abbot, and which a bishop.' No sooner said than the pages were turned, and first Gundulf found 'Wise and faithful servant, whom his lord has set over his household'.[3] Then Walter found 'Good and faithful servant, enter into the joy of your Lord.'[4] The third found some hard saying which upset him; although I once heard it, I have been happy to forget it, since it is no part of a free-spirited man to jeer at the troubles of others. There was an outburst of laughter at the incident, and Lanfranc asked what the joke was. When he was told, he forecast that Gundulf without doubt would be a bishop, Walter an abbot, while the third would have to return to the slippery paths of the world. Events proved the truth of his forecast. Gundulf became bishop of Rochester, Walter abbot of Evesham, while the third vanished into obscurity. This seemed more of a miracle later, since at the time Lanfranc had no expectations of the archbishopric or even of crossing to England.

Well, Gundulf made a holy end, and, as I have said,[5] Ralph, abbot of Seez succeeded him. When he was elevated to the archbishopric, Ernulf took over. He was French by birth and spent a long time as a monk in the monastery of St Lucian in Beauvais. But when he saw there a great deal of outrageous behaviour, which he could not reform or wished to endure, he decided to leave. But first he asked advice of Lanfranc, intending to do without hesitation whatever Lanfranc thought to command. Lanfranc knew well the industry of the man, for he had been with him for a long time as his student at Bec, and persuaded him to come to him at Canterbury, seeing that he could not save his

---

[1] For Gundulf see R. M. Thomson, *The Life of Gundulf, Bishop of Rochester* (Rochester, 1977) and Loyn, *The English Church*, pp. 78–9. Loyn sums up Gundulf by saying, 'In his combination of wise stewardship and holiness he represents the ideal monk-bishop of his period.' He was also brave enough to advise William II to mend his ways. See Hamilton (Rolls Series edition), p. 83 n. 4.

[2] In Buckinghamshire.

[3] Matthew 24:25.

[4] Matthew 25:21, 23.

[5] In ch. 68.

soul at Beauvais. So Ernulf came and was a monk at Canterbury throughout all Lanfranc's time. He was appointed prior there by Anselm, then abbot of Peterborough, and finally made bishop of Rochester by Ralph. It is a solemn thing to state how much probity and prudence he showed in all his offices. At Canterbury he rebuilt so splendidly the ruined eastern end of the church which Lanfranc had built, that nothing could be seen in England to match the light of its glass windows, the gleaming whiteness of its marble floor, its paintings of many colours. At Peterborough the number of monks was increased and their religious life strengthened by good advice, while the ruins of old buildings were cleared away and new foundations laid and columns erected. When these were all destroyed by a consuming fire, Ernulf was thinking how to replace them when the office of bishop of Rochester was thrust upon him. Although everything seemed to have been done there already (Gundulf's quickness had made the care of all his successors unnecessary), he was none the less always devising some scheme by which virtue could shine, strengthening the old and building the new. He lived a few days over nine years as bishop. He died aged eighty-four, leaving behind him many memorials to his goodness.[1]

---

[1] For a modern vignette of Ernulf see Southern, *St Anselm and his Biographer*, pp. 269–70.

Book 2 Essex, East Anglia, Wessex and Sussex

Here begins the prologue of William's second book about the deeds of the bishops of England

With Christ as my comfort, I have extended my first book thus far. And in this account of all the memorable deeds, attainable by our knowledge, of the bishops of Canterbury and Rochester I think I have kept all the promises I made. So now, according to the scheme of *The Deeds of the Kings*, the order would require me at once to go through the West Saxons, were I not persuaded by their geographical proximity to put the bishops of the East Saxons and East Angles before them. But the reader should know that I have followed a different series of kingdoms from the necessity of first mentioning the most important kingdoms, where dates and deeds are available, before finally subjoining those places, of which almost all has been forgotten because of the passage of time and the small extent of their power. Moreover I could be accused of doing wrong if I deprived those bishoprics of their place whose list of bishops is not defective and whose fame is not that obscure. So in this second book I shall list the names of the bishops of the East Saxons and East Angles, before adding all the bishoprics of Wessex. And I shall be careful not to leave out all the abbacies I know of in the dioceses of these bishoprics and the saints who lie at rest in them. Of everything I shall give just a brief account, keeping in mind as far as I can both those people who are keen to know and those who are easily bored and turned off. But I do ask my readers to grant me this request, that none of them should think it a fault in me if I transfer to this book what I have said elsewhere in exactly the same words and phrases. I have done this so that a sequence of events should be gathered together more handsomely all in one place and not have to be sought from different books. Also, if I said something well elsewhere, I did not think I could say it better here.

Chapter 73 The bishops of London (604–1108)

The famous city of London is not far from Rochester, about twenty-five miles. It is rich from the wealth of its citizens, and packed with merchants from all lands, but especially with those coming to trade from Germany. Consequently, whenever food prices are high all over England through the crops yielding a barren harvest, essential foodstuffs are retailed and bought at lower prices in London than elsewhere, whether you consider the profit of the seller or the cost to the buyer. Merchandise from foreign lands for the city is brought up the winding course of the famous river Thames. This rises from its spring eighty miles to the west of the city, and carries its name more than seventy miles further before joining the sea at Dover. The first man to take his seat on a bishop's chair here was Mellitus, who was appointed by the blessed Augustine. Mellitus, an abbot of Rome, had not come to England with Augustine, but had been sent out later to supplement the evangelists. Ordained bishop, he had his seat in the church of the apostle Paul, which had been built in London by Æthelberht, king of Kent.[1] For Æthelberht's kingdom adjoined that of Sæberht, king of the East Saxons and son of Ricula, Æthelberht's sister, whom London looked to as a ruler. For in ancient times the East and South Saxons and the East Angles obeyed the king of the men of Kent, because Hengist, first king of Kent, had obtained those lands from Vortigern, king of the Britons, not through war but by treachery. After Æthelberht indeed the South Saxons were subject to the sway of the West Saxons, while the others were ruled by the kings of Mercia, until both lots were seized and subjugated by the powerful West Saxons. But that happened later. At the time I am speaking of, Mellitus, with the cooperation of God and the help and assistance of Æthelberht, spread the Christian faith in a marvellous way in the province. For he also founded a monastery to St Peter in the western part of the city, directed to do so, according to the story, by a message from the apostle himself. St Peter, indeed, seen face to face in a vision by Mellitus, actually dedicated the recently built church himself and promised the bishop by means of a countryman the most acceptable gift of a large fish. Mellitus was not willing to have any doubts about what he had heard when he saw a simple countryman, who was not even a Christian, bringing what Peter had told him of and accurately reproducing the same physical features which Mellitus knew from his vision. So the whole thing was believed. There was no repetition of the rites of consecration, which they could see had been properly carried out from the candles burning throughout the whole church and the crosses which had been made, as well as from the sprinkling of holy water and the not insubstantial traces of holy oil in the proper places. Human care took second place to divine performance and Mellitus proclaimed with prophetic voice that the monastery would be one of great importance, seeing that the apostle had carried out pontifical rites in it. Gradually the truth of the prophecy became more and more clear, especially in the time of the last king Edward who gathered together there an unusually large number of monks and constructed a church in a new style of building.[2] Under king William, instead of diminishing, it became increasingly important. William endowed it with lands of great revenue, because he had received the insignia of a king there. So later the

---

[1] Stenton describes the setting up of a see in London as 'a precarious advance into territory beyond the sphere of Æthelberht's direct rule' (*Anglo-Saxon England*, p. 109).

[2] Edward the Confessor's church at Westminster was the first English church built in a mature Romanesque style. No traces of his church are now visible above ground, but the ruins of the contemporary Norman abbey of Jumièges give some idea of its appearance.

custom grew up that future sovereigns should receive their royal crown there, in memory of Edward who was buried on the spot.

After the deaths of Æthelberht and Sæberht Mellitus was driven from his see by the rulers who succeeded them and came to Canterbury.[1] The friends who greeted him there had their hearts troubled by a great tide of cares, so Mellitus joined up with Justus and withdrew to France, waiting there to see if the present storm clouds might perhaps clear from the sky. And the holy spirit came to his aid, softening the heart of king Eadbald into belief, and ensuring the early return of both of them. Justus, in fact, returned to his own see without any difficulty, but Eadbald lacked the power to be able to restore Mellitus. So Mellitus for a little time was without any office, but on the death of Laurentius became archbishop of Canterbury. The stain of apostasy lasted among the East Saxons until the times of their king Sigeberht. He was baptised by bishop Finan,[2] on the encouragement of Oswiu, king of Northumbria, and brought back his people to the faith, which they had renounced together with Mellitus, by means of bishop Cedd. He was the second bishop of London, but was buried in Northumbria in the monastery at Lastingham.[3] You can find more about this in Bede,[4] who also mentions that Cedd's brother Chad held the episcopal see at Lichfield and was buried there. After Sigeberht his brother Swithhelm was king. On his death, Sigehere and Sebbi held the kingship as vassals to Wulfhere, king of Mercia. Sebbi, a man of spotless faith, made a seemly end, whereas Sigehere, during a plague, broke the seal of the faith, but, at the urging of Wulfhere received it back again from bishop Jaruman.[5] After Cedd's death, this Wulfhere was bribed to install on the vacant throne a certain Wini, bishop of the West Saxons.

But as the years went by, Theodore, sent to Canterbury as archbishop by pope Vitalian, gave to the people of London the venerable Erconwald as their bishop.[6] The stories still told about him, remembered from the days of old, are evidence that he performed visible miracles. This is the most notable of them. He was visiting his parishes in a litter because his feet were bad and happened to come to the bank of a fast-flowing river. His companions stood there hesitating, as the sick man could not cross by horse or on foot and they feared that the strong waves might swamp the litter, when suddenly the waters vanished as the river at that spot totally disappeared. No sooner had the bishop and his train got across than the river, which standing to one side with its crested waves had collected itself into a pile, returned to its bed. According to Bede, many sick people were cured by touching this litter.[7] Erconwald founded two monasteries, one for himself and one for his sister. His was called

---

[1] Eadbald, son of Æthelberht, and the three sons of Sæberht had remained pagan.
[2] Finan was Aidan's successor as bishop of Lindisfarne (651–61).
[3] Cedd was a tribal bishop of the East Saxons rather than bishop with a see in London. He had chosen the site for the monastery at Lastingham himself.
[4] *Ecclesiastical History* 3:23, 4:3.
[5] Bishop of the Mercians at Lichfield 662–7.
[6] Erconwald was bishop of London 675–93.
[7] *Ecclesiastical History* 4:6.

Chertsey. Helped by Frithewald, a sub-vassal of Wulfhere, he filled it with monks and a wealth of valuable objects. Its religious life shone brightly, nor did it ever want for essentials until the coming of the Danes, who destroyed the place like they did everything else, burning the church together with the monks and the abbot. But then king Edgar, that nonpareil prince, who was not content with the new monasteries being built everywhere by himself or his bishops unless he also patched up the old ones, got it properly restored. He searched out from all corners the old documents which warranted him giving back to the monastery the estates which had been appropriated by certain nobles for their own use either through force or through the title of long-standing occupation. The convent of Erconwald's sister is called Barking and is situated about eight miles to the side of London. There Æthelburg, for that was her name, had as associates and companions in her piety and power Hildelith, her immediate successor (the most blessed Aldhelm dedicated the still-extant book *In Praise of Virgins* to her)[1] and the almost modern Wilfidis, who was only a few years before the time of king Edgar, and who by the grace of her sanctity makes up for, and I might almost say anticipates, the antiquity of the other two. For nobody ever asks a prayer of her in vain, provided that he does not lack faith. Indeed I admit that it was through the prayers of such women that the convent was never completely destroyed and that now, in the days of the Normans, like many other things, it has even been raised to a position of the greatest importance by the number of its nuns and the beauty of its buildings. So Erconwald is considered to be London's greatest saint and is by no means undeserving of the favour of the canons because of the speed with which he answers prayers.

Other bishops, though, lie buried in such a cloud of obscurity that we do not even know where their tombs are. For all their episcopates suffered from the misfortune that the citizens held in great honour the memory of the writer who merely knew enough to list the names of the bishops of London. So of their deeds or graves not a word. But here are the names of Erconwald's successors: Wealdheri, Ingwald, Ecgwulf, Wigheah, Eadberht, Eadgar, Cœnwalh, Eadbald, Heathuberht, Osmund, Æthelnoth, Ceolberht, Deorwulf, Swithulf, Heahstan, Wulfsige, Æthelweard, Ealhstan and Theodred. The memory of the last-named has not completely disappeared. The people still keep it fresh as they tell how he lived in the time of king Æthelstan and set out with him in a war against Analavus. He went with Oda of Ramsbury, whom I mentioned earlier,[2] to pray for help from heaven and to reveal it to the king. The people took the good bishop's name as an omen of his virtues. He did fail to live up to it on one occasion, though it was more a mistake than a sin. Some thieves had been captured at Bury St Edmunds, their attempt failing when the martyr himself bound them with an invisible knot, and when they were sentenced to the gallows, Theodred handed them over to the severity of the laws. When he

---

[1] For this book see ch. 196.
[2] See ch. 14.

thought about what he had done, he was sorry, and he did penance for it for all the rest of his life, as the guilt bit into his conscience. His body is placed on a platform next to a window in the crypt, and can be seen by people passing by. After Theodred an unbroken succession of bishops was maintained by Wulfstan, Berhthelm, Dunstan who later was archbishop of Canterbury, Ælfstan, Wulfstan, Ælfwig, Ælfweard and Robert, who when he was a monk at Jumièges was first made bishop of London by king Edward and soon archbishop of Canterbury. I have already described his end in the earlier pages of this work.[1] His successor, also appointed by king Edward, was William.

Then William, having risen from duke of Normandy to king of England, appointed Hugh d'Orival bishop of London. A few years after his consecration he met with an incurable illness. The 'king's disease' with its oozing sores covered his whole body, so that only his genitals could cure him. For he believed those who declared that the only remedy was to cut off the receptacles of the malignant humours, namely his private parts, and he agreed to it. The result was the bishop endured the shame of being a eunuch, without finding a cure, for he remained a leper for the rest of his life. Hugh was succeeded by Maurice, the king's chancellor.[2] For some things his reputation did not stand too high, but he was admirably efficient, and an unmistakable indication of his generosity is the cathedral of the blessed Paul, which he began in London. So overwhelming is its beauty that it is rightly numbered among the famous buildings. The spaciousness of its crypt and the extent of its upper church are such that it seems to be able to contain any number of people. Maurice's plans were so grandiose that the expenses of the vast undertaking were handed down to his successors. And even when his successor, Richard,[3] transferred all the revenues of his bishopric to the building of the cathedral while supporting himself and his people with resources from elsewhere, he still seemed to achieve practically nothing. He nobly poured all his money into the cathedral, but was just using it up with very little actually happening. So the impulses towards the good, which he had at the start of this episcopate, fell victim to despair as the years went by, and gradually died away. There is a place among the East Saxons in the diocese of London, called Cic by the heathens, which is the resting place of the blessed Osyth, a virgin famous for her miracles. Richard established a house of regular canons here with some lands adjoining.[4] Its occupants were and still are famous for their learning, and from their example, a joyful crop, so to speak, of men wearing their habit clothed the whole country. Richard was thinking of retiring there himself, once he had taken off the wrappings of the world, especially as he was being warned to do

---

[1] See ch. 22.

[2] On Maurice see Loyn, *The English Church*, p. 91, who tells us, among other things, that Maurice claimed his sexual exploits were necessary for the preservation of his health.

[3] This is Richard de Belmeis, who had been royal sheriff before being promoted to the see of London by Henry I.

[4] Several such houses were established by bishops during Henry's reign. Matthew believes the aim was for their canons to set an example to the parish clergy (*The Norman Conquest*, pp. 211–12).

so by the paralysis which had affected him for so long, but in the end the habit
of power with its allurements kept his sick mind from doing so. The first prior
of this place was William de Corbeil, who was raised to the office of
archbishop of Canterbury on the death of archbishop Ralph. The monks
had been nervous about accepting someone who was a priest, but he did
nothing to be regretted. He was a man of great piety, fairly friendly, but not
lazy or lacking in sense.

Chapter 74 The bishops of the East Angles

The first bishop of the East Angles was a Burgundian called Felix.[1] He became
a friend of Sigeberht, who was in exile in Gaul, and went with him to England
after the death of Earpwald.[2] Sigeberht became the king of the province and
Felix, ordained as bishop, fully supported the ardour of the king and by his
boundless enthusiasm and alert labours spread the Christian faith over the
whole area. He even established schools in suitable places, and so gradually
shaped a rough race into civilised Latins.[3] He reached the goal of life after
seventeen years of being a bishop and was buried in the see of Dunwich. His
body was then taken to Soham, a town near marshland, which once upon a
time was dangerous to ships wishing to go to Ely, but which nowadays can be
crossed on foot by the road built across those reedy marshes. The remains still
exist there of the church which was destroyed and burnt by the Danes, and
which covered with its ruins the inhabitants who were also burnt. Much later
indeed the body of the saint was looked for and found and buried at Ramsey
Abbey, about which I shall speak later on.[4] Felix was followed by his deacon,
Thomas, who came from Jarrow. When he died five years later, the see was
filled by Boniface of Canterbury, who held the office for the same number of
years as his predecessor Felix. Then the revered Bisi was made bishop by
archbishop Theodore, and lived a blameless life while good health permitted it.
But when he was suddenly seized by a serious illness, his place was taken by
two bishops[5] and in fact two bishops always held that see right up to the
time of Ecgberht, king of the West Saxons, one of them stationed at
Dunwich, the other at Elmham. The pairs were Beadwine and Æcci,
Nothberht and Æscwulf, Heathulac and Eadred, Æthelfrith and Cuthwine,
Eanfrith and Ealdberht, Æthelwulf and Ecglaf, Ealhheard and Heardred,
Sibba and Ælfhun, and Ealhheard and Tidfrith. Ealhheard was bishop at
Elmham and Tidfrith at Dunwich, when king Offa of Mercia created the
archbishopric of Lichfield. Hunberht and Waormund, and after Waormund

---

[1] Felix was bishop 630–47.
[2] Sigeberht and Earpwald were brothers. Sigeberht had been baptised in Gaul, and was now keen
to imitate the excellent institutions he had seen there.
[3] These schools were designed to educate men for the priesthood, teaching them the Latin
necessary for reading the Bible and the liturgy.
[4] In ch. 181.
[5] See Mayr-Harting, *The Coming of Christianity*, p. 131, for Theodore opportunistically using
Bisi's illness to further his policy of extra dioceses.

Wilred, were the two bishops of the East Angles in the time of Ludeca king of Mercia and Ecgberht, king of the West Saxons. But Ludeca and his predecessor Burgred invaded East Anglia,[1] and even the two bishops were deprived of essential supplies. Indeed when both kings were killed during this attack on the region, the two bishoprics ceased as well, and the two bishops became one with his see in the small town of Elmham. The bishops there were Eadwulf, Ælfric, the two Theodreds, Æthelstan and Ælfgar. The writer of the life of St Dunstan[2] has given a remarkable instance of the sanctity of Ælfgar, and I shall record it here in his own words.

> The feast of the Ascension was three days before the day of the glorification of St Dunstan. As dawn rose on this great feast day a priest called Ælfgar, who was deservedly famous for both his teaching and his deeds, and who afterwards we know had a reputation as an outstanding bishop of Elmham, was keeping vigil and performing the holy office for our Lord's Ascension in the church of the Saviour. While his mind was fixed on the contemplation of heavenly things, he passed out of his body beyond all the things of this world and saw Dunstan sitting on his archbishop's throne and dictating canonical laws to a clerk. And then an amazing thing! In through all the doors of the church poured countless hosts of angels, who stood in front of the archbishop on his throne in serried array and spoke to him these words of greeting, 'Welcome, Dunstan our friend; if you are ready, come and graciously join our fellowship.' Dunstan replied, 'You holy spirits, you know that today Christ ascended into heaven, and that it is our duty to refresh the people of God with word and sacrament; so today I cannot come.' They replied, 'Be ready on the Sabbath to come with us from here to Rome and, once sanctified there before the supreme pontiff, to sing the songs of heaven.' The angels departed. But the priest, who had been so clear a witness of the event, wondered in silent astonishment at their departure.

And later on the writer added,

> Also the priest, who had experienced this remarkable trance in the church, when he discovered that the trance he had undergone was not just a vision but had been translated into reality, openly revealed to all with great sobs what he had seen.

I have borrowed this account from another writer to show to my readers how saintly Ælfgar was. With the mystic eyes of insight he had seen deep secrets and he was also the right man to publish them abroad. Indeed, I would find it hard to believe that when he undertook higher office he was less vigilant for sanctity, and, as a matter of fact, you must believe that he was made bishop out of the respect felt for his virtues, and that on his own day he was received up into heaven to join the hosts of angels that he had seen.

---

[1] Burgred (852–74) in fact came after Ludeca (825–7).
[2] Osbern, a monk of Canterbury.

After him Ælfwine was bishop, then the two Ælfrics, then Stigand, but he was deposed. Grimcytel bribed his way into office and was bishop both of the East Angles and the South Saxons. However, as time went by and Stigand had given his account of the matter, he grew so powerful that he reinstated himself as bishop of the South Saxons, and made his brother Æthelmær bishop of the East Angles. But Stigand thought this quite insufficient for a man of his ambition, and ascended the thrones of Winchester and Canterbury, although he had only been prevailed upon with extreme difficulty to be ordained as the official bishop for the South Saxons. After Æthelmær the bishop at Elmham was Herfast. This appointment can be found in the proceedings of the council, which was held under the leadership of the two metropolitans in the sixth year of William's reign.[1] Herfast did not want to give the impression of having done nothing, especially as the Normans are very keen on posthumous fame, and so transferred the see from Elmham to Thetford.[2] He was a man of little intelligence, so the story goes, though with some education in the classics. Indeed people thought highly of his knowledge of these matters, before Lanfranc came to Normandy and became a monk at Bec. Herfast, who by now had become chaplain to William, duke of Normandy, who was afterwards king, came with a great retinue of companions and horses to this famous centre of learning,[3] where pupils on all sides were puffing out their cheeks and spouting forth dialectic. From their first words together Lanfranc could see that the man's knowledge was practically nil, and so arranged for the alphabet to be set before him, sidestepping the man's fierceness by this piece of Italian wit.[4] Herfast was very annoyed at this, and got the duke to remove Lanfranc from Bec and all Normandy. But the grace of God intervened, the duke was pacified, and Lanfranc allowed to stay. William Fitz-Osbern played a great part in all this,[5] though the most important factor in Lanfranc's regaining favour was the fact that his horse happened to be limping when he came to court to ask for a furlough, and this caused the duke to shake with laughter.

After Herfast, in the days of William II, Herbert, surnamed Losinga (this surname had become attached to him because of his skill in flattery),[6] bought the bishopric of Thetford. He became bishop after being prior of Fécamp and abbot of Ramsey, while he inserted his father Robert of the same surname into the abbacy of Winchester. Thus Herbert was a great encourager of simony in England: it was by money that he had obtained his abbacy and bishopric and by money that he had ensnared the attention of the king, nor were they small promises of money that he whispered for the favour of princes. But he wiped

---

[1] This council was held at Winchester in 1072.
[2] See Matthew, *The Norman Conquest*, p. 42 for the Normans' growing appetite for fame at this time, and pp. 187–8 for Herfast's attempts at getting control of the monastery at Bury St Edmunds.
[3] This visit was in 1053.
[4] Knowles suggests that this story of 'the brilliant ultra-montane using his gifts at the expense of the duller Normans, may be merely *ben trovato*' (*The Monastic Order*, p. 108).
[5] The duke's closest companion and right-hand man.
[6] The Italian for 'to flatter' is *lusingare*.

out these rash mistakes of his youth by his repentance. For when he was an older man, he went to Rome.[1] There he laid down the staff and ring of his office which he had obtained by simony, and through the kindness of that most merciful see[2] deservedly received them back: in Rome they think it more holy and proper that the revenues of all the churches should serve their own uses rather than those of some king or other. And so Herbert went back home and transferred the episcopal see to Norwich, a town famous for its trade and large population. He founded a community of monks there, famous for their piety and numbers, and bought everything they needed out of the income of his household. By bestowing no episcopal lands on the monks, he made sure that his successors would not be able to take offence and deprive the servants of God of their livelihood, if they discovered them in possession of things which belonged to their own estates. He also established Cluniac monks at Thetford, who belong to that order which is scattered almost throughout the whole world, rich in worldly goods and worshipping God in the greatest splendour. And so Herbert hid the mass of his past offences under the numerous and extensive graces of his virtues, being especially deterred from evil and spurred on to do good by the prognostic of his predecessor and by his own. For Herfast's was 'Not this man, but Barabas',[3] whereas his own was, 'Friend, do what you have come here for.'[4] When Herbert heard this, he could not refrain from tears or from words like these, 'I confess my coming here has been bad, but with God's grace helping me my going hence shall be good.' So he became highly regarded by his highness at Rome both for his wealth of eloquence and learning and for his ability in secular affairs. And the change in Herbert, was, as Lucan says about Curio, 'the crucial turning point'.[5] For, just as in the time of king William he had been an advocate of simony, so now in the reign of Henry he was its unbeaten opponent. He had no wish for others to practise that for which he now repented he had once set the fashion in his youthful zeal, always bearing in mind, so they say, the maxim of Jerome, 'We erred in our youth: let us make it good in our old age.'[6]

Finally, how can I weave into my work fitting praise for Herbert's action, as a bishop without much money, in making the monastery so magnificent that nothing was missing, neither imposing, uplifting buildings, nor beautiful ornaments, nor God-fearing monks who showed concern and charity towards all. These actions comforted him in his lifetime with hopes of happiness, and at his death carried him above the skies, if our faith in repentance is not vain. As is well known, the monastery of St Edmund belongs to the diocese of the bishop of Norwich, so, although I have spoken of it elsewhere,[7] it is not

[1] See chs. 56–7 for an earlier account of this journey to Rome.
[2] In the person of Urban II.
[3] John 18:40.
[4] Matthew 26:50.
[5] In his *Pharsalia* 4:819 Lucan uses this phrase to refer to Curio's defection from Pompey to Caesar just before the Civil War between the two dynasts in 49 BC.
[6] Letter 84:6.
[7] In ch. 56.

illogical if I mention it briefly here. For in this way I shall keep to my plan and arrangement of deciding to include, after the facts about the bishops, some mention of the saints who are at rest in their parishes.[1] And I admit it gives me great pleasure that the first saint we meet is St Edmund. As king and prince of his country, he was the first of his fellow saints to claim the palm of praise. He ruled over East Anglia,[2] a man who was devoted to God and distinguished by the line of kings who were his ancestors. He had peacefully governed his country for some years (not that he had been forced by any softness of the times to doff his manliness), when the Danes arrived, led by Hinguar and Hubba, with the aim of laying waste the lands of the Northumbrians and East Angles. Hinguar captured Edmund, who did not resist but had thrown aside his weapons and was prostrate on the ground saying his prayers. But Hinguar, after torturing him for some time, cut off his head.[3] And then the Danes burnt and levelled to the ground the episcopal dwelling at Soham, as I have described earlier,[4] and also the monastery at Ely, after driving out the monks.

But after the death of the blessed Edmund, the purity of the life he had lived blazed forth in miracles worthy of the saint.[5] When his head had been separated from his body by the cruel executioner, the Danes threw it away and it had lain hidden in some bushes. The citizens were in search of it, following the steps of the departing enemy and intending to perform the proper rites of a royal funeral, when they eagerly drank in a glad gift from God. For a voice coming from the lifeless head was heard inviting all his executioners[6] to come to him. A wild, carnivorous wolf was holding it between his paws, and guarding it to keep it safe from harm, and like some household pet it humbly followed behind the bearers to the grave, harming no one and harmed by no one. Then for the time being the body of the saint was committed to the ground, turves hurriedly thrown on top, earth scattered over them and a cheap wooden shrine erected. But as time went by briars covered the little chapel and the citizens had forgotten all about the martyr. But Edmund appeared to his negligent people and by miracles aroused their slumbering minds to show him respect. The one I shall quote is small and trivial, but nevertheless it was the first time men experienced his powers. A blind man, who was feeling his way with a stick, wandered by night into the little chapel. A light from heaven shone upon him and filled his eyes. Soon afterwards, some thieves were attempting to burgle the same chapel at night, when in the middle of their attempt the saint bound them in a net of invisible cords. That was quite a pretty sight, robbers caught by their own quarry, so

[1] William outlined this plan in the prologue to Book 2.
[2] From 855 to 869.
[3] For the evidence concerning Edmund and discrepancies in accounts of his death see *The Blackwell Encyclopaedia*, *s.v.* 'Edmund, St'.
[4] See p. 96.
[5] See Stenton, *Anglo-Saxon England*, p. 248, for the rapid growth of Edmund's cult in the quarter of a century after his death.
[6] This story of St Edmund is given in almost the identical words of *The Deeds of the Kings* 2:213, but that text does have 'searchers' instead of 'executioners', which seems to make more sense.

that they could neither desist from their undertaking nor finish what they had begun. The result was that the bishop of London[1] removed the long-standing disgrace of the humble construction and built a more dignified tomb for the venerated body, whose marvellous lack of corruption and milky whiteness testified to the glory of the blessed soul. The head was joined to the rest of the body, although a purple scar bore witness to the martyrdom. And what exceeded human miracles was that the hair and nails of the dead man were quick with life. Indeed a holy woman called Oswen cut the hair and pared the nails every year, producing objects of great veneration for generations to come. She was a woman of holy boldness who could handle the limbs to which all the world is inferior. Completely different was Leofstan, a youth of uncontrolled rashness. With boastful threats he demanded to be shown the body of the martyr, deciding, so he said, to weigh with the evidence of his own eyes what was a matter of uncertain rumour. He paid the penalty for his headstrong impetuosity, for he went mad, and after a short time he swarmed with worms and died. Edmund indeed in his own day knew how to keep the ancient custom of 'sparing the humble and warring down the proud'.[2]

By these two means he so bound all the people of Britain to himself that the man who uses his cash or wealth to beautify Edmund's resting place regards himself as the most blessed of men. Even kings, who lord it over others, boast of being his servants, and repeatedly send him their royal crown, buying it back at a great price if they wish to use it. And tax collectors, who run riot elsewhere, regarding right and wrong as the same thing, there turn suppliant and stop their lawsuits on this side of St Edmund's trench, having seen the penalty paid by their many brethren who decided to continue past it. This trench was made on the orders of king Cnut, who was warned to do this good thing by the unhappy end of his father Swegn.[3] For in the time of king Æthelred, Swegn was laying waste the whole of England and breathing out no less terrifying threats in the district of St Edmund, when, so the story goes, he was given a gentle admonishment by the martyr in a dream. Swegn with barbarian ineptitude replied with some roughness, so the saint struck him with a pole and killed him. Because he had been struck in his sleep, a long delay intervened before the author and manner of his death was revealed to those standing outside. The guardians of the body to their amazement had indeed heard a conversation between people arguing and the sound of a blow. King Cnut knew of this incident, so did all he could to mollify the saint. Besides the trench I have mentioned, whose purpose was to keep the saint's lands free from all disturbances, he finally with royal generosity built a basilica over the saint's body, of the size required by the usage of the times, and established an abbot and monks, on whom he bestowed many large

[1] Theodred, bishop of London 926–51.
[2] Virgil uses this line at *Aeneid* 6:854 as a summary of the mission of Rome.
[3] Stenton notes that 'Swegn's tepid patronage of Christianity contrasts sharply with Cnut's enthusiastic devotion to the interests of the church in England' (*Anglo-Saxon England*, p. 397).

estates. His extensive donations survive intact today,[1] since Bury St Edmunds towers above several of the monasteries of England.

In the succession of abbots, Leofstan was the abbot there in the time of king Edward.[2] He was concerned about some people who were sceptical of the incorruption of the saint's body, and at risk to himself took measures for the faith of others. So, with the abbot himself dragging it by the head and a monk by its feet, the body was brought out into the open and exhibited for inspection. Leofstan prayed to it aloud, saying, 'St Edmund, my master, you know that I have done this, not because my mind lacks faith, but for the salvation of others, and so that God's miracle performed on you should not be hidden from the world. But because I am guilty of many sins, and I ought not to have touched the vessel of the Holy Spirit, if my action displeases you, inflict some punishment on me in this world. For it is better and I prefer it that I should be marked by some bodily affliction than that I should suffer everlasting punishment.' He had hardly finished speaking, when, incredible though it seems, the fingers of both his hands were pitifully bent back or immovably twisted up in his palms, so that he was punished with the penalty he had asked for. Later, other further weaknesses assailed him and he sent messengers to king Edward, begging him to send him a doctor. The king had a monk of St Denis called Baldwin sent, who had knowledge of this art.[3] But although Baldwin cured his other diseases, he could do nothing to heal his fingers. He was surprised at this, as he had had great success as a doctor. But when the people who knew of it told him the reason for the disease, he stayed on in the abbey and with his whole heart devoted himself to a love for the martyr. During a stay of many years he got to know all the leading people, and succeeded Leofstan as abbot – or rather acceded to his urgent appeal and the wishes of the king that he should become abbot. In his time and through his efforts, the monastery was given the freedom by pope Alexander of being subordinate to no bishop in anything, merely having to take notice of the nod of the archbishop in matters where it was lawful to do so. Everything was refurbished, inside and outside. The glory of its buildings and the weight of the offerings it received were such that nowhere in England were there bigger and better. Two saints, Germanus and Botwulf, lie buried in the church. I do not remember their deeds being recounted either in Bury or elsewhere, except that the first is said to be the brother of St Æthelthryth[4] and the second to have been a bishop.[5]

---

[1] For whether or not the monastery at Bury St Edmunds was founded by Cnut, see Janet Burton, *Monastic and Religious Orders in Britain 1000–1300* (Cambridge, 1994), p. 273 n. 10.

[2] Abbot Leofstan is not to be confused with the headstrong youth, also called Leofstan, who appeared on p. 101.

[3] For monks as doctors see ch. 274.

[4] Queen of Northumbria in Wilfrid's time. See ch. 100.

[5] This sentence is a puzzle. So much was known of Germanus, bishop of Auxerre, that Bede fills five chapters of his *Ecclesiastical History* (1:17–21) with his mission to England and his miracles, and William himself records some particulars of him in *The Deeds of the Kings* 1:22. Botwulf founded a famous monastery at Icanoe in the Fens (site unknown) in 654 but does not seem to have been a bishop.

Chapter 75 The bishops of Winchester: Birinus to Æthelwald (634–984)

Now that I have gone through the names of the bishops of Canterbury, Rochester, the East Saxons and the East Angles, my next task is to give an account of the sees and the deeds of the other bishops, as far as these are known by report or in writing.

And first, according to the scheme of my plan, it is the turn of the West Saxons. To begin with they had one bishop, based at Dorchester, but soon two, one at Winchester and the other at Sherborne. In the reign of king Edward three more were added to the two, based in Wells, Crediton and Cornwall. Soon afterwards there was a sixth at Ramsbury.[1]

Because the purpose of my history is to give an ordered account of all these, I must speak first of the city of Winchester, as befits its position. So, at the time when Cynegils and Cwichelm were reigning over the West Saxons, pope Honorius persuaded Birinus (whose origin is obscure) to undertake the task of preaching the gospel to Britain. He was ordained bishop by bishop Asterius of Genoa and made his way to the sea in order to cross to Britain. While he was packing his bits and pieces, the sailors were urging him to hurry as the wind was favourable, and so he forgot those cloths which are called 'corporal cloths'.[2] He was already out to sea, with the ship happily ploughing its furrow through the calm waters, when he remembered he had left them behind. He was at a loss what to do. If he asked the sailors to go back, they would certainly laugh at him as the voyage was going so well. But if he kept quiet, he would have to put up with his apostolic worship being imperfect. And so, brandishing the weapons of his faith, he summoned all his courage, climbed down the side into the sea and with all speed made for the shore he had just left. There he found the corporal cloths, picked them up, and for the second time his daring had a blessed and happy outcome, for he returned to his companions, brushing aside by the power of his faith the crests of the waves and the thousand ways to death he encountered. They for their part had been won over by this great miracle, had cast anchor and were holding the ship stationary. They took him back on board, all competing to do him honour, and he soon reached the coast in the region of the West Saxons.

It was the fortieth year after the arrival of Augustine, and the kings I just mentioned had been ruling for twenty-five years. Birinus had promised pope Honorius to make his way to the furthest reaches of England and to sow the seeds of the faith where not even the name of the gospel had been heard. But no sooner had he landed than he found that all the inhabitants of the area were the most devoted adherents of sacrilegious rites. So it seemed pointless to venture further and to look for sick people to heal, when he found no one healthy in Wessex. He stayed there, and by his own efforts and the power of

---

[1] See the map in Peter Hunter Blair, *An Introduction to Anglo-Saxon England*, p. 171.

[2] Linen cloths upon which the consecrated elements are placed during the eucharist, and with which they are subsequently covered.

God bestowed the saving water of baptism first on king Cynegils and soon all the province as well. It was a spectacle worthy of much praise, for it happened that the day appointed for the king's baptism coincided with the day on which he had decided to give his daughter in marriage to Oswald, most holy king of Northumbria, and in a gracious exchange it was enacted that the future son-in-law of Cynegils in the flesh became first his spiritual father for the baptism. Both kings gave their officiator Dorchester for his episcopal see.[1] It was then a city, now a town, and ruled at that time by the kings of the West Saxons, though later by the bishops of Mercia. The episcopal see of Mercia remained in Dorchester right up to our own day, but now is at Lincoln.[2] And so Birinus, worn out by his labours for God and departing this life, was buried at Dorchester in the church which he had built. In later years, when the bishopric of the West Saxons had been established in Winchester, Birinus' body was moved there by bishop Hæddi, and Birinus is considered to be the patron of the city, after God.

After Birinus, a Frenchman called Agilbert held the bishopric of the West Saxons. You can read a more detailed account of his arrival and departure in Bede.[3] Here you will find just a summary. He in fact departed in a temper when a man called Wini was brought in to be bishop at Winchester. Wini was an Englishman, but had been ordained in France. However, this 'invader' did not promote peace for long, as he was driven out by the tyrannical act of the same king[4] and fled for refuge to king Wulfhere of Mercia. He bought the bishopric of London from Wulfhere and spent the remaining days of his life there. This was a bad example for posterity, and it would be hard to tell whether the greater sin and infamy belonged to him who put the sacred office up for sale or him who bought it. Agilbert was then begged by messengers of the king to return, but he excused himself from coming on the grounds that he was bound fast in the chains of his bishopric of Paris. But in order not to disappoint the hopes of his petitioner, he sent his nephew Leutherius. He was given a warm welcome by all the West Saxons, and after being consecrated by archbishop Theodore, he governed their church for seven years. Bede has left no details about the years of his bishopric, but I have mentioned it, as I thought it wrong to pass over in silence what I had learnt from the chronicles.[5]

His successor was Hæddi. Formerly a monk and abbot, he was bishop for more than thirty years.[6] Bede says his bishopric was based more on his innate love of goodness than on any endowment of learning and culture.[7] I am not at

---

[1] How could Oswald join in giving this gift? Did he merely witness his father-in-law's deed of gift? See Judith McClure and Roger Collins, *Bede: The Ecclesiastical History*, p. 388.
[2] It was moved to Lincoln in 1072.
[3] *Ecclesiastical History* 3:7. Though Agilbert was a Gaul by birth, he had studied the Scriptures in southern Ireland before coming to Wessex. He no more approved of the division of his diocese than did Wilfrid, bishop of York.
[4] King Cenwalh, son of Cynegils, both brought Wini in and drove him out.
[5] William gets Leutherius' dates from the Anglo-Saxon Chronicle.
[6] 676–705. He had been abbot of Whitby.
[7] *Ecclesiastical History* 5:18.

all sure about this. I have read his official letters, which are not in the least badly put together, and Aldhelm's letters to him, which give a very strong impression of eloquence and learning.[1] The number of the miracles sent by him from heaven made clear to men's minds the reverence paid to his sanctity. Nowadays these miracles for the time being have come to an end, Hæddi being content with the glory once obtained by him immediately after his death. Because the area of the diocese was too extensive to be governed properly by one man, after Hæddi's death it was split into two halves, one being given to Daniel and one to Aldhelm.[2] It will be time to give an account of Aldhelm and his successors[3] when, with God as my companion, I hammer out a narrative which will be good enough to profit my readers. For the moment, as I promised, I shall deal with the bishops of Winchester. Daniel lived on for a long time after Aldhelm's death and was bishop for forty-three years. In the end he resigned his office while still alive,[4] in order to finish his vigorous old age in the peace of the cloister. For the rest of his life he was a monk at Malmesbury, according to the clear tradition which has come down to us through the generations, and is said to have been buried there. The monks of Winchester claim that his burial place is in their church, but they cannot point to either his real or supposed tomb. His successor was Hunfrith, who is recorded as being present at the council held by archbishop Cuthbert.[5] Then Cyneheard was bishop. After him came Æthelheard, who was soon archbishop after being abbot of Malmesbury, Ecgbald, Dudd, Cyneberht, Ealhmund, Wigthegn, Herefrith, Eadmund and Helmstan, who was bishop when Ecgberht was king of the West Saxons.

When Helmstan entered upon the path of his fathers, he was succeeded by Swithhun,[6] who had already been ordained as a priest in the same church by Helmstan. During his priesthood the piety of his life matched his simple good sense, and his praiseworthy character and industry did not escape the notice of the king, who so far cultivated him that he transacted much business on Swithhun's advice and sent his son, Æthelwulf, to be tutored by him.[7] The happy chance of this presaged the young man's future felicity, for under this most saintly teacher he learnt how to enter upon the governing of his country as a man of experience, when his time came. As Plato well said long ago, 'A country will only be happy, if either its philosophers are kings, or its kings philosophers.'[8] Æthelwulf showed this saying to be true, when, on the death of his father, he was elevated to the kingship from being subdeacon at Winchester

---

[1] See ch. 195 for an extremely learned letter, believed by William to be from Aldhelm to Hæddi.
[2] Aldhelm's half was the diocese of Sherborne. The split was part of Theodore's reorganisation.
[3] The account of Aldhelm comes in Book 5, that of his successors in chs. 79–83.
[4] In 745. Daniel had also become blind, so that children were dying without baptism. Boniface, the English missionary to the Frisians, wrote a letter to Daniel comforting his old mentor in his affliction.
[5] The Council of Clovesho of 747. See ch. 5.
[6] In 852.
[7] The king was Ecgberht. Æthelwulf was the father of Alfred the Great.
[8] In his *Republic* 5:18.

with the agreement of pope Leo IV, there being no other legitimate heir still alive. Then indeed it became clear what theology had taught him, for he thought of the profit of the servants of God much more than his own and tithed the whole kingdom for God.[1] He did nothing which was not thought out, and ordered nothing which was not righteous.

But I have described this elsewhere,[2] and now my hands are unrolling the deeds of Swithhun. Æthelwulf had so much reverence for his father and teacher (for that is what he called Swithhun) that he did not stop until he had honoured him with the bishopric of Winchester, with the agreement of the clergy. Ceolnoth, archbishop of Canterbury, ordained him, and now the foundations for good laid in the land by the king were built upon with happy increase by the bishop, as he promoted the good schemes which the king set in motion by his own particular suggestions.

Swithhun was indeed a repository of all the virtues, but the two which he rejoiced in most were mercy and humility. My pen will give instances of both. He happened to be sitting over some workmen engaged in building a bridge in the eastern part of the town,[3] by the encouragement of his presence pricking their idle laziness into life, when a woman who was carrying eggs to market began walking over the bridge into the city. Like typical workmen, the men jumped up and down around her and by their naughty stamping broke all her eggs. This did not seem a trivial incident to people of a more sensible sort, and they immediately brought the matter to the notice of the lord bishop. The woman, a poorly dressed old crone, was brought before him. Swithhun listened to her complaint and sighed for her loss. And, as he hesitated, the compassion he felt for her aroused him to perform a miracle. Making the sign of the cross in front of him, he immediately made all the broken eggs whole. Hardly a small proof of his holiness and pity!

What about his humility? Whenever it was his duty to consecrate a new building as a church of God, instead of going on horseback or in a carriage, he would stride there vigorously on foot, no matter how far it was.[4] And to stop the ignorant laughing at him or the arrogant censuring him with an accusation of self-display, he would accomplish the whole journey as a traveller by night, hidden from the sight of men. He loved an unseen holiness and did not prostitute his good deeds by any display. And this, I suppose, is the reason why he deprived the minds of future generations of any knowledge of all his miracles, and enjoyed heaven as his only witness. Anyway, when he was now about to bid farewell to this present life, using his bishop's authority he ordered those standing around him to bury his body outside the church,[5] where

---

[1] For this grant see Stenton, *Anglo-Saxon England*, p. 308.
[2] In *The Deeds of the Kings* 2:106–7.
[3] Bishops, like other landowners, were under an obligation to provide men for the army, and to help with the building and repair of fortifications and bridges. See Burton, *Monastic and Religious Orders*, p. 12.
[4] Bede records that Aidan made his journeys in the same manner (*Ecclesiastical History* 3:5).
[5] Outside the west door of the Old Minster. For a map of the churches of Winchester see Barbara Yorke, *Wessex in the Early Middle Ages* (Leicester, 1995), p. 204.

it might be exposed to the feet of passers-by and to the rain dripping down from the eaves.

He died in 863, in the sixth year after the death of Æthelwulf. Much time went by and this jewel of God lay hidden without fame for almost one hundred years. During this period eight bishops lived out their days. Their names are Ealhfrith, Tunberht, Denewulf, Frithustan, Beornstan, Ælfheah, Ælfsige and Berhthelm. I shall be careful not to pass over those of the eight whose lives had some fame and reputation. If we can believe the story about Denewulf, until late in his life he was not only illiterate but also a swineherd. King Alfred, while retreating from his kingdom as a result of a fierce enemy attack, escaped into a wood and happened to meet him pasturing his pigs there. To cut a long story short, he discovered that Denewulf's character was turned towards the good and got him taught his letters. Nor did he stop helping Denewulf until he had been improved enough to be made a bishop – a miraculous achievement. Frithustan was one of the seven bishops consecrated in one day at Canterbury by archbishop Plegmund in the days of king Edward, son of Alfred.[1] His many virtues can still be read about today in a number of books: the grave has not buried in obscurity the sanctity of his life, as it has that of others.

Beornstan was bishop for four years only. The tradition is that he was a man of the purest piety. Every day with unbroken care he would sing a mass for the repose of the dead, and at night he would fearlessly go round the cemeteries and chant psalms for the salvation of their souls. On one such occasion, he had completed all the Psalms and added the words 'May they rest in peace.' In reply he heard from the graves the voices, as of an infinite army, saying 'Amen'. The unusualness of it made it all the more miraculous. To think that the dead should have spoken to the living, in order that Beornstan should not tire of a duty which he heard pleased so many souls! He was also a most ardent follower of the example of our Lord. Every day, having first sent away any spectators, he would wash the feet of the poor, set beside them a table with food and even clear away the remains as a lesson for his servants. When he had finished this service to the poor and sent them away, he would remain in the same place for several hours, giving the time to prayer, as was thought. One day he had gone in to pray as usual, when, without being disturbed by any prior pains from an illness, he suddenly gave up the breath of life unseen by anybody. His followers who knew his habits let him lie there all day, as they thought he was busy with his prayers on that occasion as well. But at dawn next day they broke in and found his lifeless corpse. He was bewailed and buried. But the citizens consigned his memory to the silence of oblivion, because they saw that he had been cut off by an early death. They did not know that it has been written, 'The man who has lived well cannot die badly' and 'For the good man there is consolation, whatever death snatches him away.' Their behaviour was put straight by the divine justice when Æthelwald became bishop long afterwards. It was his practice at the beginning of the night

---

[1] For this consecration see ch. 13.

to work by lamplight before the relics of the saints. One night three persons appeared to stand by him (this was not in a vision, for he was wide awake). He heard the middle one of them say, 'I am Beornstan, once bishop of this city. And this man', pointing to his right, 'is Birinus, who brought Christianity to us. And this man', pointing to his left, 'is Swithhun, the special patron of this church and city. You must know that, just as you see me together with them here now, so I enjoy an equal glory with them in heaven. So, why am I deprived of honour from men, when I am glorified by the company of these heavenly spirits?' He finished speaking and, having given this precious memory of himself to his people, he vanished with his companions into the air. Afterwards he received no small veneration, just as he deserved.

Ælfheah,[1] in addition to the pile of other laudable virtues he so abundantly possessed, was also famous for his prophetic insight. I will give two examples of this. It was Ash Wednesday, and the bishop according to custom was keeping the penitent from crossing the threshold of the church.[2] He exhorted the others to devote themselves to fasting and chastity, even giving up the pleasures of sex with their wives during that time, since for those who had done many unlawful things to refrain even from the lawful was a proper effect of penitence. The rest heard the teaching with respect, but one fellow came out with a witty remark which caused the others to laugh. He couldn't, he said, at the same time control himself at both board and bed, so as to abstain equally from food and sex. He had actually moved his wife out of his bed some time ago, but he was going to get her back as soon as possible for some night-time use, making this fatuous remark worse by using a vulgar, indecent word. The bystanders heard the bishop murmuring something, and picked up the words, 'Poor fellow, you make me sad, for you do not know what the coming day will bring.' This harsh prophecy was followed immediately by the death of the rascal. He was found dead in his bed next morning, strangled, perhaps by the devil.

On another occasion he ordained three monks to equal positions in the priesthood, Dunstan,[3] Æthelwald and a certain Æthelstan who soon put off his monk's habit, gave up celibacy and poured out his life in the embraces of prostitutes. When he had completed the ceremony, Ælfheah of blessed memory spoke thus to his close followers, 'Today in the presence of God I have laid my hands on three men. Two of them will be granted the favour of a bishopric, the one at Worcester and then at Canterbury, while the other will one day in lawful succession fill my see here. The third will wallow in the pig-mire of pleasure and meet a miserable end.' At this point Æthelstan, who was present because of his close connection with the bishop, interrupted him by saucily asking, 'I don't suppose I am one of the two to be elevated to episcopal rank, am I?' 'No,' replied the bishop. 'You will have no share or place in that

---

[1] Bishop of Winchester 934–51. It was a later Ælfheah, also bishop of Winchester 984–1006, who was put to death by the Danes in 1012. See ch. 20.
[2] People who had repented were kept out of the church until Easter Day.
[3] Ælfheah was Dunstan's uncle, and had persuaded him to become a monk.

order of which I have spoken, nor will you go on wearing that habit in which you preen yourself before the eyes of men.' What power the mind of a saint possesses, to bring forth the secrets of heaven so clearly and without any blurring. For those words did not fall to the ground. What happened next made all of them the solid truth, for Dunstan and Æthelwald trod the narrow path which leads to life and became distinguished and famous in the bishoprics foretold for them, while the third scurried down the wide pathways of the world.

A previous book[1] has dealt with Ælfsige's rash madness in buying his archbishopric and his miserable end. And so I see it is now suitable to say something, if briefly, about father Æthelwald, the successor of Berhthelm, the successor of Ælfsige at Winchester.[2] Both his parents were citizens of Winchester, neither short of money nor of contemptible descent. Æthelwald himself as a boy was devoted to learning. In his youth he became a member of the royal household and a favourite of king Æthelstan. On the king's advice he was given his tonsure as a priest by Ælfheah, and soon afterwards his cowl as a monk by Dunstan, abbot of Glastonbury. He was ordained dean of the monastery there. Some of the monks responded to his teaching, others to his piety, but all of them to his love. At this time the abbot had a truly remarkable dream about him. He saw a tree growing up inside the walls of the monastery. Its branches, spreading out through the four quarters of the heavens, overshadowed the whole of England, which was covered by the monks' habits that filled all the leaves, and the biggest habit was placed on its top and protected, as it were, the other smaller ones with the warmth of its sleeves. Dunstan was amazed at such a miraculous sight, and asked its meaning from a venerable old man with white hair who was standing near by. 'The tree', he replied, 'is this island; the bigger habit represents the life of your monk, Æthelwald; the others are those countless individuals whom he will draw to God by his word and his example.'[3] This prophecy was in harmony with a vision shown to Æthelwald's mother, when her belly was now large and she was thinking about giving birth. From her mouth there flew out a golden eagle, which for a long time flew over the city with beating wings and finally, out-topping the highest clouds, disappeared into the heavens. Fortune, which was already playing[4] about him, later showed the people a true outcome of these visions. For when Æthelwald, in his longing for a stricter life, was thirsting for exile in France, king Eadred kept him in England. It was Eadred's mother, Eadgifu, a woman famous throughout the whole land of Britain for the praises paid to her religion, who took up Æthelwald's case and persuaded her son to keep him.

---

[1] See ch. 17.
[2] Æthelwald was bishop of Winchester 963–84.
[3] This was an apt dream about a future leader of the tenth-century monastic revival in England. For Æthelwald's efforts on behalf of all the monks of England see Loyn, *The English Church*, p. 20 and Yorke, *Wessex in the Early Middle Ages*, pp. 212–18.
[4] Virgil *Aeneid* 2:684 uses a similar word in describing an omen given to Aeneas' son Ascanius.

So he was given the very small abbey of Abingdon, so that he might put the power of his wisdom to the test. His energy there was such that he did not disappoint the hopes of his patrons, but raised the abbey to the height of fame which we see today.[1] Indeed after a few years had slipped by and Dunstan had by now been made archbishop, Æthelwald himself was chosen for the bishopric of Winchester by king Edgar and consecrated by Dunstan. Then indeed he rose up to the help of his churches, and by mighty efforts rooted out vices and planted nurseries for the growth of the virtues. It was impossible to know whether to praise him more highly for his zeal for holiness, the exercise of his learning, the force of his preaching or his building activity. The secular clergy of his bishopric together with those of another nearby church called New Minster,[2] when given the choice of changing their life or leaving, chose the softer option and were moved out.[3] Æthelwald brought in monks in their place, endowing them with further estates from his bishopric which were both nearer and richer. He founded and established a nunnery and a monastery in Winchester. I shall speak of his other foundations in various places when I come to deal with their bishops. It is remarkable that he accomplished so much, though we should not forget that king Edgar, who loved him second only to Dunstan, was completely devoted to carrying out his wishes.

The appearance of St Swithhun at this time was also a great help to his projects and a cause for praise.[4] Maintaining the lowliness of his old life, Swithhun seemed in a vision to utter the following words, not to some personage of exalted rank but to a poor little man who kept himself alive by the work of his hands. 'Go to the Old Minster at Winchester. Find the sacristan and tell him to inform bishop Æthelwald that he is to open up the tomb of Swithhun, once bishop there, and bring out the remains. He will find there pearls more precious than all other treasure. The divine mercy has had regard for the days of his bishopric, and will use me to make them famous for portents from heaven. Here is a sign, to stop you delaying. There are iron rings, firmly fixed with lead to the stone of the tomb. Whenever you want, you can pull them out or put them back with the smallest of efforts. Other people, attempting the same thing, will try in vain.' The poor man departed. He spoke to the sacristan as he had promised, and was taken in before the bishop. He dealt with the matter boldly, and the bishop believed him. On an appointed

---

[1] 'He significantly increased the abbey's endowment and rebuilt and rededicated the church there' (*The Blackwell Encyclopaedia*, s.v. 'Æthelwold').

[2] Founded *c.*901, the New Minster was immediately to the north of the Old Minster. William describes the New Minster and the nunnery at greater length in ch. 78. For the charter issued in favour of the New Minster, reputedly the work of Æthelwald, and for its still-extant *Book of Life* see Loyn, *The English Church*, p. 13.

[3] For whether the expulsion of the clergy was the work of Æthelwald or of king Edgar see Stenton, *Anglo-Saxon England*, p. 451.

[4] The translation of Swithhun's remains from outside the west door of the Old Minster to a more fitting shrine inside the church on 15 July 971 increased greatly both the prestige of the Old Minster and of Swithhun himself, who up till then had been an 'obscure ninth-century prelate' (*The Blackwell Encyclopaedia*, s.v. 'Swithun').

day the bones were taken out of the tomb and placed in a box. Large numbers of people rushed up. They made their prayers to St Swithhun until there was a huge pile of them. But no one complained of being disappointed. All their prayers were granted and came true. In the end the number of miraculous cures worked there on all kinds of illness was greater than human memory can recall happening anywhere else. The saint received the surname of 'Pious' for being quick to help anyone who prayed to him, unless faith was lacking. His goodness, which began long ago, has not died out even in our own day. I myself have seen the miracle of a man, whose eyes had been gouged out by violent robbers, receive back his vision unclouded through the merits of Swithhun, when either those eyes or some others (for they had been thrown rather far away) had been replaced. His eyelids, which had been disfigured by the marks of the dagger points, were a sign of that past calamity. The constant desire of the saint is that God should be glorified in all things. He does not allow anyone cured by him to wallow in the morass of the flesh, unless he wants to be plunged back into his old disease. Once, even, when the monks were tired out from the frequency of the miracles and were making difficulties about their lack of sleep owing to some miracle happening in the middle of the night, their laziness did not escape the eye of the saint as it looked upon them from afar.[1] Straightaway he stood by the bed of Æthelwald, who was asleep at the court of the king, and threatened to take a holiday from performing his cures, if the monks persisted in thinking they should cease praising God. Why should they fall asleep praising God, when he himself was awake for their salvation?

Though not even Æthelwald himself took a rest from performing miracles. The two saints, one alive and one dead, seemed to be rivalling one another in piety, as on all sides their miracles abounded, and this man had his faith strengthened and that man his health restored. Æthelwald himself, tricked by his servants, had drunk a deadly poison, but, just when it was spreading through his body and feeding on his vitals, by faith he quenched its force. He recovered a vessel containing olive oil when it was lost, and increased its contents when it was found. With a word he bound with invisible bonds the arms of a raving monk, and just with his blessing undid the thongs when the monk confessed his sins. Another monk, standing on the edge of a high place, happened to fall over, but Æthelwald's prayer placed a hand beneath him as he fell and restored him to work. When his province was attacked by famine owing to the barrenness of the soil, he ordered the cathedral plate to be broken up and distributed, protesting that it was better that precious metals should be used for the hunger of the poor than for the pomp of the priests. After building a new church, which had long been an ambition of his, he was lifted up from this world, to the great sorrow of his monks, but with none on his own part. He himself rejoices, high in glory, but many of his religious foundations were destroyed after his death, and all were diminished.

---

[1] Æthelwald had told the monks to sing a Te Deum for each cure, and two hundred people had been cured within ten days.

Chapter 76 Ælfheah, bishop of Winchester 984–1005

Æthelwald was succeeded by that good man, another Ælfheah. I have said something about him already,[1] and now I would like to chat about him at greater length. As a bookish boy he frequented the schools. As a young man he changed his clothes and took the habit of a monk at Deerhurst,[2] then a small monastery and now just an empty shell of the past. Although he had taken on the rule of the monastic life at Deerhurst, he soon hurried to Bath[3] in his eager search for something deeper, and there, enclosed within the walls of a private cell, he tasted the spiritual food of heaven. He attracted many good monks to Bath, although, as happens in a large body, they brought with them a corrupting evil. For one of them, without father Ælfheah's knowledge, would keep up his carousing all night long and be still at his drinking at daybreak. God did not put up with this for very long, but in the middle of the night struck down dead this standard-bearer of faction in a house which breathed religion. The saint at the time had his prayers interrupted, for he heard sounds coming from the building as of men being attacked and defending themselves. Surprised at this strange event and holding his breath, he gradually approached the door. Then, through the chinks of the windows, he saw two huge demons battering the life out of a body with repeated hammer blows, while the victim begged for help with piteous cries. But his attackers said in reply, 'You did not listen to God, and we shall not listen to you.' After Ælfheah had told the others about this in the morning, it is not surprising that his drinking companions turned teetotal.

And so on the death of the bishop of Winchester, archbishop Dunstan made Ælfheah bishop in his place. Dunstan was moved to do this by an oracle he received from Andrew the apostle, who mentioned Ælfheah by name as his selection. As bishop he was wise in worldly matters, and simple in the things of God. He took care over the external, but did not neglect the internal. He exhumed the bones of his predecessor twelve years after his burial, persuaded to take this bold step by various powerful signs. And so that he might worthily adorn the see of such a father, as he followed in the footsteps of his holiness, whenever he sat at table, he would neither gorge his belly's maw nor seek the glory of total fasting. He never indulged in meat except when he was ill. He always sipped from the cup, which he brought just up to his lips. The thinness of his body, which scarcely stuck to his bones, showed how little food he ate. At night he would slip past his attendants and go on his own down to the river. Plunging in up to his thighs, he would stay there awake praising God, until the dawn grew pale in the sky, when he would return to his room past the still-sleeping attendants.

After twenty-two years as bishop of Winchester, he was translated against his will to Canterbury. This was because, so people said, he was being removed

---

[1] See ch. 20.
[2] Deerhurst (Gloucestershire) is first mentioned c.804 in the will of Æthelric, son of Æthelmund.
[3] Founded as a nunnery in 675, Bath had become an all-male community by 758.

from an honourable office with which he was familiar and being loaded with a heavier burden. In fact Cœnwulf, abbot of Peterborough, had bought the bishopric of Winchester, although he did not long enjoy this bold sacrilege, for he was dead before two years were out. Ælfheah journeyed to Rome to receive the pallium from the pope and was crossing the Alps. While staying the night in a certain village he was attacked by a crowd of country people who stripped him of all his goods. But at once a fire got hold of the houses. No one knew what caused it, but, helped by the gusts of wind it was threatening the destruction of the whole village. The rough villagers, acknowledging, though with difficulty, their crime, ran after Ælfheah and caught up with him just as he had left the village to continue on his journey. In respectful reverence they asked his pardon and restored his property. Ælfheah, who could always be easily persuaded, made the sign of the cross from directly opposite the fire. At once the flames turned in upon themselves and died down, and the whole blaze became a pile of cold ash. When Ælfheah was in Rome, he foresaw and prophesied the death of his successor at Winchester, with no one, as I have said elsewhere,[1] bringing him the news of it. Then he returned to his see and spent seven happy years as archbishop, at the end of which he was thrown into chains by the Danish invaders and was inmate of a prison for seven months. You must look elsewhere for the reasons for his imprisonment. Meanwhile a deadly virus attacked the Danes and laid low in droves the enemies of Ælfheah, death coming so speedily that it preceded the feeling of pain. The stink of unburied bodies infected the air, and the noisome atmosphere produced a pestilence even for the remainder who seemed healthy. There was no end to the countless people who collapsed until Ælfheah, in response to prayers, drove the plague away and restored health by means of the bread which he had blessed for communicants. Despite this the Danes showed no thanks for his help but stoned to death their saviour. Some indeed, being better disposed towards the archbishop, fought to get his remains buried, but for some time were opposed by his killers. But when the matter was brought to judgement, it was agreed that if the dead tree which chance had provided[2] should come to life again through the saint's blood on the day after the hearing, the Christians could bury the body as they thought fit. And this came to pass. For in the morning the tree, which had even by that time lost its bark, was found to have come to life again, clothed in flowers and swelling buds. And so permission was then given for the body to be peacefully buried at St Paul's in London. Ten years later, at the orders and under the supervision of king Cnut, the body was exhumed, found to be without any corruption, and taken to glorify the seat of his archbishopric. The freshness of the blood and the incorruption of the body has lasted to my own day and has been seen very recently. Nor indeed did any of Ælfheah's murderers escape paying the penalty. I could give the actual details of their punishments, if I did not feel

---

[1] In ch. 20.
[2] Presumably to serve as a temporary burial place for the body.

reluctant to describe the woes of the unfortunate. The unhappy persecutor is sufficiently trampled upon when the martyr in his glory towers above him.

Chapter 77 Æthelwald to Walkelin (1007–1098)

The successors of Ælfheah in the see of Winchester were Æthelwald, Ælfsige, Ælfwine and Stigand. Stigand, it was often said, was removed and then succeeded by Walkelin, king William's appointment.[1] Walkelin's good achievements, which surpassed expectation, will keep him from disappearing into the mists of time, as long as the episcopal see lasts at Winchester. Maurilius, archbishop of Rouen, when meditating on his journey beyond the grave, had advised Walkelin to pledge himself to the religious life, on the grounds that there was hope that Walkelin had the potential to achieve great things, if he once found a position in which his abilities could shine. Walkelin justified the promise which the archbishop had seen in him and achieved unexpected results in the development of religious life, in the numbers of monks[2] and in the buildings he put up. At first indeed the stranger from overseas had disliked the monks. But he was easily persuaded to change his mind, and then he often bewailed the hidden aversion he had felt for them. In the end he cherished them like sons, loved them like brothers and honoured them as lords, not denying them any help or friendship just because his clothes were different. He found fault with no one, declaring that he would spatter the glory of his episcopal position with ugly spots, if he sank so low as to abuse inferiors. He did commit one very great sin, robbing the monks of three hundred librates[3] of land and assigning them to his own use and that of his successors.

He appointed as prior of Winchester a certain Godefrey of Cambrai, a man famous equally for his life of religion and for his writings.[4] His literary abilities are shown in the easy, friendly style of his letters, in his verses in praise of the primates of England and especially in the satirical epigrams which he composed. How he polished up and made glow with the ancient customs of his own country the whole divine office which had fallen into disuse with the passing of time! He sketched the attractive outlines of a standard for the religious life and hospitality of the monks, who today still follow Godefrey's principles in both, so that we can heap our praises upon them with almost complete justification. The house provides hospitality for those arriving by land or sea. People can stay as long as they like, welcomed as they are by a never failing purse and charity that never tires. Among all this the saint had an inner core of humility. He possessed a unique treasure store of philosophy, but brought out nothing from it which did not have a fragrance of sweet humility.

---

[1] Walkelin was reputedly a kinsman of the king and his clerk.
[2] Walkelin's scheme of replacing monks by secular clergy, mentioned in ch. 44, presumably came later in his twenty-eight years as bishop of Winchester.
[3] A librate was a variable quantity of land, producing a yearly value of one libra or pound sterling.
[4] He became prior *c*.1082. There is also an account of him in *The Deeds of the Kings* 5:444.

These praises of him can only seem inadequate, although there are very few, even among those with a minimum amount of bookish learning, who do not regard others as falling short of their own powers, as they strut around arrogantly displaying their knowledge of literature. Indeed, in order that this saintly soul should not lack any element of perfection, he had to keep to his bed for many years, while his sins were burnt out of him in the furnace of a long-lasting illness.

Chapter 78 The religious houses of Winchester and its diocese

There is in this same city of Winchester a minster, built once upon a time by king Alfred. He also established secular canons in it, being persuaded to do so by a man from Flanders called Grimbald, who later was buried there with great ceremony and who nowadays is believed and said to be a saint. But Æthelwald of blessed memory removed the canons and replaced them with monks, giving them Æthelgar as their abbot, about whom I have already spoken.[1] In order to finance the offices of this monastery Æthelgar bought sufficient land from the bishop and the canons of the time, paying a standard gold coin for every foot. But the old minster and this new foundation were so close together, with their walls actually touching, that the voices of the one choir would disturb the other. So the unpleasant antipathy arising from this and other matters unearthed very many reasons why they caused excessive offence to each other. So recently this new minster has been rebuilt outside the city,[2] where the monks live a more peaceful existence and can build up their own fame more freely. Æthelwald also built a convent for nuns in Winchester, putting in charge of them a virgin of advanced years called Æthelthryth. She had often prophesied about Æthelwald, basing her forecast on the dream which his mother had had about the golden eagle.[3] There had been a convent on this spot before, in which Eadburg, daughter of king Edward the Elder,[4] had lived and died, but by then it was almost in ruins. When she was barely three, Eadburg had given a remarkable proof of her future holiness. Her father had wanted to find out whether his little girl would turn towards God or the world. He set out in the dining room the adornments of the different ways of life, on this side a chalice and the Gospels, on the other bangles and necklaces. The little girl was brought in by the nurse and sat on her father's knee. He told her to choose which she wanted. With a fierce look she spat out the things of the world, and immediately crawling on hands and knees towards the Gospels and chalice adored them in girlish innocence. The people sitting around cried aloud, pouring kisses on the girl at these signs of future holiness. Her father honoured his offspring with more restrained kisses and said, 'Go where heaven calls you, follow the bridegroom you have chosen and a blessing be upon your

[1] In ch. 20.
[2] In 1111 by Henry I, under the name of Hyde Abbey. For its original foundation see p. 110 n. 2.
[3] See p. 109.
[4] King of the West Saxons 899–924.

going.' And so, when she put on the habit of a nun, she zealously invited all her friends to share her love for her calling. Her royal lineage did not make her pause, for she considered it a noble thing to bend the knee in the service of Christ. Her holiness increased as she got older. Her humility grew as she grew, till she would even secretly at night pick up the shoes of various nuns, and when she had carefully cleaned and polished them put them again by their beds. Countless miracles during her life and after her death bear witness to the devotion of her heart and the integrity of her body. The keepers of the sanctuaries[1] will give you a better account than me of these miracles in their own words.

There are three monasteries in the diocese of the Winchester bishopric, Chertsey, Romsey and Wherwell. I have spoken about Chertsey.[2] We know that Wherwell was built in honour of the Holy Cross by Ælfthryth, wife of king Edgar, in her compunction for the cruel death of her stepson Edward, whose confidante and patron she had been. The monastery of Romsey was founded by the most excellent king Edgar. I know that the bodies of two virgins, Merewynn and Ælfflæd, are buried there. I do not know their histories, but I am not so much omitting them as reserving them for a proper account, if I happen to come across them.

Chapter 79 The bishops of Sherborne: Aldhelm to Ealhstan (705–867)

In the division of the bishopric of the West Saxons it has been a matter of public observation that the bishop of Winchester had two districts, Hampshire and Surrey, and that the other bishop at Sherborne looked after Wiltshire, Dorset, Berkshire, Somerset, Devon and Cornwall. Sherborne is a small town which does not attract either because of the numbers of its inhabitants or the charm of its position. Indeed it is a matter for wonder and almost for shame that the episcopal see lasted there for so many centuries. Nowadays it has been changed from a bishopric to an abbacy,[3] a move not unknown in our times, when strife and lust are spoiling everything, and goodness is laughed at as something to be ashamed of. The first bishop of Sherborne was father Aldhelm. I mention him here just to give his position. I have nowhere found a full account of his life. But there is a great deal of evidence for it, and, as to conceal this from posterity would be a crime, I have decided, God willing, in the final pages of this little work to deal with this material at greater leisure. The bishops of Sherborne that came after him were Forthhere, Herewald, Æthelmod, Denefrith, Wigheort and Ealhstan.

Ealhstan was bishop at the time of Ecgberht king of the West Saxons and of his son Æthelwulf and beyond that.[4] He had great political influence and was

[1] Some of Æthelthryth's bones were at Pershore Abbey. See ch. 162.
[2] In ch. 73.
[3] The episcopal seat remained at Sherborne until 1078.
[4] Ealhstan was bishop 824–67.

an important advisor on state matters. For king Ecgberht he subdued the men of Kent and the East Angles by his military campaigns, but seeing that Æthelwulf was of a softer disposition, he spurred him into a knowledge of his kingdom by his careful advice. Against the Danes, who were then invading the island for the first time, he aroused the lazy and even gathered together his own army, supplying the money from his own treasury. The reader of the chronicles will find an account there of his many exploits against the Danes, begun with determination and brought to a successful outcome. He passed fifty years of his life as bishop, happy to have been in the battle for good works for so long a time. I would be praising him unrestrainedly, were it not for the fact that, in the grip of a very human greed, he seized possession of what did not belong to him when he subjected our monastery to his schemes. To this day we feel the effects of the mischief caused by his effrontery, even though, since he died, the monastery has completely escaped the rapacity of bishops right down to our own times, when it has experienced a similar crisis.[1] It is so irresponsible to set an evil precedent. Its originator may die, but his example lives on. The perverse mind loves to learn of the evil action committed by another, and so hear of an evil action he can do himself. In fact there was less shame for the monks of that time sighing for their stolen liberty than there is for us having lost it, especially since they regained it immediately. Also Ealhstan, as our sources tell us, was as outstandingly generous as he was violently avaricious, whereas the robbers who take our property both plunder us and keep us oppressed, so that we are not even allowed to give free expression to our sorrow. You can see how powerful Ealhstan was by the fact that he kept the king himself[2] out of his kingdom when he was returning from Rome, and, with the king's son set up as shadow ruler, did not allow the old man to return to his own until peace had been established by his arbitration. Ealhstan left his church magnificently enriched by estates acquired on all sides. If I were to tell you the size of them, you would marvel at his greed – or good luck.

Chapter 80 Heahmund to Werstan (868–937)

He was followed as bishop by Heahmund, Æthelheah, Wulfsige, Asser and Sigehelm. Both the last two are known to have been bishops in the time of king Alfred, who was the fourth son of Æthelwulf. Asser was called from St Davids to be bishop. His learning was by no means completely contemptible, seeing that he expounded in simpler language the *Consolation of Philosophy* by Boethius, a task necessary then, but laughable now. But Asser had no choice, for the king had commanded it, in order that he might translate it more easily into English. Sigehelm was sent overseas on almonry duties for the king, even getting as far as to St Thomas's in India. Something which could cause wonder for people of this generation is that his journey deep into India was a

---

[1] Ealhstan appropriated the revenues of the monastery at Malmesbury. From 1117 to 1139 Roger, bishop of Salisbury, did the same thing.
[2] King Æthelwulf in 856. The shadow ruler was his son Æthelbald.

marvellously prosperous one, as he brought back exotic precious stones, in which the land abounds, and some of them can still be seen in precious objects in the church. On the death of Sigehelm the bishopric of Wessex was vacant for seven years because of enemy attacks. But later, archbishop Plegmund and king Edward, the son of Alfred, were forced by threats and edicts from pope Formosus to make five bishops instead of two. I have often referred to this,[1] but it is still sensible to repeat them here in order to give a complete list. Æthelhelm was at Wells, Eadwulf at Crediton,[2] Æthelstan in Cornwall, Frithustan at Winchester and Werstan at Sherborne. So Æthelhelm was in charge of Somerset, Eadwulf of Devon and Æthelstan of Cornwall, though I nowhere find the names of his successors. The three counties of Dorset, Berkshire and Wiltshire were left for Werstan. But soon afterwards, in the lifetime of the same king, Wiltshire got its own bishop, a man called Æthelstan, who had his see at Ramsbury. Werstan, so the story goes, was slain by the pagans in the battle fought by king Æthelstan against Analavus. The king, as I have said elsewhere, deliberately withdrew.[3] When the bishop arrived at the war with his forces, he had no fear of an ambush on the grassy, level plain and pitched camp on the exact spot from which the king had retreated. But Analavus had reconnoitred the place the day before, arrived by night with his forces at the ready and immediately wiped out all he found.

Chapter 81 Wulfsige as bishop of Sherborne (943–958)

The bishops after Werstan were Æthelbald, Alfred and Wulfsige. Archbishop Dunstan, when bishop of London, had made Wulfsige abbot of Westminster, as a small monastery for twelve monks had been established in the place where once Mellitus had founded a church for St Peter. Wulfsige carried out the office entrusted to him with such holiness and judgement that he was given the position of bishop at Sherborne. Once in his episcopal see he very soon ejected the clergy and brought in monks. Amid the flurry of activity from the bishops of his day he did not want to seem to be sleeping.[4] He did not provide for the livelihood of the monks with gifts from his episcopal revenues but raised the requisite money from outside. He also thought of appointing an abbot, but the monks protested that they could not be without Wulfsige's sweet sovereignty as long as he lived. Wulfsige gave in to them, though against his will, and openly declared that the decision would be the start of great troubles for his successors. His life gives us many clear proofs of his holiness, and his death a special one. For when death was now close at hand and he was knocking on its gates, the eyes of his mind were opened and he loudly chanted the words, 'Look! I see the heavens opened, and Jesus standing at the right hand of the

---

[1] For example, *The Deeds of the Kings* 2:129.
[2] Yorke gives reasons why Crediton was chosen (*Wessex in the Early Middle Ages*, p. 210).
[3] See p. 15.
[4] Similar replacements of clergy by monks had been carried out by Æthelwald at Winchester, Dunstan at Canterbury and Oswald at Worcester.

goodness of God.'[1] The man who could borrow the words of the first, most holy martyr was a venerable and holy soul, and happy in that he saw the heavens opened and deserved to enter. His crosier and various other episcopal insignia are still preserved at Sherborne, giving us, as I might say, a living simulacrum of his good sense and humility.

Chapter 82 The bishopric of Ælfwald (1045–1058)

Wulfsige was succeeded by Ælfwald, Æthelric, Æthelsige, Berhtwine, Ælfmær, Birhtwine and his brother Ælfwald. This Ælfwald had been a monk at Winchester before becoming bishop of Sherborne, and he placed there an image of St Swithhun, lifting high the torch of veneration. All men agree that he lived a most respected life. Since the time of the Danes meals in England were served in the most elaborate fashion, but Ælfwald always used a wooden bowl without any too oily food in it and a very small cup, which had been washed out with water so that all taste of beer had been removed. I myself have heard a white-haired priest of great reliability recalling with tears of joy his good memories of Ælfwald. He did not forget the story of how both before and after Ælfwald's death no one was ever able to fall asleep with impunity while sitting in the bishop's seat, for the sleeper would immediately spring up, terrified by grim-looking ghosts who angrily asked why he was unworthily occupying the bishop's place. Many people had had some sight of this. A bitter quarrel had arisen between Ælfwald and earl Godwine, I do not know for what cause. On the day appointed for a hearing the matter was not resolved but was heading for the courts, and the bishop, as he departed after a heated exchange, shouted this threat to the earl, 'By my Lady St Mary it will be bad for you that you have upset me.' The bishop arrived home, but had scarcely set foot on the ground, after dismounting from his horse, when to his surprise a servant of the earl turned up at a gallop, the heaving of his horse's flanks showing how fast he had ridden. Falling on his knees and with tears in his eyes he asked the bishop to return. Immediately after Ælfwald's departure his master had felt a burning within and could hardly move his tongue. The bishop was still angry and said, 'By my Lady St Mary, it will go badly for him!' But he was won over by the united prayers and petitions of the people standing around, forgave the earl his sin, said a blessing and cured his illness. The same priest also used to tell how the bishop had shown a ready devotion to the service of St Cuthbert. He would weep tears of joy at every mention of him, and hardly a moment passed when he was not holding in his heart this antiphon concerning the saint, or repeating it with his lips, or giving it expression in his deeds:

Cuthbert, holy bishop,
Perfect man in all things,
Monk amid the turmoil,
Worth respect from all.

[1] Acts 7:55, the words of Stephen.

As day by day the love in his heart for Cuthbert received sweet increase and the flame of its goodness could not be contained in it, he set out for the sacred city of Durham. This will seem very bold to you, but, when he got there, he removed the covering of the tomb and talked trustingly to Cuthbert as to a friend. Then he placed beside it a little gift as a token of his everlasting love and went away. And now when the moment of his death was at hand, for as long as his voice had strength, he sang the antiphon. When his speech failed, he signalled with his hand to the others to chant it. And so with his last breath he showed the love which he had towards the saint. After his death the diocese of Wilton with its see at Ramsbury was again united with the see of Sherborne. I will tell you what happened, when I have first given the names of the bishops.

Chapter 83 The see of Ramsbury (909–1058)

The first bishop of Ramsbury was Æthelstan, the second Oda who afterwards became archbishop, the third Oswulf, the fourth Wulfgar and the fifth Ælfstan. Ælfstan was originally a monk of St Æthelwald at Abingdon.[1] Æthelwald's biographer includes this miracle to illustrate Ælfstan's obedience.

> Among Æthelwald's monks was a brother called Ælfstan. He was a straightforward character who had great powers of obedience. The abbot ordered him to supervise the meals for the craftsmen of the monastery. He did this job extremely thoroughly. Every day he cooked the meat with his own hand, and carefully lit the fire for the workmen. He would even fetch water and get the dishes clean again, though the abbot thought he was doing this with the help and companionship of another servant. One day the abbot was making his customary tour of the monastery when he unexpectedly came across this brother standing by a cauldron of boiling water. The abbot saw that all the dishes were clean and the floor swept. He was delighted at this and said to him, 'Brother Ælfstan, you have concealed this obedience from me. But if you are such a soldier as you show yourself to be, put your hand into that boiling water and boldly pull out a crust for me from the bottom.' Ælfstan obeyed the order. The fierce heat yielded to his daring faith and he suffered no harm. Afterwards we saw Ælfstan as abbot of Abingdon. He was then even elevated to a bishopric, and finally found a holy rest in the Lord.

Sixth was Sigeric and seventh Ælfric, who both, as I have said earlier,[2] became archbishops of Canterbury. Eighth was Berhtwald, a former monk of Glastonbury, who administered the see for many years from the time of king Æthelred right up to the last Edward.[3] In the days of king Cnut, he was one night at Glastonbury, keeping a strict holy vigil as was his practice, when he

---

[1] Æthelwald became bishop of Winchester in 963. His biographer was Ælfric, a monk at Winchester. For Ælfric's writings see Loyn, *The English Church*, pp. 25–6.
[2] Ch. 20.
[3] From 995 to 1045.

had a divine vision. For he had begun thinking about the well-nigh extinct royal line of England, a subject which frequently caused him anxiety, and as he thought about it, sleep crept upon him. And, miraculously, he was swept up to heaven and saw Peter, chief of the apostles, holding by the hand Edward, son of king Æthelred, who was then an exile in Normandy, and consecrating him king. A life of celibacy was appointed for him and a fixed span of twenty-four years was allotted him for completing his period of kingship. When Berhtwald bewailed Edward's lack of descendants, Peter replied, 'The kingdom of England belongs to God, and after your death, he will provide a king of his choice.' When he had finished his life's journey, Berhtwald was buried at Glastonbury. He had added many estates and revenues to its possessions, and had also been very generous to our monastery.

Edward was king at the time of Berhtwald's death, and he thought of giving the bishopric immediately to his chaplain, Hereman, a native of Flanders.[1] But its poverty did not match Hereman's big ideas, or rather his greed, for Ramsbury did not have a college of priests or the means to support one,[2] so he begged the king, who had thought him worthy of the honour, not to allow him to live in a dishonourable fashion: his predecessors had been natives of England, whereas he was living a foreigner's life, with no wealth from his parents with which to sustain it: so he asked the king to allow him to establish his see at the monastery in Malmesbury,[3] as, fortunately for him, the abbot had recently died. The king thought this was the easy way out, a course he was always more ready to follow than was wise, and considered that the grant could be legitimately made. But two days later he cancelled the grant. For before Hereman could be fixed in possession of the monastery, the sharp-minded monks, on hearing of the miscarriage of justice which had taken place in the king's court, had gone in the utmost haste to earl Godwine and his son. They in their turn, disturbed by this novel piece of unfairness, went to the king and got him to change his mind. This was not difficult, as they were nobles with very great power, and were helped by the justice of their case and the lack of determination in the king. So Hereman was removed before he had been clearly established. Filled with shame he left England in a rage. Soon after-wards he renounced the world and became a monk at St Bertin.[4] It was an illness that persuaded him to do this, plus the fact that he was angry with fortune at the lack of success of his worldly ambitions. But as often happens on such occasions, his sudden attack of religion grew cooler by the day and he thought about returning to England. He was used to servants and to feeding on luxuries, and he was tired of being without the comforts which he had known all his life. Also an encouraging rumour had reached his ears of the death of Ælfwald, bishop of Sherborne, whose see he had been waiting to unite with his own, as promised long ago by queen Eadgyth. He came all the more quickly

---

[1] Edward had spent twenty years in exile in Normandy during Cnut's reign.
[2] The shire now seems to be too small a division to support a bishop and his household.
[3] A well-endowed abbey, as Book 5 shows.
[4] A monastery in St Omer.

because of this, and found things had happened according to his hopes. By now his bitter enemy, Godwine, had died and his son, Harold, in his panting eagerness to be adopted by Edward, had become a supporter of the king's wishes on this and on other matters.

So Hereman received the complete see of Sherborne with its three counties on the grant of king Edward. Indeed he lived so long that he outlived his benefactor and lasted as bishop until the times of William. During his reign, when canon law decreed that episcopal sees should be moved from towns to the cities, he moved his seat from Sherborne to Salisbury.[1] This is a fortress like a city, situated on high ground and surrounded by a mighty wall. However rich in other resources, it suffers from such a shortage of water that merchants have to struggle up the hill to sell it there. He began work on a new church, but old age and death overtook him before it was time to dedicate it. But under his successor, the saintly Osmund,[2] the church was finished and suitably adorned as well. Priests famous for their learning came from all sides. Not only did they find a warm welcome, but they were even treated with generosity to make them stay. In the end, more than anywhere else, Salisbury was a beacon for the fame of its canons, who were equally adept in music and literature. A supply of books was collected, since the bishop himself was never tired of writing them or binding them when they were written. He was of pre-eminent purity. Even fickle fame would blush to tell lies about his goodness. Though this did mean that he seemed harsher than was just to repentant sinners, as he punished more severely in others what he did not find in himself. He was free of ambition. He did not foolishly lose his own possessions, or seek those of others. He did not burden with heavy payments the abbeys situated in his diocese. He is believed to have atoned for whatever faults he may have caught from contact with the world's stain by the patience he showed as he wasted away before his death in a long-lasting illness.

Chapter 84 Cerne

In the county of Dorset are the abbeys of Cerne and Milton for men, and Shaftesbury for women, besides some which have been completely destroyed or greatly diminished. The story of the foundation of Cerne is as follows. After Augustine, first teacher of the English, had won Kent for Christ, he travelled through the remaining provinces of England, as far as the power of king Æthelberht reached. For he had under his control, as I have said elsewhere,[3] all of Britain inhabited by the English apart from just Northumbria. So Augustine moved in on Dorset, won many souls from being lost to the devil, and increased the number of Christians. But his goodness met an obstacle at Cerne. He had stirred up the jealousy of the devil, who was feeling pain at the

[1] Around 1070.
[2] Osmund had been one of the two bishops to ask Anselm's forgiveness before the archbishop left for Rome in 1097. See p. 63. William gives rather a brief account of his own diocesan bishop.
[3] *The Deeds of the Kings* 1:9.

numbers of souls being won by Augustine, and the inhabitants, with minds ablaze, attacked Augustine and his companions, disfigured him with serious injuries, even fixing fish tails on his clothes, forced him back, pushed him away and drove him out. He bore their insults patiently and with self-control, happy that he was acting in the name of Jesus, and in order not to increase the rage of these unhappy people, he shook the dust of his feet upon them and went some three miles off. And there, removed from the whirlwind of persecution, he regained peace of mind, and had an inward vision of the presence of God. With his face aglow, he said to his followers, 'I see God. He will give us thanks, and will pour upon these crazed people the spirit of repentance.' No sooner had he spoken than the inhabitants came up at a run, begging forgiveness for their actions and promising to believe. This event or rather this saying gave the place its name. For it was called Cernel from two words, one Hebrew and one Latin. 'Hel' is the Hebrew word for God and Augustine said that he saw or 'discerned' God. His words turned out to be true, because in an instant the people who previously had showed such rage changed their minds and believed. Also at Cerne, when there was no water for baptism, at the command of the archbishop a spring gushed forth from some hidden source. It is still today a famous spring for the people of the place, both because it was provided by Augustine and because it is a convenient water supply for them.

In a later generation Eadwald, brother of Edmund, king and martyr, lived the life of a hermit at Cerne, existing solely on bread and water. He was tired, so men said, of the delights of the world, in which misfortune had overtaken both him and his brother. For it often happens that the noble spirit is warned by the disasters of life to turn its attention more towards God, who knows not how to be disappointed or to disappoint. No doubt the highest virtue is to want the good for its own sake, but the second level of virtue is to be able to be compelled to do it, so that, in my opinion, people think as highly of Paul, who was driven to the good by the lashes of the whip, as of Peter, who willingly and without delay ran towards his master when he called him.[1] After a life devoted to religion, Eadwald was buried there, because of the high opinion men had of his sanctity, and so years later provided for a very rich man called Æthelweard the opportunity of building a monastery to St Peter on the spot.[2] It is not as small as men think, but in fact an extensive foundation. If only the people concerned were handing it to the servants of God instead of to their own worthless followers! But in our day ambition has so changed everything in England for the worse, that the resources which the men of old generously gave to the monasteries are being dissipated to satisfy the greed of their owners, rather than serving the needs of the monks, their guests and the poor. But we can be sure that the donors will not be deprived of their reward, so those bad men should think how their actions will one day be weighed in the divine scales.

[1] One is reminded of God's words at the end of George Herbert's poem *The Pulley*, 'If goodnesse leads him not, yet wearinesse / May tosse him to my breast'.
[2] Cerne was founded during the monastic revival of the tenth century.

Chapter 85 Milton

The church at Milton was built by king Æthelstan for the soul of his brother
Edwin. He had been led astray by evil advice and exiled Edwin from England. I
have described his end elsewhere.[1] Æthelstan placed at Milton many relics of
the saints which he had bought in Brittany,[2] the most remarkable being those
of the blessed Samson, once archbishop of Dol,[3] a man of very great holiness
and clearly highly regarded by God. I could recount some of his virtues here,
except that they are well known anyway and I have my hands full with my
account of the miracles done by English saints.

Chapter 86 Shaftesbury

Shaftesbury is only a town, though once it was a city. It is situated on a steep
hill. Evidence of its antiquity is given by a stone in the chapter house of the
nunnery. It was transferred there from the remains of the ancient wall and
reads, 'King Alfred built this town in 880, in the eighth year of his reign.'
Ælfgifu, the wife of Edmund, who was Alfred's great-grandson, built the
nunnery,[4] and her bodily remains were placed there after her death. She was a
woman always intent on good works. She was so pious and loving that she
would even secretly release criminals who had been openly condemned by the
gloomy verdict of a jury. For her the expensive clothes, which entice some
women to cast shame aside, were material for munificence, and she would give
away the costliest dresses to some poor woman, the moment she had seen her.
With Ælfgifu even the envious could only praise her physical beauty and her
skill in handiwork, as there was nothing they could criticise. I have spoken
elsewhere of the grace of prophecy which God poured on her.[5] In her lifetime
she performed the works of virtue, but after her death miracles glittered. I once
composed these verses about them:

> She bore sharp pain for several years,
> Then gave her soul, refined, to God.
> Her blessed remains, their journey done,
> God's mercy marked with countless signs.
> The blind and deaf, who worship them,
> Restored to health, attest her work.
> The lame who come walk upright home,
> The rich return made wise, the crazed made sane.[6]

[1] In *The Deeds of the Kings* 2:140 William describes how Edwin was sent to sea in an old open boat.
[2] Æthelstan's purpose in buying relics is clearly explained by Jonathan Boardman in the *Church Times* (6 July 2001), p. 11: 'For the medieval mind, power found its earthly expression in the authority of the monarch, and its heavenly manifestation in the abiding presence of bits and pieces of sanctity. Monarchs collected relics on a vast scale to emphasise the link further.'
[3] In the diocese of Tours.
[4] By the time of the conquest Shaftesbury and Wilton were the two richest nunneries.
[5] In *The Deeds of the Kings* 2:154 Ælfgifu makes a prophecy about the king's sons.
[6] William's verses are in trochaic tetrameters.

The body of St Edward lies in the nunnery, or rather it lay there.[1] He was the grandson of this saint by her son Edgar. He was murdered, though innocent, by a stepmother's guile, and lifted up to heaven.[2] He was first buried at Wareham, a town near the sea, and not far from Corfe, where he was killed. His body lay there for three years. His enemies had envied his royal renown while he was alive, and after his death they begrudged him a burial in holy ground. But God's power was at hand to raise to triumph the guiltless one by the fame of his miracles. For at his grave lights shone from the sky, the lame man walked, the dumb man used his tongue again, all illnesses alike gave way to health. The news telling of what the martyr had done spread through England. His murderess was worried and attempted to go to his grave. But the animal which usually carried her and which had always been quicker than the wind, outstripping the breezes themselves, as the saying goes, now at God's command stood motionless. Her servants attacked it with whips, but their efforts were in vain. She changed animals, but the same thing happened. Eventually her dull brain grasped the meaning of the omen. So she allowed another to do what she could not do herself, and the sacred remains were lifted from their ignominious grave and taken in great pomp to Shaftesbury. Later on part of his body was carried to Leominster, and part to Abingdon. His power was great everywhere but it shone especially at Shaftesbury, thanks to his virtues and its holy choir of virgins. The place took a name from him, and by metonymy was popularly called St Edward's. Indeed his lung is still miraculously on display there. His body has long since decayed, but the lung beats on, its vigour unimpaired. But because almost all miracles are open to rational criticism, some people distort this one with an unfavourable interpretation, arguing with Suetonius[3] as a witness that if a lung has been soaked with poison, you would expect it to be incorruptible, as then neither putrefaction nor even fire can destroy it. They admit that Edward was stabbed by a dagger while he was drinking, but maintain that the poison had been given him to drink because he was thirsty, and that its force was only forestalled by the sword. But I have studied the matter very carefully, and my verdict is that they are wrong, as poison could not have reached his vital parts so quickly, and especially as Suetonius makes his comment not about the lung but about the heart. So let it count as a miracle from heaven, which cannot be spoiled by the evasions of men.

Chapter 87 Wilton

The monasteries in the county of Wiltshire are Malmesbury for men and Wilton and Amesbury for women. I intend to speak about Malmesbury

---

[1] Excavations at Shaftesbury in the 1930s uncovered what are almost certainly Edward's remains. The excavator promised to donate them to whichever church would provide them with a proper shrine. Such a shrine, with accompanying veneration, was finally provided in the 1980s by a Russian Orthodox church at Brookwood Cemetery outside London, where the relics are still to be found.
[2] Edward the Martyr was king of England 975–8, his stepmother was Ælfthryth. Stenton, *Anglo-Saxon England*, p. 373, puts a case for his stepmother's innocence.
[3] *The Twelve Caesars* 4:1, where the victim is Germanicus, father of the emperor Caligula.

elsewhere. The only thing I know about Amesbury is that together with the convent at Wherwell[1] it was founded by Ælfthryth, murderess of St Edward, as an act of penitence. The body of St Melorius is buried there, though I know nothing about his family or sanctity. The nunnery at Wilton is adorned by being the resting place of the sweet remains of the bones of the blessed Eadgyth, the daughter of king Edgar, who cherishes it with her love. Wilton is a sizeable town, situated above the river Wylye, and so famous that it gives its name to the whole county. There Eadgyth, consecrated to God from her infancy, won the favour of God by her unspoilt maidenhood, and the favour of men by her careful service, eliminating any pride in her birth by the nobility of her mind, though I have heard from my elders that there was one thing about her which men regarded as a grave offence, namely that she tricked their sight by her splendid golden clothes. She would process, decked with garments more *haute couture* in appearance than was demanded by the sanctity of her profession. St Æthelwald openly criticised her for it, but it is said that she made an apt and witty reply, 'It is only men's conscience that waits for God's true and irrefutable judgement, for, as Augustine says, pride can exist in miserable rags as well. So I think that the mind can be as pure when clad in these garments of gold as in your tattered skins.'

St Dunstan was consecrating a chapel to the blessed Denis,[2] which she had built for love of the martyr, and during the ceremony he saw her across the church frequently stretching out her right thumb and painting the sign of the cross on her forehead. He was quite overjoyed and said, 'Never let this finger decay.' But at once, as masses were being said, he burst into such floods of tears that he alarmed a deacon standing near by as his voice broke into sobs. When he was asked the reason, he replied, 'This rose that now blooms will quickly wither; this bird, beloved of God, will quickly fly away, in six weeks from this day.' The events which immediately followed the bishop's prophecy proved it true. Eadgyth stuck to her noble purpose, and before her youth had ended she breathed her last on the day predicted, when she was just twenty-three. Soon afterwards St Dunstan saw in a vision in his sleep St Denis holding the virgin by the hand in friendly fashion and giving orders by heavenly edict that she should be honoured by her servants on earth just as she was highly regarded by her bridegroom and Lord in heaven. And as the miracles at her tomb increased in number as a result, the order was given that the maiden's body should be taken out. It was found to have dissolved completely into dust, apart from the finger and her belly and the parts below it. As St Dunstan was wondering about this, the virgin herself stood by him in a vision and said, 'It is no surprise that the rest of my body has decayed, since dead bodies normally dissolve into some secret recess of nature, and I myself, being only a girl, sinned with those parts of me. But no corruption justly destroys my belly, for it was never pricked by desire, and remained free of inebriation and couplings of the flesh.'

[1] In the Winchester diocese. See ch. 78.
[2] This is St Denis, martyr and patron saint of France.

Eadgyth's brother was king Æthelred, who was born almost t
England by his sloth. He was succeeded by the Dane, Cnut, a kin'
things done but who did not love the saints of England because of the hostility
of his race to them. He was at Wilton one Pentecost, when, with his customary
bloody-mindedness, he burst into a frightful peal of laughter against the virgin
herself: he would never believe that the daughter of king Edgar was a saint,
seeing that the king had surrendered himself to his vices and was a complete
slave to his lusts, while he ruled his subjects more like a tyrant. While Cnut,
venting his spleen, was belching out this barbaric crudity, archbishop
Æthelnoth, who was standing by, contradicted the king, so Cnut, more
angry than ever, ordered the tomb to be opened, so that he might see what
holiness the dead virgin could produce. The tomb was broken open, and the
dead girl, with a veil spread in front of her face, rose out of the grave up to her
waist, and seemed to make an attack on the contumacious king. Cnut took
fright and panicked at this, drew his head a long way backwards, and
collapsed in a heap on the ground, as his knees went weak and rubbery. The
fall knocked the wind out of his body. For a long time his breathing stopped,
and he was thought to be dead. But as his strength gradually came back, he
blushed for shame at the thought of death and the fact that, although severely
punished, he had been saved for penitence. So in very many places in England
Eadgyth's feast day is still celebrated,[1] and no one thinks that he could profane
it with impunity.

Her mother Wulfthryth lies buried in the same church. She was not actually
a nun, as popular opinion crazily supposes. She had merely put on a veil as her
own idea in her sudden fear of the king, before, as the story continues, the king
snatched away the veil and dragged her to his bed. Because he had touched a
woman, who had been a nun, if only potentially, he was reproved by St
Dunstan and made to do penance for seven years. Also, when Eadgyth had
been born, Wulfthryth did not develop a taste for repetitions of sexual
pleasure, but rather shunned them in disgust, so truly is she named and
celebrated as a saint.

Chapter 88 Abingdon

In the county of Berkshire there are two monasteries, at Abingdon and
Reading, both for men. The monastery at Abingdon was the work of Cissa,
father of Ine, and soon of Ine himself, king of the West Saxons, and of many
kings from the time of its beginning. But during the wanton, widespread
ravaging of the barbaric Danes in the time of king Alfred, the buildings of the
monastery at Abingdon were levelled to the ground. Furthermore the king was
pushed by the advice of wicked men to convert all the lands belonging to the
monastery to his own use and that of his advisers. Indeed king Eadred,
grandson of king Alfred, took pity on the deserted spot and gave back all

---

[1] On 16 September. There is a Latin life of Eadgyth by Goscelin of Canterbury.

the lost possessions into the hands of Æthelwald, whom he had appointed abbot there, thinking to do something for the soul of his grandfather at the same time. He developed such a love for the church that he himself had buildings measured out and the foundations laid, his plan being to construct there a monastery whose fame would spread far and wide. He would have accomplished these desires fairly well, if death had not too hastily removed him from our midst. Æthelwald, however, continued what Eadred had begun, but before he could put the finishing touches to the enterprise was elevated by king Edgar of famous memory to the bishopric of Winchester. But Ordgar, whom Æthelwald appointed abbot in his place, completed the efforts of his master, and the place grew rich and immensely famous, as each abbot added something new, so as not to be thought inferior to his predecessors. In our own day abbot Faricius has won especial renown for his improvements there.[1] Born in Tuscany as a citizen of Arezzo, he was a doctor by profession, then in fact a monk with us at Malmesbury. It seems a good idea to reproduce an actual eulogy of him. It is not my own composition. I shall quote the verses of my fellow monk, Peter, so that the goodness of the praiseworthy abbot may shine in splendour, and so that anyone who thinks it worth reading them may notice the grace of this most distinguished of poets. So here is just a small example of his eloquence. Peter himself has won a higher and more glorious fame before large audiences on other occasions.[2]

> He was good and thoughtful, a man of wisdom,
> Enriching the buildings, caring too for our souls.
> Possessing all fruits provided by learning,
> He turned his wisdom to the church's glory.
> Skilled in all laws which medicine teaches,
> He won favour from kings with his healing gifts.
> You saw kings and nobles his obedient subjects,
> Believing, at his nod, it was safe to live.
> Support from the king gave him such courage,
> He dared to fight with the rich for his rights.
> He broke them, and crushed them in such small pieces,
> That he ruled as his subjects lords of the land.
> Even Giffard,[3] inferior to none of the nobles,
> Bent his neck for the cowl of a monk.
> Estates long lost he returned to his sway,
> Greedy attempts on his lands he repelled.

[1] See ch. 67 for William Rufus' wish that Faricius should succeed Anselm as archbishop of Canterbury. Knowles, *The Monastic Order*, pp. 180–1, in his own eulogy of Faricius, calls him 'one of the greatest abbots of his age'.
[2] Peter Moraunt, a monk from Cluny, in fact became abbot of Malmesbury in 1140. Dom Hugh Farmer, 'William of Malmesbury's Life and Works', *Journal of Ecclesiastical History* 13 (1962), pp. 39–54, suggests that this unusual appointment 'probably represents Henry's choice rather than the community's'.
[3] William Giffard, who became bishop of Winchester in 1107. See ch. 57.

Why name all these nobles and lesser fry?
He drove off in triumph all attacks on his rights.
From this grew fame, and from fame grew glory,
From this his church grew to maturity.
Mindful that influx of goods was God's gift,
He converted it all to the monastery's splendour.
The added estates, the vestments and gifts,
Copes from kings, rich vessels and painted hangings,
All these are signs that I'm speaking the truth.
The gleam of rich gold adorning the ceilings,
Metals embossed and fabrics bejewelled,
Were full of wonder for those who beheld them.
Life was too short for his happy intentions,
Death broke them both. When was man so lamented?

Chapter 89 Reading

There was once a nunnery at Reading, but it was destroyed many years ago. King Henry planned to restore it as a monastery, in fulfilment of the penance enjoined upon him. He also linked with it two other destroyed monasteries, those of Leominster and Cholsey.[1] It was in honour of the mother of our Lord and of John the Evangelist, and was built between the two rivers Kennet and Thames, in a spot where it could serve as a resting place for almost all those travelling to the more densely populated cities of England. The king settled some Cluniac monks there, to give a strong lead in matters of piety and to show that the hospitality would be never failing.[2] There is no point in mentioning the bodies of the saints that are buried in these two monasteries, as they were all brought there from overseas, and now are inhabitants of a foreign land. Anyway they have received eulogies from writers in the past, and so need not heave sighs at my silence.

Chapter 90 The bishops of Wells

The third West Saxon bishopric was at Wells, a town in Somerset, which derived its name from the number of wells that gushed forth there. These were the bishops there from the time of king Edward the Elder to the time of William the younger: Æthelhelm, Wulfhelm, both afterwards archbishops of Canterbury, Ælfheah, Wulfhelm, Brihthelm, Cyneweard, Sigegar, Ælfwine, Lyfing, otherwise called Æthelstan, who later on in the time of king Æthelred

---

[1] Cholsey is in Berkshire.
[2] The first abbot was Hugh of Amiens, who had been a monk at Lewes. Loyn says, 'Henry I's most conspicuous act of patronage was his foundation of the great abbey of Reading with suitable endowments in 1125' (*The English Church*, p. 111). Antonia Gransden, *Historical Writing in England*, p. 175, reminds us that William himself will almost certainly have experienced Reading's never failing hospitality, and suggests that this chapter may even be a form of thanks for his visit.

succeeded the holy Ælfheah as archbishop of Canterbury, Æthelwine, abbot of Evesham who was later expelled, Berhtwine, Æthelwine for a second time upon the expulsion of Berhtwine, Berhtwine for a second time upon the second expulsion of Æthelwine, Merehwit otherwise known as Berhtwig, Duduc and Giso a Lotharingian[1] in the time of king Edward and William the Conqueror. All these had their sees at Wells, in the church of St Andrew.

When these were succeeded by John of Tours,[2] a doctor by profession who had made a lot of money in the practice of medicine, he decided to transfer the episcopal throne to Bath. He thought it was insufficiently glorious to live without fame in the town of Wells. While William the father was alive, his intentions remained unrealised, but he effected the move in the time of William the son. Not content with moving the see, he also bought the whole city from king Henry for £500 in silver and transferred it to his own use and that of his successors. The spring at Bath whose waters bubble up into the hot baths is supposed to have been discovered by Julius Caesar. The waters are beneficial for those who bathe in them, though when patients first arrive they find the smell of sulphur offensive, until their senses get used to it and the unpleasantness disappears.

King Offa had founded a monastery at Bath, and Edgar, as was his practice in several other places, had enlarged it. He had a fondness for Bath, both because it was an impressive place, and because he had received his royal crown there. John easily obtained this abbacy from the king. At first he was rather hard on the monks, whom he found dull and outlandish. He took away all the estates which provided them with food, and in a miserable fashion supplied them with just a little sustenance through his lay brothers. But as time went by and new monks were enrolled, he became kinder, even supplying the prior with a few lands which enabled him in some degree to support himself and his guests. John began and completed many fine schemes for books and for adornments, and especially for gathering a band of monks who were equally commendable for their knowledge of letters and their zeal in the offices of the monastery. He was a very successful doctor, relying on practice, not theory. At least this was his widespread reputation, but I do not know whether it was true. He liked the company of the learned, so as to derive some praise for himself from his association with them, although in dealing with disputants he showed a sharper tongue than should have belonged to a man of his position. His health was sound: he provided good food for himself and his guests. He died at an advanced age, though even in death he could not be persuaded to show generosity and return the lands of the monks, setting an example which should not be followed by his successors. He was buried in the church of St Peter which he himself had built from its foundations and surrounded with carefully constructed, high walls. For Andrew gave way to Simon Peter, the

---

[1] Lothingaria was the block of land between the Alps, the Rhine and the Scheldt. Giso was king Edward's chaplain.
[2] In 1088.

younger brother to the elder.[1] The whole extent of this bishopric is contained within Somerset. It has three abbeys for men, at Glastonbury, Athelney and Muchelney.

Chapter 91 Glastonbury

Glastonbury is a town situated in a marshy corner. It can be approached by horse or on foot, but it does not give pleasure by its position or its beauty. King Ine was the first to build a monastery there. He did it on the advice of the blessed Aldhelm, and bestowed upon his monastery many large estates which are still on its books today. It had its ups and downs over the years but abbot always succeeded abbot, and Glastonbury remained famous for its community of monks right down to the arrival of the Danes in the time of king Alfred. Then, like everything else, it was destroyed and for several years it lacked inhabitants of reputation. But Dunstan,[2] who earlier had lived out the solitary life there as a monk, splendidly restored all that the hurricane of war had smashed, and soon, thanks to the generosity of king Edmund, acquired for it all the belongings it had once had, and many more than these, and established an abbey unparalleled in England, now or in days gone by.[3] Its fertile farms stretched far and wide, and its library overflowed with ancient texts of great beauty. But through some evil chance, ever after the coming of the Normans it went downhill under bad abbots. There were no new buildings of note, and the inhabitants became impoverished. The abbots, concerned only with the fame of their position, acted like tyrants rather than men of God. Puffed up but powerless in secular matters, at home they upset the monks by their cruelty. It will be sufficient evidence of this just to mention the career of Thurstan. Made abbot of this monastery by the gift of king William the father, he misused and squandered its estates and revenues on his male prostitutes. He demanded a strict rule of living from his monks, but all the while kept them on pitifully short rations. From this arose ill-feeling and verbal arguments, for, as Lucan says, 'A hungry people knows not fear.'[4] From quarrels[5] matters passed to fighting. The monks were driven by some soldiers into the church and wept for their miseries at the holy altar. But when the soldiers burst in, two of the monks were killed on the spot, fourteen wounded, and the others driven out. For the soldiers were in such a mad frenzy that, while attacking the monks from long range,[6] they had made the crucifix bristle with arrows. As long as the

---

[1] In other words John's new church of St Peter at Bath replaced the old church of St Andrew in Wells.

[2] Dunstan was abbot of Glastonbury 942–57. By the end of this time 'he had brought into being the first organised community of monks which had existed in England for two generations' (Stenton, *Anglo-Saxon England*, p. 446). Many of these monks, when promoted, contributed to the English monastic revival.

[3] Glastonbury was indeed the wealthiest of English monasteries. See the table on p. 9 of Burton, *Monastic and Religious Orders*.

[4] *Pharsalia* 3:58.

[5] One quarrel was over which chant should be used in church.

[6] They had climbed up into the gallery.

king was alive Thurstan took the blame for the harm caused by this crime and was banished to Caen, but on the king's death he paid money to the officers in redemption for his sin and was restored to his office. It was scandalous and disgraceful for a man who knew he was guilty of a great sacrilege to dare to force his way back in to a place which he had violated.

Patrick is buried at Glastonbury, if we can believe the story. A native of Brittany and a pupil of the blessed Germanus of Auxerre, he had been ordained bishop by pope Celestinus and sent by him as an apostle to the Irish.[1] He spent many years converting that people, and achieved much through his own efforts and the cooperation of God's grace. But finally, just when he thought he should return to his own country, prompted by his weariness of years of travel and the old age which was now his neighbour, he died in Ireland. Indraht, son of the Irish king, who had a character of unsurpassed sweetness and sanctity, followed his teacher Patrick as a missionary. He was joined by seven Irish noblemen, but they were all attacked and killed by robbers in the same place. A credulous antiquity consecrated them as martyrs. What can I say about the other saints buried at Glastonbury? My poor speech will hardly find words to match the majesty of their deeds. King Edmund sent there the bodies of many saints, whom he had discovered and unearthed on a trip to the north, among them being Hild,[2] abbess of the priory now called Whitby, but once known as Streneshalh. In her day it was for nuns, but nowadays it is for monks. That reliable historian, Bede, will show you in his history the worth of her service.[3] Also found by Edmund was the body of Ceolfrith, abbot of the monastery at Wearmouth. Bede has written for him also his own proper account.[4] He did in fact die and was buried at Langres, when in extreme old age he was on a journey to Rome, but it is generally agreed that his body was later brought back home. Glastonbury has also some of the bones of Aidan, first bishop of Lindisfarne.[5] For because the same historian bears witness that the others were taken to Scotland by Colman,[6] it is too certain to be open to doubt. Benignus, the confessor, is said to be buried there. He had lived not far from Glastonbury as a hermit, and his celebrated miracles had persuaded the nearby monks to venerate him and to take his body to their monastery. Also buried at Glastonbury are king Edmund, the restorer of the abbey, of whom I have spoken above, and his son, king Edgar, who was not ungrateful to his memory of his father but added to the gifts given by him a pile of the broadest estates.

Chapter 92 Athelney

Athelney is not an island in the sea, but its marshes and spreading stagnant waters make it so inaccessible, that it can only be approached by boat. There is

[1] Around 430.
[2] Hild died in 680.
[3] 4:23.
[4] In his *History of the Abbots of Wearmouth and Jarrow*.
[5] 632–51.
[6] 3:26. Colman was bishop of Lindisfarne 661–4.

a very large grove of alders there, in which live deer, goats and many beasts of that kind. On the firm ground, which is a bare two acres broad, is the little monastery and the monks' outbuildings. It was built by king Alfred, who once had found a snug hiding place there for a time, when he had been driven out of his lands by the Danes. Soon afterwards he received assurance from St Cuthbert in a dream that he would be restored to his kingdom, and vowed to God that he would build a monastery there. He also built a church. In area it is only small because of the narrowness of the room available, but it was built in a new style. Four posts fixed in the ground, encircled by four apses, support the whole construction.[1] The monks there are few in number and poor, but their love of peace and solitude makes them put a high value on their poverty – or makes them feel better about it. Their patron is St Æthelwine. As they continually experience his sanctity in the benefits he gives them, they are always praising him and lauding him to the skies. There is a persistent opinion that Æthelwine was the brother of Cenwalh, king of the West Saxons,[2] and that he increased the greatness of his family by his holy character. Weakness kept him perpetually fettered and imprisoned, but he served God none the less actively. He made a good end, and now he is a ready help in trouble to all who call upon him.

Chapter 93 Muchelney

The founder of Muchelney abbey was the same man as the founder of Milton abbey.[3] The same reason led him to do it, and he provided the same buildings and gifts of relics. But the advantage which Muchelney has in addition is that the monks are quite freely able to keep vigil for the mysteries of heaven, as they are rarely visited by groups of men from outside. For Muchelney is difficult of access. In summer it is generally approached on foot or by horse. In winter there are no visitors. But enough about Muchelney. I must turn my pen away from it, as the remaining districts of this province are calling me.[4]

Chapter 94 The bishops of Crediton (909–1103)

At this point I shall give a list of the bishops of Crediton. Crediton is a small town in Dumnonia, commonly known as Devonshire, twelve miles from Exeter. The bishops who in succession held their sees here were Eadwulf, Æthelgar, Ælfwald, Sideman, Ælfric, Ælfwald and Eadnoth also known as Wini. Then Lyfing became bishop of Crediton, after being a monk at

---

[1] The style of the church, showing the influence of Carolingian France, is an example of Alfred's wide cultural contacts. The community, consisting largely of monks from France after the almost total extinction of English monasteries by the Danes, did not prosper.

[2] 643–72.

[3] King Æthelstan. See ch. 85.

[4] Having dealt with Dorset and Somerset, William now turns to deal with Devon and Cornwall. All these districts had been parts of the original diocese of Sherborne before the partition of c.909.

ınd abbot of Tavistock. He was considered to be a great friend of
ɔd to have great influence with him. He had spent much time with
ꞇmark, and had attached himself to his retinue on his journey to
ꞇ when Cnut's business in Rome was concluded[1] and the king had
hurried off to Denmark by land, Lyfing sailed to England carrying the king's
letters and to execute his commands. Before Cnut himself arrived in England,
Lyfing had wisely and skilfully completed all the tasks laid upon him by the
king, and advanced so far in the royal favour that on the death of his uncle
Burgwald, bishop of Cornwall, he united both bishoprics under his own
control. He was ambitious and headstrong, a tyrant who never suffered a
defeat in matters of ecclesiastical law, according to story, and who regarded
nothing as important unless it promoted his own wishes. Finally, so our
ancestors tell us, when he was breathing his last breath, such a terrible noise
was heard through the whole of England that it was thought to be the
destruction and end of the whole world. He was buried at Tavistock. He
had given many notable gifts to the monastery[2] and had become so popular
with the monks that even nowadays they chant fifteen gradual psalms daily for
the peace of his soul, a custom which has continued unbroken through the
succession of abbots.

In the time of king Edward he was succeeded by Leofric, who had grown up
and been educated in Lorraine. He transferred the episcopal see to the town
which is called Exeter, as its walls are washed by the river Exe on its way to the
sea. When the place was brought under the control of the English on the
expulsion of the Britons, king Æthelstan had been the first to fortify it with
towers and to surround it with a wall of squared stones. It is such a trade
centre that you would not fail to find there any item judged profitable for
human use, although the soil is hungry and poor and only just about brings
forth unproductive oats with husks which are generally empty and devoid of
grain. Leofric expelled the nuns from the monastery of St Peter and established
his bishopric and canons there. In the fashion of Lorraine but contrary to
English custom the canons were to eat in one dining room and sleep in one
dormitory. This rule was passed on to posterity, though it has now partly
lapsed owing to the luxury of the times, and the canons have a steward, though
appointed by the bishop, who provides them daily with the necessary food,
and annually with suitable clothes to wear.

Leofric was succeeded in the time of king William by Osbern, a Norman by
birth, the brother of the most excellent earl William of Hereford. In the days of
king Edward Osbern had received generous hospitality at the English court, as
he was a kinsman, once removed, of the king.[3] As a result he was more inclined
to follow English customs over food and other matters, and cared little for
Norman pomp. He continued the practices of his master, king Edward, and

---

[1] Cnut had gone to Rome to attend the coronation of Conrad, the Holy Roman Emperor.
[2] These included a great collection of English books, one of which, the Exeter Book of Old English
poetry, containing examples of all the chief varieties of native verse, is still kept in the cathedral.
[3] He had in fact been a priest in the Confessor's chapel.

when they were being carried out by others, he and his companions would show their pleasure by the gestures they made with their hands.[1] And so, just like the prelates of old, he was content with the ancient buildings, and was held to be generous of disposition and chaste in body. He lived until the fourth year of king Henry, although for many years as old age pressed upon him he had been blind.

Chapter 95 Tavistock

In Devon there is a monastery called Tavistock, near the river Tavy. Its building was started by Ordgar, earl of Devon, father of the Ælfthryth who was the wife of king Edgar, and auspiciously completed by bishop Lyfing. It is in a lovely spot with woods near by and a plentiful supply of fish. The material of the church matches its surroundings, and streams from the river flow in between the outbuildings of the monks and under the rush of their own impetus carry away all the rubbish they find in their path. Rumonus is talked of there as a saint and as a bishop he is buried there, although his exploits are mere beautiful adornments from the writing desk, there being no documentary evidence to support an opinion. You will find the same thing in many places in England besides Tavistock, just a bare list of names of saints and a record of any miracles they may have accomplished. I suppose that all knowledge of their deeds has been destroyed by the attacks of their enemies.

You can see Ordgar's tomb in the same monastery, and the huge mausoleum of his son is worth a visit. He was called Eadwulf. He was as big as a giant and immensely strong. It occurs to me to give some brief examples of his strength. He was journeying to Exeter with his kinsman, king Edgar. When they jumped down from their horses at the town gate, they found the entrance closed with bars on the outside and locked on the inside. It so happened that the doorkeeper had not known about their arrival, for they were riding at a time of internal peace, and he had gone far away. So Eadwulf took hold of the bars with both hands and with seemingly little effort threw them on the ground in pieces, at the same time tearing away part of the wall as well. Now that his blood was up, with a savage gnashing of his teeth he gave a second proof of his manliness. Weakening the doors with his kicking, he broke away their double hinges so fiercely that he destroyed their material as well. Everybody else applauded, but the king made light of the matter and jokingly attributed the exploit to diabolical strength, not to human powers.

Another example. There is a wood in Dorset near Horton. In those days Horton was numbered among the abbeys[2] thanks to the generosity of Eadwulf, although it has now been destroyed. When Ealdwulf had laid aside his cares and felt this peaceful spot calling him he would give a demonstration there of

---

[1] Stenton calls him 'a pattern of antique virtue', and cites him as 'a warning against attaching much importance to the generalisations of later writers about Norman contempt of English barbarism' (*Anglo-Saxon England*, p. 677).

[2] In Domesday the poorest house in the land, with an income of only £12 a year.

his amazing strength. It has a stream, which flows beside a fertile grove used in hunting. It is ten feet across, from one bank to the other. With outspread legs he would make both banks one, and then with gentle, almost effortless chops from a small hunting knife would lop off into the river the heads of the beasts that were driven towards him. But enough of his strength, for this strange giant, when still aglow with the heat of youth, fell victim to death, and gave instructions for his body to be buried at Horton. But Sihtricius, the aggressive abbot of Tavistock, got in first, and just because Eadwulf had ordered various gifts to be made to the church at Horton along with his body, transferred giver and gifts alike to his own abbey. Afterwards, in the reign of king William, Sihtricius turned pirate, polluting his religion and bringing infamy upon his church.[1]

I do not know the list of the successive bishops of Cornwall and so do not include it. My one piece of information is that there was an episcopal see at St Petroc. This is a place on the coast of north Cornwall, near a river called Hegelnuthe. Some people place it by St Germans on the south coast of Cornwall, near the river Lynher.

Chapter 96 The bishops of Selsey and the South Saxons

Now that I have reviewed all the episcopal sees of the West Saxons, my story takes me to the bishops of the South Saxons. Their province is bounded on the one side by the West Saxons and on the other by the men of Canterbury. Together with its chieftains it has always been subject to the authority of the kings of Wessex, ever since Cædwalla[2] routed their king, Æthelwalh, in war. Æthelwalh had been baptised in Mercia on the advice on king Wulfhere. Then, when the blessed Wilfrid was deposed from his see, Æthelwalh thought it right to give him friendly hospitality and even raised him up with the gift of an episcopal see in the place known as Selsey. This town is surrounded by sea on all sides, and can only be approached by one road. But king Æthelwalh was killed, as I have just said, and Wilfrid, who had built a monastery there, went back home when peace was restored. So for many years the episcopal see was vacant, in the interim looking for its administration to the bishop of Winchester. But then Eadberht was made bishop there by archbishop Nothhelm, and he was succeeded by Eolla. On Eolla's death the line of succession was continued by Sigga, who was present at the council of archbishop Cuthbert, Ealuberht, Oswald, Gislhere, Tota, Wihthun, Æthelwulf, Bernege, whom his ordainer archbishop Plegmund pronounced to be suitable, Cœnred, Guthheard, Alfred, Eadhelm, Æthelgar, who had previously been abbot of Winchester and afterwards was archbishop of Canterbury, Ordberht, Ælfmær, Æthelric, Grimcytel, who, although expelled from his see of the East Angles which he had bought, also acquired this one through money

---

[1] Knowles aptly refers to Sihtricius as 'this compatriot and predecessor of Drake' (*The Monastic Order*, p. 104).
[2] Cædwalla was king of the West Saxons 685–8.

but clung on to it, Heca and Stigand, but not the Stigand who afterwards became bishop of Winchester and archbishop of Canterbury. This Stigand, who was appointed bishop at Selsey by king William,[1] moved the see to Chichester, a town near the sea in his diocese, where from days of old there had been both a monastery of St Peter and a convent of nuns. Stigand was followed by William, and William by Ralph.[2] Ralph was well known for his tall body but was also famous for his keen mind. Indeed when the younger William was unjustly hounding Anselm, Ralph because of his sacred office stood up to William face to face in defence of his archbishop. William redoubled his threats, puffed up in the consciousness of his power, but Ralph, no whit afraid, held out his crosier and took off his ring, for the king to take them, if he wanted. Neither then nor afterwards would he have been deflected from his rigorous stance, if he had possessed a defender. But Anselm by his departure dampened the hopes of Ralph and the other good men that there were, so that for the moment his position was weakened and later became a lost cause. As the years went by, Ralph also showed a churchman's defiance to the commands of king Henry, when he wanted to impose a tax on priests throughout England. The others acquiesced or kept silent because they were afraid: in Ralph alone the pontifical hardness could not be softened. He gave orders for divine office to cease through his whole diocese, and for the church doors to be blocked with thorn bushes. He did not prevent the monks chanting the psalms, but merely stopped the people from entering. This extreme behaviour had an effect on the king, and he excused Ralph alone from the priests' tax, as he knew he was a man who would not take notice. Indeed Ralph's boldness in defence of his faith was so highly praised by the king that he excused him from paying all dues. Ralph kept saying that as his see was a poor one and his church had been destroyed by fire, he ought not to be plundered for taxes but enriched with donations. His determined innocence made him so remarkable that the king, who took away from others, willingly and submissively gave gifts to Ralph. Finally, when the church, which he had founded, was destroyed by the accident of a fire, as I have mentioned, it was the king's generosity in particular which got it repaired in a short time. Ralph made a most Christian end. All his goods had been divided up for the use of the poor, and, when dying, he even gave orders for his bedclothes, right down to the mattress, to be given away in bequests before his eyes. He has deservedly won a lasting remembrance as a good man. He raised his see from a poor and lowly state to the highest peak of glory. He gathered together as many priests as his see could sustain with provisions. He bequeathed to his church adornments of all kinds: I am ashamed to count up the shamefully small numbers of such things which it had before. Three times a year he would go on a preaching tour of his dioceses, never using his episcopal authority to make demands of the provincials, though always gratefully accepting what they

---

[1] He was appointed bishop at Selsey in 1070. The other Stigand was archbishop of Canterbury from 1052 to 1070.
[2] Ralph was bishop 1091–1123.

offered. He did not hesitate to rebuke evildoers, even if his rebuking was
having little effect, tempering his fault-finding with an inborn sense of humour.

Chapter 97 Battle (1067)

In his diocese there are at least two monasteries of recent foundation. There is
the monastery of St Martin at Battle,[1] founded and advanced by king William
in the place where he had fought the English. He was a generous benefactor of
it both when alive and when about to die. The altar of the church is on the spot
where the dead body of Harold was found, killed in war for the love of his
country.

Chapter 98 Lewes (1077–1078)

The founder of the monastery of St Pancras at Lewes was William, earl of
Warrene.[2] A Cluniac monk called Lanzo placed it in the forefront of English
monasticism. Its lofty position indicates Lanzo's successful work, for it is truly
claimed that no other monastery at all can outdo it in either the piety of its
monks or its hospitality towards guests or its charity towards all men. Its
widespread fame is surpassed by the truth of the deeds which fame recounts,
although the long speeches of those who praise it would tire my readers.
Indeed I would say more about Lanzo, if I had not given a not unworthy
account of him elsewhere,[3] and if his merits did not transcend all description of
them.

[1] See Loyn, *The English Church*, pp. 79–80, for an account of this impressive abbey of new design,
225 feet in length, its ruins and location since transmuted into art in a watercolour by Turner.
[2] On Lewes see Knowles, *The Monastic Order*, p. 151. William de Warenne had been entertained
at Cluny on a pilgrimage to Rome. On p. 176 Knowles notes William's generous praise of monks
belonging to a different order from his own Benedictine one.
[3] In *The Deeds of the Kings* 5:442–3. Lanzo's death scene from this is quoted by Knowles in *The
Monastic Order*, p. 152.

Book 3 Northumbria

Chapter 99 The prologue to the third book

Second in importance after Canterbury comes York, a large, metropolitan city, still exhibiting Roman elegance. Built on two sides of the river Ouse, it embraces ships coming from Germany and Ireland. Always the first obstacle to the savage tribes of the north, it also suffered under the attacks made upon it by the barbaric Danes during the whole period of their domination of England. So it had already been shaken by many falls before it finally collapsed under the pestilence brought by king William. He was angry with the townspeople, because they had taken in the Danes on their arrival in England and had negotiated with them, and so he wiped out the city, first by famine, then by fire. The villages and fields of the whole district were ravaged on the king's orders, their fruits and crops ruined by fire or water. The sinews of a once fertile province were cut by rapine, flames and bloodshed. For sixty miles and more the land on all sides was uncultivated, and the soil is completely barren to this day. Any stranger who now sees the cities which were once so famous, with their lofty towers threatening the heavens and their fields of smiling pasture watered by streams, can only lament, and any old inhabitant who sees them does not know them. Amid the ruined walls, where some remain but half-destroyed, you can see marvellous Roman buildings. For example Carlisle has a dining room arched over with a stone vault. No shock of tempest could ever have made it totter, if timber had not been deliberately piled up against it and set on fire. The region is called Cumbria and the men Cumbrians, and on the doorway into the dining room we can read the inscription 'To the Victory of Marius'. I am not sure how to explain this, unless perhaps some of the Cimbri,[1] driven out of Italy by Marius, once settled in this area.

The whole speech of the Northumbrians, especially that of the men of York, grates so harshly upon the ear that it is completely unintelligible to us southerners. The reason for this is their proximity to barbaric tribes and their distance from the kings of the land, who, whether English as once or Norman as now, are known to stay more often in the south than the north. The king himself, who in the south of England is content with an escort from his household, does not set forth without a great company of auxiliary troops whenever he is visiting northern parts. Alcuin once foresaw this calamity happening to the region from an omen which was shown to him at York. In a

---

[1] The Cimbri, a tribe of Northern Germany, were defeated by Marius in 102 and 101 BC.

letter to king Æthelred[1] he reported in these words the omen which he had seen, 'What is the meaning of the rain of blood which I saw during Lent in the city of York, capital of the whole kingdom, in the church of the blessed Peter, chief of the apostles, and which, coming from the north in a clear sky, fell menacingly from the top of the church roof upon the homes of the city? Must we not conclude that bloodshed is coming from the north upon our people?'[2] Alcuin foresaw these things happening in his own day, and later generations realised that they had clearly come about either because of the violence of the men of the north or as a consequence of the failings of the men of the north. For in the time of the English the Danes laid waste the province, and then the Normans, driven wild by the arrival of the Danes, destroyed what was left. So in this book, the third of my *Deeds of the Bishops*, I shall relate whatever has come to my notice about the archbishops of York, either from the tales of my elders or from the turning of pages. The outstanding archbishop, I believe, was the first Wilfrid, a man who for almost all his life was undeservedly tossed about on a sea of perils. I think it is suitable to include an account of his life and all his deeds in this summary, as they are not that well known and many things are missing in Bede's history.[3] Anyone with this in mind finds an immense work opening up before him, but I shall try to keep it as brief as I can. And you can always take as an excuse for my boldness the fact that the reader unable to get through whole lives of the saints can find here a selection of the more useful items. And so, cutting out long, rambling narratives, I shall go for the truth and summarise briefly what Stephen, the priest, recounted with a great army of words.[4]

Here ends the prologue to Book Three. Here begins Book Three of the Deeds of the English archbishops, written by William.

Chapter 100 The career of Wilfrid to October 679

Paulinus was the first archbishop of York,[5] and is known to have received the pallium from pope Honorius. When he had been driven out, his Scottish[6] successors, Aidan, Finan and Colman, had no wish to acquire status from the pallium or the fame of the city, and lurked in hiding on the island of Lindisfarne. When Wilfrid proved Colman to be wrong about Easter,[7] he

[1] King of Northumbria 774–96.
[2] There is another paragraph from this letter of Alcuin, written in 793, in ch. 128.
[3] Bede only devotes two chapters, *Ecclesiastical History* 4:13 and 5:19, to connected accounts of Wilfrid.
[4] Stephen, a disciple of Wilfrid who accompanied him on his many travels, probably composed his *Life of Bishop Wilfrid* within a decade of Wilfrid's death in 709. See B. Colgrave, ed., *The Life of Bishop Wilfrid by Eddius Stephanus* (Cambridge, 1927). Mayr-Harting considers that 'the discreet silences of Bede and the protestations of his own monk and biographer have both in their different ways helped to detract from Wilfrid's reputation' (*The Coming of Christianity*, p. 129). Lapidge in *The Blackwell Encyclopaedia* (*s.v.* 'Stephen of Ripon') proposes that the usual identification of Stephen with Eddius Stephanus is a mistake.
[5] From 625 to 633. For his subsequent career see ch. 72.
[6] For the people designated by the term 'Scottish' see p. 267 n. 2.
[7] At the Synod of Whitby in 664.

himself was chosen to be archbishop of York by king Aldfrith, son of king Oswiu, who sent him to France to be consecrated. As Wilfrid kept delaying his return, king Oswiu was influenced by the schemes of the 'Fourteeners', so called because like the Jews they celebrated Easter on the fourteenth of the moon,[1] and pushed Chad on to the episcopal throne of York. Chad was a very holy man, but his appointment was against the rules, and this wrong was righted by Theodore, sent by the holy see to be archbishop of Canterbury, for he enthroned Wilfrid.

Anyway, to go back to Wilfrid's beginning, he was born[2] in Northumbria of parents who were not of the lowest, and any graces not conferred upon him by his birth were made up for by the nobility of his behaviour. While his mother was in labour and bringing him forth into the light, his father's retainers, who were standing outside, thought they saw the house, in its consciousness of the birth taking place inside, burst into fire, with flames so fiery that they shot long trails up into the sky. As the retainers noisily threw water on to the fire to put it out, the maidservants dashed out, alarmed by their shouting. They told them not to disturb their mistress who was in labour, but were surprised that they did not see with their own eyes what the men claimed to have seen. For by now the flames had vanished without doing any harm, and as the building still stood in one piece, the retainers had no excuse for their shameful behaviour. Anyway it was realised that the baby would be a boy of fiery energy, seeing that so big a blaze had occurred at his birth.

He passed through his boyhood without schooling. But when his increasing age had added four years to ten, he left his father's home out of hate for his haughty stepmother, his own mother having died. He was helped by the retainers to whom he had shown obedience while at his father's hearth, and was brought to the notice of queen Eanflæd.[3] By her frequent questions she elicited from the young man the secret that he was more disposed and willing to be a soldier of God than of the state, and handed him over to a certain Cudda, who once had been a member of the king's council and his chamberlain but who was now living a life of pious meditation on Lindisfarne. Cudda looked after Wilfrid kindly for several years and sent him back to the queen. He had by now memorised the Psalms and various other ecclesiastical texts, but had conceived a desire to go to Rome in his eagerness for still further development. As Wilfrid was old enough, the queen furthered the young man's desires by sending him to her cousin, Erconberht, king of Kent, so that he might give special attention to helping Wilfrid. So Wilfrid came to Kent, and added to his knowledge by learning about Roman practices, which outstripped the lore of the Scots. In the end he collated the Psalter translated by St Jerome, which the Scots had given him, to accord with the fifth edition of the Roman Psalter and always read and kept that by him.

---

[1] The Jewish passover was the fourteenth day of the month Nisan. Early Christians had celebrated Christ's resurrection on that day.
[2] Around 634.
[3] The wife of Oswiu, king of Northumbria.

After a year, the king added him to the company of that vigorous young man, Benedict, afterwards abbot of Wearmouth,[1] and with him Wilfrid hurried on the journey to Rome.[2] But when he got to Lyons, his handsome face and steady character won him the affection of Dalfinus, the archbishop of the city. Dalfinus tried to keep him there by offering him a priesthood, or marriage with his niece, but had no success with either offer. Wilfrid excused himself from the marriage by his zeal for celibacy, and deferred the priesthood until his return from Rome. So, supported by the archbishop's advice and assisted by his purse, he resumed the journey he had begun, and soon caught up with his companion, who in anger at the delay had gone on ahead. So he came to Rome and successfully accomplished all his wishes, helped by the blessed Andrew, before whose triumphant gaze he had prostrated himself and prayed for help and ability in letters. He obtained a private audience with the most blessed Boniface, then archdeacon, through whom he won the favour of the pontiff of the supreme see. He stayed in Rome for a long time, enjoying the company of these men and from their instruction becoming learned in the computation of the paschal cycle. He then returned to archbishop Dalfinus at Lyons. As the archbishop welcomed him with a kindness which was just as warm as before, they agreed on the following plan: Wilfrid, the foreigner, was adopted as his son and made a priest, while the archbishop, who by his friendly concern had removed all thought of a return to his country from Wilfrid's mind, was chosen as Wilfrid's father.[3] But the devil begrudged France to Wilfrid, and a longer life to Dalfinus, and sent against them the hellish fury of queen Baltildis,[4] so that, having killed nine bishops, she might add Dalfinus as the tenth to her heap. She had instructed him through her servants to appear before her. He was well aware of the woman's wickedness, but his bravery was greater than her evil and he hastened to obey. When he had been dispatched immediately by the executioners' swords, the young Englishman, keeping his nerve in a remarkable fashion, thirsted to join his father in death and almost threw himself on to their swords. But although he was now unarmed and thrust out his neck towards them, the killers took pity on him and kept him safe for England.

When the news of his arrival got around, he was courteously summoned to court by king Aldfrith, son of king Oswiu, who listened to him gladly and gratefully as he told of the labours and stages of his journey, the elegance of France and pomp of Rome, and the regulations of canon law. His upright behaviour and energy, his preaching, knowledge and eloquence won him the friendship of the king, who kept Wilfrid with him for several days so that he might carefully cultivate this recent acquaintance. The king gave him a place in

[1] See ch. 186 for an account of Benedict Biscop.
[2] Mayr-Harting claims that this journey was the first known journey made by Englishmen to Rome (*The Coming of Christianity*, p. 120).
[3] Wilfrid stayed with Dalfinus for three years, and no doubt 'imbibed high notions of the status and authority of bishops', as Alan Thacker suggests in *The Blackwell Encyclopaedia*, *s.v.* 'Wilfrid, St'.
[4] Baltildis was the widow of Clovis II and the regent of Neustria 657–64.

Ripon in which to live and to build a monastery, and his nobles contributed many gifts as an offering for the work. Wilfrid was ordained priest and abbot there by Agilbert, the Frankish bishop who came down from Scotland,[1] and after a few days Wilfrid had proved the Scots wrong, got rid of their mistaken ideas about Easter and brought back the knowledge of the truth. Kings and nobles rejoiced and the whole province gloried that they had a native as their teacher,[2] as by now Scottish rawness turned their stomachs, and many offerings were made to Wilfrid to sustain his life and support the needy poor. Wilfrid indeed was just as generous as the donors in giving away the contributions of his people to the pauper and the stranger, making the challenging jest that the more he gave to the poor, the more abundantly would God bestow on the donors things to give away! Unusually restrained in his appetite but unusually ready to watch and pray, he ever preserved the chastity received from his mother, and even in his youth had not fallen into sin. Right until old age he kept up the custom of pouring cold water over his whole body when he went to bed at night.[3] But finally, though late in the day, he was stopped from doing this by the order of pope John, who was afraid that Wilfrid would fall incurably ill, if the coldness of his aged body was increased by the pouring of cold water over it.

Because of these things the whole people with shouts of support chose him as the right man to make holy the archbishop's chair at York. Wilfrid, however, persistently refused the honour. He had no wish to be consecrated by Scottish bishops or bishops ordained by the Scots, seeing that the apostolic see refused them communion. Just as he had no right to nominate any of them, in the same way it was up to him to guard his own reputation and look after his own salvation. But he suggested that the king's majesty and the religion of the people should allow him to receive the honour at the hands of French archbishops. If this was done, the consequence of this legal enthronement would be a great increase in knowledge. His plan was approved and he was sent to France to be consecrated, with an escort of great splendour and with great expectations from those who stayed at home. Twelve bishops, amongst whom stood out Agilbert, acclaimed his election, lifted him on to their shoulders as he sat on his golden seat and finally took him to the altar and consecrated him.[4]

But, as Wilfrid was returning home after the completion of the ceremony, adverse winds seized his ship and drove it on to the hostile shore of the South Saxons. The ebb of the tide left it beached there as booty for the wide-mouthed

[1] Presumably Agilbert had headed north immediately after losing the bishopric of the West Saxons (p. 104).

[2] William seems to have forgotten the opposition party at the Synod of Whitby. Thacker says that Wilfrid's championship of the Roman Easter 'caused deep offence within the Northumbrian ecclesiastical establishment' (*The Blackwell Encyclopaedia*, s.v. 'Wilfrid, St').

[3] For Wilfrid's asceticism see Mayr-Harting, *The Coming of Christianity*, pp. 133, 142. He considers both the grandeur of Wilfrid's public activities and the simplicity of his personal life as having a source in Gaul.

[4] This splendid ceremony took place at the Frankish royal palace at Compiègne. As Mayr-Harting says, 'the Gaulish church pitched the interpretation of the bishop's office high on these occasions' (*The Coming of Christianity*, p. 132).

enemy. Being savages who lived like bacchanals and who as yet knew not the true God, they were roused to frenzy and gathering their forces for war sounded the trumpet. The archbishop thought that allowance should be made for the circumstances, and offered peace and piled up promises, but the natives remained impervious and rushed to battle. Their pagan priest, standing on higher ground, tried to crush the power of the Christians by his fanatical incantations, but one of the archbishop's men whirled a stone from a sling, which smashed into the priest's forehead with such force that it penetrated the skull and injured his brain. The natives attacked the Christians all the more fiercely because of this. The one hundred and twenty of the latter were ready for both outcomes, whether fortune's wheel should give them the victory or overwhelm them in death. They charged into the close-packed mass of the enemy, and twice and three times drove them back. Meanwhile the famous archbishop and his priests were kneeling in prayer on the shore, and, thanks to their intercessions, the tide returned earlier than normal and took the party off into its sheltering bosom. They soon put into Sandwich, singing out the time for their rowing with joy, since hosts of the enemy had been killed, while they had lost barely five men themselves.[1] So Wilfrid, victorious in all his perils, returned home, but there found confusion, for Chad had been installed as archbishop in his place. It is not difficult to steal from men of great piety, especially when it is their offices that are being stolen. So Wilfrid lived humbly in Ripon for three years, exercising the functions of a priest wherever he was asked to go, but always accompanied by a great train of followers, who did not think he should be left on his own. His most frequent invitations came from Wulfhere, king of Mercia, who bestowed upon him the place called Lichfield for the founding of a bishopric or a monastery, according to his wishes. Ecgberht, king of Kent, was no less assiduous in honouring Wilfrid, and, at his invitation, the archbishop ordained many Kentish men. One of these was Putta, made priest by Wilfrid, and afterwards elevated to the bishopric of Rochester by Theodore.[2] For, after the death of archbishop Deusdedit, men were waiting for Theodore to come from across the sea.

On his arrival,[3] he realised that Wilfrid's demotion was unjust and irregular, and so removed Chad from the archbishopric. Chad took the loss humbly and calmly, and the patience of this most holy man so deeply affected Wilfrid that, thanks to his help, Chad again made his way upwards through all the offices and finally was made bishop of Lichfield. He lived on there for a number of years, before finding an end which matched his sanctity. Meanwhile Wilfrid did not promenade along the pathways of vice. His first concern was for the spread of Christianity and for the Christians to live better lives, his second to raise new churches and to repair old ones. The church at York,[4] built once by

[1] Mayr-Harting, *The Coming of Christianity*, pp. 139–40, brings out the biblical parallels in this narrative in which 'the guns of the Old Testament flash and pound'.
[2] For Putta as bishop of Rochester see p. 88.
[3] In 669.
[4] Of St Peter.

king Edwin on the advice of the blessed Paulinus, was now without a roof. Its walls, which were half-destroyed and which threatened to collapse completely, served only as nesting places for birds. The archbishop felt sad at heart at the shame of it. He strengthened the walls, and put a new roof on, which he protected against storm damage with sheets of lead. Light from the windows had come through thin linen cloths or through a lattice work of metal: Wilfrid had them glazed. The old age of the walls and the passage of many years had destroyed their beauty: Wilfrid whitened them with a wash of gleaming limestone. The church at Ripon also experienced the archbishop's energy, for he had it rebuilt from the foundations with beautifully curved arches, a stone floor, and an encircling colonnade. The new brother kings, Ecgfrith and Ælfwine, were invited to its consecration, as their father Oswiu had died during the rebuilding. They endowed the church richly and handsomely, thereby winning the prize of fame, as they were praised in fulsome language before the people, and for three days rewarded with a most lavish display of foods.

Then, as it seemed, the delight taken in this worldly pomp was linked to a divine miracle of a dead child being brought back to life. This is how it happened. On a visit to the town of Tiddanefre Wilfrid was met by a huge crowd of women, bringing their sons for confirmation. A working woman had mingled with this flowing wave of people. Bringing her dead son with her she cunningly offered him for confirmation, hiding the fact that he was dead and drying her tears. She genuinely believed that this deception would enable him to come back to life. But it was no good, for when the archbishop uncovered the lad's face to perform the ceremony, he saw that he was dead. But then the woman, now that she had failed to succeed by trickery, turned to prayers and besought Wilfrid in the name of God and his mother and all his faith and holiness to bring the dead child back to life. At the same time she threw herself in his path and in her extremity absolutely refused to be moved. Meanwhile the saint was in two minds whether to boldly attempt the unaccustomed miracle or to harden his heart and ignore the tears of the dead child's mother. In the end holiness was the victor in his virtuous heart,[1] and, murmuring to himself a few verses from the divine Psalms, he then put his right hand on the corpse and brought back the life into that little body. For immediately the child opened its mouth and showed by the swift movement of its eyebrows and the movements of its whole body that it had come back to life. The mother shouted for joy, but, restrained by the archbishop, fell silent. The boy was called Æthelwald. He later became a monk at Ripon, and was looked upon as no small addition to the miracles done by Wilfrid.

At just about the same time Wilfrid performed a similar miracle at Hexham.[2] At his expense a church was rising high there, when a monk fell

---

[1] The four Latin words which make up this key phrase in the story are emphasised by their initial letters of 'v', 'p', 'p' and 'v' forming an ABBA pattern.
[2] For Wilfrid's great new foundation at Hexham, endowed by the Northumbrian queen Æthelthryth, see ch. 117.

from the top of its walls and smashed all his bones. He was carried into the oratory. He was speechless and unconscious and, as the monks looked at him, they could not be sure whether he was completely dead. But the archbishop's eyes filled with tears. He called the monks to prayer and urged them to shake the apathy from their faith: nothing was difficult for those who believed. So as with one voice their prayers were lifted up on high, and mercy was brought down from heaven. The monk began breathing again, and the onlookers hoped for the gift of health to be restored. His broken bones knitted together, and in thankfulness the victim grew strong again.

No less attentive to his own duty was king Ecgfrith, who increased his kingdom on the side of the Picts, and protected it against the Mercians. For on the death of king Oswiu, the Picts regarded the young kingdom in its infant state as a pushover, and massing together made an unprovoked attack on the Northumbrians. The young king met the Picts under their chieftain Bernege, and with his tiny band so slaughtered their countless host that the plains lost their flatness for the bodies piled up on them and the rivers were dammed up and came to a standstill. Wulfhere, king of the Mercians, also led his army against these same Northumbrians in bitter enmity. He remembered that his father[1] had been killed by them, and he came north, confident that he would repair the loss or gain a kingdom. But fortune did not smile on Wulfhere. Indeed she was almost no more of a friend to him than to his father, except that he did ingloriously get away, after shamefully exposing his back to the enemy. Still alive, a few days later he ceded part of his kingdom to the Northumbrian king. As a result of these victories Wilfrid was given more estates, and churches with monks were set up.[2] For he was loved by all men out of respect for his virtues, and he was highly regarded for his abstinence, which is more to be praised than the examples of it I have given so far. He was famous for rarely taking more than one plateful at the longest meal, and for never draining more than one cup. Besides this he was kind and friendly to everybody, and so got them on to his side. Abbots and abbesses made him master of their possessions while they were alive, and when dying named him as their heir. Nobles entrusted their sons to him to be educated, so that, when they had grown up, they might fight for church or state.

As a result of all this, an unhappy jealousy crept into the hearts of queen Eormenburg and some of her courtiers, who cast envious eyes upon Wilfrid's great wealth. While the most blessed Æthelthryth appeared to serve the royal bed,[3] she had acted as peacemaker between her husband and the most blessed archbishop, and by her sane counsel removed the sting from any charges which were whispered against Wilfrid. And the king himself found to his delight things going just as he wanted in war and at home, while he relied on the

---

[1] King Penda of Mercia had invaded Northumbria in 655.
[2] The decade after Theodore's establishment of Wilfrid in the archbishopric of York in 669 saw Wilfrid at the height of his powers.
[3] Wilfrid had not succeeded in persuading Æthelthryth to have sex with Ecgfrith. See Bede, *Ecclesiastical History* 4:19.

kindly support of Wilfrid. But when the new bride entered the palace, the harmony with the archbishop was broken and ended, and the king's household gradually diminished in importance and finally sank right down. So the queen aroused envy against the archbishop, because he possessed all those abbots and abbeys, and got himself served from gold and silver vessels, and had walking at his side a crowd of followers who preened themselves in their gleaming garments.[1] The report of all this envy soon reached the ears of Theodore, archbishop of Canterbury. He did not hesitate. The offering of presents had weakened his firmness of purpose, and now, without consulting Wilfrid, he introduced into his diocese three bishops with different districts.[2] He claimed that there was good reason for this, as it meant that three bishops could be fed from what had fattened one. All those revenues and that massive diocese were enough for four bishops. These arguments could have seemed plausible, if Theodore had not completely robbed and deposed the man whose energy had gained all these possessions, or if he had at least acted with Wilfrid's consent. Nor could this completely open attack on Wilfrid be concealed, when Wilfrid went before the king's tribunal and asked the reason for the wrongs done to him. His enemies said, 'In no way are we making accusations against you. We just want to accomplish what we have decided.' No statement could be more ridiculous. It was as if they quoted the line of Juvenal 'What I want I command, and my will is reason enough.'[3]

Then, after Wilfrid had made an appeal to the apostolic see, he used the following remark to counter his mockers, who were standing near the king and bursting into laughter, 'The mockery you are now making about my departure for Rome will be changed into great sorrow for you, on this same day in one year's time.' The outcome of events competed with the archbishop's words for truth. For not many days after Wilfrid's departure, king Æthelred of Mercia, Wulfhere's brother, began a war in his desire to avenge the injuries done to his brother. Ecgfrith met him, full of vim and expecting to inspire the usual terror. But the Mercian put his army to flight, and routed his brother Ælfwine. The Northumbrians were turned to sorrow in their grief at this, and now lamented the absence of their one-time counsellor. And it happened that a year later, on the same day on which the young king had heard the warning at York, his body was brought into the city, showing that justice at last was done. Æthelred triumphed, having made his kingdom whole again, and he also expelled bishop Wynfrith, the successor of Chad at Lichfield, because he had been of Ecgfrith's party.[4]

---

[1] It also helped Eormenburg's cause that Wilfrid had encouraged Æthelthryth to become a nun.
[2] Theodore was following the Gregorian concept of subdividing great dioceses. Eata became bishop of the northern part with his see at Hexham or Lindisfarne. Bosa became bishop of the middle section with his seat in Wilfrid's principal church of York. The third see was created for Lindsey, the district south of the river Humber. For the crucial part played by the bishop in the church of this time see Stenton, *Anglo-Saxon England*, pp. 147–8, 165.
[3] *Satire* 6:223.
[4] Bede, *Ecclesiastical History* 4:6 says that it was archbishop Theodore who 'displeased by some act of disobedience of Wynfrith, deposed him from the bishopric'.

Wynfrith was by chance driven on to the coast of France and fell in with king Theodoric and Ebroin, a Frankish duke. Orders had been sent to these from Britain that they should take captive and despoil bishop Wilfrid. They made a mistake over the names, and killed the followers of Wynfrith while seizing his goods, but allowed Wynfrith to get away. Wynfrith paid for the mistake over the names, taking another's danger upon himself, but got away from the brigands, even though without a shirt on his back. As for Wilfrid, the schemes and plans of his enemies did not escape the notice of his intelligence. Helped by a gentle west wind, he put out to sea and turned his prows towards the east in order to sail to Frisia. He was courteously received by its king and people and spent the approaching winter there. It was indeed a sorrowful exchange, to live with greater safety among foreigners than among his own people, and to be exiled from his fatherland but to be welcomed in Frisia. As king Adalgisius' heathen pride was immediately affected by Wilfrid's preaching, an easier way was opened up for preaching to the others.[1] Ebroin sent letters attempting to persuade the king to kill or expel the man of God, but, although he promised vast sums of gold, he achieved nothing. His letter was read out in the hearing of Wilfrid, who was eating in the dining room at the time, but Adalgisius threw it into the fire with the words 'Let the same flames consume the man who in his greed for gold breaks an agreement made with a friend.'

And now the warmth of spring was opening the flowers, when Wilfrid resumed his journey and came to Dagobert, king of the French beyond the Rhine. Dagobert had not forgotten how Wilfrid had once received him hospitably, when he had been driven out by a faction of nobles and had come to him from Ireland. Wilfrid had helped him with horses and an escort and sent him back to his country. So Dagobert now made Wilfrid welcome, and begged him with many prayers to honour his country by remaining there and to accept the bishopric of Strasburg. When Wilfrid put off his answer to the request until his return from Rome, Dagobert allowed him to continue his journey, together with his bishop Deodatus. So Wilfrid was making his way through Campania, relying on the influence of his companion, and was on the point of entering Rome when he turned aside to visit Bertharius, the governor of that province. Bertharius had been told about Wilfrid's mission by messengers from his enemies and had been persuaded by promises to do him harm. But, although at first he was proud and haughty, he abated his anger when he heard the true account of the matter. So far from harming Wilfrid, he brought the matter to a good conclusion with the help he provided. He told Wilfrid that he had been prompted to do this because of the humanity of a certain king of the Huns, to whose court he had once been exiled. Although the king was a pagan, no persuasion or bribery could get him to harm the visitor, whom he had sworn to protect.

[1] Bede, *Ecclesiastical History* 5:19 writes of Wilfrid 'instructing many thousands in the word of truth' and claims that Wilfrid 'first began the work of evangelisation in Frisia which Willebrord afterwards completed with great devotion'.

So at long last Wilfrid arrived at Rome. He found the city agog with expectation for his arrival. For a humbly pious monk called Kenwald had been sent on ahead by Theodore, bringing with him written accusations and a bitter, strongly worded denunciation. The most pious pope Agatho had been concerned about it, and had summoned a council of fifty bishops and abbots to meet in the basilica of the Saviour, called the Constantinian.[1] The proceedings of the council were as follows:[2]

Agatho, most holy and thrice blessed bishop of the catholic church and the apostolic city of Rome, spoke as follows to the assembled council: 'I do not believe that you reverend brothers are unaware why I have summoned you to this august assembly. I desire your worships to find out about and consider with me the nature of the disagreement which has arisen in the churches of the island of Britain, where through the grace of God the multitude of the faithful had increased. We have been informed about it both by the accounts of envoys to Rome and by a series of letters.'

Andrew, most reverend bishop of Ostia, and John, bishop of Porto, spoke as follows: 'The governing of all these churches lies under the control of the apostolic authority of all you who carry on the office of the blessed apostle Peter. But, with our fellow bishops and servants now recently assembled, we too by your order have read the various writings which those instructed have sent to your apostolic pontificate from the island of Britain. These include the documents sent by the person of that most reverend archbishop who was once sent to Britain by this apostolic see, the reports of others attacking a certain fugitive bishop, as they call him, and the depositions made by Wilfrid, beloved of God, archbishop of the holy church of York, who came here to Rome, when he had been deposed from his see by the archbishop mentioned above. These documents contained many subjects for investigation, but neither have we found in them that Wilfrid has been convicted of any crimes for all the subtleties of our sacred canons and so properly deposed, nor have his accusers shown in their own words that Wilfrid had committed crimes for which he should have been deposed. But rather have we discovered that he showed such consistent restraint that he did not get involved in any seditious wranglings. Indeed, once bishop Wilfrid, known as a man beloved of God, was deposed from his see, he merely made known the merits of the case to his fellow bishops and hurried here to our apostolic see.'

Agatho, most holy and thrice blessed bishop of the catholic church and the apostolic city of Rome, spoke as follows: 'We have been told that Wilfrid, beloved of God, bishop of the holy church of York, waits outside the doors of our august council chamber. As he requests, let him be admitted to our council chamber, carrying the petition which he is said to have brought with him.'

Wilfrid, bishop beloved of God, entered the august council chamber, and

---

[1] The council took place in October 679.
[2] William's account of the proceedings of the council is an abridgement from the version of the monk Stephen, which is given in full by Hamilton (Rolls Series), pp. 222–6.

said, 'I beseech your pontifical blessedness to order my humble petition to be taken up and read out publicly.'

Agatho, most holy bishop, said, 'Let the petition of Wilfrid, beloved bishop of God, be taken up and read out to everybody.' John, the clerk, took it up and read out to the august, apostolic council: 'I, Wilfrid, humble and unworthy bishop of the Saxons, with God as my guide, have brought the steps of my heart to this apostolic height, as to a place of fortification and a tower of strength. Because I know that it is from here that the norms of the sacred canons spread out to all the churches of Christ, I confidently expect this place to do justice to my humility. Indeed I have no doubt that your episcopal eminence has decided upon this, both prompted by my humility and because of the words which I spoke to you orally in your presence, when at the moment of my arrival I presented myself to your apostolic gaze. For the foes of my archbishopric attempted to usurp my see, which I had held for ten years and more, although I was convicted of no crime against the decrees of the sacred canons in the assembled council of the most holy Theodore, archbishop of Canterbury, and the other prelates. Also three bishops were ordained in my bishopric, although such ordination was against canon law. Indeed the most reverend archbishop Theodore ordained bishops while I was still alive, and to a see which I was administering, however unworthily, and he did this on his own authority and without the agreement of my humble self or the consent of any other bishop. However, it is more seemly for me to pass over this fact than to complain about it, out of my reverence for Theodore, whom I dare not accuse outright, seeing that he was appointed by this august, apostolic see. But if it has become clear that, when I was driven from my former see contrary to the justice of the proper rules and anyway able to atone for any sin condemned by canonical harshness, I was seen by no one to be rebellious but merely departed after I had told my fellow servants and fellow priests, the bishops of that province, what had happened, and if indeed your apostolic eminence has already discerned that I have been deprived of my office, with humble devotion I willingly accept what has been decided. And if I am to take up my former bishopric, I accept and with my whole strength revere the decision given by the apostolic see, so much so that the infiltrators should be driven from those parishes of the church, of which I, your unworthy servant, was formerly the head. And if, on the contrary, it seems good to bring in prelates to that same district of which I was the leader, at least let orders be given for men to be promoted to these offices with whom I can in fellowship serve God in peaceful and tranquil concord.' That was the gist of it.

Agatho, most holy and thrice blessed bishop of the holy catholic and apostolic church of the city of Rome said, 'The argument of the petition presented by Wilfrid, bishop beloved of God, has completely satisfied its hearers: when he realised that he had been unjustly removed from his episcopal see, he did not rebelliously oppose the decision with secular force, but, accepting it meekly, sought the canonical help of our founder, the blessed Peter, chief of the apostles. Furthermore, in humble expectation, he promises to accept his sentence, not arguing about the justice of the verdict delivered, but declaring that with unshaken loyalty he will perform whatever decision our founder, the blessed apostle Peter, whose function we perform, shall think fit to come from my lips.'

That sacred assembled council delivered a unanimous verdict, of which this is a summary, 'We decide and decree that Wilfrid, bishop beloved of God, should take up the bishopric which he recently had. The helpers that he chooses for himself with the consent of a council assembled in his province should be ordained by the most holy archbishop and elevated to bishoprics, and those irregularly appointed to bishoprics in his absence should certainly be removed.'[1] And other things were said, imposing an interdict on those not obeying the decrees.

Chapter 101 Wilfrid imprisoned by king Ecgfrith

The bishop was elated by these decrees, and he was also commanded by order of the pope to take his seat among the number of those hundred and fifty holy bishops who were holding a council to oppose those who were preaching that there was one operation in the two natures of our Lord Jesus Christ.[2] After this Wilfrid set about returning home, and under the protection of God returned to his country, untouched by any perils. He obtained an audience with king Ecgfrith, though with great difficulty, and handed him the sealed decrees of the pope. The king had them read out to the bishops who formed his faction, but he was so far from obeying the Roman see that he robbed Wilfrid of all his possessions, sent his followers flying in different directions and handed over the blessed archbishop to a keeper, noted for his brutality, to be thrust into prison. The king too easily believed those who declared that the decrees had been bought for a price, as the Romans could be won over by those who offered them gifts. The whole court was itching with curiosity about the bishop's punishment. I shudder to say that the queen even wrenched away by force a small reliquary belonging to the bishop and thought nothing of wearing it with its relics around her neck or taking it with her when travelling.

The priest bore all this with unmoved mind and countenance. He was afraid for his followers, but he encouraged them with holy counsel to endure bravely, until the unconquerable felicity of God's goodness should bring an end to their sufferings. But although the keeper had treated other prisoners with savage cruelty, he was a gentle Englishman towards Wilfrid. He subjected him to no other punishment than darkness, as he did not dare disobey the king's commands altogether. But even this punishment was in vain, for God's

---

[1] Agatho and his council seem to have attempted a compromise. On the one hand Wilfrid was to be restored to his see, and the bishops appointed by Theodore to be removed. On the other hand Theodore's policy of dividing the Northumbrian see was approved. See Stenton, *Anglo-Saxon England*, p. 136.

[2] The council took place in Milan on 27 March 680. Bede, *Ecclesiastical History* 5:19 records that Wilfrid bore witness to the orthodoxy of the English church on the matter before the council.

regard for Wilfrid did not allow the darkness's disregard to put out the light of Britain, which the heavenly torch had marked out as being Wilfrid's distinction, when his mother was still freeing herself of her womb's weight. A light sent from on high split the thick darkness of the cell, rivalling with its brilliance the absent daylight.[1] The brightness dazzled the eyes of the jailers as they watched through the cracks and sent them running to their master. He was horrified by their story, but reported nothing unusual out of his fear for Ecgfrith. His reluctance received a push from an illness which befell his wife. The foam which she suddenly vomited forth from her gaping jaws was terrifying enough for her husband, but when she was soon also attacked by some more powerful demon and lay there stiff, bloodless and speechless, the keeper sprang up, threw himself at the bishop's feet and easily obtained a pardon from the merciful priest. For Wilfrid immediately said a prayer and poured water which he had blessed down the woman's open throat. The disease left her, and she was as healthy as before. Ecgfrith heard about this in a message from the keeper, which expressed his sorrow and begged the king not to sacrifice him undeservedly to the devil as the guilty party in the punishment of the innocent bishop.

But the king showed not the slightest change of mind. He gave orders for Wilfrid to be taken away from Osfrith (that was the keeper's name) since he was such a poor-spirited individual, and handed over to a minion called Tinber, who was more likely to obey his cruel commands. As the king's cruelty grew greater, so did the miracles. The king ordered Tinber to put Wilfrid in chains. But as the heartless jailer was preparing the iron fetters for chaining the shins of the saint, they perpetually through some never-failing trickery slipped bafflingly through his very hands as he made the attempt; for either a tighter fetter was not able to go round shins which were too big for it, or a fetter which was too big made no contact with slender shins. And if ever his expert efforts found a perfect fit, the chains flew off with such speed that the eyes of the onlookers could not follow it. So wickedness yielded to holiness. The saint was freed, and kept in free custody. Ecgfrith was not bothered by any of this. Whenever he was told about it, he either turned up his nose at it with a joke, or insulted the saint in abusive language. However, he did send frequent messengers to the bishop, carrying his commands that Wilfrid of his own initiative should invalidate the force of the decrees which he had brought back, by saying that they had been wrung from the Roman court by bribery, and not obtained by a legal decision. If he did that, the king in his kindness would give back to him part of his bishopric and all his property; but if not, the author of the schism would be responsible for his losses. Such threats had little effect on the priest's mind. So far from agreeing, he replied that not even to save his life would he do that which would impugn the authority of the apostolic see.

What in the meantime of queen Eormenburg, tinder and spark of the whole

---

[1] Mayr-Harting draws the parallel with Acts 12:7 where Peter, in prison, is visited by the angel of the Lord (*The Coming of Christianity*, p. 144).

blaze? She joined day and night in one round of feasting, and carried the reliquary around with her in triumphal procession, exulting in these spoils which she had taken from the leader of the enemy.[1] But one night, when she was visiting abbess Ebbe,[2] her husband's aunt, the devil pushed himself into her inmost being and she began to act strangely and to talk gibberish. The abbess was aroused by her cries and rushed into her chamber, enquiring soothingly what the matter was. But the queen made no reply, for by now the disease was gripping her tightly and blocking her voice. Then the handmaid of the Lord, understanding the reason, advised her nephew to return the reliquary to the saint, and for Wilfrid himself to be reclothed in all his episcopal vestments according to apostolic command. He should do this, if he wished his wife to recover. But if the king was so angry that he thought to persevere in his evil ways, he should at least give back what he had taken from Wilfrid and allow the man himself to go free. The king did this. The queen at once made a good recovery, and, on the death of her husband, changed her habit and repented of her actions as a religious.

Chapter 102 Wilfrid becomes bishop of the South and West Saxons (680–685)

So Wilfrid, driven out of his own land, made for Wessex. He was welcomed there by a certain noble called Berhtwald, but only for a very few days did he have a safe hiding place in Wessex. For Berhtwald was the vassal of Æthelred, king of the Mercians, seeing that he was the son of Æthelred's brother, and Æthelred sent him fierce messages, warning him not to keep Wilfrid for even one day. He was doing this as a favour to Ecgfrith, for Osthryth, Ecgfrith's sister, had recently married Æthelred to comfort herself for the death of her brother Ælfwine, and had established a peace between her husband and her brother Ecgfrith. So Wilfrid, having already built there a very small monastery, abandoned his monks and turned aside in flight to the still-pagan South Saxons, since no place in Christendom was left for him to hide in. The king of the South Saxons was called Æthelwalh. When he heard the reasons for Wilfrid's travels, he decided to help the priest, and so he made a most binding agreement with him that he would neither give him up to the prayers of his enemies nor remove him because of their bribes. In reliance on this protection, Wilfrid preached the gospel, first to the king and queen, and then to their people as well. Nor did he find it difficult to win them over: as soon as the king had been baptised, his example encouraged the others to do the same.[3] The king gave to the bishop his own mansion of Selsey, a house which was being lived in by a member of the king's household. Wilfrid filled it with monks and

[1] For a Roman soldier in classical times to win such spoils in battle had been regarded as the height of bravery.
[2] Abbess of Coldingham in Berwickshire, and a friend of Wilfrid and Cuthbert.
[3] The South Saxons were the last of the heathen English tribes on the mainland to accept Christianity. In less than a generation the inhabitants of the Isle of Wight followed their example.

handed it down to posterity as the episcopal see. At that time Cædwalla had
been driven out of Wessex by a faction of nobles. He frequently visited the
saint for advice and was readily received by Wilfrid who supplied both
Cædwalla and his followers with horses and money. In his rage and anger
against everybody Cædwalla killed king Æthelwalh, who had the bad fortune
to come across him. And when Cædwalla gained possession of the whole of
Wessex, he put Wilfrid in charge of the whole kingdom as its lord and master,
decreeing that nothing should be done in the whole province without Wilfrid's
agreement. Finally he also gave him vast possessions in the Isle of Wight[1] and
willingly confirmed by edict Wilfrid's former possessions.

Chapter 103   Theodore restores Wilfrid to his reduced see (686)

Many years passed away on these matters. By now Ecgfrith had been killed in
the war against the Picts, and Theodore was on the verge of death. His
conscience was smarting for the sin he had committed against Wilfrid, and so
he summoned Wilfrid and bishop Erconwald to London. He confessed all his
sins to them, and said that he was particularly worried and anxious about his
offence against the saint, in that he had allowed him to be robbed contrary to
the rules, whether by open attack or hidden, patient manoeuvring. 'My end is
at hand', he said, 'in the year that lies ahead. This I know from God's heralds
and the forewarnings of my frequent bouts of illness. And so I ask you, most
holy bishop, kindly to forgive me for what I have done and to accept the office
of my archbishopric; for you, of all the English, are most learned in Roman
law. I myself, if God grants it, will try to blot out my past offences by my
present zeal in doing my duty, for by my authority and prayers I will make
kings your friends.'

Wilfrid replied calmly to this, as befitted a saint, but he did not agree to take
up the archbishopric without the decision of the greater council. So Theodore
rose up in all his strength to make sure that Wilfrid got back his bishopric, and
sent messengers with letters to Aldfrith, Ecgfrith's successor as king of the
Northumbrians, and to Aldfrith's sister Ælfflæd, abbess of Whitby, asking that
they should put aside their quarrels with Wilfrid and without delay embrace
his love. I will reproduce here the letter which he wrote to Æthelred, king of
the Mercians, in order to make clear the fervency of his zeal.

> Theodore, archbishop by the grace of God, sends wishes for everlasting
> salvation in the Lord to the most glorious and excellent king of the
> Mercians. Dearest son, your admired holiness should know that I have
> made my peace with the venerable bishop Wilfrid. And so I advise you,
> beloved, and in the love of Christ command you to give all the support you
> can for as long as you shall live, as you always have done, to the holy, pious
> Wilfrid, seeing that for a long time now he has been deprived of his own
> possessions and has laboured hard for the Lord among the heathen. I,

[1] A quarter of the whole island.

Theodore, your humble and age-worn archbishop, suggest this to your blessedness, firstly because, as you know, apostolic authority commends it, and secondly because the saint himself has possessed his soul in patience, and, following the example of his head, has quietly and humbly waited for a cure for the wrongs which were unjustly inflicted upon him. And if I have found favour in your sight, let my eyes see your welcome face, however burdensome the long journey may seem to you, and let my soul bless you before I die. So act towards the saint, my son, as I have begged you to do. For if you obey your father, who will soon be leaving this world, it will do much for your salvation. Farewell.

Chapter 104 Wilfrid appeals to Rome a second time (703)

So, since Wilfrid came to the kings with letters from the archbishop, they ensured his safety and granted him their support. Aldfrith had known him well of old and now on his own initiative invited him to his court and generously conferred upon him first the monastery of Hexham, then, with the decision of the council, the archbishopric of York and the monastery at Ripon.[1] This friendship between them lasted for almost five years, until poisonous plottings, hatched in the bosoms of certain people, burst out into the open. King Aldfrith was turned off course by these people.[2] He robbed the monastery at Ripon of its rightful possessions and thought about establishing a bishopric there. He claimed that he had to follow the decrees of archbishop Theodore, not those produced at the first and the last times, but those which, issued in the intervening period, are known to have fomented the discord. Wilfrid could not accept them and went away to king Æthelred of Mercia as his friend. He stayed under Æthelred's protection for a very long time,[3] and upon the death of Sæxwulf, bishop of Lichfield, took over that see and was both loved and revered by all the people. But king Aldfrith and Berhtwald, who had succeeded Theodore as archbishop, devised very many plots against Wilfrid in their efforts to destroy him and finally settled upon the scheme of holding out the hope of peace and inviting him to a council.[4] Once he was there, they would either bend him to their wishes by wheedling words or crush him, if he remained obstinate. Wilfrid was oblivious of any trickery. He judged other people by his own upright behaviour and went to the council.

But he found it to be far different from his expectations. When they had worn him out with endless calumnies and false accusations of crimes, they finally asked him if he was willing to obey the decrees of archbishop Theodore. He now saw through their wickedness and baffled them by the clever reply that

---

[1] In fact Wilfrid, while in Rome in 679, had received a separate privilege from pope Agatho, which exempted his monasteries from diocesan control and placed them directly under the Holy See.
[2] Stenton says that after Theodore's death in 690 Wilfrid had again raised his claim to the whole of the Northumbrian see (*Anglo-Saxon England*, p. 143).
[3] From 692 to 703.
[4] The council took place at Austerfield, on the southern border of Northumbria.

he would gladly obey those decrees of archbishop Theodore which were consonant with the sacred canons. Then he attacked them in a long, bitter but true argument: having over a period of twenty-two years put no trust in the decrees of the three popes, Agatho, Benedict and Sergius, were they now approving the decrees of Theodore, which had not been unanimously agreed upon? Having argued thus, he fell silent. But now the hairs on Aldfrith's neck were bristling with anger and he said to the archbishop, 'If you, father, command it, I will crush Wilfrid by force.' But even Wilfrid's enemies were not happy that a man of such reputation, who had come to the meeting won over by his trust in them, should be the victim of illegal force, and so they decided to go down a different path. They set about persuading him with feigned gentleness that, because he was the cause of countless quarrels breaking out in the church of God, he should of his own free will give up his possessions and his archbishopric, and that he should confirm this renunciation in writing. It would add to his fame and increase his glory, if he should prefer to live in peace as a private individual rather than to stir up by his own actions or those of others the storms of sedition in defence of his bishopric.

Father Wilfrid saw the scheme which was inextricably bound up with these words, and replied that nothing could so increase a man's bad reputation as for him to condemn himself out of his own mouth. He had been the first man after the expulsion of the Scots to teach the true Easter in Northumbria, the first to introduce antiphonal chanting in church, and the first to command the monks to observe the rule of St Benedict.[1] In return for all this, as an old man who had been bishop for almost forty years, he was now receiving the present of being forced to condemn himself in writing. They should realise that he would not do something which would disgrace himself, dismay his people and be unpleasant for everybody. Instead, he was appealing to the apostolic see, and summoning to appear before it any of his enemies who were entering upon an ecclesiastical conflict. So Wilfrid, now an old man of seventy, began to think again about the difficulties of a journey to Rome. Without delay he crossed the sea, completed the remainder of the journey and entered the city. For several days he waited for his accusers to arrive. After their arrival, he personally argued his case in letters, seeing that it was a matter of importance to him, in the following way.

Chapter 105 Wilfrid's letter to pope John VI (704)

To my master, most blessed John, pope of the whole world, greetings from bishop Wilfrid, your suppliant and humble servant of the servants of God. I must inform your holiness that disturbances have lately been caused in Britain by those who have taken from me for themselves my archbishopric and my monasteries with their estates and all my possessions. They have

---

[1] Antiphonal chanting had been the custom in the primitive church. Stenton says that the achievements claimed by Wilfrid in this sentence constitute 'the ultimate significance of his work' (*Anglo-Saxon England*, p. 145).

done this in defiance of the decrees of the blessed pope Agatho and his venerable successors as popes. So I have been forced to appeal to this holy, apostolic see, calling upon my enemies in the name of omnipotent God and the blessed apostle Peter to come before your presence, if any of them have some accusation against me, just as was decreed in the writings of your most blessed predecessor, Sergius. And so I have taken the trouble to present my humble petition to your glorious presence, so that, in the overflowing kindness of your piety, you may think it right to confirm the decrees passed about my insignificant self by your blessed predecessors. Let any one who comes to accuse me be brought on your order into our midst, so that he may make the accusations that he wishes to make. If I do not credibly refute even the smallest accusation brought against me, I am willing to suffer the severity of canon law. Secondly, I ask you to give me a letter of commendation from your highness to king Æthelred of Mercia, asking that all my monasteries which are in his kingdom should be at peace. Also may I have a letter to king Aldfrith of Northumbria, asking him to give back all my possessions. But if it shall seem to him too serious a matter for me to have the archbishopric of York, let your apostolic see decide who should be appointed as archbishop there, provided that I do not lose the two monasteries of Ripon and Hexham which I founded and which are situated in that province. Finally I also pledge myself to obey all the decrees of archbishop Berhtwald, which do not contradict those most well-founded decrees of your predecessors concerning my humbleness.

The accusers sent by archbishop Berhtwald were ordered to speak in reply to these words, and first made this point: it was a capital offence that in a council convoked in Britain Wilfrid had contumaciously declared that he would not obey the decrees of archbishop Berhtwald. Wilfrid stood up in their midst and cleared himself on this point by saying that he had not vowed disobedience *tout court*, but that he would only obey those decrees which were not contrary to canon law; moreover it was against the rules that he should pass judgement on himself without any crime being laid at his door.

Chapter 106 The Roman see finds Wilfrid innocent

The Romans broke into delighted applause at this simple but well-argued answer, and ordered the accusers to return home. The bishops, however, did add that, although it was laid down in canon law that any accuser failing to make good the first point in his accusation should not be allowed to stand up to proceed with further charges, out of reverence for archbishop Berhtwald they would not fail to look into the whole matter point by point. Seventy meetings were arranged over the next four months either solely for this issue or with the issue as their main item, and their upshot brought glory to Wilfrid but ignominy to his accusers. The Romans had been absolutely astonished at the shameless behaviour of the accusers, contrasted with Wilfrid's eloquence, for, whatever charges were brought against him, without thinking deeply about his answer but relying on the help of God and the truth itself, at the first movement of his lips he would shatter and sweep aside these charges as if they were spiders' webs.[1] Because of this the bishops were more inclined to marvel at the effrontery of the prosecution, wondering how men who had never held ecclesiastical office, with the exception of one who had been a deacon, could presume to accuse a man of Wilfrid's venerable age, who had been a bishop for forty years and who was a torrent of eloquence. They carefully discussed the matter for a long time, talking in Greek.[2] Finally, reverting to our tongue, they condemned the delegates as worthy of prison and pronounced their sender a fool, while Wilfrid was declared to be completely innocent on all counts.[3]

Chapter 107　Wilfrid returns to England (705)

At this point I would also mention how much benefit that synod, assembled by pope Agatho, brought to Wilfrid's cause, and I would also be telling the story of how Wilfrid, while returning home, fell ill at Meaux, a French town situated to the east of Paris, but was healed by an angel appearing in a vision, if this ground had not been covered already by the venerable historian, Bede,[4] whose sober narrative every reader should think worthy of belief. I shall briefly add what was left out in Bede's account. Wilfrid had won his case, but he still sought to remain in Rome, wishing to breathe his last at the feet of the apostles, his masters. But his pious prayers had no success with pope John, who considered the matter and said that Wilfrid was needed in England, and so gave orders that Wilfrid should not pass his remaining years in foreign climes, but should spend them in the service of his country. So Wilfrid went back home and took the papal letters to Æthelred, king of Mercia, who was now a monk. Æthelred received humbly and on bended knee this honour of greetings from the pope, and, having read the papers, he made no fuss about getting their demands carried out by Cœnred, the son of his brother, Wulfhere, whom he had appointed king in his place. For Cœnred too was full of the fear of God, as he proved to the world four years later by his voluntary renunciation of the kingship. Archbishop Berhtwald also genuinely sought reconciliation with Wilfrid, and was just as keen to establish agreement and brotherly concord. Men said that he had been terrified by threats from the apostolic see, at the time when his envoys were earning a condemnation for

---

[1] William describes Anselm's eloquence (p. 59) in a similar way.

[2] In 704 the pope still presided over a Graeco-Roman court. See Southern, *Western Society and the Church*, pp. 57, 59.

[3] In fact, as is shown by the letter of pope John to kings Aldfrith and Æthelred quoted in ch. 108, the Roman see was rather more circumspect than this, ordering both sides to hold a meeting in England to try to settle their differences.

[4] In *Ecclesiastical History* 5:19 Bede says, 'His acquittal was greatly assisted by the reading of the acts of the synod of 679 of pope Agatho.' The angel was Michael, who said to Wilfrid, 'I tell you that you will be healed of your sickness; but be prepared, for in four years I will visit you again.'

themselves by their bitter complaints, although, having been adjudged guilty, they had been acquitted because of the prayers of Wilfrid.[1]

Aldfrith, king of the Northumbrians, was the only one to continue to nurse a more stubborn hostility and he persisted in his fixed opposition. For when Wilfrid had messengers sent to him, although his initial reply to them was friendly, he was led astray, it was thought, by the counsels of evil men, to whom he showed more favour than befitted his position, and when the messengers returned to him on the appointed day, he made their hearts sad with these words: for his own part, he honoured the persons of the messengers, responsible men of noble demeanour, as if they were his parents, but he absolutely refused to comply with their requests, as it was contrary to reason, just because of a papal decree, to come to terms with a man who had already twice been condemned by the whole council of the English. But Aldfrith did not live on for very much longer after this reply. For as soon as the messengers departed, Aldfrith was seized by a grave illness that brought death near. The severity of the pain awoke the good sense which had long lain dormant in the king's mind, and, as the prophet said, 'Trouble brought understanding to his ear.'[2] He realised that he had been justly punished for his disobedience, and promised to make complete amends for his actions to Wilfrid, if the bishop could be brought before him while he was still alive. And as long as his powers of speech lasted, he kept on making this promise, and making his heir swear to carry it out, if he himself was deprived of the chance to perform his vow. But untimely death carried him off, and his repentance for flouting the apostolic letter came too late, although he did not deserve to escape the threats it contained. Because I have frequently mentioned this letter, I have decided to give a summary of it here, to make clear the amount of trouble that befell mankind just because people celebrated by antiquity as the greatest saints, such as Theodore, Berhtwald, John, Bosa and even abbess Hild, attacked with venomous hatred Wilfrid, who was, as my narrative has shown, in great favour with God.[3]

Chapter 108 The letter of pope John to kings Æthelred and Aldfrith

Greetings from pope John to those most noble lords, Æthelred king of Mercia and Aldfrith king of Deira and Bernicia. We rejoice that with the help of God you have become Christians, and we see in you a fervent faith, which, with God illuminating your souls, you took up from the preaching of the prince of the apostles, and which you firmly retain. If only our joy was increased by the conversion of your nobles! Our minds are saddened by the opposition of some people which has not been weeded out, but which must

---

[1] Again, Wilfrid's behaviour echoes that of Anselm. See ch. 53.
[2] Isaiah 28:19.
[3] William seems too strongly on Wilfrid's side here. Theodore's and Berhtwald's policy of the division of the archbishopric of York had clashed with Wilfrid's aims of ruling the whole. John and Bosa had been appointed bishops because of that division (ch. 110). Hild had been on the Celtic side against Wilfrid at the synod of Whitby.

be removed if you are to be found defenders of the faith and not violators of the precepts of the apostles. For a long time ago, when Agatho of apostolic memory was pope, bishop Wilfrid brought his case to this see, and his accusers also came, sent by Theodore, archbishop of the holy church of Canterbury, who had been sent to Canterbury from here, and by Hild, abbess of pious memory. On that occasion bishops gathered here from all sides, and thoroughly went into the matter and gave their decision on it. This decision has been upheld by the successors of the same Agatho, who were our own predecessors.[1] Not even archbishop Theodore is known to have made any opposition to the verdict, for he never subsequently sent any accusation here. And now on the present occasion we have ensured that for several days there have been heard before the council of the most reverent bishops here assembled the accusations of those who have come here from Britain to attack bishop Wilfrid and the defence made by Wilfrid. The evidence has been partly from letters old and new and partly given verbally by both sides, as the principal people involved, who began the whole trouble, were not present. It is now necessary to bring the whole matter to an end. And so we advise our brother, archbishop Berhtwald, to convoke a council together with bishop Wilfrid, to summon Bosa and John to this council, to hear the cases of both sides, and to decide what the parties are able to prove in his hearing in their turn. If at that council he can conclude the matter, we shall be pleased. But if he is unable to, he should recommend that the parties hasten to the apostolic see, so that those matters still not brought to a conclusion may be decided by the greater council. Anybody who refuses to come, should know that he submits himself to expulsion, and will no longer be considered a bishop either here or there. So let your royal highnesses agree that what we have decided in the spirit of Christ be brought into effect. But whoever in bold rashness refuses, he, whoever he is, will not go unpunished by God, nor will he escape being bound by condemnation from on high.

Chapter 109 Wilfrid's restoration and death (12 October 709)

On the death of Aldfrith,[2] a certain Eadwulf plotted to obtain the kingship. He also spat out against Wilfrid the frenzy of an unbalanced mind, just as if he had sworn to be as insane as Aldfrith. For the archbishop, remembering that Eadwulf had once been a friend, declared his judgement that Eadwulf's ambition was ill-advised. At this the foolish man boiled over in such a rage that he ordered Wilfrid to leave his kingdom at once, unless he preferred to be robbed of all his possessions and driven out in disgrace. But his threats were in vain, for two months later he was deprived of life and kingdom, and as he lay dying he struck the ground with the crown which he had seized.

[1] These predecessors were Benedict (684–5) and Sergius (687–701).
[2] On 14 December 705.

The nobles of the kingdom now set Aldfrith's son, Osred, on the throne, and Berfrith, the greatest of these nobles in power and faith, accepted the advice of archbishop Berhtwald and agreed to hold a council in Northumbria, so that at long last Wilfrid's just case should reach a peaceful end. At the council[1] the bishops, according to the apostolic orders, were given the choice of yielding to Wilfrid in their part of his bishopric or of going to Rome to defend their position, with excommunication being the lot of any who refused to choose. The bishops were objecting to this in their usual way when the business was ended by these words from the blessed virgin, Ælfflæd, Aldfrith's sister, who had become abbess of Whitby after Hild, 'Away with doubts! I bring you the will of my brother. I was present in person when he made it. The will informs us that Aldfrith promised to carry out the commands of the apostolic see immediately, if he got better, or, that if death's intervention made this impossible, he handed over this task to his heir.' Then Berfrith joined his words to those of the virgin and said, 'My judgement is that we should obey the commands of the pope, especially since their force is backed up by the order of our king and the vow which we made in our hour of need. For after Aldfrith's death, when the attacks of our enemies[2] had driven us inside Bamburgh castle, we vowed to God, when the pressure of the siege put our lives in danger, that we would fulfil the Pope's command, if we managed to get out. We had scarcely finished our vow (I admit this, most holy archbishop) when the whole province immediately rushed to our help, each man trying to outdo his neighbour. The king's son was raised to the kingship, the enemy driven off, the tyrant killed. Because of this it is the will of the court that bishop Wilfrid should be reinvested with his powers.'

These words scattered the clouds of disagreement and brought back the clear skies of concord. The grave archbishop eagerly embraced the bishops and for the rest of his life he lived in agreement with them, having had restored to him his two monasteries of Ripon and Hexham. He enjoyed four years of undisturbed peace after his return, but then, as the archangel Michael had foretold,[3] he was attacked so strongly by the same illness which he had once had at Meaux that he suddenly lost his powers of mind and speech. But his people prayed to God that Wilfrid should at least be granted his speech so that he could make division of his property, and at once his powers were freely restored and he was able to speak. Indeed, a few days later, healthy vigour poured back into his body and he began visiting all the places in his diocese. As his repeated illnesses left him in no doubt that death was near, he now made up for his seemingly rather lukewarm attempts at various good works in the past. He ordained men to be set over all his monasteries. He divided his treasures into four parts. The first and best portion was to be given to the church of Rome, seeing that under her authority he had always been free from all injustice and restored to his offices. Indeed, weighed down with years though

---

[1] Held near the river Nidd in 706.
[2] The enemies were the usurper Eadwulf and his party.
[3] See p. 158 n. 4.

he was, he was thinking of accomplishing this bequest in person, provided that his plans were not cut short by the iron sleep of the grave. The second portion was given to the poor. The third he bequeathed to the heads of his monasteries, so that they could purchase the friendship of the powerful and so beat off the attacks of their enemies. The fourth portion went to his various companions during his times of trouble, for they had not yet been given lands to sustain them.[1]

When this had been done, he got permission from the people of Ripon, for whom he had always felt an especial love and affection, and from the other Northumbrians, and set off to Mercia, where he had been invited for an interview with king Ceolred: at the same time he would be able to secure the peace of his very many monasteries which through the kindness of the kings of Mercia he had founded in that region. So he spent an year and a half visiting and strengthening all the monasteries of Mercia. But then he was warned a second time of his approaching death, and when at Oundle he was attacked by the onrush of extreme weakness, he knew that his last day was at hand. He said the few words his strength allowed to his sons and shared the holy blessing with them. Then, seemingly free from all pain, he entered upon his end, just when the monks sitting by his bed had recited the whole Psalter up to the verse, 'Send out your Spirit and they will be made new.'[2] Wilfrid died aged seventy-six, in the forty-sixth year of his archbishopric. He was a man who was tossed about by many dangers because of his upright life, and who even in his periods of exile did not take a holiday but busied himself in founding monasteries and bishoprics. It was remarkable how his character won him the favour of the princes amongst whom he spent his exile, while the same man, because of his unbending uprightness, was hated by the kings of his country. He left behind him more monasteries than anybody else, dividing among many heirs the properties which he had amassed single-handedly. His body was carried to Ripon, and buried there with great reverence. At the hour in which he breathed his last, men heard without seeing them the sweet song of birds and the beat of their wings as they flew up into the sky. This happened so often during the funeral procession that the wise men present wished it to be understood that the birds were an assembly of angels, come down to the dead man according to their promise.[3] The pall, on which his body had lain, if touched by a paralytic, restored his limbs to wholeness after a bath. When men attempted to burn down the building in which he had died, the flames grew frightened, and a handsome young man was seen driving them back. When the monastery at Ripon was destroyed several years later, Wilfrid's body was taken to

---

[1] Thacker says of Wilfrid's division of his property, 'He disposed of his possessions in a manner more appropriate to a contemporary aristocrat than a Benedictine abbot' (*The Blackwell Encyclopaedia*, *s.v.* 'Wilfrid, St').

[2] Psalm 103:30.

[3] Emily Dickinson has the same identification of birds with angels in poem 1570, the two robins that visit her apple-tree after a night of storms being two Gabriels in disguise.

Canterbury, where he is ranked with the highest, and honoured among the foremost.[1]

Chapter 110 John bishop of Hexham (687–706) and of York (706–721)

But I must return to the pathway after a long detour and continue my review of the bishops of York. Wilfrid had been the bishop of the whole of Northumbria, but after his first expulsion, which I have described,[2] two bishops were set up in his place, Bosa at York and Eata at Hexham. When Eata died, John was ordained bishop in his place. Then, during the reign of king Aldfrith, Wilfrid returned, to take over the whole bishopric for five years, with John being removed from Hexham and Bosa from York. But after these five years, Aldfrith expelled Wilfrid for a second time, and John and Bosa were restored to their sees. On Aldfrith's death, when Wilfrid returned to favour and took over the see at Hexham, John moved to York as Bosa was now dead. John was a man of outstanding qualities, which have been famously described by Bede in his *Ecclesiastical History of the English People*. And indeed he lives up to these praises, for he still performs miracles.[3] The most famous one happened at Beverley, where he lies buried. The people of Beverley were accustomed to show for display some very wild bulls. Tied up in the strongest chains, they were being dragged along by some strong men, sweating profusely. But as soon as they entered the graveyard, all their ferocity was put to sleep and they were so docile you would have thought they were silly sheep. Their chains were undone and they were sent to play around the churchyard, although previously they had always attacked with horn and hoof whatever got in their way.

Chapter 111 Wilfrid II as bishop of York (722–732)

John was succeeded at York by his own priest, Wilfrid, who outlived the times of Bede. For Bede, in the year in which he died, says that Wilfrid was archbishop of York.[4] This second Wilfrid was the cause of an unresolvable dispute between the citizens of Canterbury and York. The men of Canterbury claimed that they possessed the body of the elder Wilfrid, while the men of York argued that the body was that of Wilfrid the younger, taken to Canterbury by archbishop Oda.[5]

---

[1] For assessments of Wilfrid's mixed character and career see *The Blackwell Encyclopaedia, s.v.* 'Wilfrid, St'; Mayr-Harting, *The Coming of Christianity*, pp. 107, 129–47; Stenton, *Anglo-Saxon England*, pp. 135–45.

[2] See p. 147.

[3] Bede describes miracles performed by John in *Ecclesiastical History* 5:2–6.

[4] In *Ecclesiastical History* 5:23 Bede does make such a statement, but he makes it in 731 and not in 735, the year in which he died.

[5] For Oda, archbishop of Canterbury 942–59, and his removal of Wilfrid's body to Canterbury, see ch. 15.

Chapter 112 Ecgberht

On the death of Wilfrid the younger, Ecgberht sprang into the pontifical limelight. He was the brother of Eadberht, the king of the same province, and through his own good sense and his brother's power reshaped that see into the genuine article. For as anyone picking up the *Deeds of the English* may read, Paulinus at his death left the honoured pallium at Rochester.[1] The bishops of York after Paulinus panted after nothing higher than the simple name of bishop. But when Ecgberht was enthroned at York, as a man of a more ambitious spirit he thought to himself that, although it was a mark of pride to seek after the illicit, it was equally a sign of cowardice to fail to claim one's due, and so, by appealing to the apostolic see, he won back the pallium.[2] He also established at York a whole repository, as it were, for the liberal arts, including a most splendid library.[3] I can call upon Alcuin as an apt witness to this library. He writes in a letter to Charlemagne, 'Please send me some of your choicer books of scholarly learning, like the ones I have here in my own country thanks to the goodness and devoted efforts of my master, archbishop Ecgberht. If it pleases your excellency, I will send some of my young servants to pick up the necessary volumes from your court, and to carry back to France the flowers of British learning.' Ecgberht was buried with his brother in the same colonnade at York after a bishopric of thirty-six years.

Chapter 113 Cena and Eanbald (766–796)

Ecgberht's successor, Cena, was followed by Eanbald, a hard-working pupil of Alcuin. In a letter to him Alcuin says, 'Praise and glory be to God, who has enabled me to go on living amid the blessings of prosperity, and to rejoice in the promotion of my dearest son to work in my place in the church, in which I was brought up and educated, and to be in charge of the treasures of wisdom, left to me as my inheritance by my beloved master, archbishop Ecgberht.' It was Eanbald who joined with Æthelheard, archbishop of Canterbury, and, each helping the other like the good men they were, brought to nothing the attack made by Offa, king of the Mercians, on the church at Canterbury. Alcuin appears to refer to this when he says in a letter to Æthelheard, 'I have heard that you are well and flourishing and that you have had a meeting with my son Eanbald, archbishop of York. It gives me considerable pleasure to hope that, as a result of your saintly discussions, that unity is being restored to our holy church, which in part had been dissipated, not because of rational arguments but out of a lust for power.'[4]

[1] This is described in Bede's *Ecclesiastical History* 1:65.
[2] Ecgberht is seen by Mayr-Harting as a bishop in the Wilfrid mould (*The Coming of Christianity*, pp. 242, 273). Stenton considers the elevation of the see of York into an independent northern archbishopric (symbolised by Ecgberht's regaining of the pallium) as a 'serious obstacle to the political unity of the English people' (*Anglo-Saxon England*, pp. 145–6).
[3] A suitable achievement for someone who had been Bede's pupil.
[4] See chs. 8 and 9 for an earlier account of the events of ch. 113.

Chapter 114 Wulfsige to Wulfstan (796–956)

After Eanbald the archbishops were Wulfsige, Wigmund, Wulfhere, Æthelbald, Hrothweard and Wulfstan. The last-named, bishop in the days of king Edmund, brother of Æthelstan,[1] deserved the anger of Edmund by his persistently zealous support of the Danes in their rebellion against the king. Edmund was a kind and peaceful man, but this support made him so angry that he threw Wulfstan into prison, although he was soon prompted by penitence and regard for the reverence due to a priest to let Wulfstan go free. Wulfstan, in fact indignant that a pardon had been given him, died immediately.[2]

Chapter 115 The dual bishops of York and Worcester (972–1023) and the bishops of York to the death of Ealdred (1069)

After Wulfstan this post of honour was taken up by Oscytel, who flourished in the days of kings Eadred, Eadwig and Edgar.[3] Oscytel's successors were Oswald, Ealdwulf and Wulfstan. They were all also bishops of Worcester, for this reason. Oswald was born into no mean family, seeing that he was the nephew of archbishop Oda. He became a monk at Fleury in France. It was a common custom for any Englishmen of the day who were seized with a desire for the good to take up a monk's habit in the very monastery of the blessed Benedict from which this religious rule had begun to spread abroad.[4] So it was in this place that Oswald tamed the lusts of youth, for many years devoting himself to religion and learning. He resisted several letters of invitation from archbishop Oda, putting forward as an excuse his newness as a monk and his inexperience in religion. He did in the end come to England, but only because he had been alarmed by the news that his uncle was ill and already dying. On putting into Dover, he heard that his uncle was in fact dead, and he was on the point of returning at once to Fleury. His companions, however, reminded him of the duties due to the kinsmen of his parents. And so, after paying his proper respects to the holy archbishop, he came to see Oscytel, archbishop of York, who was his next closest kinsman. He was won over by his charm and for many years enjoyed living the life of piety in his household. In the meantime Dunstan left the sees of Worcester and London and moved on to Canterbury. He was not unaware of Oswald's holiness and efficiency, and got the king to make him bishop of Worcester.

Oswald gradually realised that there was material for good in the minds of the secular clergy resident there, if only there was someone who knew how to

[1] Edmund was king of England from 939 to 946.
[2] For fuller details of Wulfstan's political activities and his relations with the kings of England during his archbishopric of 931–56 see *The Blackwell Encyclopaedia*, s.v. 'Wulfstan I'.
[3] Oscytel, a Dane, was archbishop of York from 958 to 971.
[4] For example Germanus of Winchester (ch. 156). Fleury indeed was reported to hold Benedict's body. It had been reformed under the influence of Cluny c.930.

encourage it and bring it to life, and, instead of putting them off by violent methods, he won them over by skilfully including them in his religious ambitions. Because the episcopal church of St Peter was already fulfilling its function, he built another church to the name of the mother of God in St Peter's churchyard. He established monks there, willingly spending time with them and saying the divine office as one of them. When the people saw this, they all flocked to Oswald, thinking it would be a huge mistake to miss out on the blessings of so holy a bishop. And so the clergy, left in the middle, preferred to take up the monk's habit rather than to lose out themselves and to be laughed at by the townspeople. From that time the keyholder of paradise gave place to the portress of heaven, though there was no jealousy as the heavenly dwellers made this fair exchange. When news of this was wafted on the breezes to the king and the nobles, it made a friendship between them and Oswald. So that when York was without a bishop, the king, on the advice of Dunstan, filled it with a man who by his old-fashioned way of life would have just the knowledge necessary for controlling the barbarism of the people. However, he was not allowed to give up the see of Worcester: the king did not want the newly established settlement of monks to be deprived of the support of its foster-father.[1] The nobles obeyed Oswald readily, competing in offering him possessions for the foundation of monasteries which did not yet exist and the restoration of those which had fallen down. When I get the chance, I shall give as long an account of these monasteries as seems proper.[2]

And so that he might not deprive his country of that one good without which the others seem almost pointless, Oswald invited to England outstanding scholars, whom he looked after generously. One of them was Abbo, a monk from Fleury, who brought his rich harvest of knowledge to England, and who on the orders of archbishop Dunstan added to the world's books an account of the sufferings of Edmund the martyr.[3] Later he returned home and, on being made abbot of Fleury, set himself to follow zealously a strict religious life. But when he was endeavouring to practise this regime in a cell of Fleury in Gascony which today is still called Regula,[4] he was speared to death and sent to the world above by the fierce Gascon monks, who could not stomach his way of doing things.

But Oswald for many years looked after both sees, although he went more often to Worcester. He outlived Dunstan by five years and Æthelwald by ten. He gave the English so much cause for admiration that he seemed to show forth the two of them in his one person, reproducing the authority of the one,

---

[1] Stenton thinks that an arrangement which 'annexed a rich see in a peaceful country to the ill-endowed archbishopric of a very turbulent province' was politically justified (*Anglo-Saxon England*, p. 436).

[2] In chs. 155, 162, 181.

[3] Abbo spent two years teaching at Ramsey Abbey, which Oswald had founded (ch. 181). His pupils included the learned Byrhtferth, who wrote *The Life of St Oswald*, our chief source of information about the bishop.

[4] Or in French, La Réole. The traveller on the Autoroute between Bordeaux and Narbonne can easily visit La Réole by turning off at Junction 4.

the efficiency of the other and the piety of both. On the day before his death he was standing for a long time in front of the doors of the church at Worcester, gazing up to heaven and weeping bitterly. When those near by asked why he was looking up to heaven intently, he replied, 'Brothers, let me look at the place where I am preparing to go. I shall soon set aside my body, as the time of my escape from it is at hand.' His companions were surprised. He had not previously given any indication that he was ill, but in fact had given himself to a more extensive care for his body than usual. But next day, when he had washed the feet of the poor[1] and as usual was repeating the verse, 'Glory be to the Father, and to the Son, and to the Holy Spirit', just as he was genuflecting, his breath of life departed from him. He was buried in the church of the blessed Mary, and twelve years later was lifted from the ground, after divine signs had commanded this. It was an amazing miracle that, although his whole body had turned to dust, the priestly stole which he had been wearing had not experienced the decay of corruption right up to that day, but was still intact for divine examination.

He was succeeded in both sees by Ealdwulf, formerly abbot of Peterborough, who had the reputation of being a holy and respected man. His holiness means we can pardon him for holding two sees contrary to canon law, as he certainly did not do this out of ambition but from necessity. This is not the case with his successor Wulfstan, whose character and piety were very different. Ealdwulf lies buried at Worcester. He was also venerated in the monastery at Fleury, as in the number of his gifts to it he had tried to emulate the generosity of Oswald. After Wulfstan Ælfric took up the see of York, and Leofsige that of Worcester. Ælfric was bishop in the time of Cnut and Harthacnut. He is held in detestation because it was on his advice that Harthacnut dug up the body of his brother Harold, cut off the head and ordered it to be thrown into the Thames as an example to men of infamy. Also, as he was hated by the people of Worcester for his refusal of their bishopric, he advised Harthacnut to burn their city and seize the possessions of the citizens, when they had persistently opposed the collectors of the king's taxes.

Cynesige succeeded Ælfric, and he in his turn was followed by Ealdred, who previously had risen from being a monk at Winchester to being bishop of Worcester.[2] He took advantage of the simple nature of king Edward and assumed the archbishopric of York without giving up his previous see, having put a case more by money than argument that this had been the custom of his predecessors. Then, having got his plan approved of by the king, he journeyed to Rome. He was accompanied by two bishops just elected, Giso of Wells and Walter of Hereford,[3] and by Tostig, earl of Northumberland. Pope Nicholas greeted the earl kindly, and got him to sit at his side in the council, which he

---

[1] It was Oswald's custom during Lent to wash the feet of twelve poor men daily. He died on 29 February 992. See Loyn, *The English Church*, pp. 16–17, and Stenton, *Anglo-Saxon England*, p. 450, for Oswald's part in the tenth-century monastic revival.

[2] Ealdred became bishop of Worcester in 1046 and archbishop of York in 1061.

[3] Giso from Lothingaria is first mentioned in ch. 90. Walter, queen Emma's chaplain and another foreign appointment, is described in ch. 163.

had summoned to deal with simony; he granted the prayers of Giso and Walter,[1] as they were men of no small learning and free of any stain of simony. But towards Ealdred he was severe and stripped him of all his honours, as on his own admission he was in the wrong, being found to be bishop of both sees. So they were returning home with different degrees of success when one and the same trouble came upon them all alike. For they were attacked by bandits who robbed them of everything down to their last penny apart from the clothes on their backs. But then, with their bodies only unharmed, they fled back to Rome. This misfortune gave Ealdred the chance to recover his titles. Tostig also attacked the pope with harsh, insulting words and got from him the decision he wanted. Tostig said that distant peoples would go in little fear of the pope's excommunication, seeing that it was just laughed at by brigands who lived near by. He might get angry with those who knelt before him in supplication, but he had little control over rebels. He would have to agree either that ensuring that taxes were paid to him was his own responsibility or that he had lost them through his own deceitful behaviour. For, when the king of England heard about this, he would justly refuse to pay Peter's pence to Nicholas,[2] especially as he, Tostig, would not fail to emphasise the truth of the news. This threatening thunderbolt terrified the Roman prelates, and they persuaded the pope to restore to Ealdred his archbishopric and pallium: it was wrong, they argued, for Ealdred to return to his country ignominiously, stripped of his honours. The pope listened to the voice of reason, though with this counterweight of control that Worcester should have its own bishop appointed.

The suppliants got home safely, consoled for their previous losses by the great generosity which the pope had lavished upon all of them. They were followed as they went away by legates from Rome, who with the consent of Ealdred ordained that holy man, Wulfstan, as bishop of Worcester. For no good man was accepting pontifical office from Stigand, nominal archbishop of Canterbury at that time, seeing that he himself had not entered the sheepfold through the door. Despite repeated summonses from the papal see, Stigand either by postponements or presents avoided obeying any of these until the arrival of king William, as no tricks or subterfuges could get around him. Indeed William brought widespread notoriety upon Stigand by refusing to accept from him the sacrament of the king's blessing. It was Ealdred who listened to the king's plea and performed the consecration, having previously in the presence of the whole people got William to swear an oath that he would treat his subjects with moderation and dispense the same laws to both English and French. And so Ealdred, as long as William did treat his people with moderation, loved him as his own son and honoured him as king. But when the king required of the people the payment of unreasonable taxes, the bishop sent

[1] That he would consecrate them as bishops of Wells and Hereford.
[2] Payments to Rome, probably begun by king Offa, had developed into a form of taxation known as 'Peter's pence', levied at the rate of a penny per household, payable each year by 1 August (St Peter's Day). See *The Blackwell Encyclopaedia*, *s.v.* 'Alms'.

envoys to speak to him. They only just managed an audience with the king and were dismissed with angry words. And so Ealdred immediately brandished against the king and all his descendants the weapon of the curse, having first declared that a bishop who had given an undeserved blessing could utter a deserved curse. When this was reported to the king, his heart was softened by the pleas of his friends and he sent messengers to win Ealdred round. But the bishop died before the messengers had arrived. As often happens, his distress of mind had brought on a physical illness, and he had taken to his bed and died.[1]

Ealdred's independent spirit shone forth clearly in one remark, which I shall give in English, because it is impossible to get the same jingle in Latin as in English. Urse d'Abitot, having been appointed sheriff of Worcester by king William, built a castle almost at the very entrance gate of the monastery. Indeed the moat of the castle had caused the collapse of part of the monastic cemetery. The monks complained to the archbishop, who as bishop had been their protector, and Ealdred, as soon as he saw Urse, attacked him with these words, 'You are called Urse, receive God's curse.' This is neat in English, but the word play is lost in Latin where we can only say, 'You are called Ursus, receive the malediction of God and also', which I did not put in English, 'that of myself and all consecrated bishops, if you do not take away your castle. You can be sure that your descendants will not for long have an inheritance on the ground belonging to St Mary.' Ealdred said that this would come true, and we have seen it happen. For after a few years Urse's son Roger, who had inherited his father's possessions, was driven from them by king Henry, who was gravely displeased that Roger in a moment of hot-headed rashness had commanded the death of one of his servants.

Chapter 116 The destruction of the monasteries in the province of York[2]

The death of Ealdred and his burial at York was immediately followed by the catastrophe which I have already mentioned.[3] It fell upon us at the order of king William. It was then indeed that all the nobles of the English withered away, cut down by the sickle of war; the monasteries, which twinkled like stars throughout the whole province, had already previously been destroyed in the time of the Danes.[4] Their half-ruined walls still stand, not to give pleasure to the eye, but to remind us of the sadness of their destruction. Here once was the monastery of Wearmouth, a famous place of learning for Bede and many men of letters. Here

---

[1] Ealdred died on 11 September 1069. R. Allen Brown sums up Ealdred as 'a man who had done more then most to reconcile the two worlds of England and Normandy' (*The Normans and the Norman Conquest*, p. 169). For a general assessment of Ealdred as an 'old-fashioned prince bishop' see Loyn, *The English Church*, pp. 61–2.

[2] This is the first of two Chapters 116 in the Rolls series text edited by N. E. S. A. Hamilton.

[3] In ch. 99.

[4] Knowles examines the evidence and concludes that in the reign of Æthelstan the whole of England, not merely the province of York, was without any organised monastic life (*The Monastic Order*, pp. 31–6).

was Streneshalh, renowned for its choir of holy maidens, and for its tombs of holy bishops and outstanding kings: now called Whitby, its charred ashes are being fanned into new life by the busy efforts of certain people.[1] Recently the bodies of saints have been found there and lifted up into prominence. They include bishop Trumwine,[2] king Oswiu and his daughter Ælfflæd who was abbess of this monastery after Hild, and also that monk who, according to Bede,[3] received as a gift from God the knowledge of song. The many miracles which still now are said to descend from above are an indication that his gift from God was no common one. And so I cannot go through the monasteries of this province one by one: old ones have been completely destroyed and new ones are not yet common knowledge. Anyway I have not undertaken in this work to name all the monasteries of England, but only those which have won unusual fame and high glory from the bodies buried there of our native saints. Furthermore, some have been kept from my notice through the antiquity of their story, others through the newness of their construction; some remain unknown because of the long history of this province, others because the saints who lie at rest in them did not do enough miracles to achieve fame. So even if of necessity my pen fails to perform its task for all these monasteries, they will not heave too many sighs over my silence, seeing that once upon a time they achieved fame through the will of God or through their own efforts.

In the meantime, while I am dealing with the province of York, it occurs to me to mention the names of the bishops of Hexham and of those at Candida Casa, which is called Whithorn in English. Although they were once subject to the archbishop of York, they do not still exist in our own day, and so do not have a proper place in my strict scheme. So let them slip in amongst the archbishops of York, and get a mention in the society of their company.

Chapter 117 The bishops of Hexham (671–821)[4]

The place called Hexham is eighty-four miles distant from York. It was paying taxes to the king's treasury, when Wilfrid of blessed memory got it from that blessed queen Æthelthryth in exchange for other possessions of his. At Hexham there arose buildings with walls of a fearsome height, set out with various passages linked by spiral staircases, a miracle of polished stone![5] Much of it was built under Wilfrid's own supervision, but he was

---

[1] Their leader was Reinfrid, a Norman knight who became a monk. He began the rebuilding of Whitby c.1076. See Knowles, *The Monastic Order*, pp. 165–71, for the revival of monastic life in the north after the conquest.
[2] Bishop of Whithorn 681–6.
[3] *Ecclesiastical History* 4:24. The singer was Cædmon, fl. 700, who transformed the stories of Christianity into old English verse.
[4] This is the first of two Chapters 117 in Hamilton.
[5] Stephen's *Life of St Wilfrid* describes Wilfrid's main church of St Andrew as being a building of several stories, linked by winding passages with spiral staircases, perhaps like the later Norman nave at St Albans abbey. The church was destroyed by later medieval works, but Mayr-Harting gives a description of it, based on Stephen and archaeology (*The Coming of Christianity*, pp. 158–9). See also H. M. and J. Taylor, *Anglo-Saxon Architecture*, 3 vols. (Cambridge, 1965–78).

also helped by the advice of master masons, who had been brought over from Rome by the hope of rich rewards. At that time it was frequently claimed in common talk, and even written down in books, that there were no buildings north of the Alps which could match them. People who come from Rome nowadays say the same thing: at the sight of the buildings of Hexham, they swear that they have the pomp of Rome before their eyes, for all the ravages of war over the centuries have not destroyed the beauty of the place. Wilfrid was the first bishop there.[1] After his violent expulsion, he was succeeded by Eata, then Tunberht, then John. After Wilfrid's return to England and his resumption of the see, he was succeeded, on his death, by Acca, an exceptionally hard-working and holy man. Both qualities are vouched for by Bede,[2] whom we can trust since it is well known that it was at Acca's prompting and with his support that Bede compiled many volumes of writings.[3] Acca, however, met with no greater fortune than his master, so the chronicles relate, for three years after Bede's death he was expelled from his see. We do not know whether he returned. Frithuberht succeeded Acca. Tilberht came next, to be followed himself by Æthelberht. There is a letter of Alcuin to Æthelberht and his congregation, which includes the words, 'O most noble offspring of holy fathers, successors to their honourable lives of holiness, dwellers in places of great beauty, do you follow in the footsteps of your fathers, so that you may deserve to ascend from these fairest of dwellings to share the everlasting beatitude of those who bore you.' There were only three bishops of Hexham after Æthelberht, namely Heardred, Eanberht and Tidfrith.[4] For, as I have said elsewhere and shall say again, the army of the Danes, feared since the days of Alcuin, came to our land. They killed or put to flight the people from Hexham, set fire to the roofs of their dwellings and exposed their private rooms to the skies. Hexham is now a small town, subject to the archbishop of York.

Chapter 118 The bishops of Whithorn (731–*c*.800)[5]

The place called Candida Casa is at the very end of England, next to Scotland. St Ninian, the confessor, a Briton by birth, lies buried there. He was the first to preach the gospel of Christ to those people. It was his work that gave the name to the place, for he built there a church of gleaming stone that seemed a miracle to the Britons.[6] Men of old knew that this St Ninian was a man of outstanding virtues, for Alcuin writes in a letter to the brothers of Candida Casa, 'I appeal

---

[1] From 671.
[2] Bede describes Acca, who became bishop of Hexham in 709, in *Ecclesiastical History* 5:20.
[3] The more natural way of taking the Latin of this sentence is that Bede prompted Acca to compile many writings, but this conflicts with our knowledge that Bede composed commentaries on various Old Testament books and on Acts at the prompting of Acca, who also requested Stephen to write his *Life of St Wilfrid*.
[4] Tidfrith was bishop of Hexham from 806 to 821.
[5] This is the first of two Chapters 118 in Hamilton.
[6] Ninian's church of St Martin with its gleaming stone gave the name of Candida Casa or Whithorn to this town in Galloway, as both names mean 'white building'.

to your bond of unity as holy men, that you keep alive the memory of our name in the church of your most holy father, bishop Ninian, a man famous for his many virtues. Only recently, for example, I have received poems about Ninian sent to me by my faithful disciples of the church at York, in which I recognised both the learning of their maker and the holiness of the man who performed the miracles described in the poems.' At Candida Casa in the last days of Bede Pecthelm was made the first bishop.[1] Before this he had spent a lot of time among the West Saxons, where he had deservedly won a place among the disciples of Aldhelm. He was followed by Frithwald, Pectwine, Æthelberht and Badwulf. I have not come across any other bishops of this place. In fact the bishopric soon came to an end, for, as I have said, Candida Casa was on the English frontier, and an easy victim for raids by Picts or Scots. So now that I have run through those bishops whom I thought I should not leave out, I shall return to York.

Chapter 116 Thomas of Bayeux as archbishop of York (1070–1100)[2]

In 1070 Thomas, a canon of Bayeux, was made archbishop of York by king William, and stayed in this office for thirty years. Throughout his whole life he was a man of integrity. No criticism should be brought against any of his deeds or words, except that at the start of his archbishopric he became involved in a dispute over the primacy of Canterbury, though this was caused by a mistake rather than wrong-headed stubbornness. I have described the resolution of this dispute in the first book of *The Deeds of the Bishops*.[3] People who saw him envied him his elegance and striking appearance. As a young man he had a perfect body, both in its strength and its symmetry. When he grew old, his face was a lively red, and his hair as white as that of a swan. His generosity made his successors despair. They claimed that he had been excessively wasteful in setting aside a great part of the episcopal lands for the use of the clergy. But Thomas united the clergy, now that they were properly provided for and educated.[4] He completed a new church, begun from its foundations. No wicked gossip ever attacked his celibacy. Men compared his knowledge with that of the philosophers of old, but this did not go to his head. His words and his looks were equally winning, and his manners were gentle. His singing voice and speaking voice were in no way second rate, and he composed many hymns. If anybody in his hearing made some sound by way of a joke, he immediately changed it into praise of God. He took very great trouble to ensure that the clergy should perform their music in church in a masculine

---

[1] In 731. Badwulf, the last bishop, was consecrated in 791.
[2] This is the second of two Chapters 116 in Hamilton.
[3] In chs. 25–42. William, as often, seeks extenuation for people.
[4] Like Maurice of London or Osmund of Salisbury (ch. 83), Thomas established a cathedral chapter of secular canons. As Matthew, *The Norman Conquest*, p. 191, puts it, 'he had to reassemble the canons, provide for their common needs, persuade them to improve their own holdings and to participate in common concerns'.

manner, and not spoil anything with their effeminate delivery, 'mincing the words with their soft palates', as Persius says.[1] In the fullness of years, abundantly blessed by the honours of men and the grace of God, he died in the November of the first year of the reign of king Henry, having crowned him as king in the previous August in the absence of the archbishop of Canterbury.[2]

Chapter 117 Letter of pope Paschal to Gerard of York (December 1102)[3]

Immediately Gerard was elected and made archbishop. He was the nephew of bishop Walkelin of Winchester, and had previously been bishop of Hereford. While he was hesitating to make his profession of obedience to the primate of Canterbury, he received this letter from pope Paschal.

> Pope Paschal, servant of the servants of God, sends greetings and his apostolic blessing to his venerable brother Gerard, archbishop of York. Although we cannot be unaware that you have acted badly, in opposition to us and in fact to the holy Roman church, your mother, we instruct you in this present letter not to neglect to make your professions of obedience to our venerable brother Anselm, archbishop of Canterbury. For we have heard that your predecessor Thomas once made an issue of this same matter. But as soon as the matter had been discussed in the presence of my lord, pope Alexander II, and a decision had been taken on his orders after various investigations, Thomas made this same profession of obedience to Lanfranc, Anselm's predecessor, and to his successors. So we also, with God as our authority, wish the decision then taken to be binding and adhered to completely.

Chapter 118 Thomas succeeds Gerard as archbishop of York (1109)[4]

Gerard did not read this letter which was sent to him, as it was unnecessary. On his own initiative he had forestalled the order of the pope and at the urging of the king had given himself up into the hands of Anselm, saying that as archbishop of York he would make the same profession of obedience to him as he had made as bishop of Hereford. Now the wickedness which the pope had complained of was that Gerard, on his return from Rome with the pallium, had infected the apostolic see with his own lie when he told the king that if he acted on other matters according to ecclesiastical law, the pope would be willing to allow him to make ecclesiastical investitures.[5] Gerard was not

[1] *Satires* 1:35.
[2] Anselm, archbishop of Canterbury, was in Lyons at the time. See ch. 55.
[3] This is the second of two Chapters 117 in Hamilton.
[4] This is the second of two Chapters 118 in Hamilton.
[5] See ch. 57 for an earlier account of the report made by Gerard's embassy to the pope. On the tug-of-war between Anselm and Gerard over his submission to Anselm see Southern, *St Anselm and his Biographer*, pp. 131–7.

unlettered and he was a fluent speaker. His death was unexpected. He had been ill beforehand, but only slightly. In his illness he was lying for a little while in a garden next to his house, so that he might enjoy the healthier air out of doors with its scents of sweet-smelling flowers. He told his attendants to go into the house and attend to their bodily needs for a time. They went away, but when they came back after their meal they wept for their dead master. I hope rumour made this up, and that a man with the grace given to bishops did not die in this way.[1] Certainly the canons of York opposed with the greatest stubbornness his burial in the church, and would hardly allow a humble sod of earth to be thrown on his body before its doors. However, after some years, his successor Thomas lessened the indignity of such a burial by giving him an honourable burial inside the church next to his predecessors.

Thomas was the son of Samson, bishop of Worcester. Elected as archbishop, he was invited by Anselm to come to Canterbury to be consecrated according to custom.[2] At first he politely declined: he was grateful for the invitation, but asked for a postponement, as the great retinue involved required vast sums of money to be spent on it. He was summoned a second time, but reported that he was kept back by the arguments and forcible intervention of his secular clergy. Summoned yet a third time by the bishops of London and Rochester, he gave a point-blank refusal. Anselm informed pope Paschal of Thomas's decision, and as the weakness of his bodily strength was hastening his journey heavenwards, he wrote Thomas a letter, and also sent a single copy with his seal to all the individual bishops of England, so that they might know how they ought to behave towards Thomas.

Chapter 119 Letter of Anselm to Thomas of York

Anselm, minister of the church of Canterbury, to Thomas, archbishop elect of York. I, Anselm, archbishop of Canterbury and primate of the whole of Britain, am speaking to you, Thomas, in the sight of omnipotent God, and, as spokesman of God himself, I interdict you from any priestly function which you have undertaken at my order in my parish as my suffragan. And I command you not to presume to concern yourself with any pastoral care, until you have given up the rebellion which you have begun against the church of Canterbury, and made to it the profession of obedience which your predecessors, archbishops Thomas and Gerard, made according to the

---

[1] As the text stands, it is difficult to see why William should regard such a death as a punishment from God. In fact William later deleted passages from his original manuscript. Before the words 'His death was unexpected', there was originally a sentence about charges made against Gerard, which included suspicion of interest in necromancy, seeing that he used to read the works of the obscure theologian, Julius Firmicus, in the mornings. And after 'they wept for their dead master', he had originally written, '. . . and for the book concerning strange practices found on his cushion'.

[2] As Southern points out (*St Anselm and his Biographer*, p. 36), Thomas's election was a critical moment for Anselm. As Gerard had already promised obedience to Anselm as bishop of Hereford, it was possible for Anselm to assume that this obedience still bound him as archbishop of York. No such assumption could be made about Thomas.

ancient custom of their predecessors. But if you choose to persist in this course rather than give it up, I interdict all the bishops of the whole of Britain under a permanent curse from putting their hands on you to advance you to the archbishopric, or, if you have been there advanced by foreigners, from regarding you as bishop or as being in any Christian communion with them. Also, Thomas, as God's spokesman, I interdict you under the same curse from ever receiving the blessing of the bishopric of York, unless first you make the profession which your predecessors, Thomas and Gerard, made to the church of Canterbury. But if you totally give up the bishopric of York, I permit you to perform the priestly functions, which are already yours.[1]

Chapter 120 Thomas makes his submission to Canterbury (1109)

The king at that time was in Normandy. On his return to his kingdom he opened discussions on the matter. Anselm's letter of interdiction was read out in his presence. All the bishops of England accepted and approved it. Only the earl of Mellent had tried to twist acceptance of it into being an insult to the power of the king. The unanimity of the bishops on this matter, which was not even opposed by Thomas's father, the bishop of Worcester, showed that they preferred to be stripped of all their powers rather than fail to obey the commands of their father Anselm. The bishops' piety was backed up by the support of the prince,[2] when he added these remarks to the debate, 'Whatever other people may think about this matter, my own view is that I am unwilling to lie under sentence of excommunication from father Anselm even for as little time as an hour. So, seeing that, even if we forget the letter, Anselm possesses privileges from the apostolic see, while at the same time there exist statutes, drawn up by the council of the whole realm in the presence of my father and mother, which buttress the powers claimed by the church of Canterbury, my opinion is that Thomas should choose either to make his submission to that church or say goodbye to this bishopric.' Thomas yielded, though to power rather than to reasoning: he made a profession of obedience to the church of Canterbury and accepted from its servant, I mean Richard bishop of London, what he had refused to accept from its master. Late in the day he felt sorrow for his too easy trust in his secular clergy, and as long as he lived he carried around a guilty conscience for depriving himself of benediction from Anselm.

---

[1] Thomas had been royal chaplain. Southern says, 'no one can mistake the exaggerated intensity of Anselm's feeling on the subject', as he puts out all his powers to bring Thomas to submission in this letter, the last he ever wrote (*St Anselm and his Biographer*, p. 139).

[2] Prince William, heir to the throne, who went down on the White Ship in 1120. Southern, *St Anselm and his Biographer*, p. 139, notes the irony of Anselm's wishes on this matter eventually being secured by the traditional combination of king and bishops, against which he had so often fought.

Chapter 121 Thomas receives the pallium

At that time a cardinal called Odolric was in England. He had brought the pallium for the church at York, which was to be disposed of according to the advice of Anselm. But on finding that Anselm was already dead,[1] Odolric hesitated, being uncertain what to do. When, however, the whole dispute was settled by the power of the king, it was decreed that the same cardinal should take the pallium to York. He did so, and Thomas ascended to the heights of the archbishopric, clad in this garment. From his youth up, so it was believed, he had kept free of women and all vices. He set an example of generosity to all. His piety and his support of his priests are noteworthy. He died while a young man, having performed his archbishop's functions for barely four years.

Chapter 122 Thurstan succeeds Thomas (February 1114)

He was succeeded by Thurstan, a priest who never changed his mind. When, some years after his acceptance of the office, he was still refusing to make his profession of obedience to Ralph, archbishop of Canterbury, at the king's wish he resigned from the archbishopric of his own accord. But when afterwards his priests advised him to make the journey to Rome,[2] he succeeded in bringing back this letter.

Chapter 123 Pope Paschal requires Thurstan's reinstatement

Bishop Pascal, servant of the servants of God, sends greetings and his apostolic blessing to his beloved son Henry, illustrious king of England. God has brought it about that we have great confidence in your uprightness, and shall have a still greater. And so we advise your excellency to remember all the days of your life the divine grace which has given you peace in your land and the conception of justice. So take care that you pay honour to God and his churches in your kingdom, and administer justice efficiently. If you honour God, the honour paid to you will assuredly increase. We have heard that the wise, hard-working man chosen to look after the church at York has been removed from that church without any legal hearing. This of course goes against the divine justice and the decisions of the holy fathers. We do not wish the church at Canterbury to lose power nor do we want York to be the victim of a previous judgement, but we do think that you should maintain strong and unimpaired that arrangement between these two churches set up by the blessed Gregory, apostle to the English. So the man chosen for York should without question be restored to his church, as justice demands. But if disputes arise between these two churches, these should be discussed before me, with both parties being present.

[1] Anselm died in 1109.
[2] William referred to this journey in ch. 70.

Chapter 124 Pope Calixtus consecrates Thurstan as archbishop of York

Bolstered up by this letter Thurstan returned to his see with a light heart. In the meantime the dispute between Thurstan and archbishop Ralph was escalating daily. No inducements or threats could bring Ralph to lay his hands in blessing on Thurstan, unless he first made his profession of obedience, while Thurstan vowed that he would not do such a thing, even if it put his life in danger. So when pope Gelasius succeeded Paschal and made a journey to the north of the Alps, both archbishops decided to meet him, intending to get his support for their case on the spot. But their eagerness received a check, for the death of the pope soon followed. In the end, when Calixtus, Gelasius' successor, came to Rheims to hold a council, Thurstan hurried there with all speed, having promised the king that he would contrive nothing contrary to the fair fame of the church of Canterbury. But, as soon as he saw an opportunity he forgot his promise, he broke his word and contrary to all the practices of his predecessors obtained his blessing as a bishop from the pope.[1]

In fact before Thurstan's arrival Seffrid, afterwards bishop of Chichester and brother of Ralph, had come to the pope as the king's legate to warn him against any attempt made by himself to consecrate Thurstan or his permitting anyone else to perform the ceremony, unless it was the archbishop of Canterbury according to ancient custom. Further, if the pope himself wished to use the powers of his apostolate to oppose this, he could be certain that the king would not change his intentions on this matter, even if it involved the loss of his crown. The pope replied, 'The king would be wrong to think that I am going to go against his wishes on the issue being discussed. For it has never been my intention in any way to lessen the importance of the church of Canterbury, a church presided over by countless famous fathers, as practically the whole world well knows.' Won over by these fair words the legate hurriedly returned home. But after his departure the pope caved in to the demands of those Romans who had become Thurstan's friends and consecrated him, although John, archdeacon of Canterbury, openly protested about it. The reply of the pope to John was 'It is not our intention to do any wrong to the church of Canterbury but to put our decisions into practice while keeping safe the rights and powers of Canterbury.' Those who heard this reply thought it frivolous, such was the distance between words and deeds.[2]

Chapter 125 The death of Thurstan (3 February 1140)

When the king heard of it, he banished Thurstan from all territories under his sway He was unwilling to soften this harsh decision even when the pope, who

---

[1] William here keeps the promise he made in the last sentence of ch. 70 to give an account of Thurstan's scheme.

[2] As the monks of Canterbury regarded the submission of the archbishop of York to their primacy as one of their most important rights, the reply of pope Calixtus does indeed seem frivolous.

was staying at Gisors,[1] intervened and declared that with the authority of the
blessed Peter he would remove the king from the faith by which he claimed to
be bound. So this achieved nothing and from then on the matter actually
remained unsettled. But in the following year when Calixtus was now seated
more firmly on the papal throne and was putting his own wishes into effect
with some freedom, he sent a letter with the command that either Thurstan
should take possession of his bishopric or the punishment of a curse would fall
upon the king and the punishment of suspension from his sacred office upon
the archbishop of Canterbury. Fear of this forced the king to abandon his
policy, and Thurstan was received into his see.[2] And so, although archbishop
Ralph and his successor William made many attempts against Thurstan and
poured forth many arguments, Thurstan by his own stubbornness rebutted and
made harmless all their allegations. He died a most holy death exactly four
years after Henry I, although he had previously renounced his bishopric and
become a monk at the Cluniac cell in Pontefract.[3]

Chapter 126 The bishops of Lindisfarne (635–793)

Of all the sees situated in Northumbria which once recognised the supremacy
of York the only remaining see is the one which was at Lindisfarne.[4] It is a
small island, now called Holy Island by the natives. It was chosen as the see for
his bishopric by that great saint Aidan after he turned his back on the
processions and crowds of York and was searching for silence and holy
poverty.[5] His successors, Finan, Colman, Tuda and Eata,[6] followed his example of poverty and withdrawal. Most famous was the peerless Cuthbert,[7]
who rests in his grave even now with his body uncorrupted, and was the only
one to deserve the mark of grace of this incorruption never even being
questioned. Eadberht, as the prerogative of his extreme sanctity, deserved to
be buried in the tomb which his predecessor of blessed memory had sanctified
by his body lying there for eleven years uncorrupted. When the monks brought
to him those most sacred garments, which for all those years had escaped the
taint of corruption though buried in the earth, Eadberht himself prophesied
that his own death and burial would speedily follow. Bede tells this story in

---

[1] A town in Norman Vexin.
[2] This dispute strengthened the position of Rome as legal authority in the Western Church. As
   Matthew puts it, 'Henry was justifiably outraged. Anselm's individual respect for Rome had been
   bad enough. Now Rome was invoked to protect other privileges, and a chapter of canons was
   presuming to dictate to the king' (*The Norman Conquest*, p. 238).
[3] And two years before his death in 1138 had played a dramatic part in the defeat of the Scots at
   the battle of the Standard. Knowles describes his death scene on p. 478 of *The Monastic Order*.
[4] By William's own day this see had been transferred to Durham.
[5] Aidan established his see and a monastic dependency of Iona on Lindisfarne in 635.
[6] Eata (bishop 676–85) was appointed to a new see on the expulsion of Wilfrid from York and the
   division of his diocese. See p. 147 n. 2. Cuthbert was bishop 685–7.
[7] For Cuthbert see B. Colgrave, *Two Lives of St Cuthbert* (Cambridge, 1940). Colgrave translates
   and edits Bede's prose life and a life by an anonymous monk of Lindisfarne.

great detail in his life of St Cuthbert.[1] The successors of Eadberht were Eadfrith, Æthelwald, Cynewulf and Higebald. It was Eadfrith who begged and demanded that Bede should extol Cuthbert both in rhetorical prose and in the sweetness of verse. In the time of Higebald[2] the Danes, without even sparing the sacred altars, ravaged the island. The evidence for this is a letter written by Alcuin to Higebald, which goes like this.

Chapter 127 Alcuin consoles the monks after the Danish attack of 793

> To bishop Higebald and all the congregation of the church of Lindisfarne, most excellent sons in Christ of their father, the most blessed bishop Cuthbert, greetings from Alcuin the deacon. When I was with you, your loving friendship used to make me very happy, but now, absent though I am, it is your catastrophic disaster which makes me very sad. How things have changed! Those pagans have now despoiled the sanctuaries of God, shedding the blood of saints all around the altar and trampling on the bodies of the saints in the church as if they were dung in a courtyard.[3] What trust can the churches of Britain have, if St Cuthbert and all his numerous fellow saints did not defend their own church.

Then he went on to encourage them not to fall below the standards of their predecessors by staining the purity of their commitment with extravagance in dress or gluttony. He warned them that such things happened because of transgressions of the divine law, and that still worse would happen in the future, if they thought to persist in their sins. And at the foot of the letter he also added:

> With God's help I am planning to visit our lord, the emperor Charlemagne, when, by the mercy of God, he has conquered his enemies[4] and returns home. If on that occasion I can do anything for your young men who have been led into captivity by the pagans or for your other needs, I shall not hesitate to perform it diligently.

Chapter 128 Letter of Alcuin to king Æthelred[5]

> Disaster! The church of St Cuthbert has been spattered with the blood of the priests of God and despoiled of all its objects of beauty, the most holy place

---

[1] Also in *Ecclesiastical History* 4:30. St Cuthbert had put it into the hearts of the brothers to put his bones in a new coffin. They found the garments enclosing the body undefiled and wonderfully bright, and took them to Eadberht who was spending Lent by the sea. Cuthbert's body was opulently enshrined. The Lindisfarne Gospels, written by Eadfrith and bound by Æthelwald, were one result of his rapidly growing cult.

[2] Higebald was bishop 781–802.

[3] 'as if they were dung in a courtyard' is Isaiah 5:25.

[4] Charlemagne's enemies were the Saxons, who had revolted from him.

[5] King of Northumbria 774–94. See ch. 99 for another letter from Alcuin to Æthelred prophesying the disaster.

in the whole of Britain handed over to the ravaging of pagan peoples. Lindisfarne saw the beginning of Christianity in Northumbria, after St Paulinus had left York.[1] And now it has seen the beginnings of calamitous destruction.

Chapter 129 Cuthbert's body taken to Norham-on-Tweed (c.820)

So they took counsel and decided to transfer the bodies of the saints to the mainland, seeing that the island was so exposed to the eager attacks of raiders from the sea. A group attempted to take the sacred body of the great Cuthbert over the seas to Ireland, regarding this as a holy theft. But their attempt came to nothing. Either they spent many days on the shore waiting for a wind, or, if they did put out to sea, they were immediately driven back by winds rather stronger than usual. And so they buried the sacred body with all due honours at Ubbenford[2] by the river Tweed (I am not sure whether Ubbenford is a bishop's see). The body lay there for many years until the arrival of king Æthelred,[3] although in the meantime the saint did not take a holiday from helping his people, but roamed throughout the whole of Britain, doing his miracles. If I write about one of them, I do not think it will be out of place. The miracle is the more remarkable in that the unmistakable appearance of Cuthbert in person brought back liberty to the whole of England and ended its slavery.

Chapter 130 Cuthbert's relics moved to a new cathedral in Durham (995)

King Alfred had been made so helpless by the attacks of the barbarians that he was lying hidden in inglorious fashion on a very tiny island called Athelney.[4] I have spoken about this island earlier, when dealing with the bishops of Wells.[5] So one day, while he was lying asleep at home, as his distress of mind demanded, and his companions were at various points on the banks of the river, the blessed Cuthbert miraculously spoke to him as he slept, 'I am Cuthbert, once bishop of Lindisfarne. God has sent me to bring you good tidings, for England has now paid the enormous penalty for its sins, and at long last because of the merits of its native saints God is looking down upon it with the eye of pity. You also, who have been so sadly driven from your kingdom, will after a short time be gloriously restored to your throne. Furthermore I will give you the clearest of signs. Today your fishermen will return, carrying a vast quantity of large fish in their baskets. This will be all the more miraculous seeing that during these days the unfriendly river with its

[1] In 625. See p. 140.
[2] Now called Norham-on-Tweed.
[3] In fact Cuthbert's body rested at Chester-le-Street from 883 to 995.
[4] King Alfred retreated to Athelney in May 878.
[5] See ch. 72.

frozen water has not allowed you to hope for such things. Also the cold rain falling from the sky has made all the skills of fishermen useless. You will gain the good fortune of ruling as a king again, if by the proper devotions you deserve it of God, your helper, and of me, his messenger.' With these words the saint freed the sleeping king from his cares, and also comforted the king's mother, who was sleeping near by, with the same joyful news. Both of them awoke and were over and over again telling how they had dreamed one and the same dream, when the fishermen came in and confirmed the dream by the vast quantity of their fish. And it was not long before Alfred was restored to his kingdom and all its glory, as I have described in more detail in my account of his deeds.[1]

These were the successors of Higebald: Ecgberht, Eardwulf, Cuthheard, Tilred, Wigred, Uhtred, Sæxhelm, Ealdred, Ealhdun[2] and Edmund. Edmund was made bishop by the most curious of chances. Now in the time of the Anglo-Saxons the election of bishops and abbots was in the hands of the priests and monks. In fact no monks served at the body of St Cuthbert, although by custom bishops were monks, following the example of their most holy father who as a monk had been in charge of priests. So, on the death of bishop Ealhdun the priests[3] had met to discuss the choice of their future ruler, and, as happens on such occasions, had not come to any definite decision because they were divided into two groups. As they were hesitating, Edmund suddenly appeared, for no one had thought to summon him, and with his usual facetiousness said, 'Take me and make me bishop.' They all, with their hearts set on fire by God, as it were, seized upon these words which had fallen from his lips as if they were a divine oracle. Edmund was stunned and sorry for his remark, as he preferred ball games to wearing a cowl, but they made him a monk and asked Æthelred, the king of the time, to make him their bishop. This prelude was a happy augury, as the people of Durham will tell you. The king cheerfully agreed to their request and a propitious divinity fulfilled their hopes. For in Edmund's bishopric the prosperity of the church increased greatly. The saint's body was brought to Durham and a completely new cathedral was built there.[4] Edmund did many other things, which cheating oblivion will never swallow up as the generations of citizens follow each other. Durham is on a hill. Starting from the level ground of a valley on the one side it rises up to a crest in a gentle, gradual slope. Although its site is high up and sufficiently steep and rocky to make the approach of an enemy impossible, the men of today have built a castle on the top. Right down at the foot of this castle flows a river full of fish, like very many rivers and like practically all the

[1] In *The Deeds of the Kings* 2:121.
[2] Ealhdun was bishop from 990 to 1018. By this time the bishop lived at Chester-le-Street, where he was the guardian of St Cuthbert's relics.
[3] These priests who guarded the saint's body 'fulfilled the liturgical offices, retaining many of the monastic uses which had been handed down the generations at Lindisfarne, but not constituting a monastic body in the full sense of the term' (Knowles, *The Monastic Order*, p. 165).
[4] The cathedral was actually begun by bishop Ealhdun in 995. Edmund was bishop of Durham 1020–40.

rivers of Northumbria. For in both the west and the north of England the Isis has such a superfluity of fish that country folk feed their pigs on the fishes that have been thrown up.

Chapter 131 Æthelwine rebels against king William (1070)

After Edmund came Eadred, Æthelric and Æthelwine.[1] The last of these was accused of rebellion in the days of king William, on the grounds that he had disturbed the king's peace by becoming a pirate. He was deported to Westminster in perpetual exile. For the rest of his life he lessened and washed away the charges brought against him in the past by his voluntary fasting and his floods of tears, and won a name for holiness among men. When he died, people who saw him handed down their memories of him to the next generation, and today his tomb does not go without crowds of petitioners with their vows.

Chapter 132 Walcher becomes bishop but is murdered (1080)

In his lifetime his place at Durham was taken by Walcher. As now both duke and bishop of Durham, he could rein in rebellions of the people with his sword, while moulding their morals with his eloquence. He was busily engaged in this, when he was shamefully put to death. This gave the king the chance to exterminate root and branch the remaining rebels left in that province, who just for a very short time had breathed again. The cause of his murder was as follows: the bishop had put his kinsman Gilbert in charge of secular affairs and a priest called Leofwine in charge of his household, as both of them were vigorous in action, though headstrong. Their pleasing energy led the bishop to put up with their lack of control, and because it was he who had elevated them, he now made still bigger the mountain of his kindnesses towards them. For we human beings are self-indulgent and promote our gifts with our own quiet support. A certain Ligwulf,[2] the guardian of St Cuthbert's tomb, was so loved by Cuthbert that the saint would openly stand by him as he kept vigil and tell him what he wanted doing. Well, Leofwine got Gilbert to murder this Ligwulf, since he was smitten with envy that Ligwulf by his knowledge and the impartiality of his judgements had built a stronger friendship with the bishop than himself. Walcher was shocked at the news and offered the dead man's angry family justice in a court of law, protesting that Leofwine would be responsible for the deaths of himself and his household.

---

[1] Æthelwine was the only bishop we know to have joined a rebellion against the Conqueror. He had been alarmed by William's northern campaign of 1069, and was outlawed before the end of 1070. (In Hamilton's edition in the Rolls Series Æthelwine is placed before Æthelric, but Æthelric was bishop 1046–55 and Æthelwine bishop 1056–71.)

[2] Ligwulf, a descendant of the ancient earls of Bernicia and someone who had known archbishop Ealdred, was very suited to be the intermediary between the bishop and the Englishmen of his province.

And when the matter came to trial,[1] the people were so distraught that nothing could calm them down or stop them putting the blame on the bishop: they claimed that they had seen both murderers engaged in friendly talk with the bishop in his palace just after Ligwulf's murder. The hearing became an angry shouting match, and when Gilbert of his own accord left the church, where he had been sitting beside the bishop, to buy the life of his master at the expense of peril to his own, he was impiously cut down. Even the bishop was put to death when he appeared at the doors, holding a branch in front of him as a sign of peace. And Leofwine, who had provided the spark for the blaze, himself leapt half-burnt from the church, since he had refused to leave it unless it was set on fire, and was then the target of a thousand spears. All this had been foretold by queen Eadgyth, the widow of king Edward. When she had seen Walcher being led to his consecration at Winchester, his milk-white curls, rosy cheeks and ample form prompted her to say, 'A pretty martyr we have here.' No doubt it was a shrewd guess at the ferocity of the Northumbrians which led her to make this prophecy. So Walcher departed this life, a man neither uncontrolled nor unlettered. He brought back under the control of priests[2] the secular canons who had become used to serving a monk, since they had always had a monk as a bishop.

Chapter 133 William of St Calais (1088–1096)

He was succeeded by William, who had been abbot of St Calais[3] and who established monks at Durham.[4] His power in politics and the ready eloquence of his tongue were especially seen in the time of king William II. So he was added to the company of the king's friends and made a prelate of England. But he did not remain in the favour of the king. Although there are no records now of any words or deeds of the ruler which were hostile to the bishop, William broke off his friendship with the king and joined the conspiracy of Odo of Bayeux and various others. When his side was defeated, he was exiled from England, but after two years was generously allowed to return by king William. He resumed his bishopric and took great pains to re-establish his former friendship with the king. He studied the king's character and would take the line he thought he saw the king taking. The result was that in the stormy quarrel which blew up between Anselm and king William, the bishop of Durham was the standard-bearer who roused the greatest number of troops

---

[1] For the settlement of terms with Ligwulf's kinsmen, an assembly was held at Gateshead. Walcher, refusing to plead in the open air, withdrew with his party into the church. The massacre was punished by a devastation of the countryside. See Stenton, *Anglo-Saxon England*, pp. 613–14.

[2] Walcher was a priest from the Rhineland. He found the secular canons of the cathedral following a life which included some monastic practices. He was thinking of introducing full monks into his cathedral when he was killed. See Knowles, *The Monastic Order*, pp. 166, 169.

[3] St Calais is in the diocese of Le Mans. Southern gives a useful sketch of William's career on pp. 184–5 of *Western Society and the Church in the Middle Ages*.

[4] He drew his community from the group of new arrivals in the north, who had refounded Jarrow and Wearmouth. See Knowles, *The Monastic Order*, p. 169.

against the archbishop.[1] Men say that he hoped either to win back the king's favour or to become archbishop himself, if Anselm were expelled.

But it was all in vain, for neither of his hopes came to anything. Very soon discord arose between bishop William and the king, and the bishop fell ill in Gloucester and took to his bed. The king's court was there at that time, and the bishop was ordered to appear to plead his case. When the bishop replied that his illness prevented him from coming, the king exclaimed, 'By St Luke's face, the man is shamming.' But in fact the illness which had come upon him was a genuine one, and he was near to death. When the bishops at his bedside opined that he should be buried in the cathedral at Durham, which he had so magnificently begun,[2] the bishop summoned up his strength again and breathed these words, 'It would not be pleasing to God that the reverence shown to St Cuthbert, my master, should be changed or diminished because of me, and it was in honour of Cuthbert that none of my predecessors was ever buried in the church itself. No, put me in the chapter house.' So when he died, he was taken to Durham. The monks there are a fine memorial to his industry. It was he who assembled them and adorned the church with books[3] and other ornaments. He also conferred on the prior of Durham the distinction of being the deacon and second in command for the whole bishopric.

Chapter 134 Ranulf Flambard (1099–1128)

But when Turgot, appointed by William as prior, started exercising this office too harshly, he so provoked Ranulf, William's successor, that Ranulf transferred him to the bishopric of St Andrew in Scotland and thought that no other prior should be appointed. This Ranulf (we are not sure what sort of family he came from) had once been chaplain to king William. From there his eloquence and cleverness had taken him to the top and he had been made justiciary of the whole kingdom. Whenever a royal edict was proclaimed, saying that England should pay such and such an amount of tribute, Ranulf would add that it should be double that. This made the king laugh and he would say, 'That's the only fellow who knows how to make use of his abilities in this way, not worrying if others hate him, provided he pleases his master.' Through using these skills Ranulf won the bishopric of Durham. On his arrival he at first behaved quite circumspectly, fearing to offend the saint who was said to be an especially severe scourger of sinners. But when he had committed this and that sin and not been punished, he grew so bold that he did not hesitate to drag away guilty persons who had sought sanctuary in the church of the saint, thus daring a crime unheard of in all the years of the past.[4] But he did contrive some

---

[1] See p. 58 n. 7.
[2] In 1093 he had laid the foundation stone of the building which still stands today.
[3] The titles of more than fifty books which he gave to the cathedral survive. See Knowles, *The Monastic Order*, p. 523.
[4] In his original version William included at this point accusations of Ranulf giving the monks forbidden foods to eat, and bringing in comely serving wenches. He deleted these accusations later.

glory for his name by his new buildings for the monks and his translation of the blessed Cuthbert. With general agreement the sacred body was lifted from its mausoleum and made conspicuous by being placed on high, a deed which spread the fame of Ranulf, although it was Ralph, then abbot of Seez and later archbishop of Canterbury, who with a happy daring handled the matter.[1] He exhibited the uncorrupted body for all to see, since some were doubtful whether the miracle of the flesh all joined in one and unimpaired would still continue once the body had been put on display. Also all his garments gleamed with fresh splendour, and on his chest was a chalice, with an upper part of gold and lower of onyx. His face was so tightly covered in a cloth that the abbot could not remove it, no matter how hard he tried. They found the head of Oswald, king and martyr, being held in his hands, and the bones of St Bede and king Ceolwulf, who had been a monk and a saint at Lindisfarne, in separate bags of linen. The activity in the cemetery was a great sight: the monks were all dressed in their best robes and the sky was clear with no mass of black clouds overhead. There was a long procession of people going and coming and a great crush where people jostled at the front, for having once seen the body they wanted to see it again and again. It is thought that the saint considered this public display undignified, for a heavy storm coming on unexpectedly drove everybody into the church. And there was a miracle involved, for although the monks had been drenched by the force of the storm their garments were not only undamaged but not even made wet.

Chapter 135 Praise of St Cuthbert

We hail you for your goodness, most holy bishop. It was an altogether splendid miracle and consistent with your holiness. Indeed not many days previously you had performed another miracle. All arrangements had been made for the translation of the body in the new church – chorus of monks, altar, tomb. They were only waiting for the timber packing supporting the new roof of the presbytery to be carefully taken down. But, most blessed one, you would not allow the holy desires of your saints to suffer delay, and in the dead of night you pulled down all the timber. For who else could have accomplished this great feat? The prior was awoken by the noise and rushed up, fearing for the altar and the floor. But you had preserved the objects of his fears, while the timber was in the same condition as when it was put in place. Rightly do your monks stand in such awe of you that no sinner who knows in his heart that he has rebelled against the prior or been guilty of some great wrongdoing would dare to sleep through the night unless he had confessed his sin. And so saintly lord and rightly beloved father, as your suppliant I beg you that you will deign to remember me for doing good, seeing that whenever I had the opportunity, I was unwilling to leave out your praises, however feebly expressed.

---

[1] Perhaps when Ralph was visiting the monasteries of England. See ch. 68.

Book 4 Mercia

Here begins the prologue to the fourth book

The books I write are unequal, because there is not an equally abundant supply of materials in every place. I am indeed ready and willing to praise the saints of my country, but both my knowledge and my ability are found wanting when I try to do so. It is impossible to know about all the saints, either because they lived far away from us in the remotest of districts or because there were no writers energetic enough to compose lives which we can consult. Nor can my own barren intellect and scanty eloquence describe in chapters worthy of their exploits and matching their victorious triumphs, those saints whom by the gift of God I do know something about, either because they lived in the vicinity or because there are some written records. But as I was reviewing these matters, I felt a surge of confidence which scattered the clouds of doubt and made me feel easier, when I realised that it is only a man's goodwill which can win him the eternal reward, if it so happens that envious fortune denies her helping hand. This might be false, had not the angels announced peace to men of good will. And so, even if I lack other qualities, let the devotion of my willing mind do battle for the saints. If possible, my client's tongue must be of service to those who have often saved me in the past and who recently rescued me from extreme danger by a remarkable miracle.[1] So continuing the journey I have begun, in this fourth book I shall go through the bishoprics of the Mercians, just as I once dealt fourthly with their secular power. This power was always very widespread for the times, and so was divided into several sees. This was due especially to the drive of king Offa who established an archbishopric at Lichfield,[2] inspired not by power but by the innate beauty of the region – a happy augury offered for my own work, as I travel on the journey I have set myself.

Chapter 136 The bishops of Worcester (608–1095)

The province of Mercia now has five sees, though it possibly once had more.[3] At Worcester[4] indeed the bishops were Bosel, Oftfor, Ecgwine, Wilfrid, Mildred, Wærmund, Tilhere, Heathured, Deneberht, Heahberht, Ealhhun,

---

[1] Tantalisingly, William says no more about this.
[2] See ch. 7.
[3] Namely those of Worcester, Hereford, Lichfield, Lincoln and Ely.
[4] Worcester was the seat of a diocese founded in 680 when archbishop Theodore decided to increase the number of sees in the area under Mercian overlordship.

Wærfrith,[1] Æthelhun, Wilfrid, Cœnwald, Dunstan, Oswald, Ealdwulf and Wulfstan I. The last three of these were archbishops of York. Then there were Leofsige, Brihtege, Lyfing and Ealdred.[2] In our day Wulfstan II has the greatest reputation for sanctity. So if I write at rather greater length about him, I pray that none of you will get bored.[3]

Chapter 137 Wulfstan's youth and vegetarianism

As a boy Wulfstan was well educated, and he grew to manhood among men with trained minds and such devotion to learning as there was in England at that time. At the right age he accepted a priesthood and he never through vices of character acted unworthily of this position. For some people, both now and then, after speedily singing through an early morning mass, spend all the rest of the day in eager concern for their stomachs or their profits, but Wulfstan's attitude was more serious. When he had finished the set office, he would add long prayers of his own every day. He was content with the offerings of the faithful, and with these he supported himself. He was so exceptionally chaste that, when his life was ended, he displayed in heaven the sign of his virginity which was still intact. Up to this point his standing as a secular religious was such that his reputation was greater than that of any monk you care to mention. He did not know what it was to be drunk, although he was a meat eater. But as soon as he could, he seized the opportunity to discard this as well. This is how it happened. On a certain day he had to go away to take part in a lawsuit. The importance of the matter had imposed a ban on all excuses. But he thought he should do something about his hunger, after he had sung mass. His servants made haste to ensure that their master did not depart unfed and put a goose on the fire to cook. Meanwhile the priest stood at the altar and was singing the service with his customary devotion. But as the kitchen was near the church, the smell of roast goose filled his nostrils while he was engaged on the secrets of the mass and stopped him concentrating, since his mind was ensnared by the delicious pleasure of eating. Recognising his fault, he immediately brought his attention back to the service, and struggled hard to keep his thoughts turned away from the kitchen. But when his efforts were in vain, he angrily swore an oath on the sacraments which he was then touching that he would never eat such food ever again. So, having sung the mass, he went off to his appointment without having eaten, as by now the later hour was giving him pressing reasons for departure.[4] This was the incident which

---

[1] Wærfrith, bishop 875–915, was given by king Alfred the task of translating the *Dialogues* of Gregory the Great into Old English. See *The Deeds of the Kings* 2:122 and Eleanor Duckett, *Alfred the Great* (Chicago, 1975), pp. 115–22.

[2] For Oswald, Ealdwulf and Ealdred see ch. 115.

[3] Wulfstan was bishop of Worcester from 1062 to 1095. William could write at greater length about him, as he had already produced a *Life of St Wulfstan* (ed. R. R. Darlington, Camden Society, 3rd series, xl, 1928), which was a translation into Latin of an Old English life, written by Colman, Wulfstan's chaplain.

[4] The incident of the goose took place at the church of Hawkesbury near Chipping Sodbury in Gloucestershire, where Wulfstan was the priest. See Knowles, *The Monastic Order*, p. 77.

caused him to follow rigidly for the rest of his life the lofty principle of abstaining from all meat and even from rich and oily foods. He did not, however, look down his nose at people who did eat meat. He merely declared that such food had no attraction for him, while adding his opinion that if there was a tasty meat, it was larks that provided the daintiest dish.

Chapter 138 Wulfstan's wrestling with the devil

His devotion to his way of life increased and he became a monk at Worcester, where he ascended through the various offices to the rank of prior. It was while he was prior, and all aglow with the exalted praises of his virtues, that he experienced being tempted by the devil, who no doubt envied his goodness. Wulfstan was standing praying before the altar when the devil attacked him and began wrestling with him. Wulfstan's fear made the devil's attacks fiercer and he crushed Wulfstan with his hard, enveloping arms. He did it a second and a third time, and on the third occasion Wulfstan, who was breathing with difficulty and whose insides were on fire, showed by the beating of his flanks that he had just about had enough. But God in his mercy came to Wulfstan's assistance and drove away the raging demon. As it vanished into the breezes, Wulfstan realised that it was the devil, although up to then he had thought that it was a servant of his, whose form the devil had in fact taken. Unmistakable proofs of this were given, for, whenever Wulfstan happened to see this servant, a trembling immediately ran through his body and he went completely white. But he was totally unafraid of everything else, so that he used to say that he did not know what fear was. He never got off his horse if a bridge was broken, and at the top of buildings under construction he would walk confidently across the narrowest of planks, so that rightly was it said of him, 'The good man has the confidence of the lion.'[1]

Chapter 139 Wulfstan becomes bishop of Worcester (8 September 1062)

Meanwhile, as I have described earlier, when archbishop Ealdred came back from Rome with the cardinals close on his heels, there was a reason why pressure was being put on him to ordain a bishop for the see of Worcester.[2] As the decision had been made public, Ealdred looked to his own future advantage and chose Wulfstan, no doubt thinking him a non-entity: Wulfstan's simplicity and holiness would act as a cover for his own plunder, as he took from the see whatever he wanted. So Wulfstan, with the backing and the approval of the cardinals,[3] though frightened out of his wits by their awesome solemnity, received the divine gift. The prognostic chanced to be a happy omen

[1] Proverbs 28:1.
[2] See p. 168.
[3] They had been impressed with the strict life and charity of Wulfstan who had been their host during Lent, and had fed them well while fasting himself (*Life of St Wulfstan* 17).

to thank God for, 'See, here is an Israelite, in whom there is no guile.'[1] Absolutely nothing could have been truer. Wulfstan's goodness was no make-believe sanctity, nor, again, was there any cunning trickery in him. But Ealdred did not find him as ineffectual as he had thought, as most of the things he had unlawfully got his hands on had been filched from Wulfstan by cajolery and claims of the archbishop's current poverty. Wulfstan, indeed, performed the office laid upon him more by his innate love of goodness than through reliance upon learning, though he was not so unlettered as was thought. He knew all the necessary texts, apart from the tales of the poets and the tortured syllogisms of the philosophers: these, he said, he did not know nor did he think it worth knowing them. But he had been well enough taught to be able to extemporise as eloquently as you like, and to draw tears from his hearers by his skilful description of the joys of heaven and the punishments of hell. He could persuade people to do whatever he wanted by his words, seeing that his life squared with his teaching, and he did not preach one thing, while living another. So God had given him that eloquence which increased his reputation and benefited his hearers. As I have said before, he ate and drank sparingly, although in his hall the English custom was followed of drinking all hours after the meal. Wulfstan would sit in his place among the company, chewing over the Psalms, while pretending to drink when it came to his turn. The others drained foaming tankards.[2] Wulfstan held the smallest possible glass and promoted the hilarity of the others, more to comply with the customs of the country than to satisfy his own considered wishes. For he did not neglect Norman customs either, but was escorted by a retinue of knights whose annual pay and daily food were a severe drain on resources.[3]

Chapter 140 His religious practices

This is the account handed down to us of his religious observances. Every day he would sing a mass, add the Psalter, and then over a seven hour period go through the names of all the saints, whose name days succeed each other one by one throughout the whole year, divided into seven groups. Whenever he was at Worcester, he would sing the Greater Mass,[4] saying that he was doing this as the duty officer of the week, whose tasks he did not wish to be absolved from, just because he was bishop. It also frequently happened that when he was present at meals, he would go with the others into the church, make his confession and receive a blessing, and then go back to the dining room.

[1] John 1:47.
[2] As did the Carthaginian Bitias at *Aeneid* 1:738–9.
[3] No doubt this was one of the reasons why Wulfstan, the last bishop to be appointed during the reign of Edward the Confessor, survived, on good terms with the Normans, until his death in 1095. As R. Allen Brown says, 'In the new Norman society of French chivalry to maintain a retinue of knights was a mark of status even for such a paragon of old English virtues as Wulfstan' (*The Normans and the Norman Conquest*, pp. 199–200).
[4] In the normal monastic horarium there was a sung High or Greater Mass and a recited Morrow Mass. See Knowles, *The Monastic Order*, p. 468.

Wherever he went from the dining room, he had the Psalter continually on his lips, repeating so often any prayerful verses which occurred to him that his fellow chanter would grow weary. He would never omit the benedictions commonly made by the English over their drinking, not even if he found himself in the king's hall and seated at his table, and no matter who was looking at him. If ever he was forced by necessity to be of this company, first of all he would utter a curse on unjust judges and a blessing on just judges. Then sitting down, he would be all ears, if any theological matter came up for discussion, but during political debates, which were more common, he showed no interest but nodded off out of boredom.[1] Yet anyone who thought the bishop should be opposed in argument soon discovered the quick-witted learning of his replies.

Chapter 141 Wulfstan at the cathedral

A priest called Æthelric had come to stay with Wulfstan, brought there by the fame of his piety, and from the sparkle of Wulfstan's example his own sanctity had caught fire and blazed up. For even when he was among crowds of people, Æthelric's day was devoted to non-stop prayers, so that those who saw him were amazed. Every day, when mass had been sung, he would go through the Psalms, accompanying them with just as many prayers. He was so keen on putting people right that he would even correct the bishop himself with a word or a stare from his eyes, if he ever made something of a mistake, as happens in speaking. For Wulfstan did sometimes reprimand his monks if they strayed from the pathway, but more often he would put up with their shortcomings, if honesty allowed this. He allowed no slackness at all in the saying of the divine office: if any of his clergy had missed matins through being overcome by drunkenness or sleep, he would punish them with a sharp stroke of the cane. Finally he would personally wake up the better sort of clergy and sing matins to them himself. It made no difference to him if he wore cheap clothes, and he usually kept out the cold by means of lambskins rather than those of some other animal. If someone said that he should at least wear catskins, he would smile and jokingly reply, 'Upon my word' – this had grown to be the bishop's customary manner of speaking on oath – 'I have heard of the Lamb of God being sung, but never the cat of God. So that is why I want the lamb and not the cat to keep me warm.' The fear of the Lord was so deeply implanted in him, that what others would force into a matter for display would be used by him as material for remorse.

He himself had begun the work on a completely new and larger church,[2] and when this was so far finished that the monks now switched to it, the order was

---

[1] Wulfstan shared this characteristic with Anselm. See ch. 65.

[2] As this was happening all over the country after the Conquest, Wulfstan would have found it hard not to follow the example of his contemporaries. As Matthew comments, 'For all his traditional upbringing he accepted the new magnificence: the time for small Anglo-Saxon churches was over' (*The Norman Conquest*, p. 183).

given for the old church, the work of the blessed Oswald,[1] to be unroofed and pulled down. At the sight of this Wulfstan, standing out in the open, could not keep back his tears. He was gently taken to task for this by his household, who said that he should rather rejoice that in his lifetime great honour had been brought to the church by the increased number of monks needing bigger buildings.[2] But Wulfstan said in reply, 'I see it very differently. We unhappy people are destroying the works of the saints, merely to win praise for ourselves. That age of happy men knew nothing of the construction of buildings for display, but rather they offered themselves to God under whatever roof they found themselves, and won over the members of their flock to follow their example. We are doing the opposite, neglecting souls and toiling at piling up stones.' He said more along these lines, weakening by his arguments the opinions expressed to him.

Chapter 142 A miracle of Wulfstan

I shall now say something about the miracles, which he did not fail to perform, for I have said enough about his way of life. He was dedicating a certain church, and his sermon, though saying much on other topics, had been mainly about peace. Some people, who were enemies in bitter quarrels, were touched by his words and forgave each other. But there was one man who could not be brought by any words of admonition or persuasion to forgive his enemy who was begging him to forgive him for killing his brother. He was brought before Wulfstan and spoken to for a long time, but when he still stubbornly refused, the bishop said the very words which I shall now quote, 'In the Gospel our Lord said, "Blessed are the peacemakers, for they shall be called the sons of God."[3] So it stands to reason that if the peacemakers are blessed and the sons of God, the troublemakers are men of misery and the sons of the devil. Therefore I commend you to him whose son you are and I hand you over to Satan for the destruction of your body, according to the teaching of the apostle, "So that his spirit may be saved in the day of the Lord."[4]' The saint had barely finished speaking when the devil took possession of the unhappy man. In front of all the people he began to grind his teeth, foam at the mouth and toss his locks. In the end he was dashed to the ground and rolled about in torment. They begged Wulfstan to take pity on him, but he held his hand. Finally, however, the saint yielded to the pressure of their tears and commanded the enemy to depart from him. The devil left him as easily as he had come. The man was restored to his right mind and was called upon to accept grace for his sin, but with remarkable effrontery he refused the offered peace. So the command was given for him to be taken possession of a second time and

[1] See p. 166.
[2] Wulfstan had increased the number of monks from about twelve to fifty. He had himself been at one time master of the children. See Knowles, *The Monastic Order*, p. 160.
[3] Matthew 5:9.
[4] 1 Corinthians 5:5.

a second time released, but he still refused to confess. But when a third time the devil's attacks had weakened all his limbs and got him well-nigh gasping forth his life, he did accept the peace, and ever after this right up to the day of his death he remained well and whole.

Chapter 143 Wulfstan stands up to Lanfranc and Thomas of Bayeux

In the days of William I Wulfstan was accused by Lanfranc of being illiterate, and by Thomas, archbishop of York, of refusing to submit to him as ancient law required. When in council he was commanded to answer both accusations, Wulfstan went outside so that he might think more carefully about a well-phrased response. Some monks went with him and were thinking hard about this important matter, when to their amazement they were interrupted by Wulfstan saying, 'Upon my word, we still haven't sung nones. So let's sing it.' His companions remarked that they should first do what they had come out to do, as there would be more than enough time for singing after that: furthermore, if the king and his nobles heard of this, they would not unreasonably conclude that they were being laughed at. But Wulfstan replied, 'Upon my word, we shall first perform our service to God, and after that play our part in the litigation of men.' So the office of nones was sung, and Wulfstan at once proceeded to return into the council chamber, before there had been any thoughts about shifty evasions or deliberations about how the truth might shine out. His followers tried to hold him back, as they were afraid for his case, but he would not listen to them and said, 'You are surely aware that I see plainly before me here those blessed archbishops, Dunstan and Oswald,[1] who today will protect me with their prayers and blunt the edge of my accusers' lies.' So he gave his blessing to the monk, who was a man of minimal eloquence but who had but a smattering of the Norman tongue,[2] and won his case.[3] Previously he had not been thought worthy to rule his own diocese, but now the archbishop of York humbly asked him to agree to visit those parts of his diocese which he was wary of visiting himself, either through fear of the enemy or his ignorance of the language. And what is more, Wulfstan recovered down to the last one those remaining towns of his see over which archbishop Ealdred had assumed control. In this he was consistently supported by archbishop Lanfranc, who of course was keen to weaken a rival to his primacy and power.

---

[1] *The Life of St Wulfstan* 25 says that he had been reading the lives of his two saintly predecessors during this critical council. But he had also been lent two marks of gold by Æthelwig, abbot of Evesham, to help him defeat the claims of York. See Matthew, *The Norman Conquest*, p. 184.

[2] Presumably this monk acted as interpreter, translating Wulfstan's English into the Norman French of the court.

[3] Wulfstan had succeeded in removing the diocese of Worcester from a subordination to York which had lasted since 992, and was now completely free to follow his true vocation of being a diocesan bishop.

Chapter 144 He helps William II during a rebellion

In the reign of William II Roger, earl of Montgomery, planned a rebellion against his king, and with his fellow rebel leaders set his hostile army on the march.[1] Already they had devastated all the lands from Shrewsbury down to Worcester, and were now approaching the city itself. The king's soldiers, who were encamped before the city, explained the danger to the bishop. Wulfstan hurled the thunderbolt of his curse against traitors who had not remained loyal to their lord, and commanded the soldiers of the king to hasten to avenge the wrongs done to God and his church. No doubt some will declare their amazement at what I am about to say, but I cannot ignore the authority of truthful eyewitnesses. Some of the enemy were paralysed with fear, as soon as they saw the king's troops, and some were even struck blind so that the townspeople were given a complete victory, such as they could not have hoped for. Many were put to flight by a few, some were killed and some were wounded and taken prisoner.

Chapter 145 Wulfstan's prophecies I

And what shall I say of his gift of prophecy? A man called Aldwine had been made a monk by Wulfstan, and was living the life of a hermit with his friend Guy in the widespread, desolate range of the Malvern Hills. After long soul-searchings Guy decided that it would be a short cut to glory to travel to Jerusalem, for once the hardships of the journey had been endured he would either see the Holy Sepulchre or meet an untimely but happy death at the hand of the Saracens. Aldwine also thought it a good idea, but asked father Wulfstan for his advice on the matter. The bishop dissuaded him and cooled his ardour by saying, 'Please, Aldwine, don't go anywhere else, but stay where you are. Upon my word, you would be surprised if you knew as I do the mighty works which God is about to do through you in your hermitage.' On hearing this the monk went away and from now on endured the life he had chosen with more resolution, lightening troubles of every kind by his hopes in the prophecy. The prophecy was speedily fulfilled, for soon one, then another, then a third and finally thirty followers flocked to Aldwine. They had particularly abundant food supplies, for the neighbouring people counted it a blessing to share something with the servants of God. And their faith was sufficient for any wants that remained, since men who were growing fat and sleek on spiritual joys[2] were not at all worried if they went without food for the body.

---

[1] This revolt happened in 1088. Roger, a great baron of central Normandy, had been made earl by William I in 1075.
[2] The hermits ended by adopting the rule of St Benedict (*The Life of St Wulfstan* 26).

Chapter 146 Wulfstan's prophecies II

There was a merchant called Senulf who had developed the habit of visiting Wulfstan once a year for advice on curing the diseases of his soul. Once, after giving him absolution, Wulfstan said, 'Time and time again you go on repeating the sins which you have confessed, since, as the saying goes, "Opportunity makes the thief." So I advise you to become a monk. If you do this, there will be no opportunity for such sins.' When the merchant replied that he could not become a monk because of the strictness of the discipline, Wulfstan was rather annoyed and said, 'Go away. You will become a monk willy-nilly, but only when the materials for sin have died away within you.' We ourselves in later days saw this happen. For Senulf, when he was now a broken old man, was driven by illness to become a monk in our monastery. However many times he had to repent, it only needed someone to remind him of the bishop's words for him to recall that impulse and to loose again the hardening of his heart.

Chapter 147 Wulfstan's prophecies III

A favourite pupil of his called Nicholas, who later became prior of the church at Worcester, was one day sitting at his feet. The bishop, overcome with joy, stroked with gentle hand the young man's head, which because of its loss of hair was nearly exposing Nicholas to taunts of baldness. And Wulfstan said, 'Yes, I think you will go bald.' But the young man was sad that that part of him was growing old while he was still young. He complained about the bad luck of his falling hairs to Wulfstan and said, 'Why don't you keep them in their place?' The bishop smiled and said in reply, 'Upon my word, as long as I live, your remaining hairs will never fall out.' It happened just as he had said. But in the very week in which Wulfstan said goodbye to this life, all Nicholas's hair vanished, I know not where, and left his pate completely bald.

Chapter 148 Wulfstan's death and burial

He openly gave signs and prophecies about his death. He did this often, though the clearest indication was his remark upon hearing about the death of his only sister, 'The plough has now come to my furrow, and in a few days time brother will follow sister.' He took to his bed with a fever half a year before his death, and made his preparations to enter the heavenly life. He faced fate's blow with a great heart and used to comfort his companions, who were weeping in their anxiety about the tyranny of a future bishop, with the words, 'No more sighs. Dry your tears. I am not losing my life, but changing it. I will always be with you. Freed from my vesture of clay, I will be nearer to God, and so able to help you more quickly. Prosperity will come to you at my request and adversity depart from you by my driving it away.' Happy speaker, who could dare to fill men's ears with words of such certainty, taken from the abundant storehouse of his clear conscience! Other men with sighs and sobs beg their companions to pray for them. Wulfstan promised to pray for others. What miracle is this? Was he conscious of no sin? No, it was his holy simplicity which spoke, a simplicity which did not know how to lose his trust in the mercy of God. He was lifted up by those present and carried into the church amid loud laments from the monks and the lay brethren, and for three days he remained unburied.[1] For even the appearance and form of the dead body seemed to offer the grace that had come from the living bishop, and the tears were wiped from their eyes and their sorrow comforted. His body, marked by his pontifical insignia but without any covering, lay on a bier before the altar. A sea of people flowed past, offering prayers and doing obeisance to the body before sadly departing. On the fourth day he was buried by Robert, bishop of Hereford, who had long since been connected with Wulfstan in a holy friendship.[2] He lies between two 'pyramids', with a beautiful stone arch curving above him. There is a wooden cover projecting out over his grave, held firm by iron clamps called 'spiders'. I mention this here because it supplies the setting for the miracle which I now describe.

Chapter 149 Miracles at Wulfstan's tomb

Some years after Wulfstan's death,[3] a fire, which was carelessly allowed to spread from the city, completely gutted the roof of the church. The lead was melted, and the planks were turned into charcoal as the fire raged. The roofbeams, although as big as entire trees, were burnt through and fell to the ground. The areas inside the church which had managed to escape the fire were smashed by the loud fall of this mighty mass. And amid all this the tomb of the saint was not only free from the raging of the flames but was not even stained by scorch marks or covered by ash. And a further miracle – the mat, on which suppliants at the shrine were accustomed to kneel, was found unharmed in front of the tomb. Even the wooden cover, which I described as being above his grave, was found intact, as far as it was outside the stones, while the part enclosed by the stone had turned to ash when the stone was damaged. This was not the first miracle at the tomb, but it was the most famous as everybody knew about it. For I could not enumerate those daily experiences when men find help for their particular needs, and when no one who prostrates himself in faith at the tomb returns home with his prayer unheard. Such experiences cannot be counted or put in a book. The most eloquent man alive would not have the ability to do them justice. Indeed, Wulfstan would long since have been elevated and worshipped as a saint, if the ready faith of our fathers had still existed to help the process. But our modern lack of belief, which parades itself under the protection of caution, is not willing to believe in miracles, even if seen with the eye or touched with the finger. I myself was afraid to be found

[1] Wulfstan died on 18 January 1095.
[2] See ch. 165.
[3] In fact in 1113.

guilty of silence, if I decided to omit the evidence of trustworthy authorities, and thus deprive scholars of knowledge. For I shall assume that those who remain unmoved in their reading when confronted with the love of the saint or our love for him would even turn up their noses at the holy Gospels.

Chapter 150 Samson of Bayeux, bishop of Worcester (1095–1112)

Wulfstan was followed by Samson, a canon of Bayeux, a man of great learning and a distinguished speaker. He belonged to the old school,[1] eating heartily himself[2] and giving lavish banquets for his fellow men. He did no harm to the monks, except that he took from them the monastery of Westbury.[3] Wulfstan had established monks here and protected them with the immunity that stemmed from his sanctity. Samson dissolved this monastery and a few years later died in the very place in which he had performed his culpable action.

Chapter 151 Theulf (1115–1125)

After the death of Samson, who had received the bishopric by the gift of William II, the see was given by king Henry to Theulf, also a canon of Bayeux, who was not dissimilar in character to his predecessor,[4] and who died while Henry was still king. Both bishops are buried in the nave of the church, in front of the rood screen.

Chapter 152 Simon (1125–1150)

The bishopric was then given by the king to Simon, the chaplain of queen Adela, who had married Henry after the death of his first wife. Simon is famous for his openness and the sweetness of his nature – and for his generosity, as far as this was permitted by the poverty of the see.

Chapter 153 The vale of Gloucester

The diocese of Worcester contains the counties of Gloucester, Worcester and half Warwick. The town of Gloucester is situated on the river Severn. It is thought that it was named after Claudius,[5] who was the next general of the Romans to come to Britain after Julius Caesar. The British version of the name

---

[1] Southern, *St Anselm and his Biographer*, p. 140, gives a delightful sketch of this 'old school' bishop, which includes praise for the sensible, moderate advice he gave to Anselm during the latter's struggle with Thomas, archbishop of York and Samson's son. See ch. 118 (the second one in the Rolls Series).

[2] In William's original manuscript there is a long description of Samson's gluttony at this point, though it also contains the information that Samson fed three hundred poor men every day.

[3] At Westbury-on-Trym in Gloucestershire.

[4] A passage in the original version, later deleted, described Theulf as being equal to Samson in the size of his belly but not his equal in generosity.

[5] Presumably 'Gloucester' is thought to be a shortened form of the Latin name *Claudii Castra*, 'the town of Claudius'.

is Cairclau. Also Seneca tells us in his book about the death of Claudius, 'Those barbarians in Britain worship him as a God and have built a town in his honour.' The whole region is called the vale of Gloucester[1] after the town. All the land is rich in crops and fertile with fruit trees, the fruit trees being solely due to the kindness of mother nature, while the crops are helped by the skill of their cultivators. Even the tiredest, laziest farmer would be roused again to the delights of work on these lands where his crops will repay him a hundredfold. You can see the public roads clothed with apple trees, not grafted by the work of men's hands but depending on the nature of the ground itself. Of their own accord the fruit trees spring up from this soil, bearing fruits which far surpass others in taste and look. Most of these apples do not know how to wither before a year is up, so that they supply their owners with fruit right up to the next year's crop. More than the other parts of England this district is close packed with vineyards, producing a greater yield than anywhere else and better tasting wine. For its products, which are not far behind French wine in their sweetness, do not cause the drinker to wince at their bitter sourness. There are numerous towns, abbeys of the first rank and frequent villages. All things are crowned by the glory of the River Severn. No river in the land has a wider channel, a fiercer flood or more fish for the skilful fisherman. Each day its frenzied waters, which I am not sure whether to call a whirlpool or a swirling tide, sweep up the sands from the very bottom and, piling them into a heap, advance fiercely, though the waters do not get beyond the bridge. Sometimes they even overflow their banks, and having flooded a great area of land return victoriously to their channel. Unhappy is the ship which meets this tide sideways on. Of course experienced sailors, when they see this 'bore' coming (for that is the English word for it), turn their ships towards it and by cutting through the middle of it escape its violence.

Chapter 154 Bristol

The most famous town in the vale is called Bristol. It has a safe harbour for ships coming from Ireland, Norway and other lands overseas. This is convenient, for it means that a district which is so fortunate in the richness of its produce is not deprived of a flourishing foreign trade.

Chapter 155 Gloucester

In this city of Gloucester there is a monastery to St Peter, founded there by archbishop Ealdred, as I have remarked more than once.[2] When abbot

---

[1] Malmesbury is a mere twenty miles from the vale of Gloucester, and Knowles aptly comments that William 'had doubtless often paused to contemplate its peaceful expanse from the ridge of the hills above Birdlip on his way to Gloucester and Worcester' (*The Monastic Order*, p. 181).
[2] For example *The Deeds of the Kings* 2:125. In fact Ealdred in 1058 rebuilt the church of St Peter, which had originally been founded by Wulfhere, king of Mercia, in 680, and established the Benedictine rule in the monastery.

Serlo¹ was given it as a small gift by William the Conqueror, he found few
people there and a mere three monks.² But who could find the eloquence
needed to describe how the place grew, as the grace of God worked together
with the industry of the abbot? The religious rule at Gloucester is famous for
its balance. The weak monk can take it up, but the strong monk is unable to
despise it. Their champion, Serlo, introduced it with the idea that there should
be 'nothing too much', although Serlo himself could be as threatening and
awesome towards the proud as he was gentle with the good. He did meet with
vocal opposition from the canons of St Oswald's, when archbishop Thomas³
gave to the monks the lands which belonged to their own church. For at
Gloucester in the time of king Alfred, his daughter Æthelflæd and her husband
Æthelred had built a monastery, sparing no expense and making sure the
monks did not go short of anything. They transferred there the remains of king
Oswald from Bardney,⁴ seeing that the whole of Mercia was under their
control. This monastery prospered up to the time of the Danes, and was
connected by the closest links with our monastery of Malmesbury, as you can
find in the records of both churches. But when the monks melted away before
the attacks of the invaders, the archbishops of York took over the monastery as
being bishops of Worcester as well, and brought in canons. Archbishop
Thurstan took particular trouble to restore the shrine of the saint and to
enlarge the church. In the course of this, when the old foundations were dug
out and new ones put in place, they found in the south porch the graves and
bodies of both the founders, a mark of the reverence of the men of former days.
Of course I have written a lot about Oswald in the first book of *The Deeds of
the Kings*,⁵ where I said that I was unsure whether his arms are preserved at
Bamburgh, as I remembered Bede said.⁶ But I shall mention what I have
discovered about these matters subsequently, when I come to the place.⁷

Chapter 156 Winchcombe

In the same district is the monastery of Winchcombe. It was built by king
Cœnwulf of Mercia.⁸ The great generosity he showed would not be believed by
men today. He had the church dedicated by thirteen bishops, the principal one
being Wulfred, archbishop of Canterbury. During the ceremonial of the
dedication Cœnwulf manumitted before the altar in the presence of ten earls

---

¹ Serlo's long abbacy lasted from 1072 to 1104. The great Norman abbey, begun in 1089 and
   dedicated on 13 July 1100, was an achievement of his abbacy.
² By the end of his abbacy the monks numbered about a hundred.
³ Thomas of Bayeux, archbishop of York 1070–1100.
⁴ Æthelred was an earl of Mercia. Bardney is in Lincolnshire. Oswald, martyr and saint, was king
   of Northumbria 634–42. For him see p. 104.
⁵ See 1:49.
⁶ Bede mentioned this in *Ecclesiastical History* 3:12.
⁷ In ch. 180 about Peterborough.
⁸ Cœnwulf was king of Mercia 796–821.

a king of Kent,[1] whom he had recently taken prisoner by the rights of war. Besides those gifts of inestimable number and value which the nobles took up, Cœnwulf gave to all the landless a pound of silver, a gold coin to the priests and one shilling to each monk, as well as many things to the whole people. All mortal things decay and decline, and by the time of king Edgar Winchcombe was almost a monastery only in name. But it was somewhat revived by the blessed archbishop Oswald. He made Germanus abbot there, whom he had brought with him from Fleury, and Germanus was a great help both to its religious life and the rebuilding of the church.

Cœnwulf lies buried there, as does his son Kenelm, whom Cœnwulf left to his sister Cwenthryth to bring up, as he was only seven years old. But Cwenthryth, wrongly promising the kingdom to her own greed, ordered a servant who was looking after him to get rid of her small brother. The servant took the unsuspecting lad out on an apparent hunt, killed him and hid his body among some bushes. Amazingly, this crime which was committed so secretly in England, by divine means became known at Rome. Above the altar of St Peter a dove brought down from on high and let fall a parchment, which told successively of the death and place of burial. As it was written in the English language, the Romans and men of other peoples who were present tried to read it in vain. But an Englishman stepped forward just in time to save the situation and, speaking in Latin, he broke through the language barrier. As a result the pope sent a letter to the kings of England, telling them about the martyrdom of their countryman. The body of the little boy was lifted up and carried back to Winchcombe amid a great crowd of people. The murderess was aroused by the chanting of the priests and the happy shout of applause from the people, and put her head out of the window of the room in which she was sitting. It happened that they were chanting the Psalm, 'God will lift up my praises.'[2] The queen tried to invalidate the joy of the singers by saying the Psalm backwards from the end as some kind of a trick. But then, indeed, by the power of God the eyes of the murderess were torn from their sockets, polluting with their blood the verse, 'This is the work of those who falsely accuse me before God and who speak ill against my soul.'[3] The marks of the blood are still there today, as living witnesses to the wickedness of the woman and the vengeance of God.

Chapter 157 Tewkesbury

There is also a monastery at Tewkesbury. It has recently been improved by the support of Robert Fitzhaimo. It is not easy to describe how wonderful it is now. Both the beauty of the building and the loving qualities of the monks attract the eye of the visitor and win over his mind. Originally the monastery was at Cranbourne, but abbot Gerald in his foresight realised that it would be

---

[1] This was Eadberht Præn, an apostate clerk, who had been the leader of the men who had risen for Kentish independence from Mercian authority in 796.

[2] Psalm 108:2.

[3] Psalm 108:20.

better placed at Tewkesbury,[1] both because a river happened to be near by and the monastery would adjoin its lord's lands. Also it seemed good for religious minds to applaud its name, seeing that the name of Tewkesbury is, as it were, Theotokosberia, that is house of the mother of God, a word made up from Greek and English.

Chapter 158 Malvern (founded 1050)

Our days have also seen the growth of the monastery at Malvern in the same province, a monastery which seems to me to have happened upon its name as an 'antiphrase'. For religion there is not to be described by any 'mal-' word. Rather it flourishes as a thing of beauty and worth, being a place where poverty in the things of this world strengthens the monks and draws them towards the hopes and blessings of immortality in the next.

Chapter 159 Evesham and Pershore

The province of Worcester also has abbeys at Evesham and Pershore.

Chapter 160 Evesham

Evesham was founded by the blessed bishop Ecgwine. I have not been able to discover from my own reading or to learn from others the nature of the miracle concerning Ecgwine which Bede kept quiet about. This silence is especially odd considering that Bede does mention the journey to Rome which Ecgwine made with Cœnred, king of the Mercians, and with Offa, king of the East Angles. Anyway, whatever it was that demanded this silence, it is agreed that Ecgwine was the third bishop of Worcester[2] and that he had a special affection for this place where there is now seen to be a monastery. Formerly it was a wild spot and a mass of thorn bushes, although of old there had been a little church there, perhaps built by the Britons. It was here that Ecgwine, a most holy man, kept frequent vigils, attracted by its solitude, and had the reward of being comforted by a vision in which the mother of God spoke to him. Plainly and unmistakably she commanded him to found a monastery for her there, which would be a pleasure for her and an occupation for him. He obeyed her commands, and, when he had finished the building, he strengthened it by privileges obtained from the pope and the king.

   As for the following story,[3] do we think we should believe the ancient traditions or not? According to the story, Ecgwine was one day struck with guilt for the sins of his youth and put his feet in fetters, having first thrown the

---

[1] He made the transfer *c.*1100. The total of monks rapidly rose to over fifty.
[2] From 693 to 717. In a major lawsuit in the eleventh century concerning territory claimed both by Evesham and the bishop of Worcester, the abbot of Evesham produced the bones of St Ecgwine on which to swear his oaths. See Stenton, *Anglo-Saxon England*, pp. 650–1.
[3] The story is taken from Brihtwald's *Life of Ecgwine*.

keys of the fetters into the river. He declared publicly that not until the fetters were unlocked either by God or by the keys themselves would he be saved from his sins. He made a journey to Rome thus fettered and was returning safely. When he was now sailing on that sea which ships cross going to England from mainland France, a huge fish leapt onto the ship in which the bishop was travelling, and was only caught after much straining and struggling by the sailors. When its liver was drawn out, the key was found and placed in the lock of the fetters, and it freed the saint, thus giving him a complete feeling of security. Who can deny that our father in heaven is justly famed, or that he will listen to the prayers of those who pray to him, provided that the faith of the petitioners does not waver?[1]

Chapter 161 Wistan the martyr

And you also, Wistan, happy youth, light of this same monastery, will fill part of this poor page of mine with your praises. You were the son of Wigmund, whose father was Wiglaf king of the Mercians, and of Æthelflæd, daughter of Ceolwulf who was the uncle of Kenelm.[2] I shall not keep silence about you, who were wickedly done to death by Brihtferth, your kinsman.[3] Any future scholars who think it worthwhile to read these pages will discover that the world knew nothing more famous than your abilities, which led that jealous butcher to put you to death, and God knew nothing of greater innocence than your purity, which led him, our souls' arbiter, to glorify you. For a pillar of light, sent down from heaven, broke through night's thick curtain and shone into the deep cave where the murder had been committed, thus revealing the crime of the murderer. And so your devoted parents took up your dear remains and placed them at Repton, which then had a famous monastery.[4] It is now part of the lands of the earl of Chester. The glory of the monastery departed with the decay brought by age, and your body, as I have said, now has a worthy dwelling place at Evesham, so serenely do you grant the prayers of your worshippers.

Chapter 162 Pershore

The monastery at Pershore was begun and completed in the time of king Edgar by Æthelweard, duke of Dorset. So far from counting the pennies, Æthelweard eagerly poured out his wealth in generosity. But, like other monasteries, half of it was destroyed as it pitifully succumbed to ruin. Some of it was buried by the

---

[1] One is also reminded of the story of Polycrates and his ring in the Histories of Herodotus 3:41–2.
[2] For Kenelm see ch. 156.
[3] This murder took place *c*.850.
[4] Paul Antony Hayward in *The Blackwell Encyclopaedia* (*s.v.* 'Wistan, St') cites archaeological finds at Repton as evidence for the truth of Wistan's remains being placed there. These finds 'have shown that this church was built upon a royal mausoleum which had been converted with a decade or two of the alleged death into a crypt of a type used to facilitate the veneration of relics'.

passage of time, some of it seized by the greedy rich, with a great part of its wealth being taken by kings Edward and William for their monastery at Westminster. Some of the bones of Eadburg the happy are buried here,[1] and worshipped with special reverence, as the glory of her miracles comes to life more frequently there than elsewhere.

Chapter 163 The bishops of Hereford (676–1079)

Hereford is a city, across the Severn, almost bordering Wales. It is not big now, although the remains of its steep-sided fosse show that it was once quite sizeable. Its first bishops were Putta, Tyrhtel, Torhthere, Walhstod and Cuthbert, who was afterwards archbishop of Canterbury.[2] His discourses as archbishop showed his extreme care in church matters, but also these verses, which I have lately seen,[3] will introduce you to his old-fashioned integrity and the great honours which he paid to his predecessors, as he completed with his own enthusiastic efforts whatever had been begun by them to adorn the house of God.

> This sacred cross of Christ we kneel before,
> Once bishop Walhstod planned to decorate
> With stones of gold and silver largely set.
> But all things human have their date to die,
> And Walhstod left before his work was done.
> So I, by God's grace bishop after him,
> Called Cuthbert, name from light of day derived,
> Have taken up what he so well devised
> And made his offering finished and complete.

Cuthbert also wrote these verses on a tomb of his predecessors.

> This marble slab now covers bodies six
> Of men of high renown among us once.
> Its high roofed tomb in marvellous beauty made
> Has in its care and keeping their remains.
> I, Cuthbert, bishop after them, these graves
> Have built and named that I might honour them.
> Of these, three wore a bishop's sacred robes:
> Walhstod, Torhthere and Tyrhtel are their names.
> The fourth a chieftain, Milfrith called,[4] and fifth
> His fair wife Cwenburg. Sixth and last
> Is buried Osfrith, son of Oshelm, here.

[1] For Eadburg, daughter of king Edward the Elder, see ch. 78.
[2] Cuthbert became archbishop of Canterbury in 740. See ch. 4.
[3] One imagines William copying these verses into his notebook.
[4] For the evidence that Milfrith was a seventh-century chieftain of the people called the Magonsætan in north Herefordshire and south Shropshire, see Stenton, *Anglo-Saxon England*, p. 42.

The bishops after Cuthbert were Podda, Ecca, Chad, Ealdberht, Esne, Ceolmund, Utel, Wulfheard, Beonna, Eadwulf, Cuthwulf, Mucel, Deorlaf, Cynemund, Eadgar, Tidhelm, Wulfhelm, Ælfric, Æthelwulf, Æthelstan and Leofgar. In the time of king Edward, Gruffyd the king of the Welsh set fire to Hereford, and deprived Leofgar of both his see and his life.[1]

He was succeeded by Walter, who was consecrated in Rome by pope Nicholas. Walter lasted until the fifteenth year of William the Conqueror, but then died a shameful death, if we can believe the story.[2] There lived in Hereford a working woman whom Walter had the misfortune to meet. As soon as he saw her, a long-lasting passion for her blazed up. She knew nothing about the flames consuming the bishop, and would have taken no notice of them if she had. In the meantime Walter often called to mind the line of Terence, 'Nothing is more to be pitied than an old man in love',[3] and out of respect for his age and his position tried hard to get rid of the disease. Through his valiant efforts he had just about recovered and sent his passion packing, when, through some trick of the devil, he happened to summon to his bedroom the very woman. The underlying reason was that she should cut out clothes for his servants, since she was said to be an expert at this. She arrived, and was busily engaged on the work for which she had come, when all Walter's followers, who knew his secret, left the room as one man. To cut a long story short, the bishop made an improper suggestion and was about to rape the woman, when she stabbed him in the groin with the scissors she was holding. The story of Walter's assault and the woman's revenge spread through the whole of England and even reached the ears of the king. With the dignity befitting a king he concealed his ready belief in the story, and by the strictest of edicts stopped other people from spreading it also.

Chapter 164 Robert Losinga of Lorraine (1079–1095)

The see was soon taken up by Robert of Lorraine. He built a church there after an elegant pattern, taking as his model the basilica at Aachen.[4] He was deeply versed in all the liberal arts, but his special interests were the abacus,[5] the lunar calendar and the courses of the stars of the heavens. There was at that time living as a recluse in Mainz a monk called Marimanus. In the long periods of

---

[1] Leofgar, a chaplain of earl Harold, became bishop early in 1056. Almost at once he went on campaign against the Welsh to wreak revenge for Gruffyd ap Llywellyn's invasion and burning of Hereford the previous year, and was killed in battle against them. See Stenton, *Anglo-Saxon England*, p. 64.

[2] Walter was bishop from 1061 to 1079.

[3] *The Self-Tormentor* 2:3:14.

[4] Robert was the brother of Herbert, bishop of Norwich 1091–1191. N. Pevsner, *The Buildings of England: Herefordshire* (Harmondsworth, 1987) takes the church built by Robert to be the chapel of St Katherine and St Mary Magdalene, of which there are only scanty remains, and the basilica to be Charlemagne's palace at Aachen, as both buildings were two-storeyed squares.

[5] Robert's demonstration of the use of the abacus in William Rufus' reign is used as an argument by Matthew for the view that the Exchequer possibly originated in Rufus' time (*The Norman Conquest*, p. 264).

leisure given him by his solitude he scrutinised the chroniclers, and was the first or only person to notice that the cycles of Dionysius the Less[1] differed from the truth of the Gospels. And so going over the years one by one since the beginning of our era, he added twenty-two years which were missing from the cycles of Dionysius, thus beginning to make an important, all-embracing chronicle of his own. Robert was a very great admirer of this book and because he prized it so highly had it brought to England. In the end he was so captivated by Marimanus' intelligence that he abridged Marimanus' more expansive treatment and removed the flowers of rhetoric so expertly that the abridgement seems more valuable than all the pages of the original huge volume.

Chapter 165 The deaths of Wulfstan and Robert

More than with the other bishops of the day Robert had a friendship with the holy Wulfstan, whose bishopric his own anyway adjoined. And so repeatedly putting aside his public duties, he provided Wulfstan with companionship in his home, where the purity and innocence of Wulfstan's life gave him great joy. Although Robert exalted Wulfstan above himself, their friendly relationship was not cemented by Wulfstan's death being delayed. Instead it followed at once and broke the friendship. Wulfstan was lying ill at Worcester, being near now to his blessed end, while Robert was unwillingly detained in the king's palace, dealing with royal decrees. Wulfstan stood by him in a vision, saying with complete clarity, 'If you wish to see me alive, come quickly to Worcester before I die.' After this vision, Robert got the king's permission and hurried to Worcester as fast as he could, resting neither day nor night. For he was filled with a fearful foreboding from heaven, which turned out to be true, that he would not find Wulfstan alive, and the royal palace was quite far away. And now he was sleeping in the stopping place next to Worcester, when again he saw Wulfstan saying, 'You have done all that the love of a friend could ask for; but you have been disappointed of your desire. I have already moved on. But I beg you, dear friend, to take thought for your own life and look to your salvation, for you will not stay long in this world after me. And I will give you a sign, so that you do not believe you have been tricked by some phantom of a dream. When tomorrow you have buried my body, which has already been waiting for your arrival for two days, I will cause a present to be given you which you will know comes from me.'

The bishop awoke, continued on his journey, came to Worcester and took the burial service without anyone else knowing of his vision. He had said goodbye to the monks and was thinking of departing. His horse was waiting for the touch of his spur when the prior of the monastery, reverently going down upon his knees, held out a gift to Robert and said, 'Please accept, my lord, the cope of your friend, lined with lambskin,[2] which he used to wear

[1] Written *c.*583.
[2] See ch. 141.

when on horseback. Let it bear witness to your long friendship and may it win for you the protection of the holiness of our Lord.' As Robert heard this and recognised the gift, he turned pale and a shiver ran through his frame. Straightaway he put off his departure, summoned the monks to a chapter meeting, and with the tears and sighs called forth by the affair explained how accurately dream and event squared with each other. He asked them all to think of his death and went away, glad indeed that he had been given a warning of it, but ever anxious with holy fear. Wulfstan passed over in the middle of January and Robert did not get beyond the end of June.[1]

Chapter 166 Gerard (1096–1101)

Robert's successor was Gerard, and when he was translated to York, the king commanded that he should be replaced by Roger, his pantryman. Roger, however, died in London, where the court then was, within eight days of his nomination, without having taken up the episcopal office. Archbishop Anselm had been instructed to consecrate him before he died (if, ye heavens, the folly of man can be believed!) and this demand had been anxiously and most urgently pressed. The holy priest made no reply to this human foolishness but stopped and checked it with just a smile.

Chapter 167 Reinhelm (1101–1115)

Then followed the immediate election into the dead man's place of Reinhelm, the queen's chancellor. He was invested by the king with ring and crosier according to the custom which the king then thought legal, but when Reinhelm discovered through the archbishop's refusal to bless himself or the others so invested that he had acted wrongly in accepting such investiture, he returned the ring and the crosier to the king of his own accord, without being asked or ordered to do so. So, exiled from friendship with the king, he was commanded to keep away from the court as well. He put up with this silently and with patience until a more pleasant breeze blew the clouds away from the king's heart and Reinhelm was legally inducted to his see and formally consecrated.[2] He stayed on as bishop, quite free from pride and showing all the other virtues but especially a tender conscience in his fear of God. He could be seen in floods of tears anywhere, but particularly at celebrations of the mass. No report of any evil marred his reputation, except that he was said to be less generous than he should have been or was able to be.[3]

---

[1] Of 1095.
[2] See chs. 57 and 63 for other accounts of Reinhelm's investiture.
[3] William omits the fact that it was during Reinhelm's time that the present cathedral of Hereford was begun.

Chapter 168 Geoffrey de Cliva (1115–1121)

He died a few years later, victim to the gout. His successor was Geoffrey de Cliva, and he was not bishop for more than five years. By this time people were everywhere talking about the unlucky circumstance that no one, having become bishop of Hereford, lived for very long. Geoffrey also was a good man. He ate absolutely anything put before him, and wore the cheapest clothes. He was interested in agriculture, and restored and improved episcopal lands which had suffered greatly from tax exactions previously. So he had a good supply of corn and other foodstuffs, but was rather grudging as far as the poor were concerned. Indeed he deservedly laid his reputation open to attack, in that in his lack of pity for the poor he did not bequeath a large supply of food to any heir.

Chapter 169 Robert of Betheune, bishop at the time of writing

The bishopric was given by king Henry to Richard, his clerk of the signet. Richard lived only a few years longer. Finally Robert, prior of the canons at Llanthony, was chosen and made bishop, please God, under a good omen. He is still alive today. Future generations will judge his deeds. Already his reputation for extreme piety and abstemiousness in food and dress has clearly set him on a smooth and easy path. He is certainly so well known to the papal see that, after the legate and the archbishop, he is the person who receives all the papal commands for England.

Chapter 170 The relics of Æthelberht

The see of Hereford is honoured by having the relics of Æthelberht, king and martyr. He was born among the East Angles and became its king. Offa, king of Mercia, murdered him,[1] in order, so it was thought, to strengthen and extend his own kingdom. He had been given no cause for this wicked murder, which was plotted against his own son-in-law. No sooner was Æthelberht dead than Offa invaded the kingdom of the East Angles, leaving the legacy gained by the invasion to his heirs. But the death of the innocent Æthelberht is believed to have been avenged by Offa's own death, which soon followed, and by the short reign of Offa's own son.[2] Indeed God gave such clear signs of Æthelberht's sanctity to the notice of the people that this important bishopric of Hereford was consecrated in his name. And so he is their martyr, believed in not for human reasons but because of divine powers. Nobody should think it foolish or absurd if our predecessors, who were good men and deeply religious, either accepted his martyrdom in silence or used their authority to confirm it. Leaving out everybody else, would the blessed Dunstan, upon whom book

---

[1] In 794.
[2] Ecgfrith. See ch. 8.

learning and the grace of God had been poured in full abundance, have allowed Kenelm or Æthelberht or Wistan to be revered as martyrs, unless it was clear to him that they were welcome among the citizens of heaven? Men's reason must bow down when miracles are a sign of God's favour.

Chapter 171 Modern miracles of Milburg at Wenlock

The diocese of Hereford has two religious houses, at Shrewsbury and Wenlock. Shrewsbury is a very recent monastery, founded by Roger, earl of Montgomery.[1] He established monks from Seez there. He provided them with very little food and clothing, but they in their hope of future reward joyfully made light of these afflictions. At Wenlock there had been a very ancient nunnery. The blessed Milburg, sister of the holy Mildrith and daughter of the son of Penda, king of Mercia,[2] lived and was buried there. But the place was completely deserted when Roger filled it with monks from Cluny. Nowadays we can see there virtues' seedlings striving upwards towards heaven. The new arrivals knew nothing of Milburg's tomb, for the attacks of enemies and of time had destroyed all the signs of the people of old. But when a start was made on the building of a new church, a boy kept racing up and down over the floor. He broke into the crypt where the tomb was, thus revealing the whereabouts of the virgin's body. And then, as the odour of fragrant balsam wafted through the church, Milburg's body, set on high, performed so many miracles that crowds of people flowed into the church in waves. The open spaces outside the church could scarcely contain their numbers, as rich and poor alike elbowed their way in, all thrown together by their faith in the saint. Nor were their efforts in vain, for nobody went away without their diseases cured or alleviated, while some found the 'king's disease', which by doctors was quite incurable, vanish before the powers of the virgin.

Chapter 172 The bishops of Lichfield and Chester (656–1085)

Lichfield is a small town in the county of Staffordshire, far away from crowded cities. It is surrounded by woods and has a small river flowing past. The church was built on a cramped site, showing the restraint and modest ambitions of the men of old. Bishops of our own day feel ashamed that episcopal power has to have its home in such a place.[3] As I have said, it was at Lichfield that Chad had his see and his tomb. For apart from the two bishoprics of Mercia reviewed above,[4] all the remainder of the province of Mercia and Lindisfarne in the first years of Christianity had just one bishop, one man followed by one man. Their

---

[1] For Roger see ch. 144. Seez was an abbey in Normandy.
[2] Penda was king of Mercia 626–54.
[3] On the other hand, as Mayr-Harting points out, Lichfield was easily accessible to the people of the Derbyshire Peak district, and of the Trent valley and heartlands of Mercia (*The Coming of Christianity*, p. 242).
[4] That is, Worcester and Hereford.

names are Diuma and Ceollach, both these from Scotland. After these were the
Englishman Trumhere, Iaruman and Chad, whose see was at Lichfield, as has
often been pointed out.[1] Theodore appointed as Chad's successor Wynfrith,
who had originally been Chad's deacon, and Sæxwulf as Wynfrith's successor.[2] After Sæxwulf there came two bishops, Headda at Lichfield and Wilfrid
at Leicester. When enemy attacks drove out Wilfrid, Headda held both sees,[3]
as after him did Ealdwine. On Ealdwine's death, three bishops were appointed
in the diocese, Hwita at Lichfield, Torhthelm at Leicester and Etheard at
Dorchester. After Witta the bishops at Lichfield were Hemele, Cuthfrith,
Berhthun, Hygeberht, Ealdwulf who received the pallium in the time of
Offa,[4] Herewine, Æthelwald, Hunberht, Cynefrith, Tunfrith, Elle in the time
of king Æthelstan, Ælfgar, Cynesige, Wynsige, Ælfheah, Godwine, Leofgar,
Berhtmær, Wulfsige, Leofwine, and Peter.

In the time of king William the Conqueror Peter left Lichfield and moved to
Chester, which is twenty-five miles away.[5] Chester is known as the city of the
legions, as the veterans of the Julian legions settled there. It shares a boundary
with the North Britons. Like most of the north, the district produces poor
grain crops, especially of wheat, but cattle and fish abound. Milk and butter
are the local delicacies. The richer people live on meat, and are very keen on
barley bread and white wheaten bread. Goods are taken from Chester to
Ireland, and essential supplies carried back, so that the efforts of merchants
bring in what the nature of the soil fails to produce. There was an ancient
nunnery at Chester, which has now been filled with monks by Hugh, earl of
Chester.[6]

Stories are told there of a maiden called Werburg. She was the daughter of
Wulfhere king of Mercia[7] and of Eormengild daughter of Sæxburg. Sæxburg
was the daughter of Anna king of the East Angles and wife of Erconberht king
of Kent. Werburg, who had vowed celibacy, was famous at Chester over a long
passage of years for her virtues and her goodness. I will describe one miracle of
hers, which was so remarkable that it deserved to be remembered and repeated
by the people. She owned a strip of land outside the walls, whose crops were
being gobbled up by some wild geese. The bailiff, whose department this was,
made every effort to shoo them away, but they only went a little distance.
While he was assisting his mistress at her devotions, among his other news of
the day he introduced a complaint about this matter, and Werburg said to him,
'Go and shut them all up in your house.' The bailiff was struck dumb by this

[1] For Chad as bishop of Lichfield and for Wilfrid's connection with the town see p. 144.
[2] For Wynfrith see pp. 147–8.
[3] Headda became bishop in 691.
[4] See chs. 7 and 8 for Offa raising Lichfield to an archbishopric in 787 and the reversal of this by
Canterbury in 803.
[5] A council held at Windsor in 1072 decided that bishops' sees should be in walled towns rather
than in villages. Other such moves included Sherborne to Salisbury and Selsey to Chichester. See
chs. 83 and 91 and Stenton, *Anglo-Saxon England*, p. 666.
[6] For the monks at Chester see p. 53 n. 3.
[7] Wulfhere was king of Mercia 656–75.

strange command, and thought his mistress was joking. But as she persisted and showed she meant it, he went back to his crops, and as soon as he caught sight of the wicked robbers, he told them in a loud voice to follow him, as his mistress had commanded. Then all the geese formed up, followed their enemy with bowed necks and were shut up in his house. The bailiff took one of them for his supper, as of course he had no fear that anyone would accuse him. At daybreak Werburg arrived and after scolding the geese for their theft of other people's property, told them to fly off. But the creatures showed their intelligence. They knew their number was not complete, and instead of going off somewhere else they crowded round their mistress's feet and, making such complaints as they were able, awoke her instinct for holiness. And she, receiving the revelation from God, realised that the geese were not making all this cackling for nothing, and by careful questioning of the bailiff discovered the theft. Immediately, her virgin's hand made a sign of healing and flesh and skin reappeared on the bones, while from the skin feathers began to sprout until the bird came back to life, and after first giving a little jump soon flew free up into the air. The others followed without delay as their number was now made up, having first made a sign of respect to their liberator. So this is the maid whose merits are told of in Chester and whose miracles are lauded to the skies. She grants without delay the prayers of all, but she is especially near at hand and quick to help when women and children pray to her.[1]

Chapter 173 Robert de Limesey (1086–1117) moves the see to Coventry

As I have said, bishop Peter set up the see at Chester in the church of St Peter, and established a few canons there. But his successor, Robert, made another move, taking the see to Coventry.[2] It was in the Chester diocese and a magnificent monastery had been built there by earl Leofric and his wife Godiva.[3] It had so much silver and gold on view that the very walls of the church seemed too flimsy to support the treasuries, which visitors gazed at as though they were a miracle. Robert stared open-mouthed at this wealth and actually used the treasures of the church to stop the king seizing any of his lands, and so that, bit by bit, he might satisfy the greed of the Romans. From one of the beams which supported the shrines he tore away five hundred marks of silver. He stayed at Coventry for several more years, but set the place no sort of example of goodness. When the roofs threatened to fall in, he never did anything about the danger. He stole so many church treasures that he incurred

---

[1] St Werburg's, the principal church of Chester, was dedicated to her in the tenth century and later claimed possession of the decayed remains of her corpse.

[2] John of Tours, bishop of Wells, similarly linked his impoverished bishopric with the rich abbey of Bath in 1088. See ch. 90.

[3] The monastery had been built in 1057. As Matthew points out, it was comparatively easy for Robert to get his hands on the wealth of Coventry, as it did not have the kind of papal protection or royal support which saved the monastery of Bury St Edmunds, although Lanfranc protested vigorously about Robert's usurpation (*The Norman Conquest*, p. 188).

the charge of embezzlement, and a bishop would have faced trial for this offence, if a prosecutor could have been found. He spent a miserable amount on food for the monks, and he neither bothered to fire them with love for the rule of their order nor did he allow them to aspire to any learning beyond that of the common people. He was afraid that they might be pampered by abundance of food, or roused to revolt against himself by strict obedience to the rule and vigorous habits of study. So the monks, providing they could only live in peace, were content enough with a rustic diet and light literature. Indeed, as bishop Robert lay dying, he commanded that he should be buried not at Chester but at Coventry, thus bequeathing to his successors, so he thought, not an undeserved right of censuring him, but the almost legal right of championing him.[1]

Chapter 174 Robert Peche and Roger de Clinton (1121 to the time of writing)

His successor was another Robert, surnamed Peche, who was appointed to the bishopric, when serving in the chapel of king Henry. He lived for a few years and was buried in Coventry. During his lifetime he carefully walked in the footsteps of his predecessor. The present bishop, also appointed by king Henry, is Roger, nephew of the Gausfrid de Clinton, who was once a man of importance in England.

Chapter 175 Some treasures of Coventry

Coventry possesses an arm of the great Augustine, set in a silver reliquary. On it you can read engraved this inscription, 'This arm of St Augustine was bought at Pavia[2] by archbishop Æthelnoth when he was returning from Rome for one hundred talents of silver and one talent of gold.' So it is in Coventry that bishop Robert lies. His reputation was not universally bad. He was amusing and generous and began great buildings at Lichfield.

In two porches at Coventry lie the bodies of the builders of the monastery, an excellent married couple, though the wife, Godiva, has the greater fame. In her lifetime she contributed all her wealth to the church, and when she was on the point of death, she gave orders for a circlet of gems to be hung round the neck of a statue of the blessed Mary. She had sewn the stones on to a thread, so that by touching them one by one as she began her various prayers she might not leave any of them out. But how valuable do you think these gems were? Amazingly, experts valued them at one hundred marks of silver.

---

[1] Perhaps this sentence means that if Robert had decided to be buried at Chester, his successors might have had a less secure claim on the monastery at Coventry. A line in William's original version but later deleted explained that the rule was that 'bishops should be buried in their own sees'. See also *The Deeds of the Kings* 4:341.
[2] Pavia is just south of Milan.

Chapter 176 The bishops of Leicester (*c.*737–*c.*965)

Leicester is an old city in the middle of England, so called from the river Legra which flows past it. I shall only note the names of its bishops,[1] as nothing else about them has come down to us. They are Torhthelm, Eadberht, Unwona, Wernberht, Rethhun, Ealdred, Ceolred and Leofwine. In the time of king Edgar Leofwine joined the sees of Lindsey[2] and Leicester so that it is now called the see of Lincoln and Leicester

Chapter 177 The bishops of Dorchester and Lincoln (678–1092)

Dorchester is a small town of few inhabitants in the county of Oxfordshire. But its churches are very imposing, both the old constructions and those built through recent initiatives. After Eadhæth the bishops there were Æthelwine, Eadgar, Cyneberht, Alwig, Eadwulf, Ceolwulf, Berhtred and Leofwine, who joined both sees.[3] Then there were Ælfnoth, Æscwig, Ælfhelm, Eadnoth, Etheric, Æthelric and Wulfwig.

Remigius, a monk of Fécamp,[4] gave much help to William duke of Normandy in his invasion of England, having bargained with him for a bishopric if he was successful, and William was no slower to grant him the bishopric of Dorchester than Remigius was to accept it. And when pope Alexander, as I mentioned earlier, found him guilty and displaced him, he later reinstated him at the request of archbishop Lanfranc.[5] In his first years at Dorchester he devised some excellent projects, and began to put some of them into operation, but in the end he transferred the see with all its concerns to the town of Lincoln,[6] one of the more densely populated towns of England and a market for merchants arriving by land and sea. Remigius founded a church there to the honour of our Lady Mother[7] and filled it with many canons, who themselves were conspicuous both because of their scholarship and the huge sums spent on them out of his own pocket by Remigius. He rebuilt the monastery of St Mary at Stow, and renewed another at Bardney to St Mary because of her long-lasting support of him.[8] These activities were all the more pleasing because Remigius himself was so small that men almost regarded him as a portent. His mind was always struggling to make its mark and do distinguished service abroad and, 'His virtue, coming from a smaller body, pleased the more.'[9] You would think that nature had formed him just so that we could know that that the most blessed intelligence could live in the tiniest of bodies. So he lived a happy life, but on the day before the dedication of his

[1] Leicester had been part of the diocese of Lichfield until it became an independent bishopric *c.*737.
[2] This is the see referred to on p. 147 n. 2.
[3] That is, the sees of Leicester and Dorchester *c.*960.
[4] In Normandy.
[5] See p. 44 for more details of this incident.
[6] In 1075.
[7] Only the west front of this church now remains as part of the present cathedral at Lincoln.
[8] Stow and Bardney are both only a few miles from Lincoln.
[9] William adopts Virgil's line about the boxer Euryalus at Aeneid 5:344.

church at Lincoln, amid the preparations for its consecration, jealous death removed him from this joyful scene. For indeed at the urging of the great-hearted Remigius a royal edict had summoned all the bishops of England to the city. Only Robert, bishop of Hereford, refused to come. He had seen for certain by looking at the stars that the dedication would not happen in the time of Remigius, and he had not kept quiet about this.

So the dedication was postponed, but it was performed without too much weight of ceremony by his successor, seeing that he was in the delicate position of having inherited the labours of another. His name was Robert Bloet. He was bishop for nearly thirty years. He died when far from his see at Woodstock. He was riding with another bishop at the king's side when fate suddenly snatched him away. In general he was cheerful enough with his own people, but he lacked gravitas. He was second to none in his knowledge of politics, but not so in church matters. He decorated his cathedral with the most costly ornaments. After his death his body was disembowelled, so that it might not pollute the air with foul smells. His innards were buried at Eynsham, the rest at Lincoln, for in his lifetime he had transferred to Eynsham the monks who had been at Stow.[1] We also know that the Eynsham monks were devoted to our Lady and loved by her. When one of them, a young lad, had been lying ill for more than an year, he eventually saw the Virgin coming to his help and putting to flight the swarms of demons who had assembled around him. He had pointed them out with his finger to the people by his bed, and kept asking for them to be driven away by the sprinkling of holy water, but the demons, when driven away in one quarter, popped up in another. When, however, the queen of heaven appeared in her might, they vanished every one. At once the sick man, believing he was cured, began the response 'Rejoice, Mary the Virgin'. But half way through he stopped, either because he was in great pain, or, more likely, because he had forgotten the words. Prompted by a monk who stood by, he picked up the thread, but, with the final word of the response, he breathed his last. Now that you have had a taste of this monastery from this story, my pen will give an account of other religious houses in the diocese of Lincoln.

Chapter 178 Oxford

There was a nunnery at Oxford from early times. Frideswide, virgin undefiled, lies buried there. Though daughter of a king,[2] she despised a king's throne, declaring that she was wholly given to our Lord Christ. But when her royal suitor found prayers and flatteries useless in pressing his suit, he decided to use force. Frideswide discovered his intention and sought safety by fleeing into a wood. But she could not keep her hiding place a secret from her lover, nor was his passion so feeble that he gave up pursuit of the fugitive. So the maiden,

---

[1] Eynsham had been refounded on a modest scale by Remigius. Eynsham and Selby were the only two monasteries which belonged to bishops, i.e. where bishops instead of the king elected the abbot and bestowed the temporalities. See Knowles, *The Monastic Order*, pp. 402, 631.
[2] Her father was called Didanus.

informed of the young man's passion, journeyed on by hidden pathways and, guided by God, entered Oxford in the dead of night. But when her indefatigable lover galloped up at daybreak, the girl now gave up hope of escaping. Also she was so tired that she could go no further, and so prayed to God to aid her and punish her persecutor. And just when he was entering the city gates with his companions, he was struck blind by a blow falling from heaven. Realising his stubbornness had been wrongful, he sent messengers to appeal to Frideswide and recovered his sight as quickly as he had lost it. As a result, the kings of England became afraid and took care not to enter or stay in this reputedly deadly city, individuals refusing to put the truth of the matter to the test by incurring any risk to themselves. And so Frideswide, a woman, won a virgin's triumph and established a monastery, and it was there, when her time came and her bridegroom called her, that she breathed her last.[1]

In the time of king Æthelred some Danes, who had been condemned to death, sought sanctuary in this monastery, and the English in their insatiable anger burned both Danes and monastery.[2] But the king soon repented of this and the shrine was renewed, the monastery rebuilt, old lands given back and fresh possessions added. In our own day, when the very few priests remaining there lived as they pleased, the place was given by Roger, bishop of Salisbury, to a canon called Guimund, a man of exceptional learning and acceptable piety.[3] He laboured to good effect at the charge entrusted to him, and displayed to God a great number of canons there who had sworn to live according to the rule.

Chapter 179 St Albans

The district of Bedford contains the abbey of saint Alban. The martyr, a proper one and no hireling, has Bede and Fortunatus as the best witnesses and encomiasts of his martyrdom.[4] If I wanted to add something to their accounts, it would be as though I wanted to pour water into the sea. The martyr's most sacred body, which had lain for a long time in the dust of the earth, was raised to the light and placed in a shrine by king Offa, who also honoured it by building a most beautiful church and establishing a large number of monks.[5] There is no doubt that Offa was instructed to do this in a dream which he had while staying in Bath, and that as he drew near to St Albans on his journey thither, he received encouragement from the sign of a light like a huge torch, which hovered over

---

[1] Late sources describe the foundation, ruled by Frideswide as abbess from 727 to 735, as a double monastery. For the double monastery as a feature of early English monasticism, see Stenton, *Anglo-Saxon England*, pp. 161–2.
[2] All this happened in 1004.
[3] St Frideswide's was set up as a house of Augustinian canons under Guimund in 1122, one of the many such houses set up in the reign of Henry I. See Knowles, *The Monastic Order*, p. 175.
[4] Bede writes of Alban in *Ecclesiastical History* 1:7. According to Hamilton's Rolls Series edition, p. 316, Fortunatus, bishop of Poitiers, d. *c.*709, did write a short prose life of St Albin, bishop of Angers, but not one of St Alban.
[5] Nothing survives of Offa's church apart from a few columns used in the Norman rebuilding. His monastic community was refounded in the 970s as a Benedictine Abbey.

Alban's burial place both night and day. That monastery has never been a completely roofless ruin, and in our own day under abbot Paul, who was appointed by archbishop Lanfranc,[1] it has reached its highest point.

Chapter 180 Peterborough

In Huntingdonshire are Peterborough, Ramsey and Crowland.[2] Peterborough was once called Medehamstede, but after abbot Cœnwulf surrounded it with a wall, it was called Peterborough because of its likeness to a city.[3] Here a monastery was built by the blessed Æthelwald. The expense involved was so carefully worked out and its possessions so extensive that almost the whole region round about was subject to it.[4] Those famous virgins, Cynethryth and Cyneswith, daughters of king Penda, keep the relics of their bodies cherished there. Both were dedicated to God from infancy, and walked on the road of this noble ideal until old age. The younger daughter, not content with her own salvation alone, even consecrated to celibacy king Offa, the man who wanted to marry her. He had been the king of the East Angles for a few years.[5] He was a young man with a happy soul and a happy face, in the flower of his youth and greatly loved by his people. But, instructed and advised by Cyneswith, whom he hoped to marry, he exchanged his passions for something better. He went to Rome with Cœnred, king of Mercia, and Ecgwine, bishop of Worcester, and there he received the tonsure of a monk, and said goodbye to earthly things for his lifetime. The company of these virgins is enriched by St Oswald, according to the story, for it is said that his arm is at Peterborough, complete with sinews, nails and flesh, secretly brought there from its original resting place.[6] Great show is made of the reliquary which contains this treasure, but one's faith in the story wavers, when the listener does not see for himself. I am not saying this because I am doubtful of the genuineness of St Oswald. I am simply unwilling to make a rash statement that his arm is preserved there.

Chapter 181 Ramsey

Ramsey abbey was built by St Oswald, archbishop of York. He was helped by a certain Æthelwine, earl of the East Angles. Both should be applauded for

---

[1] He was also the nephew of Lanfranc, and a monk of Caen.

[2] For the Fenland houses of Peterborough, Ramsey, Crowland, Ely and Thorney, see Emma Cownie, *Religion and Patronage in Anglo-Norman England* (Woodbridge, 1998), pp. 109–25.

[3] Medehamstede was founded by king Peada of Mercia c.650 and dedicated to St Peter. It was destroyed by the Danes and restored by Æthelwald c.966. Cœnwulf became abbot in 992. For the growth of Peterborough under Ernulf, abbot 1107–15, see p. 90.

[4] Æthelwald ensured that his monasteries were adequately endowed, issuing an unparalleled number of charters. See Stenton, *Anglo-Saxon England*, p. 452.

[5] From 704 to 709. Bede tells the story of his visit to Rome in *Ecclesiastical History* 5:19. William also mentions it in ch. 160.

[6] Bede says Oswald was originally buried at Bardney and that a year later his successor, Oswiu, buried the head at Lindisfarne but the hands and arms at Bamburgh (*Ecclesiastical History* 3:12). In ch. 155 William doubts the Bamburgh story as well.

their praiseworthy generosity, but especially the earl. One day he saw the archbishop, who was conducting the funeral of a prince, openly weeping with his eyes fixed sweetly on the ground, and through this fact alone he was so captivated by Oswald's religion that he put all his wealth at the archbishop's disposal. So encouraged by Oswald's holy support the earl built a most splendid monastery, situated in a damp marsh.[1] Felix, first bishop of the East Angles, lies buried in this monastery. He was taken there from Soham on the orders of the earl.[2] Also buried there are two brothers, Æthelred and Æthelberht. They were the cousins of Ecgberht, king of Kent,[3] who for some time had them living with him. But he was afraid that as they grew up they would hope for the kingship, and so depriving them of his attention, he finally got rid of them from his busy court. He was helped in his evil design by a sinister agent, called Thunre because he spoke like thunder. Thunre deceived the boys with daily kisses, and then, actually while he was hugging them, stabbed them with a dagger. Once they were killed, he buried them in a deep pit, which, according to the story, was under the very throne of the king, so that no one should have the idea of looking for the princes there; for who would look for them under the king's throne? But that divine eye, which sees the secrets of our hearts, brought the innocent victims into the light of day by bestowing on that place many healing forces. It also sent a terrible miracle to the king, for as he sat over the bodies he was scorched by fire. Those who were near by were alarmed. They dug away the stones which had been thrown over the bodies together with hastily cut turves, and built a shrine to honour their martyrdom. The king himself repented of the murder, and gave a large part of the isle of Thanet to the boys' sister in order to build a monastery to redeem both killer and killed. Thunre, shameless as usual, was turning this monastery to his evil ends, when the earth suddenly opened and swallowed him, so that he descended into hell while still alive and wide awake. The saints' bodies were buried somewhere in East Anglia, but the name of the place is lost. Earl Æthelwine exhumed them from this unknown church and led them in a crowded procession to Ramsey.

But Æthelwine and the princes are outdone in miracles and surpassed in signs by Ivo, bishop of Persia, who also lies buried in Ramsey.[4] One day, wearying of the luxurious way of life provided by his widespread bishopric, he secretly left it all behind for his people, and set off globetrotting, accompanied by just three friends. After many years of travel, during which the people he met wrongly assumed from his ragged clothes that he was a simple countryman,

[1] In 969. Ramsey was unusual in being a completely new foundation. Oswald was the first (titular and non-resident) abbot, and 'thanks largely to Oswald's own wealth and family connections the house prospered, and by the end of the tenth century was one of the richest of all English monasteries' (John Blair, *The Blackwell Encyclopaedia, s.v.* 'Ramsey').
[2] For Felix see p. 96.
[3] From 664 to 673. On p. 144 he invites Wilfrid to ordain many Kentish men.
[4] John Blair, *The Blackwell Encyclopaedia* (*s.v.* 'Ramsey'), says that Ramsey avidly collected relics and promoted saints' cults, especially the three mentioned in this chapter. The relics of the alleged Persian bishop, St Ivo, were discovered at nearby Slepe (renamed St Ives) in 1001.

he at last landed on the shores of England. He was delighted by the outlandishness of a language completely new to him. Everybody laughed at him as a simpleton, and so he settled in the country of the marshes, and there lived out what life remained to him. His companions followed him in death in the order decreed by God's providence. The natives did not know the name of the saint or where he was buried. Many years came and went, and this heavenly jewel lay hidden in oblivion. By now the blessed Oswald had left this earth and Æthelwine had come to the end of his life. And at the precise moment when it was pleasing to him who arranges the passage of time and who controls the size, number and mass of all things, St Ivo appeared in a vision to a simple, harmless countryman. In orderly progression he informed him of his name, rank and place of burial. He instructed him to go and describe the details of his vision to the abbot of Ramsey, and to tell him to take his own body to Ramsey but to leave his friends where they were: his body was not to be put inside a shrine, but in a place next to the altar, where all who came to the abbey would see it. This vision was strong enough to stir a belief in the abbot of Ramsey. He was in fact slow to believe fully, but, once his belief was firmly established, he quickly and speedily carried out the instructions of the saint. Having travelled to the place, he looked for, found and opened the grave. No sooner had the holy body been laid out on a linen cloth than from the complex passages of the tomb there burst forth a powerful, bubbling wave of water. To this day the fountain gushes forth, pleasant to drink from and helpful for all diseases. It is impossible to guess (much less describe on paper) the number of the crowds of people healed by St Ivo. In fact there is no saint in England who is more ready to hear the prayers of the sick or more efficacious in curing them. I saw with my own eyes the following miracle.[1] A monk was lying ill with dropsy. By now his skin had swollen and grown outwards and his heavy breaths were alarming those who stood around. He felt that he could drink up whole rivers and drain dry full water jars. But he was warned in a dream to go to St Ivo. He arrived, and after the third drink of water, he vomited forth a wave of excess water. His belly collapsed back and his legs grew thin again. In a word, he completely regained his health, and in the end proudly proclaimed that, thanks to this restorative vomit, he could at last say he had lost his thirst for water.

Chapter 182   Crowland

Crowland is one of the islands situated in the stretch of eastern fens, which begin in the middle of the land and, flowing for one hundred miles or more, are poured by their own force into the sea in many great waves. A youth of noble family called Guthlac, when he was twenty-five years old, gave up the weapons which he wielded so powerfully, and lived a hermit's life at Crowland for fifteen years. His solitary life, helped by the grace of God, won him the

---

[1] It is interesting that William had travelled as far afield as St Ives in Huntingdonshire.

approval of men, as did his position as priest, his remarkable miracles and his accurate prophecies.[1] But the grace of his virtues shone still more brightly after his death, for after a year his most holy body stayed uncorrupted and many times he showed himself to be an extraordinary miracle worker. Furthermore, the place where a monastery was built over his body experienced no troubles or losses during the great turmoils of war of a most unstable period, and this, too, was put down to Guthlac's help.[2] There also arrived at the monastery St Neot, a new guest there but an old champion of men before God. He had once been a disciple of the blessed Erconwald,[3] and had always been held in the greatest honour at St Neots. But because of a Danish invasion his body was removed from there and taken to Crowland, where, now joining shield to shield with Guthlac, he protected the natives and also listened to the prayers of visitors. For although the place could not be approached on any side except by water, the people sailing past made the space in front of the monastery gate a veritable high road. And so the monastery is almost never without guests arriving from this side or that.

Our own times have found someone to consecrate there as martyr, on the grounds that fame pronounces that he was put to death when he was innocent. I hope that fame and the truth are not in conflict. This martyr is earl Waltheof, scion of a noble house and son of Siweard, the mighty earl of Northumberland. He was arrested by king William I on the suspicion of being involved in a conspiracy against himself, kept in prison for a long time, finally beheaded and buried at Crowland.[4] I have recorded in my *Deeds of the Kings* the opinion of the Normans that he was guilty, and in my present work I shall not omit the different opinion of the English. Englishmen are outstandingly truthful. They claimed that the earl had been forced to swear an oath of disloyalty when surprised at a banquet, but that he had joined the conspiracy only with the movement of his lips and not in his heart. This, they said, had become generally known because earl Waltheof had then of his own accord confessed it to archbishop Lanfranc and the king himself and repented of his oath, which had been but the pretence of an hour. The assertion of the English seems to be confirmed by the divinity shown in the many extraordinary miracles at his grave. For they say that when he was put in prison he atoned for his misdeeds by sighing and sobbing every day. The prior of Crowland has told me that, impressed by the miracles, he touched the noble body, which was free from all

---

[1] For Guthlac, celebrated anchorite and poet, see B. Colgrave, *Felix's Life of St Guthlac* (Cambridge, 1956), and *The Blackwell Encyclopaedia, s.v.*

[2] The monastery was founded by king Æthelbald of Mercia in 716. When cast into exile in the reign of the previous king, he had sought solace from Guthlac in his 'hollowed-out burial mound' (*The Blackwell Encyclopedia, s.v.* 'Crowland'). By 1066 Crowland was the only monastery remaining in the shires of Lincoln, Leicester, Nottingham, Derby and York.

[3] Bishop of London 675–93. See p. 93.

[4] The other leaders of this rebellion of 1075 were Roger, earl of Hereford, and Ralph de Gael, earl of East Anglia. In *The Deeds of the Kings* 3:253 William has the story that the conspirators were all drunk when they plotted the rebellion at the wedding of Ralph to Roger's sister. Waltheof was beheaded outside Winchester on 31 May 1076, 'so far as is known, the only Englishman of high rank whom king William executed' (Stenton, *Anglo-Saxon England*, p. 612).

corruption, and saw that the head had been fixed back on to the rest of the body, with only a sort of red line showing the sign of the beheading. In consequence he said he had no hesitation in calling him a saint on all occasions, and offering in his name the prayers and other monastic services that people asked for.

Chapter 183   The diocese of Ely

It remains for me to review the bishopric of Ely. When I have done this, this work of mine will take a rest from its long travels around England. Ely is the largest of the islands in the marshes. According to Bede,[1] it gets its name from the number of eels there, and he agrees with the common opinion on the matter. In fact the supply of eels and of almost all fresh-water fish is so abundant that visitors marvel at it, and the locals laugh at their amazement. The waterfowl are as cheap as the fish. For one penny five men and more could buy enough fish and fowl not only to drive away their hunger but even to make them feel gorged. It was at Ely that the most blessed lady Æthelthryth first established a religious house for the handmaids of God.[2] After her death, her sister Sæxburg, wife of Erconberht king of Kent, and mother of that most holy virgin Eorcongote, grew old as a nun and as the abbess in the same place. She was succeeded as abbess by her other daughter, Eormengild, who had been wife to Wulfhere king of Mercia and mother of the virgin Werburg. I have said something about the truth concerning Werburg earlier on.[3] These three ladies were abbesses in unbroken succession, and they were followed by many emulators of their leadership and piety right down to the time of the Danes, whose attacks led them even into the marshes where they drove out the inhabitants and destroyed the buildings.[4] One of the Danes, driven to rashness by his savage heart, tore away the precious mantle which covered the mausoleum of the virgin Æthelthryth and smashed the marble of the tomb with his axe. But at the shattering of the skin of the marble from his blow, one fragment rebounded from the ground with such force that it flew back up into his eye and laid him senseless on the ground. After he was wiped out, his companions, who had been intending to defile the tombs of the other saints, left them untouched and raced each other to get away.

But the holy spot did not remain in solitude for long, thanks to the efforts of the king of the East Angles and the local people. Secular clergy were established there for a time, who performed the many acts of worship. One of them, who was more daring than the rest, tried to egg on his companions to establish more certainly the incorruption of the virgin. I doubt whether his

---

[1] *Ecclesiastical History* 4:19.
[2] According to Bede, *Ecclesiastical History* 4:19, Æthelthryth, although married to Ecgfrith king of Northumbria (655–70), determined to remain a virgin, and, having become a nun at Coldingham, in 672 returned to her own country of East Anglia and founded a nunnery at Ely. See also William p. 146.
[3] In ch. 172.
[4] The Danes conquered East Anglia 869–70.

intentions were genuine. Anyway the others used the risk involve᷉
excuse, so he approached the tomb on his own. He first of all pushed a ⌄᷉
tied to a piece of wood through the hole made by the Dane's blow, and,
following it as far as he could with his eager eyes, groped all around. But soon,
when the end of the piece of wood split off, he tried to pull towards himself the
clothes in which the sacred body was clad. He had already pulled out part of
them when the virgin, indignant that her naked body was being seen by a
rascal, tugged her clothes back in so violently that the priest, who had been
pulling the other way, was knocked backwards on to the ground. His attempt
left him a cripple for the rest of this life, but even so he did not subsequently
stop doing crazy things.

Later on the holy bishop Æthelwald stopped up the hole with stones and
cement, and also drove away the clergy and established monks there. Anyone
would be surprised at the size of the great estates which he gave to the
monastery, all of them bought out of his own pocket,[1] although you could
work out the extent of the monastery's lands in ancient times from the fact that
the present ruler, with many estates taken away and many seized, still counts
into his pocket each year the sum of £1,400. He gives barely £300 of this to the
monks, not counting his own expenses and the money spent on servants and
guests.

Chapter 184 Brihnod transfers Witburg's remains to Ely

Æthelwald appointed Brihnod as abbot of Ely,[2] and he transferred to the
monastery the body of Witburg, saint Æthelthryth's sister. Up to that time her
grave was at an unknown place in the country, where for several years she had
lived a celibate life on a very meagre diet. A tame doe, who would come to her
hand, had given her milk each day from its udders. A certain man who threw a
spear at the doe and killed it, by accident or out of jealousy, was soon attacked
by the king's disease, and wasted away and died. Well, when Brihnod put
Witburg's undecayed body on his ship and was taking it away, the inhabitants
jumped up to get their weapons when they heard about it, and I am sure that
Brihnod would have paid the penalty, if he had not hurried to plunge his ship
into the waves. For at that time the island of Ely could only be approached by
boat. But today's men, being cleverer, have tamed nature, and by throwing
supporting materials into the marshes, have constructed a road by land and
made the island accessible by foot. Anyway, Brihnod's sailors were in great
peril amid the billowing waters, since in their fear at the danger they had
entrusted themselves to a marsh previously unexplored, but a column of fire,
extending down from heaven to the ship, brought it in a direct line to land. As
for the undecayed state of Witburg's body, although some people had come to

[1] Peterborough was similarly well endowed by Æthelwald. See p. 214 n. 4. See *The Blackwell Encyclopaedia*, *s.v.* 'Ely Abbey', for the reasons behind Æthelwald's refoundation of Ely *c.*970.
[2] Abbot of Ely 970–81.

be uncertain about it, all doubt was removed when in the days of abbot Richard[1] the bodies of the female saints were being moved from one place to another. No one even dared touch the blessed Æthelthryth because of the faith received of old, whereas Witburg's clothes were removed to right down below the breasts. Her whole body was seen to be in perfect condition, and she looked more like someone sleeping than a corpse. She had a silken cushion placed under her head, and her veil and the rest of her garments shone and looked as new as the day they had been made. Her face looked calm and had a pleasant, rosy-red colour. Her just opened lips showed her white teeth. Her breasts were quite small.

Chapter 185 Hervey the first bishop of Ely (1109–1131)

There were abbots at this monastery right up to the ninth year of the reign of king Henry, but then, because the diocese of the bishopric of Lincoln was too big, the decision was taken to establish a bishopric at Ely with jurisdiction over Cambridgeshire. And so that Lincoln should not complain about diminished revenues, the king in his generosity took the town of Spaldwick from being part of the district of Ely and gave it to Lincoln, to make up for the losses sustained by its bishop and to nip in the bud any complaints. A certain Hervey was enthroned as bishop at Ely. He had been bishop of Bangor, but had given up this see in the hope of greater riches, alleging that he did not get on well with his Welsh neighbours. For Bangor is completely Welsh. Its monastery used to be so fine and so full of monks that Bede said[2] that if it was divided into seven parts, each part would have not less than three hundred men. Certainly the half-ruined church walls still there are more extensive and with greater piles of rubble than anywhere else.

Chapter 186 Æthelwald brings the body of Benedict Biscop to Thorney abbey

In the see of this bishop of Ely is found the monastery of Thorney.[3] Thorney, though compressed in space and beyond words, is the first in the list of praiseworthy abbeys. It is a copy of paradise, giving us with its beauty a picture in this life of the heavens themselves. Set in the middle of the marshes, it abounds in trees which make their way, tall and knotless, up to the stars. The flat plain with its green covering of grass is a delight to the eye, and there is no place in all its extent where a runner is likely to trip. None of it, or only a little, is uncultivated. In one place apple trees rise from the ground. In another the land is bordered with vines, which either creep along the ground or rise to the skies, supported on poles. Nature and cultivation fight it out between themselves: where nature has forgotten something, cultivation supplies it.

[1] Abbot of Ely *c.*1106.
[2] *Ecclesiastical History* 2:2.
[3] Thorney, just east of Peterborough, was founded in 972.

Who can describe the beauty of its buildings, whose foundations rest unshaken on ground which is remarkably solid, considering it is in the middle of those marshes?[1] A huge empty space is given to the monks for their peace and quiet: the restrictions they put on seeing other human beings increases their hold on heavenly things. Any woman who visits Thorney is regarded as a monster, whereas their husbands, if they pay a visit, are greeted as angels. But nobody stays there for more than a moment, and even the monks' servants go away for festivals. I could truthfully say that the island is an abode of chastity, a fellowship of goodness, a training ground for theologians.

It is called Thorney because it is covered in thorn thickets, although Æthelwald gave orders for the brambles to be rooted up and the thickets destroyed, when, at the beginning of his bishopric, he was thinking of renouncing all the things of the world and living a hermit's life there. He used to taste, as best he could, the first-fruits of the peace of heaven by spending the forty days of Lent alone and free for God in a remote church, which he had had built there. For these reasons he did not give as many estates to the monastery as elsewhere, but merely what was sufficient for himself and twelve monks.[2] And for the land that he did give to the monastery he obtained a charter from the king, agreed to and signed by all the bishops and nobles, which freed it for ever from all public obligations. He brought together so many bodies of the saints, both those who had once been hermits there and others from the whole of England, that almost all the corners of the church are full of them. I am deliberately refraining from mentioning the names of the saints because of their barbarous sound. It is not that I personally disbelieve in them or deny their sanctity, for what authority do I have to call into question that which was consecrated by the holiness of antiquity? No, it is because, as I have said, their names have an uncivilised sound and a nasty smell, at least for the foolish people that our age produces in such numbers, and I am unwilling to expose these saints to their mockery, particularly when not even the local people read their lives. And it would seem irresponsible for a writer to dwell on the merits of saints, when he has found no miracles of theirs to describe. So, saving the reverence of all of them and keeping peace with them, I shall be bold and give an account only of the Benedict, who was the tutor of Bede[3] and an abbot.

This Benedict bordered both banks of the river Wear, a not uncelebrated river of Northumbria, with two monasteries called after the apostles Paul and Peter.[4] United in love and obedience to their rule, the monasteries never

---

[1] As Knowles points out, these sentences of praise seem to indicate that William had visited Thorney (*The Monastic Order*, p. 185).

[2] Burton points out that Thorney was mainly dependent on this initial endowment, whereas Crowland extended its estates by acquiring aristocratic patronage (*Monastic and Religious Orders*, p. 185).

[3] Bede began his lessons with Benedict at the age of seven, and owed his historical knowledge to the library collected by Benedict. See *Ecclesiastical History* 5:24.

[4] William presumably never visited the north-east. The monastery of St Peter at Monkwearmouth (or Wearmouth), founded c.673, does border the Wear, but the monastery of St Paul at Jarrow, founded c.861, is seven miles to the north on the banks of the Tyne.

quarrelled. The reader of Bede's life of Benedict and his other abbots[1] will be struck by the energy shown by Benedict in bringing a library of books to Northumberland, and in being the very first man to introduce into England builders of stone houses and makers of glass windows. In doing this he spent almost his whole life in foreign lands,[2] although the hard work entailed by his enthusiasm for bringing these novelties to his kinsmen went unnoticed in his love for his land and his delight in beauty. For stone buildings had not been seen in England before Benedict, except just here and there, nor had the sun's rays ever thrown their light through clear glass windows. Benedict also showed forbearance. For when he was the ruler of the abbey of St Augustine at Canterbury, he willingly gave place to Hadrian on his arrival in England, doing it not out of fear of the angry frown of archbishop Theodore but in reverence for his high office. For Benedict had been made abbot of that monastery by king Ecgberht, but, as I have said, he submitted out of his reverence for Theodore, who had been commanded by pope Vitalian to establish Hadrian thus close to himself, so that Hadrian could see that no Greek novelties were introduced into the church. And then during a long absence ot Benedict spent travelling in foreign lands, his monks at Wearmouth had brought in a new abbot without consulting him. But, far from being riled, Benedict behaved generously towards the new abbot and on his return home gave him equal honour at meetings and in fact shared all his power with him. And when he was so badly smitten by paralysis that he could not move any of his limbs, he appointed a third abbot, because the second one I have mentioned had been struck by the same paralysis as badly as himself. So that, when his disease grew worse and was now threatening his life, he had summoned this third monk and had said goodbye to him just with a nod. But even he was not strong enough to take up the appointment any more effectively, for he came to his end more quickly and died before Benedict. So Æthelwald bought Benedict's body for a great price and took it to Thorney, adding a brilliant light[3] to its rather obscurer saints.

---

[1] Known as *The History of the Abbots of Wearmouth and Jarrow* (c.630).
[2] Benedict in fact made six visits to Rome, joining forces with Wilfrid on the first of these. See p. 142 and Bede, *Ecclesiastical History* 4:18.
[3] For this 'brilliant light' see *The Blackwell Encyclopaedia, s.v.* 'Benedict Biscop'; Stenton, *Anglo-Saxon England*, p. 85; Mayr-Harting, *The Coming of Christianity*, pp. 152–6.

Book 5 Aldhelm and Malmesbury Abbey

Here begins the prologue to the fifth book

Having travelled through the bishoprics of the whole extent of England, I am now, as it were, returning home after a long journey to carry out the promise I made about our most blessed father Aldhelm.[1] It is not an unusually rich store of material which spurs me on to fulfil this vow to the best of my ability, but rather that remarkably deep affection, which the saint has won from me. For how could it be right to refuse the publicity of my pen to one who, after God, was responsible for what little ability I do have? Am I not to give my tongue to him, for whom, had it been necessary, I would have given my life? Furthermore, the man who holds back his words is greedier than he should be. So since it would be a huge departure from justice in this brief account of the saints to pass over in silence none but my own master and protector, I have taken upon myself to say just a little about his life,[2] even if our ignorance of the facts means that the fullness of this record will fall well short of what I would have liked. Indeed, apart from Bede's mention of him in his *Ecclesiastical History of the English People*,[3] Aldhelm has always remained unhonoured, buried in undeserved obscurity thanks to the sloth of his countrymen.[4] His wonderful learning and amazing miracles make him a great man, but there are no surviving writings which illustrate this. Anyone would be glad to read more about the miracles which Aldhelm did while he was alive on this earth. Despite my most diligent researches I have found absolutely no written account which has come down to our own times apart from the craftsman's inscription on an ancient silver shrine.[5] Faricius, abbot of Abingdon,[6] did put together an account of these matters, but he relied on his own knowledge, and made no additional use of any external sources to confirm his own words. I have decided upon a different line of approach. I shall go closely into the events left out of Faricius' life, and wherever my story takes me, it will be supported by appropriate witnesses acting as posts. For

[1] See pp. 105 and 116.
[2] Aldhelm lived from *c*.640 to 709/10, and so was a contemporary of Wilfrid (634–709).
[3] In *Ecclesiastical History* 5:18 Bede devotes half a page to Aldhelm as a writer and man of learning.
[4] In fact it was only after the conquest that Aldhelm lapsed into obscurity. Until then he was an important author on the monastic curriculum, both in England and on the continent. M. R. James talks of his poetry being read in Spain and of the best ancient copy of one of his works belonging to an abbey in Limoges (*Two Ancient English Scholars*, Glasgow, 1931).
[5] The making of this shrine is described in ch. 236.
[6] For a poem in praise of Faricius of Arezzo see ch. 88.

otherwise no one is going to accept as true events so removed and distant from our own times, and which, as I have said, have been buried in obscurity for lack of a historian. Moreover, there is much evidence waiting for me, a monk of Malmesbury, to use, which Faricius either did not know about or omitted to mention. For although his powers as a writer are in no way to be despised, his ignorance of our language, as one born under Tuscan skies, means that he lacked the knowledge to research properly on this particular subject. So I ask my readers in all fairness and out of their goodness not to allow my own lack of fame to prejudice their sense of the abbot's worth. Although, if they pay attention to honours, I too have acquired something of a name and a reputation.

Chapter 187 William's programme for Book 5

My account will be in four parts. Firstly, I shall describe the lineage and learning of this greatest of saints. Secondly, I shall go through the monastic houses which he founded, and the privileges and endowments by which he made this monastery of ours so distinguished. At this point, at the very beginning of my narration I ask for my hearer's patience and for him not to give up when he is burdened with the writings of others.[1] For this little book promises not a display of eloquence but an assemblage of facts. It is not so much a description of the life of the saint as the evidence which is the tool for a knowledge of that life. Thirdly, I shall describe the very few miracles which he did in his lifetime. It is not that he did not do more, but I shall confine myself to those which no one has had doubts or scruples about. Fourthly, I shall write as truthful a history of our abbey as I can from the death of the saint down to our own day, describing the vast shipwrecks of its liberty which our church has endured, but also showing how, when seemingly most oppressed, it has always with the help of the saint successfully lifted up its head above misfortune. I am well aware that I am not equal to such a history. But led by the Holy Spirit, who up to now seems to have breathed vigorous life into my sails, I shall skim securely across even the immensity of this sea.

Chapter 188 Aldhelm's descent from West Saxon nobility

Aldhelm was of Saxon origin, born, as everybody knows, into one of the highest families, though he overcame the nobility of his birth by the nobility of his character. Faricius playfully suggests that his name should be spelled 'Ald-elm', meaning 'old kind one'.[2] I, on the other hand, if I might join in the game and encroach upon my reader's serious attention, would give the completely different explanation that the name is spelled 'Ald-helm', meaning 'old

[1] For example, in the second part of William's account, the reader has to get through seven charter-grants, describing endowments made to the monastery during Aldhelm's abbacy.
[2] In Faricius' suggestion, 'Ald-' presumably comes from the English word 'old', and '-elm' from 'almus', the Latin word for 'kind one'; William's etymology is the correct one.

helmet'. For the saint himself in the prologue to his *Mysteries*[1] clearly indicates that his name ought to be written with an 'h' in the middle. He also openly says in his letter to Wihtfrith that he is 'old helmet of protection'.[2] His life supports my interpretation, for, with his head protected by the helmet of salvation, he was trained as a soldier of Christ who fights to the end and does not know how to surrender to the enemy, and carried up to the skies the laurel wreath of victory won from the devil.

Some men say, though we do not know where they got this from, that he was the nephew of Ine, king of the West Saxons, being the son of Ine's brother Kenten. I did not like to claim this to be the truth, as it seems to me to square more with fickle rumour than with the facts of history, seeing that the chronicles clearly state that Ine had no brother except Ingeld, who died a few years before himself. I could also make the objection that Aldhelm was at least seventy when he died and Ine outlived him by more than eighteen years, indeed being still vigorous enough after this number of years to go on a journey to Rome. How could a young uncle have a nephew of seventy, especially when that nephew was the son of his younger brother? Having brought this discrepancy into the open, let me state the unambiguous truth. If you read the *Handbook* of king Alfred,[3] you will find that Kenten, father of the blessed Aldhelm, was not the brother of king Ine, but his first cousin. As for his Saxon origin, he himself, in a letter[4] to a certain Cellanus, tells him about it in these words, 'I am surprised that you, a busy, successful monk from the famous, flourishing land of France should write a letter to such an unimportant mannikin as myself, born into a family of Saxon race, and tucked up in the tiny cradle of my infancy under northern skies.'

Chapter 189 Aldhelm's education

His father, being a man of good sense and conscious of his noble birth, sent Aldhelm to learn his letters not at the school of some inferior teacher but at the hands of Hadrian, the abbot of St Augustine's (anyone who has read *The Deeds of the English* will know that Hadrian's learning towered above the rest).[5] As a boy there he learnt his Latin and Greek and soon so distinguished

---

[1] Short philosophical riddles in verse. Mayr-Harting, *The Coming of Christianity*, pp. 202–3, gives examples.
[2] See ch. 214 for a letter to Wihtfrith.
[3] This was a commonplace book in which Alfred had copied passages which interested him. According to Asser, it was 'almost as big as a Psalter'. No copies of it are extant.
[4] For full translations of the extant letters of Aldhelm and helpful introductions to them see M. Lapidge and M. Herren, *Aldhelm: The Prose Works* (Ipswich, 1979). This extract is from Letter X. Cellanus was an exile from Ireland who had become abbot of the monastery of St Fursa at Peronne (on the Somme).
[5] See *The Deeds of the Kings* 1:12. Hadrian, a monk of African origin, came with Theodore, a Greek-speaking scholar born in Tarsus, to Canterbury in 668, when Hadrian took over from Benedict Biscop as abbot of St Augustine's (ch. 186). Lapidge says the two of them 'established a school in Canterbury which represented one of the high points in Greek and Latin scholarship in early medieval Europe' (*The Blackwell Encyclopaedia, s.v.* 'Hadrian').

himself that his teachers themselves marvelled. When he was now a little older, he returned from Canterbury to the West Saxons and became a monk at the monastery of Meldunum. This monastery is in the town which according to the writings of king Alfred was originally called Maildubery, but is now known as Malmesbury. The monastery had been founded by an Irishman called Meldum, otherwise known as Maildubh, who was a monk by profession but had the learning of a philosopher. He had left his native land of his own free will, and, on arriving at Malmesbury, had been so attracted by the pleasantness of its wood, which by then had grown to an immense size, that he practised as a hermit there. When food ran short, he took pupils, in order that their high fees might improve his meagre diet. As time went on, they followed their teacher's example, became monks instead of pupils and formed themselves into a monastery of some size. Living with these monks, Aldhelm was led by their example to further study and he added the liberal arts to his already copious knowledge. Indeed, in order to drink in these arts to the full, he studied for a second time in Canterbury at the feet of Hadrian, who besides being the fountain of letters, was also the stream of liberal arts, until he was forced by ill-health to go back home. I shall back up these statements with evidence, so that my readers may have a firm belief in their truth.

We know he studied as a boy under Hadrian from these words in a letter of his to Hadrian, 'To Hadrian, revered father and respected teacher of my unformed childhood,[1] greetings etc. from Aldhelm, slave of the family of Christ, and humble pupil of your holiness.' The fact that Aldhelm was brought up and educated as a youth in the monastery of Meldunum is included in the charter in which bishop Leutherius gave him the abbacy there. 'I, Leutherius, bishop by the grace of God, have been asked by the abbots to think it right to bestow and confer upon Aldhelm, the priest, the land called Malmesbury for the living of life there according to the rule. There, indeed, from the first flowering of his infancy and his apprenticeship in letters, he has lived his life so far, instructed in the studies of the liberal arts and nourished in the lap of his holy mother, the church.'[2] That the monastery was founded by Meldum is proved by the charter which pope Sergius gave to Aldhelm, 'Your order asks us as deputy for our founder, the first of the apostles, to strengthen with apostolic privileges the monastery of the blessed apostles Peter and Paul, which, situated in the district of the Saxons, was founded by Meldum of holy memory and is even now known as Meldumsbury, and which, so we have learned, your order is thoughtfully managing. We give our assent to your humble petition.'[3] That Aldhelm studied again at Canterbury but left because of ill-health is shown by

---

[1] William's view that Aldhelm studied 'as a boy' under Hadrian is awkward in that Aldhelm was born *c*.640 and Hadrian did not come to England until 668, but Aldhelm's Latin word which William takes to mean 'childhood' could mean 'lack of eloquence', and this meaning would allow Aldhelm to be taught by Hadrian later in his life. See Letter II in Lapidge and Herren, *Aldhelm: The Prose Works*.

[2] This charter of Leutherius is given in full in ch. 199.

[3] This bull of pope Sergius is given in full in ch. 220.

his letter to Hadrian. 'My dearest friend, whom I embrace with the grace of a pure love, I admit that ever since our close fellowship ended about three years ago and I left Canterbury, my humble self has been on fire with a burning desire for your companionship. And for a long time now I have been thinking about how to bring my prayer to fulfilment, if our arrangements and the changes of the times allowed it, and provided that I was not kept back by various impediments and obstacles, or, my special fear, that I was not prevented by the diseased state of my fragile body, which sends a raging fever through the marrow of my wasting frame. For once, when I was with you again subsequent to my first period of elementary instruction, I was forced to return home because of such an illness.'

Chapter 190 Aldhelm and poetry

I think this evidence shows that Aldhelm was a master of the liberal arts, having had the benefit of sitting at the feet of such a companion. Nor indeed does Aldhelm himself fail to add to the praises given to him, when he says that he was the first of all the English to be bold enough to devote the attention of his keen mind to the study of the metres of poetry. For at the foot of the book which he wrote *Concerning Metrical Schemes* come these words of his, 'Here you have the materials which, as much as my feeble intellect allowed, I have collected with great effort and perhaps fruitfully concerning the different kinds of metrical schemes, although I am well aware that I could quote about myself these lines of Virgil,

> I, if life is given, shall be the first
> to bring the Muses to my native land,
> returning home with them from Helicon's spring.'[1]

So Aldhelm had a deep knowledge of Greek and Latin literature,[2] but he did not therefore neglect poetry written in his own language, and he was such a master of it that according to the book of Alfred I referred to earlier no age ever saw his equal. He could write poems in English, compose music for them and sing or recite them as the occasion demanded. Indeed Alfred tells us that Aldhelm was the composer of a light-hearted song, which people still sing nowadays, though Alfred adds the reason for it, thus enabling him to prove

---

[1] *Georgics* 3:10–11. Mount Helicon in Greece was the home of the Muses.

[2] William, like his master Aldhelm, spent much of his time as a monk studying the Greek and Latin classics. In a passage in his *Polyhistor* William justifies this by arguing that 'the man who reads them to the end that he may transfer to his own writings whatever of beauty or eloquence they tell him, to the honour of God and his saints (following the rule of the apostle, "Prove all things: hold fast to that which is good: abstain from all appearance of evil"), such a man I cannot believe does wrong in studying the writings of the heathen'. See M. R. James, *Two Ancient English Scholars*, p. 22. The words of the Apostle are from 1 Thessalonians 5:21. A similar attitude to William's in art is perhaps shown by the figure of Christ on the cross of bishop Heriman (now in the Diocesan Museum, Cologne), which has attached to the body of *c.*1056 a head which once belonged to a statuette of the empress Livia.

nse for the great man to turn his mind to apparent frivolities.
ople at that time, says Alfred, were semi-barbarians and not too
,e teachings in church. Indeed the very moment mass had been
uld rush off home. So the saint placed himself in their way on the
bridge, , ; country and town, pretending to be a minstrel. He did this more
than once, with the result that the people got to like it and came in crowds. The
consequence was that Aldhelm gradually inserted the words of Scripture into
his ballads and so brought the people back to their senses.[1] If he had thought to
deal with the matter with harsh words and excommunications, he would have
achieved precisely nothing.

Chapter 191 Aldhelm's fame as a scholar

Letters sent him by his friends show how loudly a favourable report of his high
learning had been trumpeted abroad. I say nothing about his compatriots who
competed in sending him their writings that they might undergo his judgement
and criticism. I pass over the Scots, very clever people in those days, who are
known to have done the same thing. Some of them whom I could name were
well-known writers, especially Artwilus, the son of the Scottish king. He
would pass on all his literary productions, which were by no means negligible,
to Aldhelm for judgement, so that any Scottish roughness might be rubbed
smooth by the file of his high-class intellect. Aldhelm's learning attracted
letters from the very heart of France, as this letter will clearly show.

> To abbot Aldhelm, master enriched by devotion to reading and crowned
> with the honey-producing labours of the night, to you who in the countryside
> of the Saxons are marvellously discovering those things which others are
> scarce obtaining with labour and sweat in foreign climes, greetings in the
> name of the complete and life-saving Trinity, from Cellanus[2] who was born
> in Ireland and who now as the lowest, worthless slave of Christ lies hidden in
> the furthest corner of the lands of France, an exile in a famous town.[3]

And a little later he adds:

> The glowing report of your skill in Latin has, as I might say, winged its flight
> to our humble ears. Keen readers do not shudder to hear about it, but accept
> it without derision or cloudy evasions because of the Alburnian[4] grace of
> your Roman eloquence. Even if we have not been entitled to hear you in
> person, at least we have read your works which are constructed with such

---

[1] As Mayr-Harting remarks, this record of Aldhelm's concern for the souls of his people stops us from regarding him as a dry pedant, only interested in his books (*The Coming of Christianity*, p. 215).
[2] For Cellanus see p. 225 and n. 4. His letter bears some resemblance to the elaborate style of his master.
[3] The town was Peronne.
[4] Alburnus was a mountain in Lucania in Italy, mentioned by Virgil in *Georgics* 3:146. Cellanus perhaps uses it to mean no more than 'Italian'.

balance and adorned with the charms of different flowers of rhetoric. But if you would gladden the sad little heart of an expatriate, please send a few short discourses written in that most beautiful style of yours to the place where the holy, uncorrupted body of master Fursa[1] lies buried. For the streams which flow from that most pure spring of your style can refresh the minds of many.

Chapter 192 Aldhelm's letter in support of Wilfrid

How generously Aldhelm replied to this letter can be seen from that letter, of which I recently quoted part to prove that Aldhelm was of Saxon birth.[2] But it is not easy to describe the influence of Aldhelm over friends and pupils, whether he was urging his friends to stay loyal to each other or his young pupils to listen with the greatest possible attention to divine teaching. I will give a single example of each kind of advice, so that his loyalty to his friends and his concern for his pupils may be clearly shown. When bishop Wilfrid (I gave a long account of him in Book 3)[3] was driven into exile, many of the abbots among his people followed the wheel of fortune and began thinking about going over to the side of his enemies. As Aldhelm did not believe in the justice of their case and was afraid for his venerable friend, he tried to lift up their failing spirits with this letter. After a suitable preface, he says:

You have recently known from experience the disturbance of that furious storm which, like a mighty earthquake, shook the foundations of the church; the noise of it, like a clap of thunder, reverberated far and wide throughout the different regions of our land. And so I am begging you, my flesh and blood brothers in Christ, in humble prayer on bended knee not to find any sort of a stumbling-block in this disturbing turn of events. Please may none of you have the lukewarm faith of the inactive sluggard, even if the force of circumstances compels you to be driven from your fatherland together with your own leader, who has been stripped of the crown of his archbishopric, and to go to whatever widespread foreign kingdoms may be necessary.[4] For, I ask you, what labours can be so hard or horrible that they separate and keep you from that archbishop, who, like a good father, by nourishing, teaching and correcting you brought you up right from the first years of your tender infancy when you were just learning your letters to the full flower of your youth? As a nurse carries and comforts her dear charges in the enveloping embrace of her arms, so did he gently hold and warm you in the lap of his love.

Look, I beg you, at the nature implanted by God in the creatures of the animal kingdom, so that, from a comparison with the tiniest, you may with

---

[1] Fursa was an Irish monk who left his home to go on pilgrimage and died in France in 649. There is a full account of him in Bede's *Ecclesiastical History* 3:19.
[2] In ch. 188.
[3] Chs. 100–9.
[4] This reference to 'foreign kingdoms' probably means that the letter should be dated to 677, when Wilfrid went as an exile to Frisia.

the help of Christ form a mode of behaviour which nothing can alter. Consider how the swarms of bees,[1] when warmth comes down from the sky in summer time, jostle each other as they emerge from their honeycombs burning with desire for nectar, and, as their leader leaves the homes which sheltered them in winter, in rapid flight form a mass in the sky like densely packed cohort bands, apart, of course, from the female servants of their old hives who are left behind to propagate their future progeny. And this is a still more marvellous story! When their king[2] leads out the swarm from winter camp, protected by the close-knit companies of his friends, and explores the wood of hollow tree trunks, if he should be stopped by the sprinkling of some dry sand or hindered by sudden showers wetting them with their drops in a cataract from Olympus, and goes back to the welcoming home of their old honeycomb, in the twinkling of an eye the whole army breaks through the familiar entrance-halls and gratefully enters the safety of its former cells.

And later on:

So if creatures, lacking reason and governed merely by the inborn, unwritten laws of nature, obey the orders of their leader in good times and in bad, tell me, please, are not those who have been endowed with the grace given by the sevenfold Spirit to be rebuked with the ill name given to an abomination of horror, if in their mad career they break the reins of the loyalty which they owe? But let me tell you why I am rushing with spluttering pen to arouse the hearts in your breasts by collecting together so many different arguments.

Look at it this way. Consider men of the world, completely ignorant of things divine. If they abandoned their devoted master, whom they loved in times of prosperity, when his rich felicity came to an end and the storms of adversity assailed him, and preferred safe ease in their own dear country to the afflictions of their exiled master, surely they would be thought to deserve scornful jeers and curses and loud mocking from everybody? So what will men say about you, if you abandon to a lonely exile the bishop who nourished you and brought you up?[3]

And there was more like this.

Chapter 193 His letter to his pupil Æthilwald

Having given an example of his utter integrity towards his friends, I shall now quote his excellent advice to a pupil.

[1] Aldhelm probably had Virgil's Fourth Georgic in mind, when he used the bees here as a lesson.
[2] The ancients in general believed the most conspicuous bee in the hive to be a male. The true facts were only discovered by the Dutchman, J. Swammerdam (1637–86).
[3] Aldhelm does not say why he supported Wilfrid. Lapidge and Herren suggest that they were both proud men with little taste for compromise who supported the Roman Church and the Roman Easter (*Aldhelm: The Prose Works*, p. 150).

To Æthilwald, both my dearly beloved son and pupil, greetings from Aldhelm, lowest of the servants of God. Just as I sometimes took the trouble to advise you on certain matters orally, so also now I feel no compunction about encouraging you in a letter, for I rely on the paternal authority given me by God. I am doing this, as the apostle says, 'because the love of Christ so constrains me'.[1] And so, my dearest son, though you are in your youth, keep completely away from the empty delights of this world, from daily parties and drinking bouts, which with more frequent and extended use become bad and unnecessary, from riding around the countryside and so incurring blame, from all accursed pleasures of bodily delight. Remember the words of Scripture, 'Youth and pleasure are vain.'[2] And do not devote yourself too much to an over keen love of money or to all the trappings of that worldly glory which is always hateful to God, but remember the sentence, 'What does it profit a man to gain the whole world, if he loses his soul?'[3] 'For the son of man will come in his glory and with that of the holy angels; and he will repay each man according to his works.'[4]

But much rather, dearest one, always devote your attention to divine readings or sacred discourses. And, of course, if you do make the effort to get to know any secular literature, make sure you do it only for the following reason: as in the divine law all or almost all the structure of the words stands completely in accord with the rules of the art of grammar, you will read and understand more easily the deepest and most sacred meanings of this divine eloquence, if you have previously fully learned all the different rules of the theory of their composition.[5] Always keep this letter with the other books you are reading, so that, as you read it over and over, it can warn you as my deputy to carry out the instructions contained in it. Goodbye.

Chapter 194 Aldhelm's advice to Æthilwald still valid

I wish that the monks claiming to be Aldhelm's disciples would gain and acquire profit and advantage from the reading of this letter, so that they might finally spit out fleshly delights and walk in the way of its holy teaching. For it is certain that our way of life would not have suffered so much damage, if we had not disobeyed its commands. But we are justly punished for our transgressions against it. Aldhelm himself all this time keeps silent in apparent ignorance, pretending not to see, while we are tossed about in perilous waters, our prerogatives laughed at by lawbreakers and trampled on by tyrants.[6] Even this

---

[1] 2 Corinthians 5:14.
[2] Ecclesiastes 11:10.
[3] Mark 8: 36.
[4] Matthew 16:27.
[5] An important sentence showing clearly Aldhelm's belief that an education in the liberal arts could only be justified on the grounds that it was a necessary preliminary to the study of Scripture. See Mayr-Harting, *The Coming of Christianity*, pp. 214–16.
[6] William is presumably referring here to the expropriations of Roger, bishop of Salisbury. See p. 117 and n. 1.

late in the day let us return to our heart's desire, so that Aldhelm may look with the eye of goodness on his servants, now so tempest-tossed, and gather them into the bosom of his mercy.

Chapter 195 The wide range of Aldhelm's studies

But, to take up the thread of my story, the finishing touch to the praise of Aldhelm's literary powers was applied by Bede,[1] who knew the facts because of his nearness in time, and was unwilling to lie because of his desire for the truth. After giving the titles of some of Aldhelm's books, he adds these words, 'He also wrote on various other matters, like the completely educated man that he was. He had a polished style and his knowledge of both sacred and secular literature was equally marvellous.'[2] Can any more exalted praise than this be given to him? Finally I will call the man himself as witness. He never lost his enthusiasm for all those arts which he attentively studied especially during his second stay in Canterbury. For in a letter to his predecessor, Hæddi,[3] he describes in these words his own field of study and commends its practice:

Most blessed bishop, I acknowledge that I had long ago decided, if fast-changing circumstances allowed it, to celebrate with rejoicing the next longed-for Christmas day in the company of my brothers in the same place, and afterwards, if life still accompanied me, to enjoy your affection face to face.[4] But I was held back by various obstacles and difficulties, of which the bearer of this letter will give you a full oral account, and so was unable to carry out my plan. Please forgive me: it was too difficult. For in this pursuit of reading, short periods away from one's books should not be prolonged, at least not if the reader is fired up and keen, and would burrow deeply into the statutes of Roman law[5] and scrutinise with the closest attention all the secrets of the lawyers. And a much more complicated subject for study and examination even than this is, of course, the hundred kinds of metre with their rules for the feet, and the right pattern of syllables for the melodies used in chanting. Even the keen reader on the subject is faced with a screen of darkness, all the more impenetrable because of the few experts that can be found. The narrow confines of a letter are the last place to allow me to put forward a lengthy argument on these matters, but I am referring to the

[1] In *Ecclesiastical History* 5:18.
[2] The second half of this sentence is more obviously true than the first half. It is a surprise to hear Aldhelm's labyrinthine sentences with their unusual vocabulary described as 'polished'.
[3] See ch. 223 for Hæddi being Aldhelm's predecessor. In fact modern scholars suggest that the letter was sent to Leutherius, Hæddi's predecessor as bishop of Winchester, as all the evidence points to a date before 676, when Hæddi became bishop. See Lapidge and Herren, *Aldhelm: The Prose Works*, p. 137.
[4] Aldhelm presumably writes from Canterbury, making his excuses for not sharing Christmas with his brethren at Malmesbury and for not going on to visit the bishop at Winchester.
[5] This reference to Roman law as a subject of study in seventh-century England is unique. James wonders if the actual book was a copy of the Breviary of Alaric, which Aldhelm then took back with him for the library at Malmesbury, as William later transcribed this book in his own hand (*Two Ancient English Scholars*, p. 17).

examination of the skills of the poet as he puts together the 'hidden' materials of letters, syllables, feet, poetic figures, lines, accents and quantities. The art of the poet, with the variations needed in such matters as beginning the line with a short or extra syllable, can be divided into seven parts. He needs to know the fixed patterns of the feet at the ends of lines, whether they cover one syllable or five or ten, and the thinking behind the striking effect of the use of lines ending a syllable or a foot short or in an extra syllable or foot. Even the taking of a short break means one can never master these subjects and others like them. And then there is what needs to be remembered about the principles of calculation. All that computation produced a despair which enveloped me and weighed down my mind like a yoke. I regarded all my past labours in reading as of no account, although for a long time I had believed that I had arrived at a knowledge of its secret chambers. So then I repeated to myself this appropriate quotation from St Jerome, 'When it struck me that my knowledge was superficial, then I began to be a pupil again', and in the end supported by God's grace and through my persistence in reading I understood those supremely difficult theories and the reckonings and calculations which they call fractions. But I think that I should remain silent about the zodiac and the theories about its twelve signs which follow each other in the high heavens. This dark and deep subject, requiring a lengthy discourse for its exposition, will only be cheapened and vilified by publishing some elementary textbook on the subject. Anyway, knowledge of astrology and of the vexed question of the casting of horoscopes needs the midnight investigations of a professor.

Chapter 196 The works of Aldhelm

Such studies gave him intense personal pleasure, but he also published books of nourishing learning from the sacred storehouse of his mind, lest he should never reveal the treasures he had spent so long amassing or never pass back to others anything of what he had heard. He gave the first proof of his intellect in the book which he wrote to persuade the Britons to return to the true Easter; some stroke of jealous fortune has robbed us of the pleasure of reading its teaching.[1] There is also the delightfully eloquent work which he put together called *In Praise of Virgins*.[2] In this he first of all describes the glory of virginity and then, with examples from the celibacy of the saints, shows that it is not difficult. He wrote another book on the same subject in epic verse, to which he added a third, also in verse, called *The Battle with the Eight Chief Vices*. There is also extant that noble work, which he wrote in emulation of the poet Symposius, called *Mysteries*; this poem of a thousand lines is divided into a hundred sections. For both books he cleverly composed an acrostic verse

---

[1] William gives more details about this book, or rather letter, in ch. 215.
[2] In ch. 73 William says that it was dedicated to Hildelith, abbess of Barking. It takes up seventy-one pages in a translation in a modern book. For a description of this and Aldhelm's other works see Mayr-Harting, *The Coming of Christianity*, pp. 193–5.

preface, so that in *In Praise of Virgins* the individual letters of the line, 'Now let these verses bring into view pure young poets' begin the individual lines of the preface from its beginning to its end, and, reversed through the number of the verses, also give a line ending in a letter of that particular line. But then in his *Mysteries* he adopted the different device of making the line, 'Aldhelm composed poems of a thousand verses' supply both the beginning and end letters of the individual lines of the preface, with the same letter being used at the beginning and end of the line. He displayed in these prefaces the playful cleverness of ancient literature, but a powerfully eloquent rhetoric went hand in hand with such trivialities.

He also sent to a certain Aldfrith, king of the Northumbrians,[1] who, according to Bede, was well versed in letters, a book made up of the following chapters: 'The importance of the number seven, as found in the inspired pages of Old and New Testaments and the teachings of the philosophers. – A recommendation of brotherly love. – The nature of things lacking senses which are made to speak by a metaphor. – The rules for metrical feet. – Grammatical changes – The contraction of two syllables into one. Scansion and elision in poetry. – Alternate verses of Question and Response.' He also wrote many letters. Most of them are not extant, and some which we do possess have parts missing, thanks to the carelessness of our predecessors.[2] His *Discourses* are not as lively as would be wished for by people who scrutinise the verbal expression but neglect the subject matter.[3] But such experts are mistaken. They do not know that styles of writing vary in different countries, so that the customary Greek style is intricate, the Roman brilliant and the English showy. In all ancient writings one can see how pleased the writers were with rare words derived from the Greek. But Aldhelm showed more restraint and did not use out-of-the-way words except on a few occasions when he was compelled to. Statements everybody would agree with are expressed in fluent language, while a rhetorical colouring makes his more violent assertions stand out. If you read him properly, you will think him a Greek because of his sharpness, you will swear him to be a Roman because of his brilliance, and you will realise he is an Englishman because of his sense of display.

Chapter 197 Aldhelm's church to St Saviour, St Peter and St Paul

Now that I have patched together as best I can the first part of my undertaking, I shall attack the second part, which promises to describe the monasteries founded by St Aldhelm, the privileges by which they were honoured and the lands by which they were enriched. This will be an easy task, seeing that the main bulk of the material will be taken from the works of others. I would like to say some essential, preliminary things in my own words, taking the opportunity of speeding up my work, and then with a lighter heart to process

---

[1] For Aldfrith see chs. 103–8. Bede refers to him in *Ecclesiastical History* 5:12.
[2] Only thirteen letters survive, written by or addressed to Aldhelm.
[3] Cellanus at least was keen to have some of Aldhelm's discourses sent out to France (ch. 191).

up and down the writings of others. So, from what has been said already,[1] you know that Meldum built or rather began the monastery of Meldunum, which is now called Malmesbury by a more decadent age. The monastery was so short of the necessities of life that its members could scarcely scrabble together their daily bread. But this lack of provisions was rectified by the noble Aldhelm, as my narrative will show. A few years ago a quite small church could be seen at Malmesbury: it is uncertain whether the men of old said that it was built by Meldum. Aldhelm is said to have built beside it a more impressive church, in honour of the Lord, our Saviour, and the first of the apostles, Peter and Paul. And it was in this church, as the headquarters of the monastery, that the band of monks lived from ancient times: the authority of the documents which I shall subjoin will prove the truth of this statement and silence the doubters. Further, because it was the custom at the time to compose an honorific epigram at the dedication of new churches in praise of the heavenly bridegroom and the church, his mother, St Aldhelm composed this epithalamium[2] in honour of the apostles:

The fame of our rough temple here be praised,
which spreads and shows heaven's banners bright in triumph.
Paul and Peter, fathers best, a dark world's lights,
The reins of government holding,
In our blest court we sing your praise unending.
O you who hold the key and heaven's gate
Unlock and open up the Thunderer's bright realm
To worthy men, in mercy hear the prayers
Of us who wet shrunk cheeks with watery streams.
Please hear our sobs as we lament wrongs done
And scorch our sinful acts with burning prayer.
And you, once Saul the proud, with name now changed
Called Paul, mild lamb of God, your fury set aside,
Lend kindly ear to us who speak these prayers.
With Peter stretch your covering hand on us
Who, trembling, pack and throng these holy halls,
That we may get swift pardon for our sins,
From heaven's bounteous, holy spring still flowing
And never drying up for worthy men.

Chapter 198 Aldhelm's monastic foundations

He also founded another monastery near the river which is called the River Frome.[3] We can read about it in the charter of privilege which pope Sergius

[1] In ch. 189.
[2] For such poems recording the dedication of a church see *The Blackwell Encyclopaedia, s.v.* 'Tituli'.
[3] There is more than one river Frome. This monastery could be at Wareham or in the town of Frome.

gave to both monasteries.[1] This church, which he built in honour of St John the Baptist, still stands there today, surviving and living on after many centuries. The common opinion is that he founded also a third monastery at Bradford-on-Avon, and this seems to be confirmed by the name of the town occurring in the course of the charter, which the then bishop gave to his monasteries, and being written in an ancient script. The little church dedicated to St Laurence, which he is said to have founded there, exists to this day.[2] But although the church survives, both monasteries, at Frome and at Bradford, have followed the fashion of mortal things and disappeared, leaving only an empty name, although it is hard to decide whether we should blame the fierce wars with the Danes for the destruction of these great buildings or the rapacious altercations of the English. Only Malmesbury lives on, still packed with monks, its buildings still beautiful. In my opinion, it was because of the holiness of the saint who on that spot renounced self and the flesh that it was allowed to emerge from and outlive the numerous calamities of those times of trouble, and to exhale traces of its long-lost liberty, faint though they now are. And so, as the lands conferred on the monastery by Aldhelm have been subject to widespread ruin along with the destruction of other things, I also have no personal knowledge of them at all. But anyone who wants to give an account of the extent of his land-grants to the monastery does have available for quoting as a primary document the charter which Leutherius, bishop of the West Saxons, granted to Aldhelm. It was Leutherius who spotted that Aldhelm was aiming for the top as the successes due to his virtues pushed him into the limelight, and who raised him to be priest at Malmesbury and then abbot. Here follows the document in which he handed over the possession and control of Malmesbury into the hands of the abbot.

Chapter 199 Charter-grant of Leutherius to Aldhelm

It is a customary, general occurrence that, when the fierce heats of autumn depart, the wintry blasts of the tempestuous winds follow them by turns in alternating succession, upheaving in storms on this side and on that the blue waves of the sea and the mighty expanses of the ocean, so that nobody sails across the pathways of the sea without peril as the furious blasts tear at his sails. In the same way, indeed, now that the pomp and glory of the world have been brought low as its end approaches, we see from the evidence of our own eyes tempest and upheaval falling upon our age so that in very truth and without any possibility of doubt those forecasts of our Lord are at last being fulfilled in our own day in which he thus spoke words of heavenly prophecy, 'Look at the fig tree and the other trees',[3] and so on. From now on it is the

---

[1] See ch. 221 for the full text of this charter.

[2] The present church of St Laurence was rediscovered in 1856. Pevsner, *Buildings of England: Wiltshire*, is inclined to think that it represents a late Saxon rebuilding rather then Aldhelm's original church. For a photograph of the present church see *The Blackwell Encyclopaedia*, p. 73.

[3] Luke 21:29.

tiller of the Scriptures that must be turned during these stormy tempests of our lifetime, and from Scripture's pages that we must procure armour and equipment for the whole voyage, so that, deaf to the sirens' persuasive song, our boat may be brought straight and safely to our homeland's haven.

Therefore I, Leutherius, bishop by the grace of God, helmsman of the pontificate of the West Saxons, have been asked by the abbots, who are known to have pastoral care and charge of the whole body of monks under the jurisdiction of our diocese, that I should think it right to bestow and confer the territory called Malmesbury upon Aldhelm the priest for the living there of life according to the rule. There, indeed, after the first flowering of his infancy and his apprenticeship in letters, he has lived his life so far, instructed in the studies of the liberal arts and nourished in the lap of his holy mother, the church. This seems to have been the chief reason why the abbots in their brotherly love made this proposal. And so I grant the prayers of these abbots, and, persuaded by their brotherly request, I of my own free will bestow the aforementioned place upon Aldhelm and upon his successors, as they follow the requirements of our holy rule with careful devotion, so that down to future generations the servants of God may fare well without hindrance in unbroken quiet and perpetual peace, with all upsetting disputes and arguments set aside. But lest by any chance some occasion for dispute should some day arise, I interpose this considered ruling and confirm that no bishop or king in the future, relying on his despotic power, shall make any violent attacks on this, our charter of donation, by making the stubborn assertion that Malmesbury seems to have been taken away and removed from the jurisdiction of the episcopal power. And so let it be known and publicly stated against any opponents that I have much more increased the benefits and powers of the episcopal church than forcibly removed them. Finally, so that the donation of this bequest may for ever remain the firmer, we have ordered the aforesaid abbots to sign it with their own hands. But if anyone tries to annul the rulings written in this our decree, let him know that he will give an account before the judgement seat of Christ. Given in public, by the River Bladon, 26 August 675.

Chapter 200 Aldhelm wins patrons

Once made abbot, he led the monks to a life of prayer, increased their reputation for goodness and before all else desired the glory of God. As the support of the bishop matched the abbot's energy, the affairs of the monastery flourished exceedingly at that time. Down all the roads people came running to Aldhelm, some in search of the holiness of his life, others in search of his learning. For although, as I have said, his erudition was wide-ranging, as a man of God he was approachable and simple. He could overthrow opponents with a thunderbolt of rhetoric or charm pupils with a honeyed stream of instruction. In dealing with both classes, a discourse of wit and humour flowed from his lips, admirable in its single parts and of singular excellence as a whole. This was the reason why the kings and earls of the Mercians and West Saxons, won over by the holiness of a man who was also commended by his blue blood, gave to the monastery several endowments, to the advantage of the monks' income and the salvation of their own souls. The first to do so, according to tradition, was Cœnfrith, earl of Mercia and relation of the king, a man who fought for his country with his body and for his God with his soul. This is his charter granting ten hides of land to abbot Aldhelm at Wootton Basset.

Chapter 201 Charter of Cœnfrith

The wanton fortune of the deceptive world is not loved for the milky whiteness of its unwithering lilies but hated for the poisonous bitterness of its lamented corruption, as it bites and shreds its sons in this vale of the tears with venomous rendings of stinking flesh. Although it may give a smile of favour towards poor human beings, yet it will shamelessly sink as low as the depths of Acheronian Cocytus,[1] unless the Son of the High Thunderer comes to the rescue. And because this world is itself subsiding into mortal ruin, we must hurry with all our strength to the lovely fields of indescribable happiness, where the good and the blessed experience the immeasurable sweetness of the angelic organs with their jubilant hymns and the honeyed scent of roses. Consumed by a love for this felicity, I, Cœnfrith, earl of Mercia, with the consent of my lord, king Æthelred,[2] give in perpetuity to abbot Aldhelm, a portion of land, estimated at ten hides, in the place called Wootton Basset for the service of God and St Peter. 680, Indiction 8.

Chapter 202 Charter of king Æthelred

By this gift the most worthy earl awoke and aroused the generosity of the king, who in the following year himself bestowed two estates upon the monastery, confirming his gift in the following single charter.

In the name of our Lord God Jesus Christ our Saviour! As the voice of the prophet has testified, 'We brought nothing into this world, nor can we take anything away.'[3] Therefore things lasting and eternal must be bought with things earthly and transitory. So I, Æthelred, king of the Mercians, at the request of my nobleman and relative Cœnfrith, do freely bestow upon abbot Aldhelm and his successors, in return for the prayers of the brothers serving God at Malmesbury and the redemption of my soul, thirty hides to the west of the public highway, and not far away in another place fifteen hides by

---

[1] Cocytus and Acheron were both rivers of Hades in classical mythology.

[2] King of Mercia 674–704. Malmesbury is on the Wiltshire bank of the river Avon, which was the boundary between the spheres of influence of Mercia and Wessex. The land grants of Mercia in chs. 201–4 may represent a move towards Mercian control of Malmesbury. As Barbara Yorke says, 'Patronage of religious houses in areas which they hoped to take over was a Mercian policy which can be paralleled elsewhere' (*Wessex in the Early Middle Ages*, London, 1995, p. 61).

[3] 1 Timothy 6:7.

Tetbury monastery,[1] these lands to be perpetually free from any serfdoms imposed by man. I have confirmed this gift of mine with the sign of the holy cross made by my own hand and corroborated it with the clear consent of my lords. So, after my death, let no bold king or temporal lord attempt to nullify our decree. Should anyone wish to increase and enlarge this gift, may God increase his entry in the book of life. But if anyone, in reliance on his despotic power, tries to take it away, let him know that he will give account before Christ and the nine classes of angels. This charter is written by hand in 681, Indiction 9.

Chapter 203 Gift of Berhtwald

The same king's nephew, Berhtwald, son of his brother Wulfhere, mentioned previously in my account of bishop Wilfrid,[2] did not indeed have a king's power but was merely a chieftain in one part of the kingdom. Inspired by love of God, he gave the following noble gift to the blessed Aldhelm:

Chapter 204 Charter of Berhtwald

Although word of mouth should be sufficient on its own to publish the details of grants made with holy devotion in the fear and love of God, because of the uncertainty of the future such grants need also to be confirmed publicly in writing and documentary records. So I, king Berhtwald, in the reign of our Lord, have determined to confer and bestow upon abbot Aldhelm, for the redeeming of my soul and the remission of the sins I have committed, a portion of land of forty hides, on the eastern side of the river Thames, near the crossing called Somerford.[3] I specifically declare that this parcel of land is for supplying the needs of the monks serving God in the monastery called Malmesbury, and is to be perpetually free from all serfdom imposed by secular powers. So that this grant may more surely and certainly remain for ever unshaken, I have also called upon Æthelred, our most worthy king, to witness it, for this generous act has been performed with his consent and confirmation. If anyone, relying on his despotic power, tries to make a move or an attack against this grant, he should know that he will give an account in the awesome general judgement before Christ. Given publicly at the synod held near Burford, 30 July, Indiction 13, 685.

These three documents were signed by archbishop Theodore, Æthelred king of the Mercians, Berhtwald the chieftain, Cœnfrith the earl, and by Sæxwulf and Bosel, bishops of Lichfield and Worcester.'

---

[1] Tetbury is five miles north of Malmesbury.
[2] Wulfhere was mentioned on p. 144 as giving Lichfield to Wilfrid as a place to found a monastery or an archbishopric.
[3] Somerford Keynes, on the upper Thames, is ten miles north-east of Malmesbury. Aldhelm was a builder of churches and David Verey thinks that the Anglo-Saxon doorway surviving on the north side of the church could well be the remains of a church built in Aldhelm's day (*Buildings of England: Gloucestershire, the Cotswolds*).

Chapter 205 Gift and charter of king Centwine

At the same time Centwine, king of the West Saxons,[1] weighed down by illness and old age, had marked out the young prince Cædwalla as his successor. Although Cædwalla[2] was not yet king nor Christian, he anticipated the kingship in advance, and, easily falling into belief, sought baptism.[3] As a result he enjoyed being called king and his generous gifts to many monasteries round about included a handsome grant to this monastery, as is clear from this document.

Chapter 206

In the name of our Lord Jesus Christ! All things 'which are seen are transient, and all which are not seen are eternal'.[4] And the same apostle again shows the uncertain fragility of the world when he says: 'We brought nothing into this world, nor can we take anything out of it.'[5] Therefore the transient things of earth must be used to win heaven's badge of the everlasting crown. And so I, Cædwalla, in the reign of our Lord, for the redemption of my soul and the remission of my sins, have decided to confer and bestow upon abbot Aldhelm the following lands: 140 hides, extending from both parts of the wood called Kemble and from the eastern part of the end of the roads right up to the famous river known as the Thames; thirty hides in another place, that is from the eastern part of the wood called Bradon; and five hides, especially for the brothers' fishing, at the confluence of the rivers Avon and Wylye. So let this grant remain undisturbed and unshaken down to future generations, with no one daring to nullify the privilege accorded by it. But if anybody, puffed up by despotic power, should try to attack this generosity, let him know that his interference is incurring the wrath of God, and that he will give an account before Christ and his angels at the last judgement. This generosity was happily recorded in Indiction 13, 19 August 688.

Chapter 207 An exchange of property with Baldred and its charter

In the same year Aldhelm exchanged part of these lands with a certain Baldred[6] in return for others which seemed would give a richer return and to be nearer of access. But, because for some reason or another the gift of Cædwalla stayed ratified, the exchange after a few years became invalid. This, then, is the charter of exchange.

[1] Centwine was king from 676 to *c*.685.
[2] Cædwalla was king from 685 to 689. He extended his kingdom to include much of south-east England, including the Isle of Wight, and gave Wilfrid a share of his new acquisitions. See ch. 102.
[3] Bede, *Ecclesiastical History* 5:7 says Cædwalla was not actually baptised until his visit to Rome described in ch. 209.
[4] 2 Corinthians 4:18.
[5] 1 Timothy 6:7.
[6] A West Saxon sub-king.

Chapter 208

In the name of our Lord God and Saviour Jesus Christ! I, Baldred, have decided to hand to abbot Aldhelm a piece of land of a hundred hides, which is near the river Avon and round the wood called Stercanley and Cnebbanberg; and I have received from him in return a hundred hides from the district of the eastern wood which is called Bradon. This exchange has been ratified and confirmed by the consent of king Centwine and all his princes and nobles. If anyone tries to attack these arrangements, let him know that he will give an account before the tribunal of the eternal judge and in the presence of the holy angels. This gift, or rather mutual exchange, has been recorded in the month of August, Indiction 1, 688.

These two documents were signed by Hæddi bishop of Winchester, king Centwine, and Cissa father of Ine, who was later king.

Chapter 209 The kingship of Ine (689–726)

Cædwalla became king after Centwine. Bede has described in some detail Cædwalla's hard work for his kingdom and his devotion to God, and told the story of how, after triumphing over his foes and gaining the kingship, he journeyed to Rome, and there was baptised and went happily to meet his last judgement;[1] I myself have touched on these matters in my history of the Kings.[2] When he went to Rome, Ine took up the kingship. Ine was wisdom personified.[3] You would never see anyone braver or know his equal in holiness: witness the wars he despatched, witness the monasteries he built.[4] These gifts of mind of the king were encouraged and stirred into life by advice from father Aldhelm; Ine listened humbly to the advice, put it into operation on a grand scale, and carried out the projects with efficiency. Following Aldhelm's suggestion, Ine built the monastery at Glastonbury, as I described in *The Deeds of the Kings*,[5] and gave to Malmesbury lands of no small value. Here is one example of the munificent charter-grants which accompanied his gift.

Chapter 210 Estate given by Ine to Aldhelm

In the name of the Lord Jesus Christ our Saviour! In the reign of our Lord, I, Ine, king of the Saxons, having in mind the reward of eternal life and fearing the everlasting punishments of hell, for the salvation of my soul and

[1] *Ecclesiastical History* 4:12 and 5:7. Cædwalla died on 20 April 689.
[2] See *The Deeds of the Kings* 1:34.
[3] Ine issued the earliest known written West Saxon laws.
[4] Besides Glastonbury Ine also founded the nunnery at Wimborne, where his sister Cuthberg was the first abbess (ch. 225). Bede records that after ruling for thirty-seven years Ine, like Cædwalla, went to Rome 'to spend some of his time on earth as a pilgrim in the neighbourhood of holy places' and died there (*Ecclesiastical History* 5:7).
[5] 1:35.

release from my sins have decided to give to the revered abbot Aldhelm a parcel of land for the increase of his monastery at Malmesbury. It consists of forty-five hides in various places, as named below by their inhabitants: five hides in the place called Garsdon, twenty hides at the source of the stream called the Gauze brook; ten hides in another place near the same stream; and ten hides near the spring called Rodbourne. Given in 701, Indiction 14.

This charter was signed by bishop Hæddi and by Wynberht, clerk to the king, who had dictated both this charter and other charter-grants of Cædwalla. Aldhelm had once written to Wynberht, asking if he could depend on his support at the court of Cædwalla. This is the letter.

Chapter 211 Aldhelm's enlargement of the monastery's estates

Greetings from Aldhelm, servant of the servants of God, to my lord, most beloved Wynberht, in the name of the Lord of lords and of the corner stone of the two testaments, which, cut off from the very tops of the mountains, smashed the statue made of the four kinds of metal signifying the four kingdoms of men, and destroyed it from its golden head down to the legs.[1] The bearer of this letter, whom I have sent into your holy presence, will give fuller details to you by word of mouth of the root of our present problem. It concerns the land which the revered nobleman, Baldred, gave into our hands at an agreed price. It is a handsome estate and especially suitable for catching fish. And as its grant and donation seems to have been confirmed by the power of your king, we earnestly beseech you that we may be able, with the support of your affection, to have and to hold this piece of land in firm possession, and that we may not, seeing that justice's laws are often found weak, be deprived of this land through fraud and violence.

And so on.

These, then, are the lands which the energy of the blessed abbot got added to the monastery. Delightfully situated, they are pleasantly large and conveniently close by. Indeed, a person leaving the monastery at dawn can easily go round all of them in the one day and return home while it is still full daylight. After his death other people, of course, gave other lands, but robbers have stripped us of all except these, and they got their hands even on some of these. Anyway, Aldhelm increased the lands of the monastery to more than four hundred hides, although they had previously been scarcely forty. For this is the number of hides that is the assessment of the town, customarily now called Brokenborough by the country folk, which adjoins the place which contains the monastery.

[1] See Daniel 2:34, 35.

Chapter 212 The justification for recording miracles based on hearsay

Now that I have made considerable progress, with my second promise fulfilled, and as it were have reached mid-sea point, I need still more strength, so that, helped by the breezes not of my brain but of the Holy Spirit, I may bring my boat to the shore of silence. In this section I am afraid I shall disappoint the expectation of any reader who thinks that I shall cite ancient documents as proof of the miracles I include. But although I fail him in this respect, I can command his belief by giving him a reliable guarantee of their truth. For I shall only include those miracles which have gained universal support from ancient times right down to today. They will be the miracles championed by the common assent of the people of Malmesbury, an assent handed down without a break to later generations. God has implanted them in the minds of men instead of on paper, so that the saint's miraculous deeds should not be forgotten and wasted. And deeds spoken of by the whole people through succeeding generations should not be regarded as of no importance. If anybody does think he has a right to be angry with me for writing of what I have heard but not seen, he should bring to trial those famous fathers and illustrious heroes who did the same thing, namely Luke in his Gospel and Gregory in his *Dialogues*[1] and make the same accusations against them. If a reader judges me rash, I ask him why I am not allowed to do in my small work what they did in their great ones. And it is not as though these miracles of ours lack visible proof, since we can see them engraved on the silver of that ancient casket, in the kind of workmanship known as 'anaglyptic'.[2] And so, relying on this indulgence, I shall begin my undertaking, however homespun the language may be. The love of the saint will weaken criticisms of my daring, so that a reader disappointed in my eloquence may still find pleasure in the subject matter.

Chapter 213 Aldhelm's virtues

After Aldhelm became a monk, this is how, according to my knowledge, he lived his life. His devotion to reading was so frequent and his devotion to prayer so intense, that, as he himself said in a letter, while reading he heard God speaking, and while praying he was speaking to God. He nourished his mind by voluntarily making do with little food. He never left the monastery unless he had to. He had not the smallest desire for money. If he was given any, he would immediately put it out to some useful work. Then again he got his rebellious body under control by immersing himself up to the shoulders in a spring which was near the monastery. Impervious to the winter's icy cold or the summer's mists arising from the marshes, he would pass the nights there uninterruptedly. Only when he had sung through and got to the end of the whole Psalter did he bring his labours

---

[1] The *Dialogues* consist largely of stories of miracles told by Gregory in response to the remark by his deacon Peter that few men in Italy have been famed for their miracles.
[2] In low relief, like the wallpaper of that name.

to an end. This spring, called after the name of the saint, is in a dell in the monastery grounds. Its waters bubble up gently. It is a delight to look upon and its water has a pleasant taste. In another part of the city is a spring called Daniel's Spring, as the Daniel who received the episcopal chasuble together with Aldhelm used to pass his nights keeping holy vigil there.[1]

After all this, I am almost reluctant to describe in my narrative Aldhelm's remarkable continence, if it had not been in actuality the opportunity for glorious victories. For whenever physical desire tugged at his sleeve, he would not only stop the lustful thought dead in its tracks, but even win a triumph uncommon elsewhere, since at those times Aldhelm did not shun the company of women, as do other monks who are afraid the opportunity will make them fall. Just the opposite. Sitting or reclining, he would keep the woman with him, until the lust of the flesh died down and he could go away with a calm and quiet mind. The devil realised that he was being mocked, when he saw the woman clinging to Aldhelm, and the man with his mind miles away, concentrating on singing the Psalter. He would bid good day to the woman, with his chastity intact and his purity unsullied. The inconvenience of the flesh died down, and the tempter was vexed that he was being made fun of. The truth of my claim that he cherished such a great love of chastity is supported by his outstanding work *On Chastity*,[2] in which he gives a clear picture of its honourable estate, praises its beauty and awards a crown to the one who perseveres with it. Also, it is not right to believe that a saint did not practise what he preached, or said one thing and lived out another. And so that no one shall have any difficulty with my claim or doubt its truth, let me tell you how Aldhelm warned a pupil of his against reading the erotic love songs of the poets, or spending his time in the company of courtesans, or letting the allurement of fine clothes weaken his mental vigour.

Chapter 214 Aldhelm's letter to Wihtfrith

To master Wihtfrith, you who are worthy of reverent love and delightful veneration, greetings of everlasting salvation from Aldhelm, humble servant and suppliant in Christ. News has been brought me by rumour-carrying reporters that your dear self, all on fire with a keenness for reading, has energetically decided to take a journey across the sea, with our Lord as helmsman. And so, when you reach your desired harbour in Ireland safe and sound,[3] I ask you to turn your back on the meretricious works of the philosophers and to pay especial attention to the sacred writings of the

---

[1] For Daniel see p. 105.
[2] See p. 233.
[3] The reader feels that Aldhelm is not in favour of Wihtfrith's journey to Ireland, and this feeling is corroborated by Aldhelm's asking another pupil why he has bothered to spend six years studying in Ireland, 'as if here in the fertile soil of Britain teachers who are citizens of Greece and Rome cannot be found ... namely Theodore ... mature in the arts of learning ... and Hadrian, equally endowed with pure urbanity' (Lapidge and Herren, *Aldhelm: The Prose Works*, p. 163, Letter V to Heahfrith).

prophets. For it seems to me madness to spurn the norms laid down in the New and Old Testaments from which there is no way out, and to make your way down the slippery byroads of the brambly countryside, following the difficult windings of the philosophers; or indeed to forgo the clear waters of crystal springs and to gulp down those marshy, salt, muddy waters, in which bands of the black army of toads are everywhere to be seen and chattering frogs crackle and croak. I ask you this question. How does it help you keep your oath to the orthodox faith to sweat and strain, reading and poring over the details of the incestuous rape of the defiled Proserpina,[1] which it is an abomination to speak of? Or by your reading to commend and show respect for Hermione, wanton daughter of Menelaus and Helen, who, so the trivial works of antiquity tell us, was long since betrothed to Orestes with a dowry properly given, but who changed her mind and married Neoptolemus? Or to write in the epic style of history about the priests of the raving Luperci,[2] behaving like the parasites who sacrifice to Priapus?[3] For these priests, when once the serpent on the top of the staff had been lifted on high and shown to the gaze of the Hebrew assembly, that is, when the Blessed Death of death had been fixed to the wood of the cross, were destroyed into nothingness right down to the ground.[4] Moreover, like a tumbler with arched knees and bent legs, I beg you by your discipleship, driven as I am by the filthy rumours about you, to keep right away from prostitutes or the tawdry amusements of brothels, in which lie hidden in alluring richness glossy courtesans, adorned with the red gold of an anklet and polished bracelets on their arms, just like curule magistrates[5] flashing their medals. No, you must rather keep away from lofty roofs of great houses which belong to nobles and governors and let your lucky gift for fellowship find enjoyment, contentment and happiness in the hospitality afforded by a humble hovel. Also, to deal with the icy blasts of winter, as they come from their original home in northern climes, as befits a follower of Christ, put aside your garments dyed purple, and wear a simple cloak and the rough covering of a sheepskin.

Chapter 215 Letter of Aldhelm to Geraint, king of Dumnonia, and his clergy

His holy way of life produced the fruit of miracles. And in order to try his hand at them, he first proceeded to convert and correct the Britons. Once upon a

[1] Daughter of the goddess Ceres, snatched down to Hades by Pluto, king of the underworld.
[2] A group of priests at Rome who assisted at the festival of the Lupercalia in honour of the god Pan.
[3] God of gardens and the sexual organs.
[4] Aldhelm refers to Numbers 21:6–9 where Moses cures the Israelites' snakebites by erecting a bronze serpent on top of a pole 'so that when a snake had bitten a man, he could look at the bronze serpent and recover'. This was taken as prophetic of Jesus (the Blessed Death of death) on the cross. The roundel on the centre of a walrus ivory cross, possibly made in Bury St Edmunds *c.*1150 and now in the Cloisters Museum, New York, depicts Moses and the bronze serpent.
[5] The highest magistrates in ancient Rome. Alternatively this phrase could mean 'just like curule chariots ornamented with metal bosses'.

time they had possessed the whole land now called England, but at that time they were the slaves of the Angles, this duty being the repayment given by the Angles to the people who had invited them over. Indeed the Angles had kept an eye open for opportunities and had then driven from their ancient homes those they had come to protect and herded them into rough, forested districts, where they lived a miserable, half-wild life. Those who were called the North Walians, that is North Britons, had fallen to the lot of the West Saxon kings. They had long since grown accustomed to the proper performance of their tasks as slaves, and it was many years since they had retaliated in any way. But when they did plot rebellion, king Centwine then crushed them with a slaughter so horrific that their hopes were ended.[1] Indeed the ultimate evil of being compelled to pay tribute was added to their woes as a result, so that people who before could feel at least just the shadow of freedom now groaned openly under the yoke of subjection. These unhappy people were also wrong in a matter of religious belief: living, as it were, outside the orbit of civilisation, they observed their own traditions rather than those of Rome. Their many refusals to follow catholic practices strikingly included the failure to celebrate the festival of Easter on the proper day. The complete agreement of the whole church on this had had no effect on them, nor had they thought there was any need to change when admonished to do so by the blessed Augustine, archbishop of Canterbury, but had stubbornly kept the controversy alive.

As a result the West Saxons were brought together in frequent, repeated gatherings and assemblies to decide how the Britons might be turned again to walk in the right path of church practices. The matter was discussed at great length over many days and the conclusion was this: the heretics should not be driven by force, but led by reason. A letter should be written containing all the points that could scatter error and deal with stubbornness, so that the Britons would correct their opinions through accepting its arguments. There was nothing to stop this happening, if abbot Aldhelm would regard the heretics as worth his own words of admonishment: his way of life meant he should be willing, while his learning gave him the ability to dispel the disease of disbelief, however long-seated. The saint was persuaded by these universal prayers to shoulder this burden for the conversion of the heretics, for the praise of his fatherland and for the common safety of all. He took up the task which the loving hearts of his brothers had suggested, and his efficiency in carrying it through was no less than his obedience in taking it up.[2] This was his method for refuting their wrong views about Easter and teaching them the truth. He seasoned his own words with quotations from the Gospels, and followed his thunderbolt of cast-iron argument with a shower of statements from the fathers. The work was finished to great praise and sent to the Britons. Aldhelm

---

[1] The Anglo-Saxon Chronicle for 682 records of Centwine that 'he drove the Britons as far as the sea.' See Stenton, *Anglo-Saxon England*, p. 68.

[2] For the full text of this letter which Aldhelm wrote to Geraint, king of Devon and Cornwall, see Lapidge and Herren, *Aldhelm: The Prose Works*, pp. 155–60. Its destination hardly fits with William's description of the recipients as 'North Britons'.

added to the end of it prayers to God that he would bountifully fulfil his requests for the people for whom he had poured out these words. For herein is the twofold task of the official of the church, that words of reproof for the correction of schismatics should not be found wanting on his lips, and that his prayers for them should not slumber in his heart. The saint's efforts could not be deprived of success. They achieved their laudable aim and converted those who had erred to a true belief. Right down to this day the Britons owe their correction to Aldhelm, although, with their ingrained wickedness, they do not recognise the man and they have destroyed his letter.

Chapter 216 Aldhelm's new churches at Malmesbury

As I have said,[1] the headquarters of the monastery was in the church of St Peter. But the noble mind does not know how to take a holiday from busy labour, and Aldhelm planned to build another church in honour of Mary, mother of God, in the grounds of the same monastery. So he built the church, and next to it another in honour of St Michael. Of the latter only traces are visible, though the whole fabric of the larger church has remained famous and untouched right down to our own day,[2] surpassing in size and beauty any of the churches built of old that could be seen anywhere in England. Once the stone floor was laid, no expense was spared in collecting a supply of timber for the church to be built more splendidly. The saint's efforts to please God by this willing act of service were increasing the cost. And now the time had come to join together these expensive timbers, whose price had been increased by the length of the journey and the difficulties of transport. All of them had been cut to the same length apart from one which by its shortness had played games with the skill of the craftsmen. Or perhaps they had been careless, or, as I would more readily believe, God willed it to happen, so that the holiness of the illustrious Aldhelm might shine out brightly. When the builders noticed late in the day the defective timber which had been cut off short, they at first muttered among themselves, and then brought the matter to Aldhelm's notice. He put up with their criticism calmly, though he was somewhat disturbed by the difficulty of getting a new piece. For he had provided no contingency fund, and it seemed an immense job to take the timbers down again. But when human help had been despaired of, he put his hopes in God and began thinking of short cuts to remedy the situation. He was inspired to perform a miracle. He had previously often experimented to see what his virtues could achieve, though always in secret lest the breeze of public acclaim might destroy the flowers of the purity of his conscience. And so, praying with only a movement of his lips and striving with a slight effort of his arms, he made the shortened timber equal in length to the others. He immediately concealed the miracle by gently chiding the workmen for joking with him about the defective timber,

---

[1] In ch. 197.
[2] This larger church of St Mary does not survive. The present abbey at Malmesbury is all that remains of a church which was built just after William's lifetime.

which in fact was just as long as the others. The workmen measured it by putting a plumb line against it, and when they saw the alteration, they blushed happily, for they felt no annoyance at Aldhelm's words of annoyance, but were glad that they had been outwitted by the virtue of the dissimulating saint. The beam was lifted by the windlass up on to the roof with the others and completed the timbering. The story which our ancestors told about this beam is true, for in the two fires which destroyed the whole monastery in the reigns of kings Alfred and Edward it never suffered any damage, until it rotted away, overcome by age and decay.

Chapter 217 Aldhelm prepares to go to Rome

So by now the monastery had arisen, and the adjoining church of the blessed Mary gleamed still more brightly. Aldhelm could be thought and said to be happy, father of so many monks and lord of so many possessions. But with his far-seeing prudent eye, he decided to go to meet the misfortunes which would one day come and made up his mind to journey to Rome. His intention was to obtain apostolic privileges for his monasteries, especially Malmesbury.[1] It had been advanced by the generosity of bishop Leutherius,[2] but it was possible it would meet with malicious treatment from his successors. Aldhelm, as I have said, foresaw this with his prophetic eye and thought how he might remove or weaken such threats. So he communicated his intention to Ine, king of the West Saxons, and Æthelred, king of the Mercians, whose friendship he enjoyed and through whose munificence he had risen high, and when they raised no objection he set out on the path to Rome.

But in order to put together the things necessary for the journey more freely, he went to the estates under his control in the county of Dorset. And while he was waiting for a favourable wind, he built a church there, in which he himself might commend his journey and return to God, while his companions were busy with the necessary preparations for the voyage. The still-surviving walls of this building lack a roof and are open to the sky, except that something roofs the altar and protects the holy stone from defecating birds. And, no matter how great the force of a storm which may be raging all around outside, not so much as a drop falls inside the walls of the church. The shepherds tending their flocks in the fields near by are now so accustomed to using it that they do not think it miraculous. When the fleecy clouds thicken and the storm threatens a downpour, the whole crowd of shepherds congregate there in hasty flight, and as soon as they are standing inside the walls of this roofless church they feel not a drop of rain. It takes a very shameless man not to believe this, seeing that so many eyewitnesses beat their fists against the sceptic's brow. The nobles of the province were several times induced by this miracle to try to roof the building, in their wish to show their support of the saint and do him some

[1] For such apostolic privileges, the most important of which was freedom from episcopal jurisdiction as is shown by ch. 221, see Southern, *Western Society and the Church*, pp. 113–14.
[2] See ch. 199.

service, but they found that their efforts came to naught and they gave up: they realised that the by-play, by which the miracle could be repeatedly shown, was pleasing to the saint. The quantity of the miracles brought the people each year to his feast day there, and the gifts that were offered and the miracles that were displayed were more numerous than those in the place where his most sacred bones are kept in reverence. I suppose that God is indicating by this that the glory of having his body ought to be more than enough for the people of Malmesbury, provided that they are not jealous of other people having his presence. The place is two miles from the sea in the county of Dorset, near to Wareham.[1] The castle of Corfe also overlooks the sea at that point.

Chapter 218 The miracle of the chasuble

But, as I had begun to say, Aldhelm survived the dangers of the sea, overcame the difficulties of the long journey and arrived at Rome. Sergius was supreme pontiff at that time.[2] He welcomed our hero on his arrival with appropriate kindness and made his stay comfortable in true bishop's style. His respect for the abbot was awoken when he saw that his knowledge was all of a piece with the holiness of his life, and that there was no discrepancy between his behaviour and his scholarship. A kindly divinity increased the fame of his good reputation and in this vast city raised its favourite to prominence by the praises bestowed on his miraculous acts. There is at Rome an assembly building called the Lateran. The emperor Constantine had made a palace for the papal pontiffs there out of his own palace. Aldhelm stayed there with the pope, and had many friendly talks with him. No day passed without Aldhelm chanting mass. By its rites he whiled away the tedium of his stay and commended himself and his people to God. He had done this as usual one day, and mass being now over, he threw his vestment, which they call a chasuble, over his shoulder. He wrongly supposed that someone was standing there to catch it, his thoughts no doubt being directed elsewhere and his mind still full of the divine ecstasy. The attendant had quite failed to foresee this and was examining something or other at another part of the altar. But, no matter, for 'he who guardeth Israel neither slumbers nor sleeps',[3] and he showed his greatness when human activity failed. For at once a sunbeam gleamed brightly through the clear glass of the window, inserted itself under the chasuble and carried it, held somewhat above the ground, across the empty space.

I can hardly describe the excited buzz of chatter there among the people when they saw nature serving the servant of Christ contrary to nature. It deservedly held up the vestment in the air for a man who was always lifting up

---

[1] The Britons built a church at Wareham about the same time as Aldhelm's new church, thus showing that they could coexist with the West Saxons. Geraint's grant to the West Saxon monastery at Sherborne is also evidence of friendship. See Mayr-Harting, *The Coming of Christianity*, p. 120.
[2] Sergius was pope from 687 to 701.
[3] Psalm 120:4.

his thoughts to the skies, and made emptiness solid as an act of reverence for a man who despised all earthly things as changing and transient and thirsted only for the heavenly. We are not sure whether he had taken this vestment with him from England, or whether he had borrowed it there for the occasion. Anyway, it is preserved at Malmesbury to this day, and very great care is taken of a garment which knew such goodness.[1] The sacristans do all in their power to enable future generations to enjoy the sight of it unblemished. It is made of a very fine thread, dyed a full, deep scarlet colour from the juices of shellfish. It has black roundels with pictures of peacocks worked inside. Besides being beautiful, its length is also enormous, thus showing that the saint was a man of tall stature. The bones of his arms and various other things, which we have been entitled to see, bear witness to the fact that Aldhelm in his day had grown to that size which we can describe not as bulk but as a proper bodily height.

Chapter 219 Aldhelm defends pope Sergius

Aldhelm was still in Rome, and God continued to bestow the grace of miracles upon him by repeatedly fashioning occasions by which he might display his love for his servant. The days passed and an event took place which provided the opportunity for his second miracle. A boy had recently been born in the house of one of the pope's chamberlains. The rumour had gone out among the people and was being noisily repeated that the mother was a woman who had taken the profession of a nun, put on the habit and veiled her head, and there was no sign of a father. Soon, not just in unsure suspicion but amid a public outcry the pope was being pointed at as the guilty person. The woman, it was said, had been accustomed to visit him for rather private conversations. Then came the usual human unhappiness that anyone who suffers the blow of some misfortune is immediately the target of hatred from all sides. Next he was said to be guilty of all crimes, then that he merited a crucifixion as bad as could be imagined. So the people in their madness were assailing with their suspicion a pope who deserved praise, and disgracing with their outcry a man who had never had an equal for the sharpness and facility of his learning, or for the observable orthodoxy of his faith, or for the sanctity and perfection of his life. All his actions were holy, his words catholic, and he had never cowered in fear before any earthly power. He had even openly delivered his opinion, and condemned the mutterings against the catholic faith made by the emperor at Constantinople,[2] and had involved in the same charge any nobles of the same mind who did not return to their senses.

Other documents can be consulted by anyone wishing to know the lengthy letters he wrote on this subject or the labours he endured, but I shall return to Aldhelm. In his heart he felt compassion for the wronged pontiff, and before the people he pleaded his wavering cause with all the eloquence at his

[1] The miracle may be legend, but the chasuble was real.
[2] Justinian II, emperor of Constantinople 685–711.

command. It was wretched and shameful, he said, that Romans should suspect and attack with such charges their own pope. What influence would a Roman pope, who was attacked by his own citizens, have in Britain or any other far-flung country? It beggared belief that a man who was aware of being pontiff for the whole world should get bogged down in the mire of such a sin. These words were wasted upon the wind, for the frenzy of the people, once aroused, cannot be easily damped down, so Aldhelm, getting a little more angry through his knowledge of the pope's purity, said 'Bring the child here, so that he may disprove with his own lips the charge against the pope. And then you must cease from your silly suspicions and return into favour with the pope. I myself shall not fail to do my duty in a matter which so concerns my peace.' Some greeted his words with jeers, for a foreigner seemed to be promising to do unheard of things and interfering in matters which were not his concern. But the infant, barely nine days old, was brought before him. Aldhelm first gave the baby new birth in the waters of baptism and then asked him publicly whether the people's opinion about his father was true. At that moment you would have seen the grace of God in action, for the little lad, making an effort, undid the knot of doubt and in the clearest voice declared that Sergius was pure and innocent and had never had any dealings with the woman. The crowd cheered the miracle. The innocent pope rejoiced in his triumph. Rome rang with the praise of Aldhelm's worth, and the shouts of exultation struck the stars themselves and echoed back redoubled. But when Aldhelm was asked to hand over the real father to the cognisance of the people, now that he had freed the false father from infamy, he refused to do so. He said that it was his job to save the innocent from ruin if possible, but not to punish the guilty with death.

Chapter 220 Pope Sergius issues a bull

The pope was so extraordinarily pleased with this display of Aldhelm's miraculous powers that he made no difficulties about Aldhelm's request but freely gave from his mighty power the privilege to the monasteries for which it was being asked.[1] I shall give the bull in its entirety at this point so that it may be made clear without a shadow of doubt that those who in our own day think they can trample on it and transgress it with impunity will become the victims of weighty curses and the slaves of the severest punishments.

Chapter 221 The bull of pope Sergius (*c.*701)

Sergius, servant of the servants of God, greetings to abbot Aldhelm and his successors and through you to your respected monastery. Those gifts which are given by the bishops and priests of the God-founded Christian religion, with their insight into the religious life, to those servants of God, the monks, so that they may have the opportunity of living freely, are bestowed upon

---

[1] See chs. 34 and 35 for other possible bulls of Sergius. Modern scholars suspect all three of being forgeries.

them, not in order that they should have freedom for vices, but so that they might concentrate on living well and, of course, on devoting themselves to the divine service. The gifts are: that they should be freed from the ties of human life, made immune from all performance of secular duties, and, as the rule of their profession declares, be completely free for God; and that they should concentrate on the service of him alone, for the worship of whose majesty they are not only set free from the burdens imposed by temporal powers but also regarded as worthy of the highest honour for their love of religion. And so, your order asks us, as deputy for our founder, the blessed Peter, first of the apostles, on whom our creator and redeemer, Lord Jesus Christ, thought it worthy to bestow the keys of binding and loosing in heaven and on earth (whose function we, though unequal to it, also perform and whose church we govern because of God's regard for us), to strengthen with apostolic privileges the monastery of the blessed apostles Peter and Paul, which, situated in the district of the Saxons, was founded by Meldum of holy memory and is even now known as Meldumsbury, and also another monastery, built in the same province near the river called the Frome in honour of John the Baptist, both of which we discover from reliable reports are being thoughtfully managed by your order with the help of God.

We approve of your holy devotion, and we urge you to be zealous and vigilant in praise and prayer to God, holding fast to abstinence, chastity and the purification of the body, given to works of hospitality and mercy, dedicated to following the obedience and humility of Christ, and living lives in which, as his lovers, you aim at the mutual harmony which comes from holy charity. We urge you also to preserve unimpaired the orthodoxy of the apostolic faith by your obedience to spiritual commands and the rules of the holy fathers, giving time to improving study, showing kindness to strangers and those in need, displaying a proper veneration for the prelates and priests of the churches of God, having space and time for God, shunning the concerns and money-making of the world, loving self-control and poverty, keeping up a conversation with God in psalms, spiritual hymns and constant prayers, in all the pursuits of life maintaining the abstinence which purifies the body, encouraging one another in all the commands of God, making progress by copying those who are concerned for their salvation, trusting in the help of God, and keeping yourselves unspotted not only by the contagion of the flesh but also by harmful words and thoughts so that the chastity and sobriety of your body and soul together may shine before the eyes of God, your inner man being lit up by the grace of goodness and your outer man winning praise for good behaviour and reputation.

So, seeing that it is to such people that the benefit of our pontifical mercy is due, our decision is to protect the aforesaid revered monasteries here and now with our apostolic privileges, so that they may be now and remain for ever as your order requests, under the jurisdiction and protection of the same saint whose servants we also are, the blessed apostle Peter our founder, and of the church of Him which is in our care. They are to be subject to the control of no other jurisdiction. No bishop or priest, no cleric of any ecclesiastical order is to presume at any time to claim for himself any rights of jurisdiction whatsoever over them, or to extort or demand maintenance or any dues from the congregation of your order. Neither is he to set up an episcopal chair in their sanctuaries or to celebrate the rites of the mass there, unless he goes at the summons of the abbot and congregation of the order. If they find it necessary for a priest to be ordained for them for the rites of the mass, or a deacon, they are to ask the most reverent bishop who is close at hand to perform the ordination, providing that under the divine judgement he searches out those things which belong to the sacred rule and performs the ordination as a gift which is given him. And if it happens that the abbot of the order dies, and the monks have proceeded to the election of his successor, the man chosen by the general agreement of the order's congregation of the servants of God is to be promoted forthwith, so that no damage may be done to the discipline of monastic life or the affairs of the monastery go to ruin through lack of an abbot. Also a prelate, who in the same way is in the neighbourhood, is to offer prayers for that abbey according to the authority of the apostolic pontiff. Since these things are so, if any bishop, priest or cleric of any ecclesiastical order or any layman, whatever his position, attempts to transgress or defile our decrees made under the divine judgement, he must know that he is guilty in the sight of God and barred from sharing in the saving body and blood of our Lord. His lot will be the condemnation which was the lot of Judas Iscariot, and, like Ananias and Sapphira, he will be struck down by the first of his apostles, unless he repents of his attempted act of rash presumption.[1] But life, salvation and perpetual blessedness be to those who preserve our decrees and give orders for their preservation. Fare well, most beloved brothers.

Chapter 222 Aldhelm returns to England

Aldhelm set out energetically on his journey home. He felt triumphant about the privilege awarded by this document, and at the same time the blessing of the pope and the support of some sacred relics gave him confidence. He was also carrying with him many different pieces of valuable foreign merchandise, intending to bring to England a quantity of splendid novelties. Among these was an altar of gleaming marble, white in colour, six feet thick, four feet long and three hands wide, with a lip jutting out from the stone and beautifully decorated all around. A camel, so it is said (for what animal of our country could shoulder such a burden?) carried it safely all the way to the Alps. But there the camel (or whatever animal it was, for it does not matter which particular beast carried it) collapsed, injured by the excessive weight or undone by the steep slopes of the track. The fall crushed the animal and broke the

[1] In Acts 5:1–12 Ananias and Sapphira drop dead when Peter exposes their lies.

marble into two parts. His friends lamented the damage done to both, but the saint, with a secret inward mutter, stretched out his right hand in benediction and mended them. Vigorous health flowed back into the animal, which, immediately shaking itself with a rapid motion, stood on its feet. The broken stone, which had not cracked in a straight line but had split jaggedly, immediately became a solid whole again. But so that the memory of this remarkable miracle should not fade, the mark of the split can still be seen, visible if you look closely, however miraculous the mending. Their gloom evaporated and they resumed their journey. And so with his whole train intact Aldhelm arrived at the sea which separates France and England.

There he was welcomed by a calm sea for his ship and after a safe journey across the channel was restored by a smiling fortune to his countrymen who were longing for his return. As he landed he was met on all sides and greeted by long lines of people in splendid procession. Some of the monks charmed the air with their melodious chants, others carried the tree of our Lord, others filled the roads with sweet-smelling incense. Some of the lay people beat the ground with their feet in the dance, others showed their inner happiness by different bodily gestures. All together praised God for bringing back the light of Britain, which for a long time now had been spreading its rays over other lands abroad. Nor did kingly pride stop Ine and Æthelred, rulers of the West Saxons and the Mercians, from sharing in this rejoicing, especially when to their former love for Aldhelm had been recently added a respect for his audiences with the pope. So they received Aldhelm with great joy and a ready approbation and respect, and he showed to both kings the privileges for his monasteries. For the matter demanded that both should give their support and agreement to those things which lay within the gift of them both. Without delay the decrees of the pope received the sanction of the kings, and no stumbling block prevented them from following out his commands with a similar foot of obedience. They both decreed that the monasteries concerned should stay at peace in the service of God, whether the West Saxons and the Mercians happened to be at peace or at war with each other.[1] These two famous kings would not have made a fuss about the matter out of their innate, gracious kindness, but in addition to this Aldhelm won their willing consent by giving them handsome presents. Various presents were made to Æthelred, but Ine got the altar. He placed it in a town then belonging to the king called Bruton,[2] as a mark of his reverence for the most holy mother of God. It remains placed there to this day, providing a living witness, so to speak, of the holiness of Aldhelm.[3] There is another larger church in the same town dedicated to St Peter. There is good reason for the view that this church was built and consecrated by our saint. Recent ambitious building plans have enlarged its east front.

---

[1] See p. 238 n. 2.
[2] In east Somerset.
[3] Like the chasuble of ch. 218 and the bible of ch. 224, the visible altar is a peg on which to hang a story.

Chapter 223 Aldhelm chosen as bishop of Sherborne (705)

So in this way, as I have described, his praiseworthy labours went forward, which he had undertaken for the honour of holy church. But by now he had reached the days which lie on the border of old age. Some years had gone by and passed. Hæddi, bishop of all the West Saxons who had his see at Winchester, departed this world.[1] His death was welcome to those in heaven, as the sanctity of his past life meant an increase in their number, but to men it was a cause of sorrow: they would hardly be able to find another such, who would be willing to govern such a far-flung diocese. For what is now looked after by four bishops[2] was in those days controlled by that one man, crushing rebels with his authority, and comforting suppliants with his simple openness. So by a decision of the synod, this diocese, which had become over-large, was divided into two sees, one at Sherborne and the other at Winchester. It was an unfair and unequal division that one see should control only two counties[3] while the other controlled all the huge extent of lands contained within the country of the West Saxons. In appointing bishops for the two sees, the synod members considered the worth of the learning of a candidate and the nearness of his birthplace to the see. Daniel was elected to Winchester. He had been born in those parts and was not without scholarship.[4]

The choice for Sherborne fell upon Aldhelm. The special claim of his wisdom and his advanced years made him an aspirant for greater honours. Also his love for his birthplace was a recommendation, as he was a native of that province. And so, under the leadership of God, as was the belief, they unanimously chose Aldhelm and made approaches to him in his blessed old age to see if he thought himself worthy of the bishopric. All ages and classes concurred in thinking him right for the position because of the gravity of his weathered age, his abundant learning and his unequalled holiness. And if anyone thinks birth and rank should have been taken into account (the blessed apostle did not ignore them in these matters), there was no one of more noble birth than Aldhelm, who was closely related to the family of the king.[5] His life and reputation had always been such that that there had never been the slightest scandal spread about him. But the man himself resisted as best he could and put forward forceful arguments to assist his rejection and weaken the unanimity of the synod. But his efforts were of no avail, since the very point which he had thought up for his protection was refuted. This was the weight of his years. As the years of his life were now looking at old age from just across the boundary, Aldhelm argued that they were warning him to rest peacefully and quietly, and not to plunge into dangerous action. But as soon as they heard this argument, the members of the synod countered it by the opposite view that

[1] For Hæddi see pp. 104–5. He died in 705.
[2] Those of Winchester, Salisbury, Wells and Exeter.
[3] Winchester was left with just the counties of Hampshire and Surrey. See ch. 79.
[4] For Daniel see p. 105.
[5] See ch. 188

a person of his mature years was thereby all the more drained of his impurities and more available for giving advice. So Aldhelm avoided extremes. He resisted as long as seemed consistent with reason.[1] But when he saw that their opinion continued to be unanimous, in obedience to his brothers he released the reins holding back his life, for he was afraid to oppose the divine oracle which had made all their hearts one and filled their lips with the same view. So the bishops welcomed him as their colleague, the priests as their father and the lay people as their protector. Amid the shouts of approval of all and with no dissentient cries, he was taken before Berhtwald, archbishop of the primal see, to be consecrated according to custom.[2] The two of them had in fact been fellow students and fellow travellers down the road of the religious life, and Berhtwald's pleasure in accepting Aldhelm's election increased the popular support for his old friend and companion. Berhtwald not only willingly performed his consecration but even kept him at his house for many days afterwards, lightening the load of his own archbishopric by taking Aldhelm's advice and examining with him the reasons and causes for the load.

Chapter 224 Aldhelm acquires a bible at Dover

And it so happened that during this period Aldhelm visited Dover, which is on the coast about twelve miles from Canterbury, since he had heard that some ships had put in there. The harbour there, being narrow, is always busy, as in most coastal towns. The Morini are only a few miles away across the water, and from them the crossing to Dover is the quickest one. The waves, which pour racing and crashing into that narrow area, make the sea rough at the slightest opportunity and sailors run into the greatest danger just where they were hoping for an escape from it. But when the ships have come to anchorage, it is a most secure haven in any storm. I have written this much for a preface, as it is relevant to my story. The saint was strolling along the harbour front, and gazing keenly at the merchandise to see if the sailors had happened to bring anything suitable for church use. In fact, on their voyage to England from the French coast, they had even brought a store of books with them. Aldhelm spotted a complete Old and New Testament bound together in one volume. He forgot about the rest and concentrated on buying this volume, but while he was turning the pages with an expert's eye and trying to lower the price, the foreign crew jeered at him, making merry as sailors will. Why was he thus devaluing the goods of others and lowering the price of articles which were not his own? He could depreciate his own wares if he liked, but he should leave goods which did not belong to him at their own price. In reply to their taunting words Aldhelm only smiled. Finally, as he kept questioning the price of the

[1] Aldhelm's reluctance mirrors that of Anselm in ch. 48. One strand in this may have been the fear that they would lose their humility amid the splendours of the office being offered. See Mayr-Harting, *The Coming of Christianity*, p. 87.
[2] Berhtwald succeeded Theodore as archbishop of Canterbury in 691 and held the see until 731.

book, they rudely pushed him off and with tightened ropes sailed a distance away from the shore.

But it was not long before the vengeance of the Lord sharply punished the insult done to the saint. A storm arose, a hurricane raged. The clouds thickened, the daylight was withdrawn, darkness over the sea and wildness in the sky brought in the night. The fury of the winds and the whistling in the rigging redoubled their terror. The sail-yards could not take the savagery of the storm and the ship's side was knocked this way and that as the waves crashed into her. The skill of the rowers was useless, the sailors' experience of no avail. They were heading for destruction. All the elements seemed to be conspiring to bring death to these unhappy souls. But then, rough though these fellows were, the idea dawned on them that they were paying the penalty for the wrong they had done to the saint with their insults. They shouted and wailed and they stretched out suppliant hands towards the shore. They begged for help and promised amendment. As the blessed bishop had not been upset by their insults, it was easy for him to forgive their fault. To begin with, he stretched out his hand in the sign of the cross over the tempestuous blasts and lessened and stilled the storm somewhat. Then soon he got into a boat himself and when, through the skill of the oarsmen, he reached those in peril, everything changed for the good. The storm died away completely, the hurricane was at an end. A changing wind brought the ship to shore. The waves, which a moment ago had been threatening destruction, were now gently gliding along and promising assistance. The sailors gained their longed-for anchorage on the beach,[1] and of their own accord offered the book to Aldhelm, asking him to consider accepting it as a free gift from his servants, whom he had brought back to dry land out of the very jaws of death. He weighed up the problem. His even scales suggested the midway course of neither cheating poor men so that they made a great loss nor rejecting the prayers of suppliants. The book can still be seen at Malmesbury today, providing a venerable specimen of antiquity.

Chapter 225 Aldhelm provides for his monasteries after his death

Aldhelm returned to his province as holder of his new position. In all matters his performance matched his reputation, but he showed especial concern for the freedom of his monasteries. His see was at Sherborne, where he also built a magnificent church, which I have seen with my own eyes.[2] In his fear of the uncertainties of human life, his first wish was to appoint abbots in charge of his monasteries, but his monks used the gentleness of their accustomed father as an argument against this scheme. He outlined his plan in writing, threatening

---

[1] The description of the storm-struck sailors has reminiscences of Virgil rather than direct quotations. See *Aeneid* 1:102–5 and 172, 3:192–7 and 592.

[2] Aldhelm's church was rebuilt and extended by bishop Ælfwald (1045–58), a fact not mentioned by William in his account of Ælfwald in ch. 82. A large part of Ælfwald's church is still to be seen at Sherborne.

with perdition those who were under a divine obligation but did not obey it. This was to stop his plan from falling into disuse or his successors perverting necessity into tyranny.[1] This is the text of the document.

There is nothing in this world which enjoys lasting happiness, nothing which wins lasting domination, nothing which does not in the course of time move towards death, the terminus of life. For that reason, we must so enjoy what we have inherited in the world that we are never robbed of the rewards of our everlasting homeland. This is why I, Aldhelm, after my enthronement by the divine grace into the seat of my episcopal office, unworthy though I was and vouched for by almost no suitable virtues, proposed in the secret motions of my mind to appoint according to canon law and the sanctions of the rule an abbot from the order, chosen unanimously by the free choice of my brotherhoods, over my monasteries, the ones which I myself as their instituted abbot had ruled and controlled with the help of God. But these plans and wishes of mine were opposed by the stubborn piety of my monks. On several occasions I carefully gave confidential details of the scheme to my assembled brothers, but no one gave an unconcerned agreement to these prayers of mine. They said, 'As long as you are quickened by the breath of life, and are allotted to the course of this present life here with us, we shall never refuse to bow our humble necks beneath the yoke of your rule. But as suppliants we all ask and pray that you confirm under the attestation of holy Scripture and with the clear consent of the men of authority that after your death no man, unless willingly chosen by us, may lay any claim to rule over us, neither bold king nor powerful pontiff nor the holder of any ecclesiastical or secular office.'

To this petition, duly presented by monks who are both mine and outstanding servants of God, I gave my most willing agreement. In the nunnery situated by the river Wimborne, and governed by Cuthburg, sister of our revered king, I accepted the devotion of my monks, shown most handsomely in this petition which they presented, and confirmed with the sign of the cross the request made by them as servants of God, together with the desired consent of the most famous king Ine and the agreement of Daniel, my most revered brother and fellow bishop. And the venerable king and aforementioned bishop repeatedly signed these documents with the same hand of devotion. Soon afterwards in the council of the church, which is known to have met by the river Nadder,[2] this same agreement was given by all the appointed bishops of the Saxon people, together with the assent of the royal power and the consent of episcopal precedence. But if anyone plots and schemes against the decrees of these famous people and takes upon himself to transgress the sacred regulations contained in this document, he must know that he will be struck down by the mournful verdict of

---

[1] Perhaps the second half of this sentence means that Aldhelm aimed to stop his successors as bishop of Sherborne arguing that it was necessary for themselves to be in charge of the monasteries.
[2] In Wiltshire.

condemnation before the terrible throne of the divine majesty, together with other transgressors of the decrees of the Lord. Malmesbury, Frome and Bradford are the names of these monasteries. The charter of this confirmation was written 705, indiction 3.

The document was also signed by king Ine, bishop Daniel and the noble Æthelfrith.

Chapter 226 Aldhelm provides for the churches of his diocese

Although it seemed that Aldhelm had provided for his monasteries by this charter and averted the threat of tyrannical behaviour from his successors, his great mind was not satisfied until he had also obtained a decree for all the churches of the West Saxons. Putting pressure on the trusting mind of the king by gentle admonitions, he secured the following edict.

> In the name of the Lord God, our Saviour! In the rule of the Lord, I, Ine the king, with the advice and decree of our bishop Aldhelm, and also at the suggestion of all the priests of God and in reply to the petition of the monks who live in the diocese of the Saxons, bestow upon the churches the following freedom, and to the monasteries I give the following valuable privilege, that, without hindrance from worldly matters and with minds set free from financial considerations of tribute, they may serve God alone, and that with the gift of Christ's support they may in their monastery live the disciplined life of monks according to the rule, and that they may think it right to pour out prayers before the face of the divine majesty for the state and prosperity of our realm and for pardon for sins committed, and that they may strive to intercede for our weakness by frequent hours of prayer in their churches. If anyone tries to contravene the agreement contained in this decree, let him know that he will give an account at the awesome judgement in the presence of Christ and the nine orders of angels. This charter, willingly given by us, we decree must be so kept and acknowledged that the firm strength of its unassailable legality is felt both by us, as long as life lasts and we hold the reins of government with the help of God, and by our successors in the future who hold the monarchy by the right to rule of heredity. For further proof of the power of this charter we have had it signed by princes and statesmen, judges and noblemen. Given in public and signed in the place called Everleigh, the second indiction, 26 May 704. Good luck to it. Signed by king Ine. I, Aldhelm, servant of the servants of God, have confirmed this decree by my own signature.

Also signed by ten abbots and nine noblemen.

Chapter 227 His last years

The holy bishop carried through these matters without tiring, although he was quite well aware that his end was near. For by now earthly things seemed trivial to him, and he thirsted for heaven. So he thought it best to complete the course of his life by doing what would win praise and remembrance for himself and please and benefit his people. And although his body was worn out with age and refused to perform its duties, his mind was unimpaired. It was already outside the door of the body and close to the very gates of heaven and so overcame the decay of his years, supporting with its spiritual exercises the weak performance of the body which was soon to desert it. Day and night alike were one unbroken round of busy travelling around his dioceses and preaching, with Aldhelm himself managing as completely as in his green springtime the repeated fasts and other good things of that kind. And so after four years of his episcopate, during which he lived a life which brought peace to men and pleasure to God,

> Heaven's friend and priest withdrew to heaven's realms,
> Exchanging earth for stars and fields for skies.
> His spirit safe above, his limbs were wrapped
> In friendly earth, and earth and heaven alike
> Claimed Aldhelm as belonging to itself.
> Ten times had Phoebus put the twins to flight,[1]
> When Aldhelm left, from ties of earth set free.

Chapter 228 Aldhelm's death at Doulting (31 May 709)

There is a village in the county of Somerset called Doulting,[2] and it was here that Aldhelm ended his life. He had long ago given the village to the monks of Glastonbury, though arranging to have the usufruct of it himself. The building which witnessed his end was a wooden church. As he was drawing his last breaths he gave orders for his body to be carried into it, so that he might die in that particular spot, as succeeding generations, down to the villagers of today, have asserted he did. Later on the church was rebuilt of stone. A monk from Glastonbury was attending to its consecration in the name of God, when a woman, who had been blind in both eyes for a long time, came up to the packed crowd and with remarkable faith pushed her way through the mass, shouting for someone to lead her to the altar, as she had a total belief that the saint, whose church was being consecrated, would cure a widow's blindness, seeing that throughout his life he had always given the customary alms to widows. Her bold belief brought down help from the sky and a clear light filled her widowed eyes. A miracle performed before so many people could not be hidden, especially as the woman and her blindness were very well known in the area. It is also said that the saint as he was dying rested on a stone in this church, which is known to have cured many sick people with the water in which it had been washed.

---

[1] The Latin word translated 'twins' literally means 'Spartans', and refers to the zodiacal sign of Gemini who are the Spartan twins, Castor and Pollux.

[2] Doulting is on the A361, halfway between Glastonbury and Frome.

Chapter 229 Ecgwine's vision

Next the blessed Ecgwine, bishop of Worcester, was told of the death of his friend by a vision, shining in the heavens, which commanded him to go to Doulting.[1] He journeyed in haste, spurred on by grief and love, and quickly arrived at the village. He put up a prayer for the repose of Aldhelm's soul, and gave orders for the body to be taken on to Malmesbury, just as the saint had desired and commanded. With the assurance of faith he checked the tears of the mourners and quickly accomplished his mission, assisting in person to speed up the work. The happy remains were carried forth, accompanied by a great company of people before and behind, each man thinking himself more blessed, the nearer he got to the body. It was a great consolation to the crowds that they could at least see the bier, even if they could not touch it. For the beauty of the appearance of the dead body removed much of their grief, and the grace which remained and its enduring shape dried their eyes.

Chapter 230 The funeral procession from Doulting to Malmesbury

That funeral procession became famous. All along it stone crosses were erected at seven-mile intervals, which led to a batch of miracles. For many incurable invalids, when they went up to the crosses in faith and prayed with all their might, found a speedy cure. The crosses which brought about the cures can be seen to this day. My story should not be too much for my readers to accept, seeing that there were almost as many witnesses to miracles as there were people in the area. I cite the blessed Ecgwine as the most reliable of these witnesses. In one of his writings, after various other matters, he says this, 'After two years the holy bishop Aldhelm migrated[2] to the Lord. When I was told of this in a vision, I called together my brothers and servants and told them of the death of our dear father. I quickly went to the place where his sacred body lay, about fifty miles further on than Malmesbury abbey. I brought his body back there for burial and buried it with all honours, giving orders that holy crosses should be erected to mark the places on the journey where his sacred body had rested.' All the crosses are still there, none of them having suffered any damage over the years. They are called 'biscepstane', that is bishop's stones. One of them can be seen in the cloisters of the monastery.

This fact has reminded me not to pass over the true story often told about Bishops Trees. This is a village in a valley, to which Aldhelm is said to have gone, in order to fulfil his responsibility of preaching there. While he was addressing the people, he happened to have fixed in the ground the staff of ash, which he used for a support. During the sermon the staff, through the goodness

---

[1] For Ecgwine, bishop of Worcester 693–717, see ch. 160. Lapidge and Herren consider Aldhelm's appearance in a dream to Ecgwine to be a fiction invented by Dominic of Evesham to magnify Ecgwine, the founder of Evesham (*Aldhelm: The Prose Works*, p. 181).

[2] The gravestone of the actor Ralph Richardson in Highgate Cemetery bears the one Latin word *emigravit*, 'he has gone to another country'.

of God, grew to a marvellous size, all quickened with sap and covered with bark and having put forth young leaves and beautiful branches.[1] The bishop was intent on his preaching, but when told to do so by the shouts of the people he looked behind and worshipped the miracle. The staff he left there as a gift from God. From the growth of this first tree sprang many other ash trees, indeed, so many that, as I have said, that village is commonly known as Bishops Trees.[2] Now, I am not asserting that this story is the solid truth, but I have included it so as not to be criticised for omitting something. My proof of other matters rests on ancient documents or inscriptions. As God is my witness, I have not made any additions of my own, with the exception of a word which may have flown into my mind to make my writing a little more polished and elegant. For Aldhelm has no need of being championed with lies. So amazing are the stories about him which lead the hearer into a sure belief,[3] so numerous are the stories which do not admit of any dispute. And countless miracles, which are happening now as a memorial to him, show the sanctity of his life in the past to men of the present day.

Chapter 231 Aldhelm's burial at Malmesbury

Meanwhile the monks of Malmesbury received their patron with loud laments and with affection and respect. Their love and veneration of him went hand in hand, but their faith fought with their observance of his funeral rites. They found it impossible to know whether to choose affection towards a father or joy in having such an advocate.[4] If they rejoiced in a patron sent on to God before them, they were also compelled to mourn for a comforter lost to them in their lifetime. After some days had dragged by amid these conflicting emotions, they at last permitted him to be buried in the church of St Michael, where the saint himself had once provided a tomb for his burial. He died in 709, eighteen years before Ine, twenty-five years before Bede, thirty-four years after being made abbot by Leutherius and five years after being made a bishop by Berhtwald. There is no document which has calculated his actual age; but it is a safe guess that the saint was very old. He remained in ecclesiastical office for just under thirty-four years, and he would not have taken up the post except at the proper age, especially in those days.

That year was a sad one for Britain. Many of its leading lights were extinguished or left its shores. For in this year came the death of bishop Wilfrid, of whom I earlier roundly declared that he surpassed all in England for his firm grip on justice and his readiness to perform it. Also Cœnred, king of

---

[1] In Numbers 17:8 the staff of Aaron had similarly sprouted and blossomed as a prefiguration of the Virgin Birth.

[2] Hamilton in his Rolls Series edition suggests that this may be the Gloucestershire village of Stoke Orchard.

[3] The translation of the first half of this sentence assumes that William originally wrote *quae in indubiam*.

[4] Compare the words of the dying Wulfstan in ch. 148.

the Mercians, Æthelred's successor, set out for Rome with Offa, king of the East Angles, and completed his life's course while on the journey. As I have written earlier,[1] sparkle was added to their company by the blessed bishop Ecgwine, who, after performing the funeral rites for the blessed Aldhelm, attempted that arduous journey voluntarily bound in fetters and got through to the end of it. Anyone wanting more information about this will find it elsewhere both in my writings and those of others.

Chapter 232 The beginning of Malmesbury's post-Aldhelm history

The body of the blessed Aldhelm lay in the church of St Michael for 246 years. Jealous oblivion has wiped out and buried all the miracles performed by it during this whole time, though I believe them to have been neither few nor trivial. The monks indeed moved to the church of St Mary so that they might the more fittingly murmur their intercessions to the saint as being nearer to his tomb, although as I shall show from documents, St Peter's was regarded as their primary church right down to the time of king Edgar.[2] And now, with God's help, I shall attempt to complete the fourth part of my promise, showing how changeable fortunes affected the development of the monastery of Malmesbury, and how in fact it would often have been destroyed, had not the saint stretched forth a helping hand. I shall proceed king by king, quoting documents. Æthelheard succeeded Ine for fourteen years, and after him Cuthred reigned for the same length of time. We possess the following charter of Cuthred's gift.

Chapter 233 Charter-grant of Cuthred, king of the West Saxons (740–756)

I, Cuthred, king of the West Saxons, compelled by the chain of the love of Christ and my feeling for this indivisible love, as the Holy Trinity is my witness, cheerfully and freely and bountifully give to abbot Aldhelm and the monks living in the love of his rule for the monastery at Malmesbury a parcel of land in perpetual right at the place called Wootton, valued and assessed as being of ten hides. I do this with the knowledge and consent of the excellent bishop Daniel and my lords and nobles, in order, of course, that the monks may remember me in their prayers and for the redemption of my soul, that I may be placed among the fullness of the chosen of God.

And a little later on:

A copy of this deed of gift was set up in the aforesaid monastery in 745 in the presence of king Cuthred.

---

[1] In ch. 160.

[2] For these churches, all built by Aldhelm, see chs. 197 and 216. For the end of St Peter's as the primary church see ch. 253.

So it is clear that this was done in the last year of king Cuthred's life, while bishop Daniel, who had been made bishop together with the blessed Aldhelm, was still alive, and thirty-five years after the death of Aldhelm.[1] From this it follows that the abbot Aldhelm to whom king Cuthred gave Wootton was somebody different from the great Aldhelm. Indeed it is said that this second Aldhelm was the first's nephew.

Chapter 234 Charter-grant of Cynewulf (759)

Sigeberht succeeded king Cuthred for one year, and Cynewulf succeeded Sigeberht for thirty-one years. In the third year of his reign Cynewulf enlarged the monastery with this notable gift.

> In the name of Christ! I, king Cynewulf, with the agreement of my nobles, for the redemption of my soul, give the perpetual possession of a parcel of land of about thirty hides to the family of Christ established in the monastery at Malmesbury. This land is at the confluence of the rivers Marden and Rodbourne with its limits and boundaries round about them, as they are known to be familiar to the inhabitants themselves. It includes the village at whose foot it lies, and it consists of pasture, arable, both dry and wet lands and woods. Given in 758, indiction 11, forty-eight years after the passing over of lord bishop Aldhelm. Signed by Cyneheard, bishop elect of Winchester, and Herewald bishop of Sherborne.

Chapter 235 Ecgfrith, king of Mercia, restores lands taken by Offa

When this same king Cynewulf had now been ruling for twenty-three years he was met in battle near the village of Bensington[2] by Offa, king of the Mercians. The battle was won by Offa, who seized both Bensington and a very large part of the lands of the West Saxons. Finally that plundering enemy seized the village of the monastery of Tetbury, which Æthelred king of the Mercians had given to the monastery, and the village of Purton, which had been the gift of Cædwalla, king of the West Saxons.[3] Offa gave the first to the bishop of Worcester, but the second was given back to the monastery by his son Ecgfrith, as recorded in the following charter.

> In the name of the Lord! I, Ecgfrith, king of the Mercians, in the first year of the kingship granted to us by God,[4] at the request of Berhtric king of the West Saxons and archbishop Æthelheard, have given back to abbot Cuthbert and the brothers in the monastery at Malmesbury the land of thirty-five hides in the place called Purton, starting from the eastern part of

---

[1] Bishop Daniel of Winchester died in 745, so the copy could have been set up 'while Daniel was still alive', but not 'in the last year of Cuthred's life', as Cuthred did not die until 756.

[2] On the River Thames.

[3] For the gift of Purton see ch. 206.

[4] That is, 796.

the wood called Bradon, for the forgiveness of my own sins and for the rest of the soul of my father Offa, who took this land from the monks in his lifetime. The aforesaid land is of course granted under the condition that it is exempt from secular service to kings. It is to serve the needs of the brothers who serve God in the aforesaid monastery. I do this so that our memory may stay alive for ever in the holy prayers of the brothers in that holy place. Furthermore, the abbot and the brothers of the monastery have given me two thousand shillings of unmixed silver as a purchase price of that land. I have done this after consulting the bishops and those nobles of mine whose names are written below. Given in 796, indiction 4, eighty-seven years after the passing over of father Aldhelm. May God preserve and bless the man who adds to my almsgiving. But the man who diminishes and spoils its fame, a thing which we do not want to happen, will be rooted out from the land of the living and excluded from the company of the saints, unless he makes proper recompense.

This charter was signed by archbishop Æthelheard,[1] who obtained the highest honour after being first abbot of Malmesbury and afterwards bishop of Winchester, and who had instituted this Cuthbert as abbot of Malmesbury. It was also signed by Berhtric, king of the West Saxons for sixteen years after Cynewulf, and by Cyneberht, bishop of Winchester, Denefrith, bishop of Sherborne, Heathured, bishop of Worcester, and Eadwulf, bishop elect of Hereford.

Chapter 236 Æthelwulf's gift of a silver shrine

After Berhtric came thirty-seven years of rule by Ecgberht, who subjected all the kingdoms of the English to the sway of the West Saxons, where they remain right up to this day. His son Æthelwulf, whom some call Athulf, succeeded him for eighteen years.[2] Æthelwulf was a man who gave freedom to the churches and who with his unprecedented generosity surpassed all his predecessors and those who followed him. For he made a shrine in which to place the bones of the holy confessor. Its front was of solid silver with figures engraved.[3] Its back in raised metal told the story of the miracles of Aldhelm, which in our day are passed on in speech. So it is thought that in those days the book of *The Life of Aldhelm* was at Malmesbury, and that Æthelwulf read about the miracles in it, but that later in the time of the Danes the book was lost. King Æthelwulf had a crystal pediment placed on the shrine, on which you can read Aldhelm's name in gold letters. Some say that Aldhelm's revered remains were translated by the king, but I shall follow the more common opinion when I come to deal with the matter.[4] Now let me list the gifts which king Æthelwulf gave to the monastery.

---

[1] For Æthelheard, archbishop of Canterbury 790–805, see ch. 8.
[2] Æthelwulf died in 856. For his earlier life see pp. 105–6.
[3] William referred to this silver shrine in the prologue to Book 5.
[4] In ch. 251.

Chapter 237 Charters of Æthelwulf's gifts of lands to Malmesbury I

Our Lord Jesus Christ reigns for ever, high and ineffable creator of all things! I, Æthelwulf, by the grace of God king of the West Saxons, at this holy and most famous time of Easter, for the forgiveness of my soul and the prosperity of the kingdom and people committed to me by God, together with the bishops and earls and all my nobles have taken the healthy decision of not only giving to the holy churches a tenth part of the lands throughout my realm[1] but also of granting my servants the right of perpetual freedom. This gift is with the condition that it remain fixed and unchangeable, freed from all service to kings and from servitude to any secular person. Also, Ealhstan, bishop of the church at Sherborne, and Swithhun, bishop of Winchester, have agreed that every Sunday their whole company of monks shall sing fifty psalms for king Æthelwulf and his nobles who have supported his decision, and that every week each priest shall sing two masses. Et cetera. This charter written 854, indiction 2, on Easter Day, in our palace called Wilton. And the land which we give to the free use of the church at Malmesbury is this: thirty-five hides at Purton, fifteen at Lacock, five at Sutton, five at the Gauze Brook, ten at Crudwell, ten at Kemble, and two at Dauntsey.

Also, in 843, the first year of his reign[2] and 134 years after the passing of the blessed Aldhelm, he had made a charter of freedom for the churches alone, which I have omitted here, because I recorded it in my *Deeds of the Kings*.[3] In this he had designated the following lands as belonging to Malmesbury: thirty hides at Elingdon, fifteen at Elmstead, ten at Wootton, twenty at Charlton, five at Tockenham, five at Minety and ten at Rodbourne.

Chapter 238 Charters of Æthelwulf II

Our Lord Jesus Christ reigns for ever! I, king Æthelwulf, have given to God and St Peter and the monks at Malmesbury part of the land of the West Saxons, that is five manors in the place called Tockenham, in order that the monks themselves may continually pray to almighty God for us, asking that he grant to us prosperous times for keeping safe our faith and the government of our kingdom, as long as the English people shall last. Let no one dare to remove this gift from the monastery of Malmesbury without incurring the anger and punishment of almighty God. This gift given 854. May it be preserved in peace. Signed by bishops Swithhun and Ealhstan.

---

[1] Barbara Yorke suggests that one purpose of this gift may have been to ensure the loyalty of the country on the eve of his departure to Rome (*Wessex in the Early Middle Ages*, p. 197).
[2] In fact Æthelwulf became king in 839.
[3] 2:114.

Chapter 239 Charters of Æthelwulf III

Our Lord God and Saviour Jesus Christ reigns and rules us for ever! He has saved all the generations of man, redeemed the human race with his blood, and through a true faith and the sacrament of baptism freed it from the everlasting destruction of condemnation through the devil! I, Æthelwulf, king of the West Saxons not by my own merits but as a gift from God's grace, and also ruler and governor of Kent through the gift of the same God and of the whole people of the South Saxons through the smile of God's grace, have given to almighty God for the use of the monastery of Malmesbury the perpetual possession of a small piece of land, namely five manors in the place called Minety, under the condition that the man who tries to take this land away from the church itself shall be condemned for ever. Given in 855. Signed by Ceolnoth archbishop of Canterbury, Ealhstan bishop of Sherborne, Æthelstan king of Kent, son of the same king Æthelwulf.

Chapter 240 John Scot, scholar and monk at Malmesbury

Æthelwulf was succeeded by three sons, who ruled in an unbroken series for fifteen years.[1] And then Alfred, the fourth son, ruled for thirty years, less six months. In his time, John Scot[2] came to England. He was a man of clear-sighted intellect and great eloquence, who had long ago left his native land and crossed over to the court of Charles the Bald in France.[3] Charles had welcomed him with great respect, and considered him one of his household. John exchanged jokes as well as serious ideas with the king, and was his inseparable companion at table and as his chamberlain. Many of his *bon mots*, with their frank charm, are still preserved to this day. Here are some examples. He was seated at dinner opposite the king, at another part of the table. After the courses of the meal were finished and the drinking cups were being passed around, king Charles, whose face was merrier than usual, made various other remarks, and then, when he saw John do something which offended French taste, wittily rebuked him by asking, 'What separates a sot from a Scot?' John turned this grave insult back on its author by replying, 'Just a table'. What could be wittier than this remark? The king had asked about the difference in customs regarded as important: John had replied about the spatial difference in their positions. But the king was not at all angry; he had been so captivated by the miracle of John's knowledge, that he did not want to offend his master even in word. 'Master' was what he used to call him.

---

[1] They were Æthelbald (858–60), Æthelberht (860–5) and Æthelred (865–71).
[2] 'Scot' here in fact means Irish: well into the medieval period, 'Scots' was the designation for the (one) people who inhabited (northern) Ireland and western Scotland, distinct, originally, from the Picts in the rest of highland Scotland. The scholar John Scot Erigena is also mentioned by William in *Deeds of the Kings* 2:122.
[3] Charles the Bald, son of Louis the Pious and Judith (see ch. 6) and grandson of Charlemagne, ruled the West Franks 855–63.

On another occasion a servant during dinner offered the king a dish which contained two huge fish and one very tiny one alongside. The king passed the dish to his master so that he might share it with the two priests who were sitting next to him. The priests were men of enormous bulk, while John was very small in stature. Now John was always on the lookout for some respectable means of making the table merry, and on this occasion he kept the two bigger fish for himself, and divided the smaller one between the two priests. When the king protested at the unfairness of the sharing, John said, 'Not at all! I made a fair and equal division. 'For here is one small', referring to himself, 'and two big', touching the fish. And then turning to the priests he said, 'Here are two big', nodding at the priests, and 'one tiny', still touching the fish.

So, on Charles' request, John did a word-for-word translation of the *Hierarchia* of Dionysius the Areopagite[1] from Greek into Latin, though the result was that the Latin version was barely understood either, Latin being much more like Greek in the flexibility of its word order than our own word order by position. John also wrote a book to which he gave the Greek title *Peri Physion Merismou*, that is, *Concerning the Divisions of Nature*. On account of the obscurity of some of the issues needing clarification, this would have been a very useful work, if only he could have been forgiven certain passages in which he deviated from the pathway of the Latin church through keeping his eyes firmly fixed on the Greeks. The result was that he was regarded as a heretic, and Florus wrote an attack on his work.[2] For in truth there are very many points in the *Peri Physion* book, which unless they are examined carefully, do appear to contradict the catholic faith. Pope Nicholas[3] is known to have shared this opinion. In a letter to Charles he said, 'Our apostolate has been told that the work of the blessed Dionysius the Areopagite, which was an eloquent description in Greek *Concerning the Divine Names or the Heavenly Hierarchies*, has recently been translated into Latin by a certain John from Scotland. This book should have sent to me for my seal of approval, as is the custom, especially as we frequently hear rumours that this same John, for all his reputation for wide learning, once displayed unsound views on certain matters.'

I suppose that this criticism was the reason why he tired of France and came to the court of king Alfred. John was won over by Alfred's generosity, given the important job of being his teacher, as I have discovered from the writings of the king, and settled at Malmesbury. But after a few years there he was stabbed to death by his pupils with their pens. It was a cruel and bitter twist of

---

[1] Dionysius the Areopagite, fl. 50, was a member of the court of the Areopagus at Athens, and according to Acts 17:4 was one of the few Athenians converted by Paul's preaching in their city. Despite its difficulty, John's Latin version of the *Hierarchia* is said to be the text which inspired Abbot Suger *c.*1140 to create in consultation with his master mason the light-filled east end of the church of St Denis in Paris.

[2] Florus, a deacon of Lyons, wrote his *Pamphlet against the Heretical Definitions of John Scot Erigena* in 862.

[3] Nicholas I, 858–67.

fate that he should meet this gloomy end, considering that the powers of evil, when the hands of its agents are weak, are frustrated as often as they strike home. John lay for some time without proper burial in the church of the blessed Laurence which had witnessed his horrible murder. But over many nights there shone around him a fiery light from the mercy of the divine favour, and the monks, warned by this, transferred his body to the larger church. They buried it to the left of the altar and proclaimed his martyrdom in these lines:

> John, holy sage, lies buried here,
> In life, now past, enriched with learning rare.
> At length, a martyr, he his way has won
> To realm of Christ where all the saints for ever rule.

Chapter 241 A gift to the abbey for the future from king Alfred

King Alfred and his son Edward gave no gift to this monastery, unless an exchange[1] seems greater than a gift. Anyway, I will append here the documents. They show that this church was originally dedicated to St Saviour and St Peter,[2] and that it is worthwhile in this way to read and scrutinise the writings of the men of old.

> In the name of the Lord! I, Alfred, by the grace of God king of the Anglo-Saxons, with the consent of the respected brotherhood of the church of Malmesbury, grant to my faithful subject, Dudi, a small parcel of land, namely four hides belonging to this same church, in the place called Chelworth. But after the days of three heirs this land is to return indisputably to the church of St Saviour and St Peter in Malmesbury. This document given in the same place, called of old Meldunum, but by us Malmesbury.

Chapter 242 Ordlaf intervenes

But in the passage of time in the reign of Edward son of Alfred,[3] Ordlaf, a very powerful duke, bought the land from Dudi and gave it back to the monastery in exchange for another piece of land. Ordlaf was a good and peaceful man and when he entered the road of death he ordered both lots of land to be restored to the monastery without possibility of complaint. Consequently he was rewarded with a noble burial at Malmesbury and an everlasting memorial. These are the documents.

Chapter 243 Charter-grant from the abbey to Ordlaf

> With the agreement of Edward, most glorious king of the Anglo-Saxons, and the nobles who were present as his retinue on that occasion, the household of

[1] This presumably is the exchange described in ch. 245.
[2] See ch. 197.
[3] Edward the Elder reigned from 899 to 924.

the servants of God at the place called of old Meldunum, in the church of St Saviour whose most beautiful masonry construction can be seen in the same place, freely grants to the venerable duke Ordlaf a parcel of land of five manors for his own possession in the place called Mehandum, in exchange for another piece of land of three manors in the place called Chelworth by the country people. When the days of four heirs have come to an end, the aforesaid land is to return indisputably to the brothers of the church.

Chapter 244 Charter of Ordlaf

I, Ordlaf, freely grant to the brotherhood of St Saviour at Meldunum a piece of land, called Chelworth by the country people, legally owned by me, which I bought from the venerable Dudi with the permission of my most glorious king Edward, in exchange for another piece of land which is called Mehandum.

Etc. This document was given in 901, and 191 years after the death of the most holy confessor.

Chapter 245 Edward gives the abbey Hankerton in return for Fernberge

In the name of the Lord! I, Edward, by the grace of God king of the Anglo-Saxons, have granted to the venerable brotherhood of the church at Meldunum a piece of land in the place called Hankerton in exchange for another piece of land of the same size, namely ten hides, in the place called Fernberge by the country people. The aforesaid lands are exempt from all secular usages. I have made this exchange for the benefit of the brothers and at their own request, seeing that the land which I gave to the said brothers is only two miles distant from their monastery, while the land which I received is almost twenty miles away from the said monastery.[1] This document written in 901, in the first year of my reign.

His mother Ealhswith and Ælfflæd the wife of the king added their signatures.

Chapter 246 Gifts of king Æthelstan to Malmesbury and his burial there

Edward reigned for twenty-four years, and was succeeded by his son Æthelstan for sixteen years. Æthelstan was so attached to the blessed Aldhelm, whom he said was his kinsman as was so in fact, that he devoted his body and soul to his service. Indeed the saint himself at that time was gradually showing a disposition to perform more famous and more frequent miracles, giving notice it would seem that he was tired of his ignoble burial in the earth. And he did not cease from them until a few years later he was unearthed and placed in a shrine.

[1] Fernberge is in Somerset.

Meanwhile Æthelstan had had carried to Malmesbury the bodies of Ælfwine and Æthelwine, sons of his uncle Æthelweard, of whom he had been particularly fond. They had been lost in the war against Analavus, and Æthelstan now had them buried to the left and right of the altar in the church of the holy mother of God. The often repeated reason for this was that once upon a time Æthelstan, having called upon the name of Aldhelm, had been given his sword from heaven and thus snatched from the grasp of the enemy.[1] Since that day he had bestowed upon the monastery several estates, many altar cloths, a gold cross, reliquaries[2] also of gold, together with a piece of the Lord's cross, which had been sent him by Hugh, duke of the Franks.[3] It would take a long time to describe all his devotion in building and repairing monasteries,[4] the numbers of the barbarians whom he put to flight with the smallest of armies, the bounds which he set to our power in Scotland.[5] Also I would seem to be making easy use of readily available material and to be repeating for rhetorical display things said elsewhere.[6] And at the same time in repeated praise of Æthelstan I would appear to be singing the praises of our own church, seeing that he honoured it with many gifts in his lifetime, and with the remains of his revered body at his death. But I will venture to say that, even though he was the one man who surpassed all his predecessors (or, to speak more moderately, equalled all of them), what he did was nothing compared to what he would have done, for the early departure sent him by fate broke off his mighty achievements. He was snatched away from the world at Gloucester by an untimely death, which would have been ill-suited to a man of his capabilities, if God had so willed it. His body was taken to Malmesbury and buried there under the altar of St Mary in the tower. This refutes those who say that abbot Ælfric built that tower, as he is known to have been abbot more than thirty years after the death of Æthelstan.

Here lies the pride of all, his country's grief.
The bolt of justice, purity's pattern, virtue's track.
His soul ascends the skies, from fleshly fetters freed,
An urn contains his glorious remains.
Twelve times the rising sun on Scorpio shone,
Before with flick of tail it finished the king.[7]

---

[1] See ch. 14 for a longer account of this incident of the sword and the victory at Brunanburg in 937 against the invading army of Analavus, king of Dublin.

[2] Strictly the word translated 'reliquaries' refers to small coffers in which relics were preserved and which were carried in procession slung around the neck with straps.

[3] For Æthelstan as a collector of relics see Yorke, *Wessex in the Early Middle Ages*, p. 209 and chs. 85 and 93. Stenton describes him as a 'mixture of devotion and intellectual curiosity' (*Anglo-Saxon England*, p. 356).

[4] For example, his foundation of Milton (ch. 85).

[5] Æthelstan's fleet got as far as Caithness. See Stenton, *Anglo-Saxon England*, p. 356.

[6] In *The Deeds of the Kings* 2:131–5.

[7] The sun is in Scorpio from 24 October to 22 November, so William gives the date of Æthelstan's death as 4 November 939. See also *The Deeds of the Kings* 2:140. Æthelstan's tomb can still be seen in Malmesbury Abbey.

Chapter 247 Æthelstan's gift of relics of St Paternus

Æthelstan increased the number of his services to the monastery by bringing there the relics of many saints. He got through a prodigious amount of his father's treasures in spectacular fashion in buying up these relics, having been told to do this by a vision from heaven. Many saints' relics, including those of St Paternus, bishop of Avranches, he purchased from Brittany and Normandy, being bound in a treaty of friendship with count Rollo. Paternus had been born in Aquitaine, become a monk when a young man, and later in life a hermit. Then, when he had derived considerable profit from his rather lonely philosophical studies, he went back into the public eye, being now a fit person to become a governor of souls as he knew how to govern himself. As abbot of Coutances and later bishop of Avranches[1] he performed his share of miracles.

Being thirsty, he lightly struck his stick against a rock and the water gushed forth. It was in every way awesome that when nature was not helping, a holy human being should strike jets of water from veins of marble. A girl had been deprived of the use of her tongue. Paternus poured oil on to it and made it work again. Once, a woman, whose fingers had been bent back into knots towards her palms, had them loosened by the saint's touch. A boy who had been bitten by a poisonous snake was becoming increasingly swollen and was about to die. Paternus put him on his feet again by pacifying his unruly skin and reducing it to its proper size. Evil spirits fled from their victims in whom they had made their home when they sensed the approach of the saint, their timid flight being excused by their inability to withstand the force of Paternus. Little birds, who had fed on grain seasoned by his blessing, followed him on the oarage of their wings[2] for many miles when he went away. They could never be parted from the love of the man who had given them life. There are also other miracles which we can read about in Fortunatus, a writer famed for his eloquence and graceful wit.[3]

Chapter 248 St Paternus and the thief

Æthelstan put his remains next to holy Aldhelm, so that they could be together, and Paternus' miracles were so frequent that he never disguised the fact that he was a saint. The story I am about to tell was a favourite with our forebears, who remembered it in remarkable detail. A thief stole a gold plate from his shrine, got away from the church, and spent its proceeds for whatever purposes he fancied. The saint had been patient on other occasions, but he was not taking this lying down. For when the culprit imagined he could re-enter the church without harm, he stuck fast in the doorway in a net of invisible thongs. If he tried to go forward, the poor man was scorched by an unseen flame of great power which made him wail piteously. If he tried to retreat, he was

---

[1] Paternus became bishop of Avranches *c.*557.
[2] The ornate phrase 'on the oarage of their wings' is taken from Virgil's *Aeneid* 1:305.
[3] See ch. 179 for Venantius Fortunatus. He wrote a life of St Paternus.

pulled back by a noose twisted round his neck. The bystanders were amazed at the thief's cries and struggles, for they saw neither flame nor noose. But when they learnt of his crime and punishment from his own confession, they offered prayers to the saint. And so when the loss was cancelled, so was the victim's punishment. You can read the following words on the shrine, 'King Æthelstan, ruler of the whole of Britain and of the many peoples which encircle it, ordered this shrine to be made in honour of St Paternus.' . . .[1] I will append the letter, sent because Æthelstan had won these relics from lands overseas.

Chapter 249 Letter of Radbod, prior of St Samson, to Æthelstan

With the honour of the high, indissoluble Trinity and the most excellent intercessions of all the saints, glory in this world and blessedness hereafter to Æthelstan, glorious and generous king, from Radbod, prior of the monastery of archbishop Samson. Men of piety here, king Æthelstan, have become very well aware of your benevolence and your most sacred high position which wins greater praise and fame than that of all other earthly kings at this time, since our region's stability still endures because your father Edward by letter entrusted himself to the fellowship of the confraternity of St Samson high confessor and of Jovenian senior archbishop, my cousin, and his priests. As a result still today we untiringly pour forth prayers to Christ the king for his soul and for your salvation, and, since we see that your great hand of pity is visibly stretched over of us day and night, we promise to pray to merciful God for you in our psalms and masses and prayers, just as much as if I and twelve of my canons were on the ground before your knees.

And now I send you relics, dearer to you, we know, than all earthly goods. They are the bones of St Senator and St Paternus and St Scubilion, teacher of St Paternus, who migrated to Christ together with Paternus on the same day and at the same hour. Those two saints, I can assure you, lay together in a tomb with St Paternus, on his right and on his left, and we celebrate the festival of all three on 23 September. And so, glorious king, holy champion of the church, humbler of the wicked heathen, pattern for your subjects, example of all goodness, scatterer of the enemy, father of your priests, helper of the needy, lover of all the saints, invoker of angels, we humbly beg and pray that the great mercy of your most happy bounty may not forget us, who for our sins deservedly live in exile and captivity in France. From now on you can without any hesitation pass on to me as a command the things you think it right to entrust to me.

This letter was found in a shrine in the monastery at Milton, built and founded by this same king Æthelstan and where he had placed the relics of St Samson.[2]

---

[1] There is damage, causing a gap in the manuscript at this point.
[2] See ch. 85.

Chapter 250 Charter of king Æthelstan

But I see that I should now append the evidence for the estates which the king gave the monastery. There are many copies of the charter, but they are all identical. He wrote as follows.

The wanton fortune of the deceptive world is not loved for the milky whiteness of its lilies but hated for the poisonous bitterness of its lamented corruption, as it bites and shreds its sons in this vale of tears with venomous rendings of stinking flesh. Although it may give a smile of favour towards poor human beings, yet it will shamelessly sink as low as the depths of Acherontian Cocytus, unless the son of the high Thunderer comes to the rescue. And because this world itself is thus failing and subsiding into mortal ruin, we must hurry with all our strength to the lovely fields of indescribable happiness, where the good and the blessed experience the immeasurable sweetness of the angelic organs with their jubilant hymns and the honeyed scent of spring roses, and where the pleasant songs of the happy are endlessly heard and listened to. Consumed by a love for this felicity,[1] I, Æthelstan, king of the English, by the right hand of the Almighty elevated to the kingship of all Britain, have given the perpetual right of certain parcels of land to God and St Peter to be used by the venerable brotherhood of Malmesbury on behalf of the souls of my cousins, Ælfwine and Æthelwine, sons of prince Æthelweard. These are assessed as ten hides in the place called Wootton, forty hides in the place called Bremhill, five hides in the place called Somerford, and five also in the places called Norton and Ewelme. I do this with the caveat that none of my successors are to make the slightest attempt to interfere with this gift of mine, as long as Christianity lives. If anyone does try, he should know that he will be condemned by God for ever.

Also wise men in our kingdom should know that I did not seize these lands illegally and then hand the plunder to God, but that I received them according to the judgement of all the nobles of the kingdom of the English and also of John, apostolic pope of the Roman church.[2] This happened after the death of that Alfred who, as an enemy of our life and good fortune, conspired with my wicked opponents in their plan to blind me in the city of Winchester after the death of my father. But God in his goodness rescued me, and, with their schemes laid bare, Alfred was sent to the Roman church to defend himself by oath there in the presence of John, apostolic father. He did this at the altar of St Peter, but, having sworn the oath, he collapsed in front of the altar and was carried in the arms of his servants into the School of the English,[3] where two nights later he died. The pope then sent the body back to me, and asked my advice on what should be done with it. At the

---

[1] Up to this point the charter is similar to the one in ch. 201.
[2] John XI, pope 931–6.
[3] For the School of the English at Rome see *Deeds of the Kings* 2:109, 137.

request of our nobles we agreed that Alfred, for all his unworthiness, should be buried next to other Christians. This is how possession of all his lands, both great and small, was assigned to me. Etc.

The charter recording this decision, made by me with the inspiration of God and the Lord Jesus Christ, given 21 December 937, in the eleventh year of the kingship freely entrusted to me, indiction 8, epact 14, concurrent number 3,[1] in the turning month's tenth moon, in the very famous city called Doncaster, with all the generality of my nobles under my protection and rejoicing in my royal bounty.

Signed also by the princes Eugenius, Howel, Morcant and Ludual. By Wulfhelm archbishop of Canterbury and Wulfstan archbishop of York. By the following bishops: Burgric of Rochester, Theodred of London, Æthelgar of the East Angles, Ealhfrith of Winchester, Æthelgar of Crediton, Alfred of Sherborne, Wulfhelm of Wells, Oda of Wilton, Eadhelm of Selsey, Sæxhelm of St Cuthbert, Tidhelm of Hereford, Ælfwine of Worcester, Cynesige of Lichfield and Wynsige of Leicester.

Chapter 251 King Eadwig introduces secular clergy at Malmesbury

Æthelstan was succeeded by his brother Edmund for six years and by his brother Eadred for nine years. After Eadred Edmund's son Eadwig ruled for four years. As I have described in more detail elsewhere,[2] Eadwig was led astray by the enticements of one courtesan, and when Dunstan rebuked him most severely for his folly, he expelled Dunstan from England. Then, once he had dipped his toe in the waters of evil, he inflicted cruel indignities on all men belonging to monastic orders in the whole of England just to cause Dunstan sorrow. First he deprived them of help from constitutional enactments, and later he drove them into exile as well. For he even made the monastery of Malmesbury a stable of secular clergy, 245 years after the death of father Aldhelm and 275 years after Leutherius had put him in charge of the monks there.

But you, Lord Jesus, our creator and recreator, skilled craftsman, and with great power to straighten out our crookedness, you used those men who were living no ordered life under a rule to bring into the light of day your treasure which for so many centuries had been hidden away. I am referring to the body of the great saint Aldhelm which they lifted out of the ground and placed in the shrine which I have described earlier.[3] The fame of these clergy was increased by the king's generous gift to the saint of an estate which was ideal for them because of its proximity and size. I would give the name of the estate,[4] except that it is well known and many parts of it were given by previous kings, thus

[1] An epact is an intercalary day. A concurrent number is one corresponding to a year letter.
[2] In ch. 17, and also in *Deeds of the Kings* 2:147.
[3] In ch. 236.
[4] It was probably the large grant of land at Brokenborough made to the monastery by king Eadwig in 956.

stopping Eadwig from claiming for himself alone the whole of the glory belonging to all or even from filching a part of their bequests.

But all the wickedness of his times quickly departed when he was succeeded by his brother Edgar, who would easily have outshone all his predecessors, if Æthelstan had not won this prize before him. In the end one does not know whom to put first except to say that Edgar continued what Æthelstan had begun, that Æthelstan was the braver and Edgar the luckier, and that Æthelstan relied on self-help and the help of God whereas Edgar gave ear to the counsel of wise men. So Edgar abolished the decrees enacted by his brother in his kingly extravagance and youthful impetuousness. His own words will reveal better than mine what he gave to our church and what he took from it.

Chapter 252 Charter of king Edgar in favour of the monasteries

Seeing that a fixed goal awaits the universality of the general mass, and, as the apostle says, things visible are temporal but things invisible are eternal,[1] it remains for each one of us to be rewarded there for what he has done here. Therefore I, Edgar, monarch of the whole of England and of the kings of the seas and islands round about it, by the presence of the bountiful grace of God elevated above all my forefathers in the extent of my sway, have often taken some intelligent thought concerning what part of my power in particular I should give to the Lord, the king of kings, when I remember the honours he has heaped upon me. As I was lying awake studying the matter, my pious devotions were helped by the holy thought from above suddenly entering my mind that I should renew all the sacred monasteries in my kingdom.[2] Not only are they visibly destroyed down to their wall tops with moss-covered tiles and rotten roofbeams, but also and more importantly their insides have become almost completely neglected and emptied of worship of God. Indeed I have ejected the uneducated secular clergy who were not subject to the discipline of a religious life lived under a rule, and in very many places installed pastors of a more holy lineage, that is the brotherhood of monks. And, in order that they might renew all these ruined temples, I have provided them with wealth in abundance from the revenues of the treasury.

One of these, called Ælfric, a man of the church to his fingertips, I have appointed as abbot of the very famous monastery, which the English call by the double name of Malmesbury. For the saving of my soul and in honour of our Saviour and of Mary his ever-virgin mother and of the apostles Peter and Paul and of our bountiful abbot Aldhelm I have with abundant generosity restored to Malmesbury a piece of land of ten manors called Eastcott with its meadows and woods. This land, once leased out by the aforesaid secular clergy, for a long time has been in the illegal possession of

---

[1] 2 Corinthians 4:18.
[2] For Edgar's restoration of the monasteries see Loyn, *The English Church*, p. 15, and Stenton, *Anglo-Saxon England*, pp. 367, 449.

a line of people, ending in a robber called Æthelnoth. But now that my council have listened to his subtle but blasphemous statement of his case and in my presence disproved as false his arguments laying claim to it, I have restored it to the use of the monastery, 974, in the fourteenth year of my reign, the first of the royal consecration, and the two hundred and forty-fifth after the death of our most precious confessor Aldhelm. At the request of the aforesaid abbot I have given orders for this schedule of restitution to be written out, so that future generations may have it firmly fixed in their minds, and so that, as long as the Christian faith survives among our countrymen, no powerful tyrant may violently deprive (absit omen!) that holy place of the aforesaid piece of land.

Signed by Dunstan archbishop of Canterbury, Oswald archbishop of York and the following bishops: Æthelwald of Winchester, and the three Ælfstans of London, Rochester and Wilton and others.

Chapter 253 Ælfric abbot of Malmesbury (970–979)

The Ælfric mentioned is the man who transferred all his devotion to the blessed Mary and entrusted the possession and name of the monastery to her control so that she might be seen as the sole ruler of the place on her own, with the name of the most blessed Peter in the mean time being passed over in silence.[1] Our glorious Lady did not disdain the gift of the illustrious and famous Ælfric. Indeed even today she still presides over the church, enfolding in her power the community of the most holy Aldhelm. The traditions of old are quite correct when they speak of him as being a man of letters and a particularly fine interpreter of them. They also tell of his knowledge of building, and indeed he initiated and completed the construction of all the offices of the monks, which were outstanding for those days and even now are not so very contemptible. Abbo of Fleury[2] refers to him without giving his name in his preface to the *Passion of St Edmund* composed for the blessed archbishop Dunstan. I quote, 'Your holy self recounted in my presence the history of the passion of the saintly Edmund. It had never been written down and most people were ignorant of it, but you had put it together from the oral traditions of the ages. Also in the circle around you were the lord bishop of the church of Rochester, the abbot of the monastery called Malmesbury and other brothers, as is your custom . . .'[3]

Chapter 254 Ælfric becomes bishop of Crediton

When Ælfric was now old he was promoted to the bishopric of Crediton, but survived for barely four more years. He left behind some books as a not

[1] See ch. 232.
[2] For Abbo of Fleury see p. 166 and n. 3.
[3] There is dmage, causing a gap in the manuscript at this point.

insignificant testament to his intellect: a *Life of St Æthelwald*, written before the more painstaking treatment of him by Wulfstan,[1] a shortened *Passion of St Edmund*, and many books translated from Latin into his native tongue.[2]

Chapter 255 Dunstan's gifts to Malmesbury

It was in the time of king Edgar that the most holy archbishop Dunstan paid especial attention to the repair and decoration of our monastery. His love for St Aldhelm and the West Saxon people was prompted by his affinity with them, for he had been born in those parts, and by the increasing succession of miracles which made him rejoice that at that time especially it was a saint of his own place that had been lifted to the heights. And so he generously made frequent offerings to the place of many gifts which were a marvel and a wonder in the England of that time and which showed the handsomeness and the thoughtfulness of the giver.[3] Among them were bells notable for their sound and size, and an organ with bronze pipes carefully arranged in their dimensions for music, through which 'the anxious bellows squeezed the air long held within'. Written on a bronze plate on the organ was this couplet of dedication from archbishop Dunstan,

> To holy Aldhelm I this organ give,
> May heaven destroy the man who'd take it hence.

The truth of my account can also be supported by these lines which I have seen engraved on a vessel, used for providing water for the attendants at the altar.

> Archbishop Dunstan had this vessel cast,
> To serve the church of Aldhelm, man of God.

In these verses Dunstan had ingeniously used a poet's licence to make the lines scan by removing the first L from the name of the saint. For in neither couplet was he engraved as Aldhelm but as Adhelm.[4]

In the meantime Dunstan foretold with prophetic spirit the calamities that would fall upon England from the marauding Danes after his death and even warned the king himself about them, not in dark riddles but in plain speech. Also, he was afraid for the most holy bones of Aldhelm the confessor. Thinking in advance about the greedy cruelty and the cruel greed of the Danes, he mentally pictured them sacking the monastery in their lust for wealth. What caused him most fear and dread was the thought of someone

---

[1] Wulfstan was a monk at Winchester.
[2] William makes a mistake here. The Ælfric who wrote these books was a monk at Winchester who later became abbot of Eynsham. See p. 120 n. 1.
[3] Dom Hugh Farmer, 'Two Biographies of William of Malmesbury', in *Latin Biography*, ed. T. A. Dorey (London, 1967), p. 159, wonders if these gifts of Dunstan, reputedly made with Dunstan's own hands, may have fired the imagination of the young, impressionable William.
[4] In its place in the Latin verse the first syllable of 'Aldhelm' needs to be short, and this is achieved by removing a consonant.

making off with the shrine, attracted by the gleam of its metal, and greedily hugging to his bosom its precious adornments while throwing away somewhere else the bare wood and the bones. Having thought long and hard about it, he took the revered remains from the shrine and put them in a stone tomb.[1] A place was built high up for it on the right of the altar, visible to all who looked down the church. The bones themselves were wrapped, first in delicate, shining linen, then in very precious scarlet cloth, and next to them Dunstan placed a glass phial full of the purest balsam. This was indeed a fitting aroma for the bishop who had always offered up to heaven whole offerings of his good deeds and his prayers. Also some of the supports for the tomb came from an ancient sarcophagus, in which the whole body had disintegrated, as mortal bodies do. Nor did he refrain from verses to adorn the outside of the tomb's surround, the gist of them being that Aldhelm should regard his lover, Dunstan, as worthy of pardon for his sins, and not hold it against him that he had removed the body from a higher position. The saint, he was sure, would know that he had done this as a precaution, not as an insult. Events did not prove the prophet wrong, nor did any of his words fall to the ground. I will give a brief account of what happened, by returning to the succession of the kings which I had interrupted.

Chapter 256 Aldhelm saves Malmesbury from the Danes

Edgar ruled for sixteen years and was succeeded by his son Edward who ruled for three and a half years. His brother Æthelred then took over, but in his reign of thirty-seven years his unhappy kingdom was sore beset, and brought by him to ruin and destruction. I intend to include just some of the abundant material about him at this point, especially as I have made my way through the labyrinths of the troubles he caused elsewhere.[2] But I shall not pass over in silence the key point that after the death of Edgar, who had claimed that he had dominion over more lands than any of his predecessors, not in the extent but in the security of his rule, things moved in the opposite direction and the happiness of the kingdom stood on the edge of a high precipice. For, as the poet says, great power is not allowed to last long.[3] And indeed there was a storm of invasion along the whole coastline of England as the Danes poured in, men accustomed to live by plunder. To put it in a nutshell, they ravaged all the coast, and began feeding on the marrow of the inland parts. Their ignorance of the true God increased their savagery towards the inhabitants. Some of them, with their leader at their head, came to Malmesbury. Expecting to terrorise it in the usual way, they burst furiously into the church, but, when they looked all around, they saw nothing which could slake their thirst for loot apart from the shrine of the saint. The monks had had the foresight to carefully remove everything else from the prying eyes of these lunatics, and had left just the shrine to take its chance, or, to speak more truly, to the protection of the saint.

---

[1] This took place in 987.
[2] *Deeds of the Kings* 2:164.
[3] Lucan in his *Pharsalia* 1:70–1.

He would protect it, if he wished. Alternatively, he could allow himself to become a laughing stock. The Danes rushed in with frantic haste, their mouths wide open in expectation. One of them, whose shameless greed for silver had made bolder than the rest, snatched out his dagger and tried to cut out the precious stones of the shrine from their casings. He had just put his hand on the shrine when the virtue of the saint sped to the rescue and checked the pestilent, greedy robber. He paid for his rash attempt. He was knocked back senseless on to the floor, as if a spear had been driven hissing into his heart. One man's punishment brought the rest to their senses. They stopped their frenzied yelling and ran away, leaving the holy place inviolate. They fled as fast as they could along the level roads or through trackless country, glad that they had saved just their bodies from this perilous situation. They did not stop running for many a mile, giving the appearance of having experienced a terror greater than any caused by man, since no one was chasing them from behind, and no one was blocking their way in front. The story of the affair spread through the ranks of the enemy and made them less keen on booty and more fearful to show reverence to the saint. The result was that all the monasteries round about were plundered or pillaged, while Malmesbury alone had no such heavy calamity to lament.[1]

Chapter 257 Charter-grant of king Æthelred

King Æthelred gave a town of ten manors to the monastery of St Aldhelm in the abbacy of Æthelweard, who had succeeded Ælfric. For in his early days as a king, he was spurred on by those famous heroes who were still alive. But when they died, he completely faded away, living the life of a profligate and ruining his kingdom. The abundant wealth left him by his father was an enticement to lust. His sins merited the anger of God. The anger of God brought his people to destruction. However, this is his deed of gift.

> It is clear and obvious to all men who make a habit of pouring over the works of the philosophers that we know that the end of our present life is never far away because of the various troubles brought by various calamities, and that at this present moment that end is terrifyingly imminent. And so I, Æthelred, king of all England with the help of the grace of Christ, following the advice of my nobles and wishing to buy things eternal with things transitory, have given the perpetual right of a piece of land of ten manors in the famous place commonly called Redbourne by the men of this land who know these things to our Lord Jesus Christ and to his mother, the ever-virgin Mary, in veneration of the blessed abbot Aldhelm who founded the very place usually called Malmesbury, this piece of land to be for the use of the monks living there under the rule of abbot Æthelweard. Etc.

[1] Abingdon claimed a similar rescue when a crucifix in the refectory came to life and began pelting the intruders with stones extracted from the walls. See Yorke, *Wessex in the Early Middle Ages*, p. 140.

This charter given in 982, 262 years after the death of the same father Aldhelm. Signed by those who signed the earlier charter, plus Ælfric, now bishop of Crediton, and Æscwig, bishop of Dorchester.

Chapter 258 Cyneweard to Brihtwald II (980–1067)

Æthelred died after ruling for thirty-seven years, and was followed by Cnut for twenty years, by Harold, Cnut's son, for four years, by Harthacnut for one year and by Edward for twenty-four years. In these eighty-six years the abbots of Malmesbury after Æthelweard were Cyneweard, Brihthelm, Brihtwald, Ederic and Wulsine. We know from English documents that Brihtwald did many things that were disadvantageous to the monastery, completely alienating some of its estates, and making inroads on others for a small price. But we should not blame him for he could find no other remedy for his troubles when under the burden of providing those big sums of gold which were then given to the Danes. He did not see that his lack of thought for the future could bring trouble to those coming after him. Wulsine restored to its former healthy state the religious life of the monks, which had been much weakened by the advent of the Danes. There were still monks alive in our own day who saw Wulsine in the flesh, and who found it sweet to go through their memories of the man and to pass them on to others. Relying on the tales told me by these monks, I have stored away in my mind many marvellous doings of Wulsine, but I hesitate to relate them, as they do not fit in with the scheme of my work. Wulsine was followed by Æthelweard, who was abbot for ten years. Later Ælfwine was abbot for a year and a half, then Brihtwald for seven years. Ancient tradition has it that Brihtwald, being slow to do good but quick to do evil, came to a pitiful end, dying in the town surrounded by the materials for a drinking bout, and was buried among his predecessors in the church of St Andrew, which is right next to the big church. It is generally believed that the watchmen at the church were disturbed by dreamlike shadowy shapes, until they dug up Brihtwald's body and sunk it in a deep marsh far away from the monastery. At intervals a noxious smell rose from the marsh and spread its noisome stench over the surrounding countryside.[1] But I will leave these unpleasant matters and roll up my sleeves to write of the miracles which during these years were revealed by the Godhead at the tomb of the blessed confessor.

Chapter 259 Aldhelm cures Ælfidis of paralysis

The Danes persisted in their plan to invade England, and invited the Norwegians to share in their victory. Both nations were unbelievably barbaric, but the Norwegians were more greedily rapacious and more violently lustful. During the widespread looting a girl called Ælfidis was given to a Norwegian count as part of his booty. She was of good English birth, and there was

---

[1] The second half of this sentence resembles Virgil's description of a forest at *Aeneid* 7:84.

nothing slavish about her face or form. All this fanned the count's desire to
divorce his legal wife, while he strained every sinew to marry his captive,
although, if he had not been a barbarian, he should have protected her chastity
and pitied her captivity. When he had used up all his persuasive flatteries the
villain assaulted the chastity of the struggling, desperately pleading girl by
night and raped her. But he did not live for long, and so, after his attack on the
woman, got no pleasure from his expectation of the birth of a child or from a
long life.

After the death of the count, talk of the beautiful Ælfidis reached the ears of
the king of Norway.[1] Just like all his race he was soon panting with a desire to
possess the woman. From being a king he became a lover, and from being a
man of power a suppliant. Using messengers, he pleaded with his noble captive
to think of him as a loved one. He promised mountains of gold, and a love
lasting for ever, finally offering anything that could win over a woman or
entice a captive. All these attempts he concealed from his wife, for he was
desperately afraid of angering her. Ælfidis's reply was a refusal: she had her
mind fixed on other loves and intended to serve God. The count, who had
tasted her first-fruits while alive, and in death had buried them with him, had
taken away all her love for his own.[2] When the king heard this, he was hurt
that the woman had turned him down, and as she refused his offer, he forcibly
attacked her and one night worked his way into her embraces by violence
when she feared no such thing. Conception took place from the one coupling
and a son was born whom neither wanted. For the king was willing enough to
take his pleasure, but, out of fear that his reputation would be put at risk, was
not willing reap its harvest. As for Ælfidis, she both feared God's reaction to
her adultery with a married man and was wary of the jealously of the queen.
But, as I have said, a son was born who soon found favour in the eyes of both
of them, and this brought them together. The king jibbed at casting aside a
woman whom he had made a mother, especially when she was beautiful, of
good birth, a captive, and restrained enough to confine herself to the man with
whom intercourse had happened, while Ælfidis wanted to win the king's love,
both by repetition of the deed and the delightfulness of their son. And so, now
that pleasure was an ingredient, she willingly fostered the sin which had been
begun against her will. To escape the queen's notice she had a hideaway with a
bishop of the land, from which she would be taken by the king for their nights
of love whenever he so wanted.

But the death of the king soon put an end to these alluring pleasures, and
Ælfidis was left alone on the stage with her tiny son. As she was well aware of
the lengths that women would dare to go in their anger at a mistress, she took
to flight and fled to Norway's remotest parts. The bishop, who had been
entrusted by the last words of the dying king with the sole care of the orphan,
faithfully arranged things for her and supplied her with the necessary

---

[1] The king was Ólafr, who died on 31 August 1030.
[2] One is reminded of Dido talking to her sister about her dead husband Sychaeus (*Aeneid* 4:28–9).

provisions. In the end the nobles ignored the scorn shown by the queen as a woman and the bishop explained the whole matter to them. And so by general decree the lad was placed ostensibly at the head of the kingdom, with his guardians transacting everything according to his wishes. But after not more than eighteen months the boy, whose name was Magnus, was snatched from life by an untimely death, the thread of the Fates having run out for him.[1] It is said that his death was plotted by the nobles, but I do not think that they would kill by force the innocent lad whom they had made king.

To cut a long story short, Ælfidis, at her wits' end, then decided to retreat to her own country. And so that God might prosper such a perilous voyage, she vowed that if she arrived safely in England, she would never eat the flesh of an earthly animal and would never take up greasy foods except on festival days.[2] God dutifully gave his consent. She obtained a happy outcome for her voyage, and set about keeping her vow with great thoroughness. Out of the money which had come to her from the generosity of her husband and her son she bought three estates, whose revenues supported her life and that of her servants. But, when a few years had passed, she gave an unusually splendid banquet, and, growing rather merry, encouraged her guests to join in her mirth. They responded by asking her to eat just a mouthful of meat. For a long time all their words were a waste of breath, but in the end she was overcome by appeals from some priests at the banquet, who promised prayers and masses and said that the singing of masses could wipe away the guilt of even great offences, and so Ælfidis, touching a little bit of meat with the tips of her fingers, put it to her mouth, although her senses recoiled at the idea. Immediately the strict justice of God sent her a merciful punishment, for, as she chewed the meat, she was struck so strongly with the disease which the Greeks call 'paralysis', i.e. a loosening of the limbs, that none of the limbs of her body could perform their functions. The only movement was of her tongue in her throat, confessing her sin and pleading for forgiveness. Her pardonable lapse was admirably punished by a penalty which lasted only for a time. Had she committed some heinous sin, her punishment would not have been pardonable.

For three whole years, wasting away under this infirmity, she went the circuit of the saints' shrines in her litter, knocking for help at the doors of those made more famous than the rest by the fame of their miracles. The powers above withheld all their charity, giving the blessed Aldhelm an opportunity for glory, so that his fame might flit still more finely from mouth to mouth,[3] now that he had cured so important a person. So after three years Ælfidis came to the saint's shrine upon his birthday, a festival celebrated by great crowds of country folk on 25 May. There was no delay. As she prayed at Aldhelm's tomb

---

[1] There were three Fates in Greek mythology. Clotho, the youngest, presides over our birth. Lachesis spins out the thread of our life. Atropos, the eldest, cuts it off.
[2] Such vows in times of peril were a common medieval practice.
[3] These words are a reminiscence of some lines of the Roman poet Ennius, describing how his poetry would keep him famous after his death. They are quoted in Cicero, *Tusculanae Disputationes* 1:15:34.

during the actual vigil of the festival she was touched by the master's virtue. Her health returned, the loosened framework of her limbs grew firm again, and the paralytic got up whole from her litter. Her friends praised the saint in their amazement, the monks noisily asked questions about the happening and everybody was glad. Ælfidis showed gratitude to her healer and gave all her goods to the monastery. She took the vows of a nun. While alive she lived near the church, and at her death she was buried in a famous tomb in the cloister. This miracle, which tradition has handed down to us because of the importance of the person and the comparatively short interval of time, makes me believe that there were many more miracles which are now hidden in darkness because of the destructive passing of the years and writers' neglect.

Chapter 260 The story of a Greek monk called Constantine

At the same time there came to Malmesbury a Greek monk called Constantine. It is not known where he was from, or whether necessity or choice took him away from home and country. It was he who planted the vineyard situated on a hill near to the monastery on the north, which lasted for many years. He was of a proper height, of a sweet disposition and very conversable. He was sparing with food, and drank little or practically nothing. The holidays given by festivals he spent in prayers, all the hours of the other days in work in the vineyard. When he lay dying, with his voice stopped and everyone thinking that in a very few more breaths he would breathe his last, he rallied and with a slow struggle sat up. He opened the scrip which he always wore at his side, and took out a pallium, the mark of an archbishop.[1] As best he could while lying down, he put it on in the manner he knew. But at once he fell back before the force of death, breathed his last, and passed away. So the monks realised that he had been an archbishop, but they still did not know why he had once said goodbye to his native land. We can turn this uncertainty into a good interpretation, by arguing that it was his love of religion which caused an archbishop to go on his travels. So he was buried reverently among the tombs of the abbots in the church of St Andrew, which was in existence at that time. But in the passage of time, when the need for new buildings caused Constantine and the others to be disturbed from their ancient resting places, his bones were found to be of an unusual whiteness and most sweet smell, indicating that he had not been a holy man of plebeian origin.

Chapter 261 A demoniac healed on the eve of Ascension Day

There was a countryman near Malmesbury, well known to the monks and to the town, who suffered torments from being possessed by an evil demon. He would gnash his teeth at people standing near by whom he could not touch, while those who were closer he would strike with his fist or his heel. He spat

---

[1] See p. 5 n. 2.

out jets of foam on those standing further off. He would whirl around whatever came to hand, as though he were a ballista.[1] His madness supplied him with weapons,[2] so that no one approached him in safety or went away without being hurt. Also he spoke gibberish, hurling his abuse up to the stars themselves. Such different, mixed-up sounds were heard coming from the one mouth, that now you would think him a dog from his barking, and now a cow because of his mooing, and then again an owl because of his screeching. He engulfed in his vast maw of a stomach food which was neither that of ordinary men nor prepared by cooking. His madness had so sharpened his teeth that it seemed an easy business for him to demolish anything of bone, wood or iron. Then he would loosen with one belch the raw, undigested results of his gluttony and vomit out amid wraiths of smoke whatever he had eaten.[3]

His neighbours were upset by his cruel misfortune and decided to take him around the shrines of the saints. But his madness prevented this, so that they had to tie him up first. But he was too strong to be tied up, and the scheme seemed in danger. No one, even if he was a man of tested strength, tried to put the ropes on him without being knocked senseless by just one blow from the madman. But necessity is the mother of invention and they spread out rope nets in front of his wild dashes and got his feet entangled in them. So, netted by their ingenuity, he who surpassed them in strength succumbed to their cleverness. But, although his body was tied up, the evil spirit in his mind could not be tamed until his neighbours, having made the necessary preparations, began to take their patient round the saints.

On their journey they came to Malmesbury on the very eve of the festival of the sacred Ascension of our Lord and Saviour. Having heard and believed that holy Aldhelm had once been quick to cure such diseases, they stopped there. They approached the monks and told them about their pilgrimage and its cause. The monks promised the help of the saint, and were generous with their advice: the day was at hand, they said, on which the flesh of the Lord was taken up to heaven in joyful triumph. The hope of following their head had been given to all the other members, well, to those whose works had not belied their faith. And Aldhelm, a very special member of our Lord's body, had assuredly attained to the presence of his head through the merits of his deeds. So, for him no request was too difficult, as experience had often shown. The suppliants then poured forth their prayers to the merciful saint, not doubting that he would be ready to help all who prayed with complete faith. Visitors, uplifted by this supplication, were not lacking in giving the encouragement of which men of their type and education were capable. And the cure of the sick man which immediately followed showed that the prayers of country folk had not been unfruitful. For, once laid before the altar, he soon lost the wild savage look from his face and eyes and the writhings of his neck stopped as he fell into a gentle sleep. In this way he was freed from servitude to the devil, and restored

[1] An ancient military engine, used to hurl stones.
[2] A phrase used by Virgil of a crowd getting out of control (*Aeneid* 1:150).
[3] A description reminiscent of Virgil's description of the sleeping Cyclops (*Aeneid* 3:632).

to freedom of mind. And when his calm speech showed that he had regained his wits and sanity, the hearts of the bystanders were lifted up and their tongues loosed in praise of God and the saint.

Chapter 262 Miraculous cure of a cripple

There was another man in a similar condition. His hamstrings had stiffened up and reduced him to such misery that his only way of getting about was by using just his knees. If ever he went anywhere, it was on his knees that he shuffled along the pathways rough with dust, and on his knees that he made his way across muddy ground. And because his legs were bent close to his bottom, he appeared to be an animal rather than a human being. All looked upon him as a shapeless monster, just a lump of flesh, you might say, sent forth by nature in an untimely birth. He hardly ever lifted his face to the sky. He spent all his time looking down, a man condemned to the soil. It was a struggle to stay sane. All life had for him was an extension of his misery.

But he did consider carefully which saint he might ask for help: at one time this saint was efficacious, at another time that one. Some were good at driving out devils, others came to help by curing diseases. But Christ, the author of all, was pre-eminent in all. And at that time there was a particular rumour abroad, which was in fact true, that at a certain place, called only by the name of Christchurch, that is the church of Christ,[1] great deeds of goodness were being done. No human trouble was too great for Christ to drive away there. So the cripple hired a carriage and determined to travel to Christchurch. Malmesbury provided him with a stopping place on the journey.

It happened to be three days after a festival and the recent talk about the miracles of the saint was still fresh. For during that festival need had brought together more sick people than usual at Malmesbury, and the holiness of the blessed father had sent them home cured. The cripple listened to the stories, and in the meantime went into the church. If his prayers were unsuccessful, he would continue on his journey in the morning. It was then Saturday, and men were waiting for the dawn of the Lord's day. The goodness of the saint was completely amazing. Almost as soon as the cripple passed under the roof of the church, the weakness of his limbs was somewhat reduced and he felt a kind of healing course through his whole body. This gave him confidence and more eagerness for what remained. He stayed awake there throughout the whole night

And now the day was at hand,[2] which was to bring the poor fellow more help than he could have hoped for. While the monks were processing through the cloisters as usual, the cripple, spotting from afar the empty choir, crept thither, moving his hams along with the help of small cushions. His whole body collapsed in a heap before the altar, just as if he had experienced an

[1] In Hampshire.
[2] For this phrase see Virgil's *Aeneid* 2:132.

ecstasy, his eyes closed and he fell asleep. But he was awoken by the noise of the singing of the returning monks, and all of a sudden sprang quickly up. He was cured. He looked at the monks and they looked at him. He was as surprised as they were at the unexpected cure. He told them frankly why he had come, but did not know how he had stood up so quickly. The happening was believed and praises given back to God, the miracle being made much of especially by the guest master, who the day before had welcomed their visitor as a cripple and now saw him standing upright. Healed of his debility, the cured man gave thanks to his healer, and for all the rest of his life remained a soldier sworn to his service.

Chapter 263 Malmesbury acquires a relic of St Ouen

This was the time that the remains of the blessed Ouen, archbishop of Rouen,[1] were brought to our monastery. This is how it happened: queen Emma, on the death of king Æthelred, had crossed over to her brother in Normandy, thinking that there was no safety for her among the Danes, who had gained possession of England.[2] So she stayed in Rouen for a long time, and by her gifts won over to friendship some monks of St Ouen including the sacristan, her intention being precisely to buy for herself the body of the blessed archbishop. Christianity has become so cheapened while greed has grown so great that we treat the bodies of the saints as merchandise, and put up for sale their blessed remains. To begin with, the sacristan held up his hands in horror at the monstrous proposal. But later he was forced to concur by the needs of his nephew, who had been taken prisoner in France and was looking for a ransom, and made the sale for which the queen asked. Being now the owner of these rich spoils, she returned to England when calmer times smiled upon the land and placed the remainder of the body at Canterbury, but kept the head in her own secret possession.

When after many years her son Edward became king, his royal spirit was woken to hostility against his mother by the memory of past events.[3] She had not been very generous in her treatment of her son, while he was passing through his teenage years, and so he ordered all his mother's effects to be ransacked, down to the last pennyworth. This actually happened, and, while the others were gaping at the treasures, a goldsmith who had been in the queen's secret, made off with the head of the saint in its shrine. He deposited it with his brother, who was a monk at Malmesbury, thinking that a monk was the most suitable recipient for such relics. And when he died soon after, he left it as a lasting memorial of himself to the monastery which he had distinguished with such riches. This story does not come from scattered references in untrustworthy writers, but from eyewitnesses of mature years and the greatest

---

[1] 640–83.
[2] Emma's brother was Richard II, duke of Normandy. Æthelred died in 1016.
[3] Edward the Confessor became king in 1042. Stenton discusses the reasons for the bad relations between mother and son (*Anglo-Saxon England*, pp. 426–7).

reliability and learning. But that is now enough about Ouen, as anyone who reads the large volumes relating his deeds, carefully compiled by our forebears and deservedly very famous, will conclude that it is no part of my job to write about the miracles of this archbishop.

Chapter 264 Turold, the first Norman abbot of Malmesbury

Meanwhile, upon the death of abbot Brihtwald which I have mentioned,[1] bishop Herman thought about filling the vacant abbacy with his own see. But his attempt was scotched by the monks, with the help of earls Godwine and Harold,[2] and their leader, Brihtric, the prior, was made abbot and ruled the monastery over a golden period of seven years. But when William, duke of Normandy, became king of England, although Brihtric was still alive, he pushed in as abbot a monk of Fécamp called Turold, to whom he was indebted for his great services to him. But when William later realised that he had done something wrong and was unhappy that he had been persuaded by the ambitions of a man in a hurry, he consoled the exiled Brihtric for his loss by the gift of the abbacy of Burton. As for Turold, who was ruling his subjects like a tyrant, he was removed by the king to the rich abbey of Peterborough, which in its marshland site was then being attacked by Hereward and his band of outlaws. William said about the matter, 'Because Turold is behaving more like a soldier than an abbot, for the splendour of God I shall find for him a foe who is a good match for his attacks. He can have Peterborough as a field for his courage and generalship, and practise his fighting there.'[3]

Chapter 265 Abbot Warin (1070–1081) shows little respect for English saints

Turold's place was taken by Warin, a monk from Lire,[4] who showed his capabilities best in accustoming the monks to the rule. But otherwise he was of little use to the church, being swept off his feet by his hopes for greater distinction. He was apt to empty the monks' purses and purloin funds from all sources. But he did not just hide away these greedily acquired acquisitions. No, he squandered the property of the church both at home and overseas, in order to increase his favour among the nobles and to be able to make a display before men who had once seen him as a poor man. As soon as he became abbot, he showed no respect for the deeds of his predecessors, and bodies of the saints affected him with a sort of fever and nausea. Buried at Malmesbury were the bones of Meldum of blessed memory and of others, who, once abbots there

[1] At the end of ch. 258.
[2] For a full account of this incident see ch. 83.
[3] Turold arrived at Peterborough and 'with him one hundred and sixty Frenchmen, all fully armed' (Anglo-Saxon Chronicle, *s.a.* 1070). He subsequently saddled Peterborough with the military service of sixty knights, a very high figure. See Knowles, *The Monastic Order*, p. 114.
[4] An abbey on the river Risle.

and later bishops of many places, had given orders for themselves to be buried at Malmesbury out of respect for their patron Aldhelm. And men of old had shown them respect by reverently placing them in two stone containers on either side of the altar, with wooden partitions between each man's bones. And now it was these bones that were all piled together like a heap of rubbish as though they were the remains of low-caste slaves, and thrown out of the doors of their church. And to complete his villainy, he even showed the door to John Scot,[1] whom the monks had revered with almost the same veneration as they showed to St Aldhelm. Warin showed them no consideration and gave orders for all of them to be tucked away and blocked in by stones in a far corner of the church of St Michael, which he himself had ordered to be widened and heightened.[2] The deed was bad enough, but he made it worse by the words of this witty piece of sarcasm, 'Let him who can do any better help others.'

Men of today behave so badly.[3] It is impossible to find a reproach suitable for castigating the audacity and boundless effrontery of the fellow. Are we mannikins, creatures born only to mock, going to destroy all that the blessed Dunstan and the other giants of scholarship and holiness made themselves or allowed to be made? But I will check my pen and rein in my indignation. Even Warin, by his great reverence for St Aldhelm, alleviated or wiped out his offences against the other saints. Admittedly, he was doubtful and uncertain about his sanctity to begin with, since he did not give his backing to prayers made to Aldhelm asking for a miracle to be shown, but in his hour of doubt he was brought up against the following act of holiness by the saint, which dispelled the clouds of uncertainty and flooded him with the clear light of certitude.

Chapter 266 The cure of a fisherman converts abbot Warin

An inhabitant of the Isle of Wight earned a livelihood by his skill in fishing. He was well known to his fellow fishermen, and had built up a good store of possessions at home. But one day while he was working hard at his usual job, he was struck by a blast of wind, and thick cloud arose and filled his face and eyes as he rowed. At first, when visibility was removed, he just laughed, thinking that the sudden darkness of the day would soon go away. But when the darkness kept getting thicker and thicker, he realised that he was truly blind and shouted out the news of his calamity to his friends who were engaged in the same occupation along the sea coast. His disaster was a sign to the others to take a break from their fishing. They threw away the catch they had taken, and all with one effort worked together to bring him back to shore. Having

---

[1] See ch. 240.

[2] Warin's action was not unique. Even Lanfranc had to be converted by Anselm to the attitude towards English saints which he shows in ch. 269, and Knowles gives other examples of disrespect shown by Norman abbots (*The Monastic Order*, p. 119). On the other hand, there were Norman abbots who thought differently. See Loyn, *The English Church*, pp. 82–3. The matter is also discussed by Burton, *Monastic and Religious Orders*, pp. 24–5.

[3] A sentence used by Cicero in his prosecution of Catiline in 63 BC.

landed him on the bank, they led him by the hand and got him back to his house. This happening gave the fishermen plenty to talk about. They had long talks and debates among themselves, discussing whether the wind which took the light from the innocent fisherman and plunged him into night was accidental or sent by the devil. He himself, with his sight gone, wept over each bit of his sorry situation, but still persistently went on questioning people about a cure for it. The answer was that he had no hope in human aid, and that he should hasten for succour to the arms of God and the saints:[1] this he could do, very conveniently, in the church of Christ which I have mentioned,[2] as it could be reached by a short crossing from the island to the mainland.

The blind man thought this was a good idea and got into a boat with his friends. The efforts of the rowers and the favouring winds helped equally to land him on the mainland shore with very little delay. In his desire for a cure, he spent three whole years there, but in vain. The Lord Jesus was postponing his cure in order to arouse his burning desire for it, so that when the remedy at last arrived, the long delays and the trouble caused by his wishes for it might make it all the more pleasing to him. At the end of three years his uncertainty was ended, for a heavenly vision in his sleep advised him to waste no time in going to Malmesbury, if he wanted to be made well. As soon as day broke, he set out on his happy journey, full of joyful hope. With a companion going in front to guide his tottering steps, he came to Malmesbury. He stayed there for seven days, waiting for the divine promise to be fulfilled, keeping hunger at bay in the meantime by the food obtained by his prayers from the almoner.

The eighth day, a Sunday, had arrived, when, prostrate before a crucifix in the church, he realised that he had dreamed no empty vision. His eyes recovered their sight, as blood burst out and dripped from them, just as, when milkmaids are milking, a jet of copious milk shoots from the udders of the cows. The man who had been blind let loose shouts of joy, and asking for a vessel, so that the holy floor should not suffer damage from the blood, he caught it in the vessel as it flowed out. All this happened in the presence of the people of the town and before the eyes of all the monks. The honour paid to the saint by the Normans was greatly increased. The islander threw away in contempt the stick with which he had felt for dangerous objects in his path, and set off on the return journey to his familiar fireside without it.

Chapter 267 The second translation of the relics of St Aldhelm (1078)

The abbot had no excuse left for delay after seeing this, and began busily making plans for paying proper honours to our most valued confessor. The late whirlwind had died down, and there was no fear of the enemy. So it seemed a good time for the saint to come forth from his stone cell, in which he

---

[1] For an eloquent sermon on this text see Eamon Duffy, *The Stripping of the Altars* (New Haven, 1992), pp. 198–200.
[2] In ch. 262.

had been imprisoned for fear of the Danes.[1] It was not right that stones should be pressing down into the ground those bones which the glory of their miracles was lifting to the skies. So Warin's plan was to dig them out of their tomb and place them in the shrine. And so that this holy happening should proceed with all due ceremony, he ordained a three-day fast for the people. Then on the day of Pentecost itself, helped by Serlo abbot of Gloucester,[2] he went to the tomb, lifted various things out of the way and removed the stone. He looked inside and saw that the bones were still whole and together. Realising that this truth supported the story of the monks, he shut the tomb up again until a week from that day. They were waiting to celebrate the saint's birthday then, as the changes of the paschal moon which bring round that festival mean that the birthday has sometimes to be celebrated before Pentecost and sometimes afterwards. Also present at the show to help in the work and share in the lifting of the burden was a monk called Hubert, who for a long time had been suffering from an internal disease. He was racked by the pain even more fiercely than usual on that day, but as he began examining the relics more carefully, their fragrance hit him in the face and made him step back. The fragrance sent a current of health running through his bones, which reached his inmost marrow. And right up to the day of his death this monk experienced nothing else which tore at his vitals and disordered his insides. The story spread, as it was frequently narrated both by Hubert and also particularly by those others who had often seen him previously almost in danger of death because of the seriousness of the disease. The following Sunday, the venerable Osmund, bishop of Salisbury,[3] was brought in, and the finishing touches were put to the whole scheme as the bones were laid decently in the shrine, amid outpourings of joy from the people. No supply of eloquence would be sufficient to write of all the miracles which have taken place there since that day, whether poured forth in full view or felt privately by people in need. At this point, with the help of Christ, I shall include some which seem to be germane to my undertaking. This second translation happened ninety-one years after their translation by the blessed Dunstan, 368 years after Aldhelm's passing, in 1078, twelve years after the arrival of the Normans.

Chapter 268 A fratricide from Cologne finds forgiveness at Malmesbury

The large city of Cologne is the mother city of Germany, as crowded with merchants as it is packed with the shrines of the saints. A citizen of this town, who more by bad luck than by design had killed his brother, concealed the deed for many years so that no one should know of it. But it was no good, for, as Augustine says, 'The guilty mind is its own torment and in life anticipates the punishments for the dead.' The taint of his guilt fed on the poor fellow's

---

[1] See ch. 255.
[2] For Serlo see ch. 155.
[3] For a short general account of Osmund as bishop of William's own diocese, see ch. 83.

mind and the denizens of hell were present to his imagination. At long last he showed the wounds of his ulcerated conscience to a doctor, Anno, archbishop of the city, a man as severe as any.[1] But when he had fiercely condemned the guilty person, as the atrocity of the deed demanded, he then added gentle advice. This was excellent and followed the Gospel example of first pouring wine on the wounded man to wash clean the festering wounds and then adding oil, to comfort the sinner with the hope of forgiveness.[2] He sentenced him to a seven-year repentance, in which he was to go round the churches of the saints, with his arms and his chest bound in chains. He was to wear on his chest the very breastplate and on his arms the very spear which had spilled his brother's blood in his murderous attack on him, so that the weapons which had caused his guilt should also be the penalty of his punishment. He was to grow accustomed to fasting and silence, lightening these heavy burdens with his hopes of the good, and by the lessening of his vices to build up a bank balance of virtues. Only let him endure, and what he was now undertaking for his pardon would one day be for his glory, and what was now his punishment would be his reward.

The penitent carried out these orders, adding some other crosses in addition and personally inflicting strong pain on his own body as though it were an enemy. He went to Rome. He got as far as Jerusalem. This was a bold and remarkable undertaking at that time, when the roads thither had not yet been opened up by the courage of our fellow Christians. While he was praying before the sepulchre in Jerusalem, having just managed to gain admittance, his breastplate split into fragments through the goodness of God. He returned and travelled round the whole of Europe, storm-tossed by many perils on land and sea.[3] He sought out our own monastery, and this was the goal of his labours. For here, while he was lying face down before the blessed tomb of our confessor, he won his pardon. His vehement prayers knocked on heaven's door, entered the starry sphere and brought down help from the powers above. His arms were set free of the chains; indeed these iron bands, when struck from on high, were knocked more than fifteen feet away from him. The penitent was in a turmoil as he fainted. But when he was sprinkled with cold water, he came to and gave thanks and praise to almighty God, and all who were present joined in his song. They could have no doubts about the miracle, for they had noticed him in his dreadful chains for many days previously being fed by alms from the monks.

Chapter 269 Aldhelm helps Folkwine and bishop Osmund's archdeacon

And now it should not be a trial of my readers' patience, if I recount a similar kind of miracle, as it happened to a different person and I shall recount it in a

---

[1] Anno was archbishop of Cologne 1055–75.
[2] As in the parable of the Good Samaritan, Luke 10:34.
[3] Virgil uses a similar phrase of Aeneas at *Aeneid* 1:3.

different style. Recently I described the cure of a crippled man of advanced years;[1] I shall now tell the same story about a boy. He was called Folkwine, and he had come misshapen from his mother's womb. His upper part down to the waist was that of a man, but the rest of him, unspeakably, was a horse or something indescribable with no name. The calves of his legs had no natural flexibility and they were so firmly fixed to his buttocks that they could not be unjoined. So certain persons, driven on by spite or incredulity, laid hands on him in order to make the division. But this caused great pain to the unhappy lad, who let out dreadful shrieks and called down savage curses on his assailants. For they saw a harmless boy without any cares, who was always ready for a laugh and a game, and they remained uncertain whether he might not have learned from his teacher how to pretend that his calves were fixed to his buttocks, so that by this device he might attract more alms from people taking pity on him. But when, as I have said, their attempt at a cure proved fruitless, they believed the deformity was genuine and pitied him like everybody else. By now the boy had gone from ten to twelve or thirteen, and the older he got, the more unable he was to walk as his tendons stiffened the more inflexibly. He was a particular object of pity to the townspeople of Malmesbury, where he was fed by the monks, since in his attempts to crawl somewhere his deformity caused him to stick to the spot in the mud of the roads. He would thrash away in the mire, filling the air with his cries until someone was moved by pity to pick up the lad in his arms.

But Aldhelm, two years after his second translation, undid the stiffness of that awful fastening. Aldhelm's birthday fell that year on the first day of Pentecost, but its celebration had been postponed to the second day, and on that day the lad lay down behind the choir, and gentle sleep stole over his limbs.[2] The monks, having finished their night offices, had begun their morning praises. They were singing the verse,

> Often at his sacred tomb
> The limbs of the afflicted sick
> Are then restored to health.

While this was being sung, the lad saw in his sleep a person, who did not exceed the normal height but who was taller than the smallest, come and sit beside him in a kindly fashion. His beard and hair were white, his face not intimidating or threatening but promising good things, and from his clothing and staff he looked like a bishop. Sitting down beside the lad, as I have said, he was seen to stroke his legs gently and gradually to straighten them out and restore them to their natural form. The bystanders were amazed to see the sleeping boy stretch out his legs and to hear his tendons creak, just like the cracking in the finger joints if someone tries to stretch out his hands too abruptly. The miracle and the singing of the monks happening together woke

---

[1] In ch. 262.
[2] Compare Virgil's phrases at *Aeneid* 4:522 and 8:405–6.

Folkwine from his sleep. With no effort he stood on his feet, as everybody stared in amazement. At once with the delight of a child but the determination of a man he broke into a run and threw himself down before the altar. Then the people, applauding the miracle, ran up from all sides. They gave thank-offerings for the healing and made a pile of them for the saint.

This miracle was regarded as such a wonder that the monks quickly sent a letter to announce it to the abbot, who was absent at the royal court. The abbot thought he should show the letter to archbishop Lanfranc, and that famously learned man, measuring Aldhelm's merits from the miracle, promulgated a law throughout all England which ordered that Aldhelm should forthwith be regarded and worshipped as a saint. Also immediately an annual fair was instituted on his festival,[1] so that those who were not attracted by the confessor's sanctity might at least be brought in by their desire for a bargain.

It was at this time that the most respected Osmund, bishop of the same diocese, begged for some remains of the saint. He thought it was fitting, and said so, that he should have a share in the relics of his most famous predecessor, whose see he had filled: it would be advantageous to himself, and pleasing to the saint, who with a small impairment of his wholeness would gain new honours and win great favours. Nor did abbot Warin have any difficulty with this request, for he saw himself being won over to agreement by Osmund's reasoning. And so he gave the bishop the bone of Aldhelm's left arm, which the bishop always held in especial love and honour. Indeed Osmund acquired a silver coffer, made with cunning craftsmanship out of sumptuous materials, to enclose the bone. It was now the festival of All Saints, the day marked out for the dedication ceremony at Salisbury. The bishop was engaged in this when there came into his mind the illness of his archdeacon Everard, who had taken to his bed and was completely wasting away. Orders were sent to him to get himself brought to the church by whatever means. The sick man obeyed, and came to the place, carried on his servants' shoulders as if they were carrying out the lifeless body of their master for burial. Everard himself was unable to move either his feet or any of his limbs by himself except his tongue in their natural service. The bishop's hopes for a cure rather failed him when he saw the whiteness of his face and the weakness of his whole body. But he soon recovered his confidence and struck a flame of faith on the tinder of Aldhelm's past goodness. He also by his encouraging words struck sparks of belief in the sick man's breast,[2] to stop him doubting that he could be healed by the virtue of the saint. The outcome of the event added strength to their faith. They both obtained the result they longed for – the bishop as he held out the water which had been seasoned by the dipping in it of the sacred bone, and Everard as he gulped down salvation together with the water. So that the

---

[1] For the valuable privilege, granted to some monasteries, of holding a fair, see Burton, *Monastic and Religious Orders*, p. 245.

[2] Virgil uses both 'struck flames on the tinder' and 'struck sparks' of the lighting of a literal fire at *Aeneid* 1:174 and 175.

miracle might be better witnessed to and nobody left in any doubt about it, at this same mass, in addition to the singing of alleluias, a sonorous organ pealed forth in its own distinctive fashion. It was not unlike Peter's mother-in-law, when she was careful to wait on the Lord after he had healed her, except that she won back her health through the prayers of others, while Everard got it through his own belief.[1]

Chapter 270 The double cure of archdeacon Hubald

The same bishop had another archdeacon called Hubald. He was a man with no small experience of the liberal arts, but who, because of his stammering, could only expound them inadequately to an audience. He had shown the saint long-lasting devotion and support, ever since he had been cured of a painful disease by Aldhelm's efforts, while once staying at Malmesbury on his feast day. At that time the attacks of pain in his neck and shoulders were so bad that they stopped him sleeping or eating, but just by touching the bier, which he had approached all huddled up, he, as I might say, stole back his health. For the usual custom of the sacristans is, after the procession, so to fit the shrine across the doors of the church that nobody can gain open access to it unless his body is lowered under the shrine. But whoever comes up to it then in the fullness of faith gains his desires. It hardly ever happens that someone goes away with his prayer unheard. The bold faith of those making offerings strives to obtain from the saint for just a farthing or a penny the whole total of many prayers.

Well, this same archdeacon Hubald, while at Salisbury, was groaning aloud when troubled by the same illness as before. The pain had exceeded its previous extent. Now it was so persistently affecting not only his neck and shoulders but even his arm right down to the end of his finger nails that he could not even lift his hand to his mouth or make use of it for anything. It was then the day of the Ascension, on which throughout the whole of Christendom a properly prepared solemn procession takes place. The relics were brought out of their cases, and the arm of the blessed Aldhelm was put to be carried with the rest. The sight of the arm strengthened the archdeacon's wavering faith and awoke his dormant memories, making him confident that he would be cured of the same disease by the merits of Aldhelm, who had cured him once before. He pleaded with the bishop, begging and praying that he should be allowed to carry the arm in the procession, however little that had to do with his office: for he believed that his carrying of this sacred burden would greatly help him to win back his health. The bishop was glad to see such faith. And as he also strongly desired the recovery of one who was his friend and, as I have said, a man with more than a smattering of scholarship, he picked up the relic

---

[1] The healing of Peter's mother-in-law is described in Luke 4:38–9. Everard's cure was permanent. He was bishop of Norwich 1121–45. Matthew comments, 'once again it is the saints of England's monastic past who steal the limelight from the Norman bishop' (*The Norman Conquest*, p. 182).

from the altar with his own hand and gave it to Hubald to carry. What I am going to say may seem incredible, except to those of us who are accustomed to these works of Aldhelm. The moment the archdeacon put out the fingers of his bad hand to touch the relics, the pain vanished from his arm, the use of his fingers suddenly returned to normal, the affliction of his shoulders disappeared and the swelling in the sick man's neck subsided. He was just on the point of bursting into eager speech, when he was stopped by the bishop asking him why he had such a happy smile on his face. Hubald told him the good news, as far as his joy permitted, and stayed a long time, effusively praising the saint and celebrating his power.

Then there are the daily works of Aldhelm, the preludes to his major miracles. In any account of these small cures the goodness of our praiseworthy father would be just as visible, for we can see him not disdaining the petty, although, as we know, he had power over the big. Though I am not sure whether it is any less virtuous to make easy demonstrations daily than to put on a grand show once in a while.

Chapter 271 Godefrey as abbot (1081–1105)

On the death of abbot Warin, he was succeeded immediately within a fortnight by Godefrey, a monk of Jumièges. During his abbacy his hard work increased greatly the reputation of our church. The religious life was improved. A vast quantity of beautiful objects were obtained, considering the very little opportunity so busy a man could have for this. Some books were written, or rather the foundations for a library were laid.[1] If I draw attention to this activity of his, I think I am acting within my rights, seeing that in this particular department I take second place to none of my predecessors. Indeed, if it is not boastful to say so, I have easily surpassed all of them. I hope there will be someone to look after what has now been built up. I myself have collected much material for reading, in emulation of the vigour of the man who deserves praise in this regard at least.[2] I have done my best to further his laudable beginnings. We now need someone to see that our labours are not wasted. The monks, who could only stammer out their vernacular writings, had their education completed. The work of God was planned on generous lines, and immediately put into effect, with the result that no monastery

[1] These presumably were the books which enabled William to become a polymath. The first Norman abbots in general provided a real impetus to the foundation of libraries. Knowles cites Paul of St Albans, Lanfranc at Canterbury and William of St Calais at Durham as others who made a similar contribution (*The Monastic Order*, p. 523). At the same time it must be remembered that in William's time a 'library' meant a collection of books rather than a special room. See F. Wormald, 'The Monastic Library', in *Gatherings in Honor of Dorothy E. Miner* (Baltimore, 1974), pp. 93–109.

[2] William was much younger than Godefrey (see the last two sentences of this chapter). In his own day he followed Godefrey's example in building up the collection of books at Malmesbury. The 'material for reading' could well include some of William's own compilations, e.g. his book of Roman history with extracts from different authors. For his compilations see James, *Two Ancient English Scholars*, p. 17.

throughout England did it better than Malmesbury, and many were worse. Godefrey himself would be among the first to arrive, and among the last to leave. His amiability won over the good, and his severity terrified the guilty. He was prone to anger but could immediately by a gentle response check or stop the very anger which he had stirred up himself. He was restrained in his frugality, or, as was said, over-restrained. He was often content with just one dish for himself, and between breakfast and dinner would only drink once rather than whenever he felt like it. He was so keen on elegance that he would allow nothing to be brought to the table which had not been carefully prepared in the most exquisite fashion, and uncouth words or actions were kept severely in check.

After he became abbot he was completely celibate, though before this there were a few stains on his character, but his abbacy was disgraced by one sin, and that a huge one. King William II had imposed an impossible tribute upon England with which he planned to buy Normandy from his brother Robert, and Godefrey, so that he might have an easy way of collecting his share, shamefully despoiled his church of the treasures amassed by the care of the men of old. He was following the advice of his worst counsellors, whom I could name, if the sin of the leader could be alleviated by his having companions in crime, but, 'They are equal who bear crime's stain.'[1] Indeed on one day twelve copies of the Gospels, eight crosses and eight shrines were stripped of their encrustations of gold and silver. But it turned out well, for the meagre sum obtained, a mere seventy-two marks, frustrated his greed and was not sufficient for his wishes. But the following night in a dream he saw a man with threatening face and gestures attack him by throwing boiling hot water on his face together with the jar. Awoken by his fright, he soon realised that his dream was true from the punishment that followed, for first his face and soon his whole body was attacked by that horrible illness, the king's disease, and he passed away. It was not the milder type of the disease but that particularly disfiguring one, in which pustules break out over the whole body and which is caused by melancholy, the worst of the humours. It was the saint's customary, well-known way of acting in all matters that he would put up with insults for a long time, but that when he had once decided to endure them no longer, he would expose his attacker to the gaze of the whole world. In many cases we had laughed at this actually happening, and in many others we anticipated its happening with eager hope.

On the body of the dead abbot was found a bronze hoop which went round his whole belly. The skin by now had grown over it, and it had penetrated his very vitals. When it was being shown to the people as a miracle, a monk came forward who had been in the abbot's secrets and said that an iron hoop, which had been driven into the flesh in the same way, had been recently broken by the divine virtue, and so a bronze hoop had been fitted, since that kind of metal lasts for ever. The idea had been to impose a limit upon his appetite, so that if

[1] Lucan, *Pharsalia* 5:290.

his belly protruded more than usual it would not indicate the pleasures of the table but a punishment: he had bound himself with an oath not to reveal it, as long as the abbot enjoyed the breath of life. But because nothing is so good that it cannot be given an unfavourable interpretation, his practice was criticised by these spiteful lines,

> To mortify our flesh from vice is right
> But not with iron's use to gain this end.
> Our abbot should have died a natural death;
> The which forestalled, it means he killed himself.

To which one could reply in the same number of lines,

> To tame the body every means is right;
> Examples teach it, our dear faith upholds it.
> He did not seek an early death with iron,
> But iron reins to put upon his vices.

Our most dear confessor did not have a holiday from performing miracles during the time of this abbot. In fact it seems his splendour flashed out all the more, so that our hard-working abbot might smile with glad joy at all the miracles. Two miracles which I shall record happened before my time; the others I saw with my own eyes and am glad to have done so.

Chapter 272 Cure of a wife with a spinal condition during Godefrey's abbacy

There lived a woman in the neighbourhood, who was not so lowly born that she was a complete plebeian nor so exalted by her birth that she had lofty aspirations. Her middle-class station had led to the usual middle-class collection of belongings. Once beyond the years of puberty she found a husband of the same class, and by her careful attentions won his love. They thought alike, she had a pretty face, and she easily became pregnant. They took pleasure in their moderate means, and had no desire for anything else, seeing that they had enough to live on, got on well together and were both healthy. But as generally happens in this life, something occurred to spoil their happiness The woman fell ill. All the muscles in her body stiffened up. At first she crept through the house at a snail's pace, but soon was flat on her bed, unable to move. She wasted away with this disease for five years. During this time she used up on doctors and their expenses all the essentials which she thought she had scraped together for the house. When the frequent demands had used up all their money and no more was coming in, this house, once so carefully managed, even went in want of its daily bread. Once hunger had arrived, it drove out the old tenants and brought in new ones.[1] Her fickle husband, forgetting her loyalty and putting no value on their intimacy, divorced the woman and ran

---

[1] A reminiscence of Virgil: *Eclogues* 9:4.

away from his wife's affection. So, once he had departed and rented out their rooms in a shameful transaction to get money for food, the sick woman had to be supported by the charity of others.

But at long last God looked down upon her with eyes of pity and encouraged her in a dream with this pronouncement, 'If you want to get better, go to the monastery at Malmesbury. There, through the merits of Aldhelm, you will get what you are looking for.' She did not see the speaker, but she took the words she had heard as a good omen, shook off her sleep and, finding she could move her limbs, rejoiced that she was already a lot better. She thought she was over her trouble and hurried to put her dream to the test. But when she tried to walk around the house, she made very little progress, and so she was put in a cart to be taken to the abbey. She arrived there in high hopes a few days before the saint's feast day. Soon she made her way through the very densely packed crowd and lay down before the altar. She asked the saint, who had made a promise to her in her dream and given her a pledge in the movement of her limbs, to restore her to perfect health. Her passionate prayer and unrestrained cries did not fail her. To the praises of men, she was speedily restored to wholeness by God and his saint. Perfectly well again, she had as many witnesses to the genuineness of the miracle as there were townspeople present from near by or country people from outlying parts. She went on to live a long and happy life. By a decree of the courts she got her runaway husband given back into her arms. For his part he was happy to accept the decree, seeing that he had heard she had never been unfaithful to him, however extreme her poverty and no matter how much pressure had been put upon her by lustful men.

Chapter 273 Cure of a young girl with a similar condition

The misery of a similar, or worse, spinal condition was being endured by a girl not yet old enough for marriage who lived in a village called Pucklechurch. For the spine of her back was so bent that her cheeks almost touched her knees. And, what is more, her knees themselves were bent up into a cone shape so that she could not crawl along using cushions, like most people with that disease, nor go anywhere unless she was carried in somebody else's arms. She was twelve and had had the disease for six years. Her life had been divided into two halves of sickness and health, and the disease had got worse as she had grown older. But then her twin brother, out of pity for his sister's misfortunes, to which the further complication of poverty was adding its weight, put her in a cart and took her to Malmesbury.[1] He did it once, and he did it a second time, just when the year was getting round to the saint's anniversary, but in vain. On both occasions the girl went back home without being cured and without the gift she was seeking. Not that there was anything sluggish about the saint's holy powers. They were always readily available to come to the aid of all who

[1] Pucklechurch is just to the east of Bristol. This was a cart-ride of some fifteen miles.

called upon him in faith. I suppose it was either because the belief of those who carried the girl wavered as their faith grew cold (for what does a girl of twelve know about belief or disbelief?) or it was so that any miracle might have wider publicity, since the town could not fail to be aware of a girl who had been so often brought to the shrine and so often taken away. So she was brought a third year, and a third outpouring of prayer met with no answer. The brother got fed up, lost all his belief, and went back home.

But the girl stayed on until the day of our Lord's Ascension, which was to follow our festival in two days time. And now the solemn day of the triumph of Jesus Christ had arrived, on which our famous patron saint rarely or never refused to perform some outstanding work. On this day the shrine was brought forth to the people, and the doors were shut, as I have said,[1] so that no one could enter the church unless he bent up double and went in under the shrine. The vergers had done their customary job and brought the saint's body out of the church; but the life-giving force which bestows health stayed inside with the sick girl. She lay prone on the floor in front of the crucifix. She heard the joyful shouts of the pilgrims, and she wept all the more in the depths of her heart, her own sorrow made double by the gladness of others. But in a moment she was touched by the divine healing and rose to her feet. The stiffness in her knees unwrapped itself, her spine straightened and she sprang forward to meet the saint and give him thanks as he returned into the church. It is impossible to describe all the joyful congratulations she received or all the cries that witnessed to the miracle of 'I have seen it with my own eyes! I know it's true! This is the girl who was doubled up, and is now well!'

But it is not good enough to make known what one has heard, unless a writer is also keen to add those things which God has granted him to see.[2] And when I do this, my reader, if he is a fair and unprejudiced judge, ought to believe me, just as much as he himself would want to be believed, if he were telling or writing the story of some famous event of his own day. I do not suppose that anyone will say that I should not have trusted my eyes, or that I should not have praised God by writing down what I saw. The first would be unbelievably stupid, and the second arrogantly ungrateful. Indeed I seem to have discharged a great debt of gratitude to the saints of my country, but at the same time not to have left without honour my own master and patron, who has thought me worthy of praising him so far by giving me the life which makes it possible and the necessary learning and knowledge. And praise for his famous acts ought to be given to a man of so many obvious virtues, whose equal could not be produced from among the philosophers of old, for all their longings. They taught what ought to be done. Aldhelm actually did it, and the second is greater. A simple belief in the truth is more than eloquently expressed, fine-sounding lies. The miracles performed after his death bear witness to Aldhelm's devotion to God while he was alive. The ones which I

---

[1] In ch. 270.
[2] Namely, the miracles described in chs. 274–8.

have seen for myself compel me to believe in the truth of all of them. For those in the past merit our belief in those of the present, and recent miracles confirm the account of those of old.

Chapter 274 Aldhelm cures Ernulf de Hesding

Let there be brought on to the stage Ernulf de Hesding, one of the most illustrious of the nobles of England,[1] admired for his knowledge of agriculture, and admired for his generosity in alleviating the needs of the poor. He was so exact in paying his tithes, that if he found a barn untaxed and untithed, he would give orders for everything to be taken out of it and tithed on the spot. He had discovered more than once that his keenness in avoiding infringements of tithe led to an increase in the yield from his estates through the divine favour. His hands became so badly infected by disease that besides black ulcers dripping with pus they were bent up, their nerves twitching and moving convulsively. He could not put them to any use. He could not, shameful though it is even to tell of it, use them to wipe away the remains of food from his mouth. In his helplessness he had to be fed, and to his shame another's hand had to wash him. And so he decided to go to Malmesbury, to try the services of a very famous physician there called Gregory.[2] This physician used all the tricks of the trade, as abbot Godefrey had commanded this and the patient had paid for his services, but in vain. In the end he said that the disease was incurable and would have to be left to chance, but he did show himself a good man by not taking the patient's money, and so not cheating a sick man desperate for a cure by taking his gifts of money with no result. Anyway, abbot Godefrey thought that Ernulf should make some trial of the saint's miracles, and ordered his servants to bring out some balsam found in St Aldhelm's tomb and rub it on the earl's hands. A beautiful thing happened. As soon as a drop of the precious liquid touched his hand, the trembling in the nerves stiffened into stillness, the flow of pus dried up, and, to put it in a word, in a few days he was completely well. It can be seen that this miracle brought about an increase in the earl's faith, for ignoring his personal ties and not bothering about his pile of possessions, he set out on a pilgrimage to Jerusalem, not expecting he would ever return.

Chapter 275 Cure of a lewd demoniac when William was a boy

Among the crowd of genuine pilgrims who came to the festival there was also a sprinkling of scallywags who earned an easily won crust by making their audience laugh at the jokes they thought up. When I was a boy, there arrived at

---

[1] The Domesday Book records Ernulf as owning land in six counties. He was the father-in-law of Matilda, natural daughter of King Henry I.

[2] Other monk-physicians were Faricius, abbot of Abingdon (ch. 88), and Baldwin (ch. 74) who became abbot of Bury St Edmunds. See Knowles, *The Monastic Order*, pp. 516–18, for the near monopoly of medical learning by the monks at this time.

Malmesbury one of these scallywags whose biting humour made him wittier than the rest. Indeed he was even expert at producing obscene gestures, if ever his verbal sallies fell flat and failed him. Even telling the story smacks of impropriety, but this scoundrel, when the saint's shrine had been brought outside the church, stood in front of it, and first of all bared his groin and polluted the bronze, and then disturbed the air with a loud fart. This of course got a laugh from the silly crowd, but the monks were deeply pained and hurt that the scallywag was rattling on unpunished.

Anyway, the confessor's ear did not fail to be at hand as they prayed for punishment, for the scoundrel had only just taken down his trousers, when in front of all the people in startling fashion he was possessed by a fierce devil and payed the penalty for his scandalous behaviour. Since he was spinning round like a top, foaming at the mouth like a boar surrounded by barking hounds and grinding and gnashing his teeth, it was obvious that he had passed into the control of the one who had inspired him to start on this horrendous sacrilege. His good friends laid strong hands on him and dragged him home willy-nilly. There they bound him to a post until it should seem that he was somewhat quieter in his mind, but he unexpectedly broke free. Knocking over the table on some guests who were dining in the house, he battered some with his fists and knocked others senseless with the vessels, placed near by, which he used as weapons. They all scattered, but his friends, judging that the poor chap should not be left alone, formed a tightly packed wedge, seized the madman a second time, tied him with tighter bonds and dragged him to Aldhelm's tomb. There after three nights' vigil and three days' fasting, while the monks prayed for him and won another's salvation with their own laments, he was cured not only of the devil but also, you might say more remarkably, of his lewdness. Ever afterwards he was self-controlled and gentle, although his eyes were frighteningly bloodshot so that he could always terrify us boys by rolling them round. We remembered that while he was sitting by the tomb before he was cured, he would rush at us with a staring look on his face, if he could not reach us with his filthy spit.

Chapter 276 Cure of a paralysed spinster from Killingham

A woman, who was a native of Killingham,[1] was spinning on a Saturday evening, as the day declined towards sunset. When the women who were spinning beside her advised her to put a stop to her work and show reverence for the Lord's day, she was so far from doing as they said that she even accused them of arrogance, in that they rebuked her when she was only doing what was necessary, and of folly and laziness, in that they did not do the same thing. Punishment followed her words, for she at once fell to the ground with part of her body paralysed and was within inches of death. She came to after her friends had repeatedly sprinkled her with water, and, recognising her fault, she

[1] In Lincolnshire.

wept at her calamity and prayed for pardon. But we do not catch hold of forgiveness as easily as we commit a sin. Our pleasures are transitory and fleeting, but sin fixes its root deep within us. So this woman spent very many years in going round and seeking assistance from many saints, with two crutches supporting her steps, which were now almost buried in a living corpse.

At last, when it seemed that all her efforts had failed and got her nowhere, she heard of the miracles done by the blessed Aldhelm and hurried to Malmesbury. She arrived just before Lent, and she spent all its forty days inside the church, never going outside more than once a day, while her fasting diminished her pile of sins. And now the acclamations of the Easter joy were making glad the hearts of men, and on the second day of the festival we were leading the pilgrims in procession. We were singing the hymn in which bishop Fulbert of Chartres[1] had very nicely put the Jews in the dilemma of giving back the buried Christ or worshipping the risen Christ. At this moment the woman, who was standing in front of the crucifix supported by her stick, fell to the ground more heavily than usual and crashed into the paving stones. Many rushed up to her, wishing to lift up the prostrate woman, as they were afraid that the violence of the fall had broken the limbs of the paralytic, but others of wiser judgement stopped them, saying that the outcome of the affair should be left to God, who would know how to deal with the matter properly. All, with expectant hearts, were keeping their faces fixed upon the woman,[2] when, with sparkling eyes and fingers that quivered, and finally with her whole body restored, she rose to her feet. The people of Malmesbury had got her firmly fixed in their minds because of the length of her stay, and in their certainty that a miracle had happened they opened their mouths in praise of God and their confessor.

Chapter 277 Cure of a dumb man from Calne

Calne is a village ten miles away from Malmesbury. Its territory shares a boundary with the abbey. A native of Calne, who was completely unable to speak, came to the festival in the same year, if I remember correctly. He was very well known in the area because of this distinguishing disability, and many experiments had proved that he was truly dumb. Indeed the governor of the province had more than once subjected him to torture so that a confession extracted by force that he was pretending to be dumb might establish the truth of the matter. That was a cruel thing to do, but cruelty is called for by the faking of some beggars, who will fake any disease you like to the mockery of God and men, just so that they can beg a penny or two by this play-acting and fill the hole in their belly. But the man from Calne would emit pitiful groans as

---

[1] Bishop of Chartres 1007–29.
[2] 'All were keeping their faces fixed on him' are words used by Virgil in *Aeneid* 2:1 of Dido and her court as they wait for Aeneas to tell the tale of Troy.

he was being tortured and his bruised spirit longed for the end to his troubles which was pleasing to God.

Well, although his tongue was dumb, there was nothing wrong with his brain, and he joined the crush of people hurrying to the festival. And to him alone was it granted to behold the saint. On the first occasion he saw him in front of the high altar walking near its base, and the monks as they sang were struck with amazement at the joy in his face which was closed to speech. For he tried desperately by finger signs and by opening his mouth as wide as he could to show what he had seen to the others, the clarity of whose vision had been dulled by the mass of their sins. But no words came out and his wish to speak was frustrated. And as the people near by were not gods so as to understand him, he was full of indignation and rushed into the crypt, which had then just been built. But he saw the same thing there as well, and as he was making a huge effort in his longing to speak, a monk who was present, guessing that something divine was afoot, plunged the fingers of the blessed Aldhelm's hand into his mouth as he tried to shout. Then indeed the dumb man, drawing his teeth far back out of reverence for the holy fingers and heaving up deep sighs, with a great struggle vomited forth a mangled lump of flesh, and together with the blood out came the words, 'Holy lord Aldhelm, help me.' That utterance was a happy augury for his speech being loosed both then and subsequently. And he did live on for some years afterwards, speaking without difficulty, except that the narrow passage of his throat meant that his vocal organs produced rather a harsh sound.

Chapter 278 Cure of a blind woman from Calne and close of the work

In the following year a woman who also lived at Calne though not a native recovered her sight at the festival of father Aldhelm, after being blind for eighteen years. I do not know the reason for her blindness, and in my anxiety not to lose the confidence of my readers by my long-windedness, I am unwilling to construct one. But this much is known that as she was standing before the crucifix, a beautiful sight with her blond hair tumbling over her shoulders but with the deformity of blindness, her sightless orbs began to be stirred by repeated prickings. This annoyed her, but when she began rubbing them gently she caused them to bleed. Soon, as the itching got greater, she scratched much harder with her finger nails to stop it, and a much larger stream of blood poured out, so that a bowl had to be called for to catch it. But then, with the obstacles removed, a clear light flooded the cavities of her eyes. The people present showed themselves true neighbours. They rejoiced at the miracle, and to this day they have provided the money to keep her alive. She herself took the veil of a holier condition, and ever since has suffered no loss of vision, apart from the debility which is brought by increasing age.

She is still alive in the year in which I am writing this, 1125, 415 years since the death of our most holy confessor, and the twenty-fifth year of the reign of king Henry.[1] The year has been noteworthy for the execution of coiners, who have contaminated the money supply throughout England. This coining of false money led to the other disasters of the year, namely the high price of corn, a pinching famine and the deaths of countless of the masses. It has also seen the deaths of the famous, particularly pope Calixtus and Henry V, emperor of Germany: neither office has ever had a more capable occupant. It has also been a black year for weather. Every month has had thunder and lighting. It has rained almost every day without stopping. Even the summer months were wet and muddy.

[1] It is strange that William says nothing about Eadwulf who succeeded Godefrey as abbot of Malmesbury in 1105.

Select Bibliography

Bede, *The Ecclesiastical History of the English People*, ed. Judith McClure and Roger Collins and trans. Bertram Colgrave (Oxford, 1999).

Blair, J., and R. Sharpe, ed., *Pastoral Care before the Parish* (Leicester, 1992).

Blair, P. H., *An Introduction to Anglo-Saxon England*, 2nd edn (Cambridge, 1997).

Brown, Allen, *The Normans and the Norman Conquest*, 2nd edn (Woodbridge, 1987).

Burton, Janet, *Monastic and Religious Orders in Britain 1000–1300* (Cambridge, 1994).

Chibnall, Marjorie, *Anglo-Norman England 1066–1166* (Oxford, 1986).

Colgrave, B., ed. and trans., *Two Lives of St Cuthbert* (Cambridge, 1940).

Cownie, Emma, *Religion and Patronage in Anglo-Norman England* (London, 1998).

Davis, R. H. C., *A History of Medieval Europe* (London, 1989).

Dorey, T. A., ed., *Latin Biography* (London, 1967).

Duckett, Eleanor, *Alfred the Great* (Chicago, 1975).

Duffy, Eamon, *The Stripping of the Altars* (New Haven, 1992).

Eadmer, *Historia Novorum in Anglia*, ed. M. Rule (Rolls Series, London, 1884).

Eadmer, *The Life of St Anselm*, ed. and trans. R. W. Southern (London, 1962).

Eddius Stephanus, *The Life of Bishop Wilfrid*, ed. and trans. B. Colgrave (Cambridge, 1927).

Farmer, Dom Hugh, 'William of Malmesbury's Life and Works', *Journal of Ecclesiastical History*, 13 (1962).

Felix, *The Life of St Guthlac*, ed. and trans. B. Colgrave (Cambridge, 1966).

Gransden, Antonia, *Historical Writing in England c.550 to 1307* (London, 1974).

James, M. R., *Two Ancient English Scholars* (Glasgow, 1931).

Knowles, Dom David, *The Monastic Order in England 940–1216*, 2nd edn (Cambridge, 1963).

Lapidge, M., *et al.*, *The Blackwell Encyclopaedia of Anglo-Saxon England* (Oxford, 2001).

Lapidge, M., and M. Herren, *Aldhelm: The Prose Works* (Ipswich, 1979).

Lapidge, M., and J. L. Rosier, *Aldhelm: The Poetic Works* (Ipswich, 1985).

Loyn, H. R., *The English Church 940–1154* (Harlow, 2000).

Matthew, D. J. A., *The Norman Conquest* (London, 1966).

Mayr-Harting, Henry, *The Coming of Christianity to Anglo-Saxon England*, 3rd edn (Pennsylvania, 1991).

Morgan, Kenneth, ed., *The Oxford History of Britain* (Oxford, 1988).

Pevsner, N., *The Buildings of England: Herefordshire* (Harmondsworth, 1987).

Pevsner, N., and B. Cherry, *The Buildings of England: Wiltshire*, 2nd edn (Harmondsworth, 1985).

Poole, A. L., *Domesday Book to Magna Carta 1087–1216*, 2nd edn (Oxford, 1986).

Southern, R. W., 'The Canterbury Forgeries', *English Historical Review*, 73 (1938).

Southern, R. W., *The Making of the Middle Ages* (London, 1953).

Southern, R. W., *St Anselm and his Biographer* (Cambridge, 1963).

Southern, R. W., *Western Society and the Church in the Middle Ages* (Harmondsworth, 1970).

Stenton, F. M., *Anglo-Saxon England*, 3rd edn (Oxford, 1971).

Taylor, H. M., and J. Taylor, *Anglo-Saxon Architecture*, 3 vols. (Cambridge, 1965–78).

Thomson, R. M., *The Life of Gundulf, Bishop of Rochester* (Rochester, 1977).

Thomson, R. M., *William of Malmesbury* (Woodbridge, 1987).

Verey, David, *The Buildings of England: Gloucestershire, the Cotswolds* (Harmondsworth, 1979).

William of Malmesbury, *De Gestis Pontificum Anglorum*, ed. N. E. S. A. Hamilton (Rolls Series, London, 1870).

William of Malmesbury, *De Gestis Regum Anglorum*, 2 vols., ed. and trans. R. A. B. Mynors, R. M. Thomson and M. Winterbottom (Oxford, 1998–9).

William of Malmesbury, *De Gestis Regum Anglorum*, 2 vols., ed. W. Stubbs (Rolls Series, London 1887–9).

Wormald, F. 'The Monastic Library', in *Gatherings in Honour of Dorothy E. Miner* (Baltimore, 1974).

Yorke, Barbara, *Wessex in the Early Middle Ages* (Leicester, 1995).

Index

(Names of places and people are almost all included apart from names of bishops who only appear in a list and who have no additional information given about them. For a more detailed index see Hamilton's edition in the Rolls Series)

Lightning Source UK Ltd.
Milton Keynes UK
UKHW022200120220
358617UK00005B/200